College London. She obtained a PhD from the University of Sussex investigating children with eating disorders, and trained as a clinical psychologist in London. She has specialised in feeding and eating difficulties in children for many years, has taught and published widely in this field and is an internationally respected expert. She is recipient of the 2012 Academy for Eating Disorders Leadership Award for Clinical, Educational and Academic Service.

KU-778-728

Z919564

Eating Disorders in Childhood and Adolescence

cpr

In the fourth edition of this accessible and comprehensive book, Bryan Lask and Rachel Bryant-Waugh build on the research and expertise of the previous three editions. First published in 1993, this was the first book of its kind to explore eating disorders in children and young adolescents, a population that is very different from those in their late teens and adulthood.

The contributors' experience and knowledge have increased and the field has moved forward over the past 20 years. This fully revised edition offers a distillation of current information in the younger population, and contains brand new chapters on areas of experience, research and practice including:

- the perspective of a young person going through an eating disorder
- experiences of a parent
- updated information regarding advances from neuroscience
- therapeutic engagement
- cognitive remediation therapy.

Eating Disorders in Childhood and Adolescence offers the reader knowledge, insight and understanding into this fascinating but challenging patient group. It has both a clinical and research focus and will be an essential text for a wide range of professionals, as well as being readable for parents of children suffering from eating disorders.

Bryan Lask trained at the University of London and was a consultant in child and adolescent psychiatry at Great Ormond Street Hospital for 25 years. There, with Rachel Bryant-Waugh, he initiated the first early onset eating disorders programme in the UK. Subsequently he has written 11 books and over 200 papers. He is Past-President of the Eating Disorders Research Society and recipient of a Lifetime Achievement Award from the Academy for Eating Disorders.

Rachel Bryant-Waugh is Lead Consultant Clinical Psychologist and Joint head of the Feeding and Eating Disorders Service at Great Ormond Street Hospital. She is also Honorary Senior Lecturer at the Institute of Child Health, University

Eating Disorders in Childhood and Adolescence

Fourth edition

Edited by Bryan Lask and
Rachel Bryant-Waugh

Routledge
Taylor & Francis Group

LONDON AND NEW YORK

First published 2013
by Routledge
27 Church Road, Hove, East Sussex BN3 2FA

Simultaneously published in the USA and Canada
by Routledge
711 Third Avenue, New York, NY 10017

Routledge is an imprint of the Taylor & Francis Group, an informa business

© 2013 Bryan Lask and Rachel Bryant-Waugh

The right of the editor to be identified as the author of the editorial
material, and of the authors for their individual chapters, has been
asserted in accordance with sections 77 and 78 of the Copyright,
Designs and Patents Act 1988.

All rights reserved. No part of this book may be reprinted or
reproduced or utilised in any form or by any electronic, mechanical,
or other means, now known or hereafter invented, including
photocopying and recording, or in any information storage or
retrieval system, without permission in writing from the publishers.

Trademark notice: Product or corporate names may be trademarks or
registered trademarks, and are used only for identification and
explanation without intent to infringe.

British Library Cataloguing in Publication Data
A catalogue record for this book is available from the British Library

Library of Congress Cataloging in Publication Data
    Eating disorders in childhood and adolescence / edited by Bryan Lask
    and Rachel Bryant-Waugh. — 4th ed.
        p. cm.
    Includes bibliographical references and index.
    ISBN 978-0-415-68640-2 (hardback) — ISBN 978-0-415-68641-9 (pbk.)
    1. Eating disorders in children. 2. Eating disorders in adolescence.
    3. Anorexia nervosa.   I. Lask, Bryan.   II. Bryant-Waugh, Rachel.
    RJ506.E18A565 2012
    618.92′8526—dc23

                                                            2012022072

ISBN: 978-0-415-68640-2 (hbk)
ISBN: 978-0-415-68641-9 (pbk)
ISBN: 978-0-203-07641-5 (ebk)

Typeset in Times
by RefineCatch Limited, Bungay, Suffolk

Printed and bound by CPI Group (UK) Ltd, Croydon, CR0 4YY

Bryan dedicates this book to Renee and
Gordon Carlton for a lifetime of love and
support.

Contents

Figures

Tables

Acknowledgements

We thank all our contributors for their skilled and timely chapters. We are indebted to so many of our colleagues, past and present, in the UK and abroad, far too many to mention in person, who have not contributed directly to this book. Nonetheless their ideas, creativity, support, encouragement, enthusiasm and hard work are reflected throughout the book.

Without the financial support of the following much of our research could not have been completed and we are very grateful to all of them: Medical Research Council; Health Foundation; Garfield Weston Foundation; Child Growth Foundation; Gordon Carlton Memorial Fund; Lord Ashdown Charitable Settlement; Reg Burns Trust; Psychosomatic Research Trust; Society for the Advancement of Research into Anorexia; the City of London; Sanity UK; Huntercombe Hospital Group, UK; Ellern Mede Eating Disorders Service, UK; Bartle Charitable Trust; the University of Southampton; Hampshire Partnership NHS Trust; Great Ormond Street Hospital NHS Trust; Great Ormond Street Hospital Special Trustees; Joseph Rosetree Trust; the Regional Eating Disorders Service, Oslo, Norway; and Helse-Sør Øst, Norway.

Finally, warmest thanks to Lucy Watson, our Editorial Assistant, who did miraculous work in an absurdly short time frame!

Contributors

Rachel Bryant-Waugh is Consultant Clinical Psychologist and Joint Head of the Feeding and Eating Disorders Service at Great Ormond Street Hospital for Children, London, and Honorary Senior Lecturer at the Institute of Child Health, University College London.

Caroline has lived in London all her life, taking time out to do a degree in English at Exeter University. She has worked in food service and food retail management for the whole of her career and now lives with her fiancée who is a chef.

Ian Frampton is a Consultant in Paediatric Psychologist in Cornwall UK, where his chief clinical interest is the development of children's brains. He is Clinical Co-Director of the Centre for Clinical Neuropsychology Research at the University of Exeter, UK and visiting Research Consultant to the Regional Eating Disorders Service at Ulleval University Hospital, Oslo, Norway. His main research interest concerns the neurobiological basis of early onset anorexia nervosa.

Simon Gowers is Professor of Adolescent Psychiatry at the University of Liverpool and Consultant to the Cheshire and Merseyside Eating Disorders Service for adolescents, (CHEDS). He has published widely on aspects of eating disorders research including pathogenesis, psychology and treatment and has recently published a textbook: *Eating Disorders; CBT with Children and Young People* (Routledge 2009) with colleague Lynne Green and completed a large HTA funded treatment trial of adolescent anorexia nervosa, *Health Technology Assessment* (2010), 14(15): 1–98. He chaired the NICE guideline development group which published its recommendations for eating disorders in 2004.

Melissa Hart is an Eating Disorders Coordinator for the Local Health District, based in Child and Adolescent Mental Health Services, and a Conjoint Lecturer with the University of Newcastle, Australia. Melissa has many years' experience working as a clinical dietician in both Australia and overseas. More recently, Melissa has worked as a Statewide Coordinator for Eating Disorders (child and adolescent), Statewide nutrition consultant and senior mental health dietician. Melissa has a special interest in nutritional management in mental health and research.

Cecile Rausch Herscovici is Professor of the Masters Program in Family Studies at the Universidad del Salvador, Buenos Aires, Argentina. Approved Supervisor and Clinical Member of the American Association for Marriage and Family Therapy and Researcher of the International Life Sciences Institute, Argentina.

Debra Katzman is a Professor of Pediatrics, Head of the Division of Adolescent Medicine, Department of Pediatrics and University of Toronto (UofT), and Senior Associate Scientist at the Research Institute at the Hospital for Sick Children. She is Past- President of the Academy for Eating Disorders (AED) and president-elect for the Society of Adolescent Health and Medicine (SAHM). She has published over 100 articles, abstracts, book chapters, and editorials.

Bryan Lask is Emeritus Professor of Child and Adolescent Psychiatry at the University of London, Honorary Consultant at Great Ormond Street Hospital for Children, Academic Director at the Ellern Mede Centre, London. He has also been Visiting Professor at the universities of Oslo and British Columbia. He is Past-President of the Eating Disorders Research Society and recipient of a Lifetime Achievement Award from the Academy for Eating Disorders (2011). His main area of clinical and research interest is early onset eating disorders. He has published ten books, nearly 200 peer-reviewed papers and numerous chapters in books edited by others. He has also been the Editor of 'the Journal of Family Therapy' and 'Clinical Child Psychology and Psychiatry' and is Co-Editor of a new journal: 'Advances in Eating Disorders – Theory, Research and Practice'.

Camilla Lindvall Dahlgren is currently working with Professor Lask and is a trained research psychologist at Oslo university hospital. She is undertaking her PhD at the University of Oslo, conducting a feasibility and piloting trial of cognitive remediation therapy (CRT) for children and adolescents. She has presented her research at a number of national and international conferences and is the leading author of the chapter 'Implications for Treatment' in the recently published book *Eating Disorders and the Brain* (Eds. Lask and Frampton, 2011). Her work with CRT for children and adolescents can also be found in the online version of the 'CRT Resource Pack for children and adolescents with anorexia nervosa' (Lindvall, Owen and Lask, 2011).

Dasha Nicholls is Consultant Child and Adolescent Psychiatrist and Joint Head of the Feeding and Eating Disorders service (FEDS) at Great Ormond Street Hospital, London. She is both a clinician and researcher and has authored over 50 articles, as well as producing UK guidelines on the care of seriously ill young people with anorexia nervosa. She is President Elect of the Academy for Eating Disorders.

Jenny Nicholson is a clinical psychologist at Great Ormond Street Hospital. She worked for five years with the Feeding and Eating Disorders Service, and is currently the clinical psychologist for the inpatient Mildred Creak Unit. She works with children and adolescents with eating disorders, somatoform disorders and other complex mental health difficulties on an in and outpatient basis.

Kenneth Nunn is a paediatric neuropsychiatrist at the Children's Hospital Westmead, Sydney, Australia. He is Senior Consultant Psychiatrist in the Neurodevelopmental team and Clinical Director of the Molecular Neuropsychiatry Service. He has a special interest in causal models of mental illness and the translation of basic scientific research into clinically usable and publicly accessible forms. He is affiliated with the University of New South Wales, the University of Newcastle and the University of Sydney. He is one of the three authors of the noradrenergic hypothesis of anorexia nervosa.

Isabel Owen is both a qualified teacher and a research psychologist writing up her PhD on a phase one trial of Cognitive Remediation Therapy under the supervision of Professor Bryan Lask. She currently lives in Johannesburg, South Africa, where she works as a Remedial Therapist.

Mark Rose is the UK co-ordinator of the Ravello Profile, National Research Co-Ordinator, Huntercombe Group and Researcher at the Feeding and Eating Disorders Service, Great Ormond Street Hospital for Children, London. Previously he was a Systematic Reviewer at the Centre for Primary Care and Public Health, Queen Mary, University of London. He is currently writing his PhD by Publication on the neuropsychology of eating disorders.

Fiona Simons is a pseudonym. Fiona has two daughters, is married to, and lives with, the father of both children. Her eldest daughter became unwell with anorexia nervosa in her very early teens, was acutely unwell, and was treated as both an in-patient and an out-patient.

Cathleen Steinegger graduated from the University Of Nebraska College Of Medicine. She completed a pediatric residency and an Adolescent Medicine fellowship at the Cincinnati Children's Hospital Medical Center. During her time in Cincinnati she also obtained a master's degree in nutrition science. She is currently the Medical Director of the Eating Disorders Program and a staff physician in the Division of Adolescent Medicine at The Hospital for Sick Children in Toronto.

Anne Stewart is a Consultant Child and Adolescent Psychiatrist in the Oxford Health NHS Foundation Trust and honorary Senior Clinical Lecturer, University of Oxford. She has worked clinically with eating disorders in young people for over 20 years, both in outpatient and inpatient settings, and has a longstanding interest in ethical and legal dilemmas which arise out of clinical work. Her research interests include prevention and treatment of eating disorders, including ethical issues in care and patient perspectives on treatment.

Jacinta Tan has a multidisciplinary background of medicine, child health, philosophy and psychology, and sociology. She is a Child and Adolescent Psychiatrist who is also a medical ethicist and empirical ethics researcher at Swansea University, Wales. She specialises in empirical ethics research using sociological methods and her research interests are the development of autonomy and consent, the ethics of eating disorders, eating disorders in elite athletes, research ethics in legal minors and psychiatric ethics.

Cathy Troupp is a Child and Adolescent Psychotherapist, trained at the Tavistock Clinic, where she now teaches. She has over 10 years' experience working psychotherapeutically with young people with eating disorders and their families, in specialist eating disorders services. Other special clinical interests comprise working with children with both psychosomatic problems and physical illness, in hospital settings. She has also worked as a psychotherapist in schools, court services and general CAMHS. More recently, she is developing her academic interest in the change promoting processes in psychotherapy and is undertaking a research degree at UCL in this field. She is active on the Research Committee of the Association of Child Psychotherapists.

Beth Watkins is a Clinical Psychologist with the Feeding and Eating Disorders Service at Great Ormond Street Hospital for Children, London, and previously worked in the child and adolescent in-patient eating disorders service at South West London and St George's Mental Health Trust.

Trine Wiig Haag is Nurse Consultant to the Regional Eating Disorders Service in Oslo, Norway. She has been working with children and adolescents with eating disorders for 10 years and has been involved in teaching and training of a wide range of professionals throughout Europe. She is currently preparing her PhD in nursing science.

Preface

In the prologue to the first edition of this book we raised the question of why there should be yet another book on eating disorders. We justified the first edition on the basis that it was the first book to deal with early onset eating disorders, i.e. eating disorders occurring in people below the age of 15. This is a distinct population, quite different in many ways from those who develop eating disorders in their late teens or adult life. Obviously some of the issues are similar, but many are different. In various important respects the aetiology, clinical presentation, phenomenology and treatment all differ. Further there is a wider range of eating disorders in the younger age group. The second edition was written at the end of the twentieth century, when eating disorders, including those of early onset, had become a major public health issue. Referral rates had continued to increase and the need for more and improved services was manifested by the expansion in specialist services for this population. The third edition published in 2007 attempted to keep abreast of all the exciting developments in the field. If anything the rising trajectory of knowledge has been even sharper since then.

Our own experience and knowledge have been greatly enhanced by the passage of time, concerted research endeavours, advances in understanding of aetiology and the development of innovative treatments. We believe that the time is ripe for this fourth edition in which we offer a distillation of current information about eating disorders in this younger population. The contributors to this book are all people at the forefront of work with this fascinating but challenging patient group. Between us we have tried to convey our knowledge, perception and understanding of these problems, and to share our clinical experience of assessment and treatment. The chapters in this fourth edition are completely new or have been thoroughly revised.

Part I of the book, provides three different perspectives. It opens with a contribution from Ken Nunn which considers the concept of sensitivity, so central to those with eating disorders. With his own empathic sensitivity he conveys the pain, the shame, the fear, the self-loathing, the isolation and the many other emotions that engulf those with anorexia nervosa. He then moves on to show how sensitivity can be utilized to enhance the recovery process. Chapter 2 offers the child's perspective written by Caroline Sebastian, now a young adult but many years ago a patient. She vividly describes her childhood experience of anorexia nervosa, her torment and suffering. Caroline clearly demonstrates that anorexia nervosa is only superficially about weight, and far more about inner distress. Chapter 3, by the mother of a teenager who had anorexia nervosa, provides the parent's perspective. She conveys only too vividly the bewilderment and torment of seeing her daughter so ill, the frustrations of negotiating the health care system, the loneliness and anxiety and the ups and downs of the difficult and lengthy process of treatment. She provides helpful tips for clinicians working with young people with eating disorders and their families and provides hope for all concerned.

Part II deals with assessment and course. It starts with an overview of eating disorders in this younger population followed by a detailed examination of what is known about aetiology. Subsequent chapters deal with physical and psychological assessment, followed by an overview of the very latest knowledge on the neuroscience of eating disorders. This section finishes with a chapter on outcome.

Part III is determinedly practical and devoted to clinical issues. The first chapter provides an overview of treatment, with succeeding chapters dealing with therapeutic engagement, nutrition and refeeding, family approaches, cognitive-behavioural therapy, individual psychotherapy, cognitive remediation therapy, and legal and ethical issues.

Here are a few technical points:

1   Where we made use of case illustrations, for obvious reasons we have changed the children's names to preserve their anonymity.
2   For ease of reading, and because far more girls than boys experience eating disorders, we have referred to the children as girls unless we are specifically discussing boys.
3   The age group represented in this book ranges from about 7 to 16. There is no totally satisfactory term to cover this group. In consequence we have used various terms such as 'children', 'young person', and when appropriate 'adolescent'. In a number of places we have used the word 'patient' to describe the young people we see. It seems difficult to get it right and we hope that we will be forgiven if we have appeared condescending or inappropriate in our terminology.

We hope that readers will find what follows of interest and value. Although we do not expect agreement with all we say, we trust that we have conveyed some of the fascination and challenges we have experienced in working with these children and their families.

Bryan Lask and Rachel Bryant-Waugh
March 2012

Part I

Perspectives

Chapter 1

The sensitivities that hinder and the sensitivities that heal

Kenneth Nunn

The pain of shame and self-loathing

If you have ever been embarrassed about people seeing you naked; if you have ever felt uncomfortable about being overweight; if you have ever wished you looked different in some way or other; if you have ever experienced pain at the way others viewed you and your body; if you have ever felt your life was not really yours to control – then you may have some capacity to empathise with children and young people who suffer from anorexia nervosa.

The pain they live with day after day is the deep conviction that they are ugly, loathsome, bloated and distended. To be sure, in some this is mild and creates background noise only in their emotional life. But in malignant anorexia nervosa it is an intense, unrelenting, tortured self-concern that renders life unliveable without the most intensive support from those around. For these, starvation is extreme, self-injury is common and death is never far away with casualties at around five per cent per decade of the illness. Seriously delayed growth, brain blood-flow shutdown, osteoporosis (sometimes permanently damaged bones), infertility and unstable heart rhythms are commonplace. Many of these complications are normally only encountered in the Third World or the very elderly. The sort of medications that are usually only needed to settle the overwhelming distress of psychosis are increasingly required to quell the distress and psychiatric complications of anorexia nervosa that are unresponsive to any other intervention.

The eating disorder that is more than an eating disorder

Anorexia nervosa is a disorder associated with difficulties of eating, together with weight and shape concerns. But it is much more. It is an illness that can cripple a young girl's ability to get through to the world around her about how she feels. She may be 'locked in' emotionally. It is also an illness that prevents young girls from understanding how those they love feel about them – others are 'locked out' emotionally. It is above all else an illness of communication between the world inside themselves and the world outside – an illness of emotional communication in which they have difficulties expressing and receiving what matters most – their own feelings and the feelings of others.

They have no shortage of feelings, no poverty of emotion and no emptiness of real intentions or motivation. However, feelings are segregated from words, emotions remain all too often disconnected from the tears and choreography of their facial movement. An expressionless, seemingly unconcerned face may mask a tumult within. The usual desires, thoughts and driving forces in young people are utterly captured and held hostage by weight and shape. Like the delusions and hallucinations of a person trapped in the completely dominating world of psychosis, the world of anorexia nervosa is a prison tightly bound by walls of distress at every turn. In the same way, parents may be deeply concerned and this concern may not register or may be misunderstood by children with anorexia nervosa. Parents may be perplexed, bewildered and overwhelmed as to what is happening within their child; sensitive to their distress but at a loss to understand the source of the distress. It is to the sensitivities that may fuel this distress or heal this distress that I want to turn.

A needed pain

The first time I saw a child with hereditary insensitivity to pain, like probably thousands of new medical graduates before me, I was struck by the need for pain. The little two-year-old boy had already injured himself many times and there was a danger he would lose some of his toes and fingers through his injuries before he was ready to go to school. Of course, I knew that leprosy affected sensation in feet and hands and that specific nerve damage might lead to particular insensitivities, but it never occurred to me that a child might grow up largely without pain because of a rare condition and that this inability to feel pain might make the child contin-uously vulnerable. In the same way, the young person with anorexia nervosa may be entirely unaware of the disease that is destroying them and even of the threat this poses to parents as they are traumatised by their child's condition. This inability to personally register anorexia nervosa is one of the most perplexing aspects of the illness and increasingly appears to be medically (brain based) rather than psychologically based. It is this inability to see 'the enemy', that makes 'the enemy' all that more dangerous. The insatiable demand from within about weight, weight loss, shape, the amount and type of food eaten, is so absorbing and over-riding of all other concerns that even concerns from loved ones about survival retreat to the background.

A futile pain

At the other extreme of experience, throughout my medical career, in both general and child psychiatry, I have been involved in the treatment of pain, especially chronic pain – the long-term pain that remains unresponsive to the many forms of pain relief that have been so successful in acute medicine. Here the pain may have gone on for months or years. The pain no longer signals acute tissue damage or threat of tissue damage but has become a problem in its own right. Sometimes it signals troubles in the life of the person, past or present. But even where this is so, the pain is yet another burden. Of course, like all my psychiatric and psychological colleagues, I will search out the possibilities that the pain is 'serving a function', 'fulfilling a meaning' hitherto unseen and of which everyone has been unaware. The reality is, however, that for many of those with longer term pain no cause is found, no meaning made and pain is just pain, quietly, inexorably grinding down its owner who searches for any relief we might offer. Sometimes the immediacy of pain obscures its own origins. We are asked to help these patients cope with pain, even when we cannot make sense of the pain, to provide support in the struggle with pain, even when we cannot eliminate the struggle, and to provide what comforts we can, even when the fundamental comfort of relief from pain is not forthcoming.

Responding sensitively to a futile pain

Strangely, anorexia nervosa is a bewildering mixture of insensitivity and sensitivity, a lack of awareness of their underlying condition that renders them vulnerable and a distress with their shape and weight that is overwhelming. Young people with anorexia nervosa can be exquisitely sensitive to an increase in weight or calorie intake and completely unaware that anything is wrong with them. Parents can be utterly overwhelmed with the distress of their child but also unaware of the medical disaster that has crept upon them by stealth.

How can we know to which distress we should respond in these young girls and their families and which distress we should see as a 'futile pain' which only distracts us from what is threatening? How can we help? How can we build treatment around their sensitivities and insensitivities so that it is likely to work more effectively? How can we understand this condition so that parents will feel confident to trust us and not find themselves 'fighting against us' and us, 'against them'? What are the sorts of sensitivities, 'the pains', from which they suffer? We may become so concerned about what this pain and distress mean that we forget that sometimes no meaning can be found, or the meanings that are found, are elaborate, ill-fitting interpretations that say more about what we are thinking, and where we are coming from than about the young person with anorexia nervosa. There is a relief that comes from acknowledging that we do not understand but we do care, that we cannot make sense of what is happening but we are not judging, and that we do not have the answer, but we will continue to be available to provide smaller answers to particular difficulties.

The varieties of sensitivity

Most children with anorexia nervosa love their pets – dogs, cats, goldfish and more recently electronic pets and babies. They are deeply distressed if anything untoward happens to them. They feed them regularly. They do not injure them but nurture them lovingly, tenderly and sometimes tenaciously. I have sometimes asked these young people what they would think if someone starved their kitten to death and injured their tiny paws and ankles. They are distressed at even the thought. Then I have said that this is how it feels for us when we see them starving themselves as so many do when overwhelmed with the inescapable distress of anorexia. Of course, there are no clever words that can cure anorexia nervosa anymore than there are clever words to cure cancer. Treatment is a slow, hard slog with a host of obstacles on the road to recovery. But some of the girls remember these words and try to be just a little kinder to themselves as a result.

To see how 'this might happen to me' or to those we love, to somehow appreciate it even if we are not really aware of what the person is going through, is called *identification* in the jargon of psychiatry. It means we feel for ourselves and those we love when we see their distress – we identify with their distress. There is nothing wrong with this. It is the beginning of feeling for others but should not be confused with the feeling for others that is called sympathy or empathy. Identification is the distress that people communicate when first we tell them our bad news. Many people at funerals want to be reassured and comforted by the bereaved loved ones because they become distressed that 'it might have been them' or someone 'close to them'. When we have shared bad news with others this is also the reason why many people tell us the worst story they have recently heard, of which our story reminded them. We of course do not need to hear or want to hear their worst story.

To see someone else suffering, to feel for them and with them in their distress and to register their pain is *sympathy*. It is to become aware that they are in pain and to want to relieve it. Sympathy is what we often feel when watching starving children on television and we want to relieve their starvation and distress. We feel for them even though we are clear that we will not starve and will not be in their position.

To see someone else suffering and to feel the pain as they feel it, at least in part, is *empathy*. To experience the discomfort that they are feeling in their situation, the pain in their troubles, and to wince with the embarrassment and heartache they must endure, is to understand in a different way, not merely to identify or sympathise. All of us have been children and distressed as children at some time. When we see children we can feel for them and with them.

Who owns these feelings?

There is a deeper, more difficult to put into words variety of this feeling, which often is an experience very close to empathy. It is the confusion between our own feelings and the feelings of those who are suffering. When we spend time with others, feel close to others, have things in common with others, care for others, especially when they are young and vulnerable, we may confuse our feelings, our thoughts and even our predicaments with theirs. Well-trained clinicians learn to use these confusions in ownership of feelings creatively to help those for whom they care. But they can complicate our care and before we know where we are we can find ourselves caring for our own needs, our own problems and our own predicaments. We are taking on the problems of others as if they were our own, and acting as if their problems were no longer theirs but ours. In short, we are no longer helping troubled young people and their families. We have become troubled ourselves.

The normal tangle of feelings between children and parents

Well, all of this may sound very complicated and pathological but there is a particular type of confusion of ownership of feelings between parents and children, which is very common, very normal and very powerful. Our children may not want to talk with us about their feelings because they are worried. We might be worried but we may be reluctant to talk to our children about our feelings because we do not want to worry them. We as a family might become so worried for each other that we cannot say that we are worried for each other for fear of worrying each other. When we see each other saying 'we are all fine', we cannot feel reassurance or comfort. We are not reassured. We are not comforted. I know that I am worried but cannot talk about it. I become worried that they are not talking about their worries. Each person becomes more and more worried to the point that no one is talking. There is a danger that each person in the family may come to the conclusion that the unmentionable problem must be much bigger and more worrying because no one is discussing what is happening.

This tendency to worry about our loved ones' worries is based upon parents caring for their young children and not wanting to worry them; children caring for their parents and not wanting to worry them. It is also based on the belief as a parent that 'I feel what my child is going through'. It is based upon the understanding of children of what they believe their parent is going through. The problem is that sometimes we as parents get it wrong about our children and sometimes our children get it wrong about us as parents. Sometimes those who are close miss the very obvious things that strangers can see and become convinced of problems that are our own, not our children's. It is only with time and experiences, both good and bad, that we as parents and children can disentangle our feelings from each other. So when I talk about sensitivities it does not make sense to talk about individuals alone. We all find ourselves aware and unaware, sensitive and insensitive, to the supports and threats, nurture and pain of loved ones around us.

Young people with a problem being superficial or a superficial explanation for the problem?

In anorexia nervosa some people find it easy to identify with these children and young people. On the other hand, more than a few become convinced that this is a self-induced, boutique disorder, in indulged upper middle class girls who are saturated with a materialistic and narcissistic culture that causes women to compete in a senseless rivalry of bodily perfection. Dealing with children and young people themselves moves us beyond this to an appreciation and sympathy that they are victims of an illness that is clearly not self-induced at all and not always middle class; they are often far from indulged or saturated with materialistic lifestyles. They are not simply vain or trying to attract boys. In fact, it would often be a real sign of progress if they were well enough even to contemplate how other people, especially young men, felt about them. They are usually so distressed and self-loathing about themselves that they are unable to consider how others might feel about them. When we see how sensitive they are to the imperfections of their own bodies we can begin to sympathise with these girls.

An emotional malignancy

Anorexia nervosa is not a trivial side effect of an over-indulged western society. It is a malignant disease of children with parents usually trying to do more than could be expected of any parent – damned if they do and damned if they don't. Some parents will sit on their hands for far too long while their daughter loses weight, not wishing to overreact, minimising the gravity of her weight loss, ignoring what is 'attention seeking' and hoping that 'she will grow out of it'. Others do become obsessed with food and preparing whatever she might eat in the hope of coaxing her back to food and normal eating. Still others, especially fathers, become angry and even violent, feeling helpless and useless in the face of their daughter's decline. When we are desperate, we do not look as normal, sensible, balanced and open to suggestion as others. If obtaining help has been difficult, if some have been thoughtless or misunderstanding toward us and if miscommunication within the medical system has led to a sense of loss of control and threat to our children, our composure is not as complete as it might be if it was someone else's daughter. When assessing parents with ill children the first question of the assessing clinician must be 'how much of the presenting picture is due to a worried parent of a troubled child?'

Of course we require experience to answer this question accurately and helpfully. However, it remains a good rule of thumb: *when in doubt, parents are best seen as normal, caring parents who are worried about their daughter.*

The sensitivity and insensitivity that save life

When dehydration sets in because drinking is restricted, we must be sensitive to vital signs and much less sensitive to pleas of distress about shape and weight. A young girl can semi-starve for years, almost unnoticed; but just a few days of not drinking and the body will deteriorate quickly. Changes to vital chemicals within the blood – potassium, sodium and phosphate – alter the basic message systems that keep the body's systems working and the energy production that keeps each cell alive. If life is in danger, there is no kindness in listening to a distress, which will soon die along with the child who owns it. If life is in danger it is kind to replace fluids, though unwanted, restore chemical deficiencies, though unnoticed, and refeed, though food is rejected with an outpouring of distress. There is a time to be insensitive to distress in order to save life; there is a time to be cruel to be kind.

The sensitivity and insensitivity that threaten

I once attended an international meeting in London on eating disorders at which an open debate was held on the value of nasogastric tube feeding in anorexia nervosa. The debate was vigorous and the discussion slowly settled on the Dutch position which at that time was that there should be no coercive feeding of those with eating disorders with complete respect for the ill individual's wishes. The Dutch position contrasted with the British and Australian positions. Members from these countries took a strong stand on refeeding when survival is threatened and permanent damage from prolonged starvation is imminent. Of course there were professionals from each national group who did not agree with their fellow nationals' point of view. The audience sentiment was definitely swinging strongly towards the Dutch position with a concern amongst professionals and consumers alike that individual rights should not be overridden. Then someone asked the obvious question: 'What happens when the young person repeatedly and deter- minedly chooses not to eat or be fed?' The principal Dutch discussant then said that after much consultation and discussion euthanasia is considered, describing a 25-year-old who had opted for and was given euthanasia the previous year. Silence moved across the audience with a sense of consternation. The consensus of the meeting changed dramatically.

What each society, clinician and family decide to be sensitive to and insensitive to opens up new issues with new concerns. Increasingly, anorexia nervosa is seen to be a life-threatening mental illness which is often long term but also treatable. Like other mental illnesses, anorexia nervosa requires laws for the provision of protection and treatment, even when the person who is ill does not recognise the need for treatment. We do need to be sensitive to young people's rights to freedom, but there are other rights that compete with those of personal liberty: the right to be cared for when ill; the right to be protected from harm when judgement is impaired; the right to have a future when the present threatens to take it away. Families and loved ones also have rights that compete with individual rights: the right to prevent their children from suffering where possible; the right to protect those they love who can no longer protect themselves; the right to provide needed care and to obtain expert help for loved ones. 'It's my life and I can do with it what I want' may make sense in an academic argument about individual liberty, but against the background of the solidarity of suffering that occurs in most normal families and relationships it smacks of being superficial, insensitive and naive.

Perhaps more, it indicates an impaired judgement as to the personal consequences of choosing not to eat.

Tough minds and tender hearts

Where does this leave us? Thomas Jefferson once said that what we often need in this world is a tough mind and a tender heart. We cannot afford to be weak in our appraisal of danger to those we love and for whom we care, nor can we afford to fail to respond with compassion. Physicians and surgeons in former centuries knew this all too well. Surgery without anaesthesia was agonisingly painful but so was the relentless progress of gangrene. The choices were stark and sometimes the treatment offered only a little more benefit than the illness. In the case of anorexia nervosa, we can offer much better alternatives than our forebears could and better than the Dutch solution of preserving individual liberty now does. There is pain, there is distress and there are hard decisions to be made that do not always fit with the wishes of the person in pain. Why is it so hard to find those with clear thinking and compassion? Perhaps those who are more tough minded find it hard to sustain compassion. Perhaps those who are tender-hearted have difficulty making tough decisions.

A time to hurt

There is a time to be hurtful, to allow distress, to save a life and to prevent long-term harm. There is a time to be aware of the exquisite sensitivity of these young women to their own bodies and the opinions of others. We cannot ignore fears and distress rooted in shape and weight. But we can become aware of the deeper problems: the problem of being unable to express and receive, accurately, emotional signals from others; the problem of a crippling sensitivity in girls who can nevertheless fail to see their own illness.

To be blind or partially sighted to the world around is a terrible disability. To be emotionally blind to what is going on in those around is often even more crippling than the loss of vision in blindness. The emotional blindness in those who are suffering with anorexia nervosa sits side by side with an anguish in the families that cannot be put into words. When we see the illness that these girls and young women cannot see; when we appreciate the damage that is being done that they cannot feel; when we are sensitive to the heartache of their families that they barely perceive, we are compelled to act on their behalf.

A time to heal

Healing begins as we understand the condition afflicting these girls and their families. It is not yet the healing of cure but of acceptance. However, throughout the world there is a slow recognition that anorexia is not a given of existence which must forever be with us. The sky is blue. The grass is green. But anorexia nervosa is not immortal any more than smallpox or poliomyelitis. It is time to systematically, tenaciously and strategically seek a cure, just as our colleagues in oncology seek a cure to the malignancies they face. We must confront the reality of what we cannot do at this point in time but we must also begin to slowly but surely challenge that reality. There is much that we can do today that even a decade ago we could not have achieved. There is much more we could do if all those who suffer and have loved ones who suffer combined forces with clinicians to 'crack' this malignancy of mind and body. There is so much more suffering that could be relieved by the simple recognition of the community as a whole that those who suffer with anorexia nervosa should be accorded the same dignity as those who suffer with other malignancies. The dream of healing anorexia nervosa will only be realised at a very substantial cost; the cost of us as a community becoming aware of the pain of those who suffer from anorexia nervosa, the anguish of those who care for these young people and our responsibility to relieve their suffering and anguish.

This chapter is based on a paper originally published in Nunn, K.P. (2004). Sensitivity and Anorexia Nervosa. *The Clinician*, 3, 4–8.

Chapter 2

A child's perspective

Caroline

Trapped in the darkened crowd I thought I was going to die. The noise beat away at my insides and the jostling children felt like an assault. I could see no way out and no way to make it stop. I was invisible, naked; drowning in a world that was merciless and hateful. There was no escape.

Crowds have always felt that way to me. When growing up loud music and throngs of people felt aggressive and painful. My body felt alien to me in that environment as though the outside noise was amplified inside, and the world around me had somehow infiltrated my whole being and was violating me.

I have to link that terrified little girl to the emaciated figure who stared back at me from the bathroom mirror for so many years. What I cannot combine in my head is that image with the happy little girl everyone else saw. I remember her; I know she existed once. What I cannot pinpoint is the moment when, even for her, the world became too terrifying a place in which to remain and both little girls started to disappear.

I am sure the story starts the same way for so many people. There are the doctors' visits, the psychotherapists who let me weigh myself as if I have the power to change what I did not start in the first place. There is the stay on a hospital ward when my body starts to fail me and there is the desperate rush for the specialist clinic when the weight continues to drop off. The descent is fast, devastating and rock bottom hurtles towards me before I have noticed I am falling.

I think that it is unimportant to describe my physical body as I tell my story. Of course my weight will feature but I feel very strongly that this should not be a sensationalist issue. Weight loss is not an illness. Like hair loss after chemotherapy, weight loss for me can only be described as the outward appearance that something much worse is happening inside. We all know that the most frightening things are those that we cannot see or do not understand.

My story started at Easter when I was nine years old. My sister and I sat watching films and eating our chocolate eggs. As she settled down I slipped upstairs and stuck my fingers down my throat. The relief was immense. I cannot say it was guilt that led me to do this . . . it felt like fear.

Four years later, aged 13, that fear had taken me to a small eight bed dormitory on the top floor of an old mock-Tudor style house. My mother and I drove past the clinic when we first arrived. It was not sign posted and was down a leafy driveway tucked on the edge of a busy main road, like a secret.

I had spent three weeks in a general children's ward at a local hospital on the orders of the psychiatrist I had at the time – a man whose attitude and techniques were as ineffective as they were abhorrent. I do however see his reasons for this hospital stay. My kidneys were failing me, my heart rate was low and my aorta was beating dangerously close to the surface of my skin. But hospital is not the place for an illness like anorexia nervosa for which there is no immediate medical cure; no miracle drugs or tests to be run or even as far as I could see, no need of observation. I am not making judgements as to the type of care I received – the facts can speak for themselves. Every day I was able to escape to the toilet to run vigorously on the spot for at least half an hour without being noticed. I was able to pour meals into plastic bags under my bed, having been left alone to eat and as a result I was left to continue losing weight.

During that stay I would not consider myself as being depressed, but when I hear how other people perceived me I must have retreated into some kind of trance. I would spend hours on my bed dreaming of old family holidays in France and looking forward to being back there, feeling happy and safe among the lavender and pine trees. However I was unresponsive to the world around me. To me it just felt too difficult to engage. I had no energy to communicate and would lie on the bed barely registering anything the psychiatrist was saying apart from noting that his glasses resting on my bed made my skin crawl ever so slightly.

There are many miracles that take my story to where I am now. There are many moments of luck, many extraordinary people and many moments where fate or god or just perfect timing has helped to save my life.

One such moment that did not appear significant until weeks later occurred in those numbing days of hospital and perhaps because of the psychiatrist that decided that the only care I could be given was palliative. In one of those last appointments with him as I sat in the waiting room next to my mother I saw someone walk by into another office. When I looked at her I remember a desperate urge for her to take me in her arms and tell me it was all going to go away. At that moment I was just a sick child who did not know how to ask for the love and care she needed but saw it all pass by her in the woman's face. I whispered over to my mother 'she would be able to make me better'.

Those first days in the clinic smelled like new paint and freshly sanded wood. They felt comfortable and safe. There were three of us there and it was easy and quiet and far away from the life I had escaped.

I have no way of knowing how after those first optimistic weeks the stubborn hold of illness began to envelop me. Many people think that an institution can do this to you; that those around you can condition your actions and your feelings and edge you closer to the parapet. I think for me it was all or nothing. It always is in my life, I have to be the best and when there came a point when being ill was all I was anymore I had to be the best at it. I had to push myself further and faster.

For four months I got used to a routine. I slept with a nurse watching me, I ate, I went to the toilet and I walked in furious laps around the garden. I put on weight. Little by little, every Monday and Thursday morning I watched the scales go up and I waited for the nurses to assess my meal plan for the next few days.

I started therapy sessions – endless, endless therapy. There was group therapy, art therapy, one-on-one therapy and, perhaps worst of all, family therapy where my parents and siblings would sit looking at me, all traumatised, terrified of the incomprehensible grip within which I seemed trapped.

When I met my individual therapist for the first time I saw my lifeline. It was as if fate had answered me. The woman I had seen in hospital, the women that I had known at first sight could help me was standing in front of me. She was offering me a way out.

Perhaps the refeeding process is the most traumatic time of all. It is like standing at the edge of a really high diving board, considering whether or not to jump and before I can decide I am pushed; the decision is taken from me.

The physical impact is uncomfortable and humiliating. There is the chronic diarrhoea, the distended stomach and the cold shakes that happen after a meal. But emotionally it feels as though, in feeding myself, I am fuelling the fire of illness. The more I eat the more it rages inside me. Anorexia needs to control me like a candle needs oxygen to survive. I cannot blow it out. It clings to me like an aggressive tumour.

After a few months at the clinic they allowed my parents to come and visit on Saturdays and have lunch. It is a terrifying thing to have to eat in front of the people to whom I communicated everything through the act of starvation. There were so many things that had made me feel scared and angry and hurt for so long and it was finally being recognised, even if I wasn't ready to say it out loud. To me eating meant that I was OK. Without the physical manifestation of illness what hope did I ever have of letting everyone know that whatever was broken inside me was still not fixed.

After that there were the Saturdays out. The only person I allowed to come and get me was my mother. She would drive up and more than anything I would long to run over and throw my arms around her. Instead all I could do was pull on my standard oversized black jumper and wait until we had left the clinic before grabbing the lunch bag they had provided and throwing it out the car window.

I would spend the next ten minutes screaming and raging at her to take me to the park. Overcome by a kind of panic which would start in my stomach and sting my eyes and my tongue, I would beg her to let me stop the pain just for a few minutes; just a quick walk to quiet that incessant voice in my head which reminded me of how disgusting I was and what I had allowed into my body that day.

Once we arrived at the park I would run off like an addict in search of the next fix. I would run and run in circles, my body bent like an old sparrow, my eyes fixed on nothing except the ground pounding beneath me.

One Saturday in late autumn I must have lost track of time. The park was dark. The wind sliced at my body and I could not see the path that would lead me out to the gate. I don't remember being scared. Worse than that I was completely calm; my head was quiet. For a few minutes I hoped this was the end. Maybe I could just lie down here and sleep until the cold froze me into the earth. Maybe no one would ever find me and I could just let the world slip away from me and it would all be over without me having to do anything. The Park keeper found me and drove me back to my mother. Her red eyes and shaking hands made me want even more to die.

That winter was a dark time. Death seemed to edge closer. The whole world slipped away in a misty haze of activity. I spent my days standing staring out the window, unable to think or feel; barely existing. Maybe it sounds predictable but that winter was the first time I cut myself.

I hear a lot that people self harm because they feel in control and it takes away the pain that they are feeling. For me it was for attention. Not for people to crowd around pityingly but for someone to hear me screaming out for help. For someone to notice that I was losing myself; my soul; my life. I was dying and even in those days my survival instinct still flickered somewhere. I just wanted someone to make it better; to hear my plight and my pain and to realise that the silent figure at the window was overtaken by a force that was bigger and scarier than anyone knew. The cuts on my arm were just another form of starvation; another way of begging for help without being able to ask for it.

I was so scared. Scared of needing, of wanting more than I deserved – be that love, or food or human contact. I was scared of that basic human need for all those things because the further entrenched in illness I became, the less I believed I deserved any of it. I felt greedy.

After months of inertia there was no sign to anyone that the clouds were parting for me. If anything I was worse. It was time for a change. So I was sent home. The clinic would provide me with day care and I would sleep at home.

I think there were other sufferers in the clinic who were jealous of this – jealous that I would be able to exercise freely or run away. I was simply terrified. The clinic cocooned me safely away from a world which was too loud, too daunting, too complicated to be part of. I did not want to be home; to be in the same room where I had hidden so many meals or made myself sick or hidden for fear of having to eat. I did not want to be reminded of the time when my life was just starting to unravel and where the ghosts of all my lies and secrets on the path to illness were still languishing.

I went home. I exercised every night for a week until I passed out. I went to the clinic and endured the snide comments and cruel notes that the other patients passed around me. I let the bullying happen. I let the other sufferers speak openly in group meetings about my 'attention seeking' behaviour and my selfishness. I sat head bowed, letting it seep into me, believing every word.

So I stopped going. I refused to leave the house and I refused to eat. I was cruel, manipulative, driven. I brandished a kitchen knife at my mother when offered a carton of juice and I sat in my bedroom, waiting. Those were the worst days of my life. I was ready to die. I was so tired. My bones ached, my head ached, my eyes were blurred and I was simply too drained to fight anymore. My treat of the day was the dregs of water I sucked out of my toothbrush. That was my only sustenance. It is fascinating how quickly the body can deteriorate. Within six days my skin was white and would bruise when touched. My ears rang constantly and my eyesight was compromised. I had lost ten kilograms. I do not know why I did not die.

I do not know for sure what jolted me out of that trance between living and dying. I can believe that I lived a miracle and that whatever tiny glimmer of hope that was dormant inside me managed to flicker more brightly than before. I remember one morning, being unable to lie in the half light any longer and creeping downstairs to the kitchen. The world was still and for a minute I understood that nothing would change. The nights would turn to day, people would work and laugh. Whether I lived or died the world would carry on regardless; it did not notice my reflection in the window and it was not coming to save me. If I wanted to be part of that world I had to choose it for myself and suddenly I ached to be part of it. It was as though just for a moment I had woken before the illness and I could see what a waste it was. It was all just a pathetic, lonely waste of an existence and in that moment I was so tired of it. I have a diary entry from around that time which might help to understand the change. (I never wanted to re-visit that diary. I know it is there and it has remained untouched for ten years but I needed to remember exactly what saved my life, even if it just gives some other girl, somewhere else some hope)

'Remember how this feels. I want you to remember that this is what death feels like; slow and painful. You are alone and bruised all over. There are disgusting scabs and scars on your arms and legs that will always be there. You can barely speak or see and your family are broken. Is it worth it? Is it worth dying to be thin or to be in control or for anything? You are fifteen; is this all you were ever meant to be? Remember this if you ever want to do it again'

It does not happen in a moment like you might expect it to. Getting well was not a one-time decision but a choice I had to make over and over again every day. The struggle back to being me was more horrendous than anything I had experienced before. I remember lying on the floor in front of the fridge sobbing, furious with myself and with an illness that would not allow me to reach inside. Perhaps that is what helped. Suddenly I was so angry that I had the strength to fight back, rather than disappearing into my former comatose state of despair and oblivion.

I went back. I started to talk to my therapist. She guided me through the tangle inside, and tiny parts of me seemed to come back. I still felt guilty and scared and like a bad person, but the more she listened the more I understood that I was being heard, and that whatever was broken inside me had been seen and might be fixed.

It would be another six months before I left the clinic, and another six years before I felt like my real self again. Rejoining life is almost worse than isolating myself from it. I had to re-learn who I was. My mind had been overtaken by something else and I no longer had a sense of who I was; what I liked, what I believed in.

I left the clinic having taken some school exams whilst there and embarked on the next step of school life. But I was different. I had missed that stage of experimentation and development that my peers had gone through between fourteen and sixteen, and I lurched blindly through a wide and often dangerous variety of sexual encounters and substance use. I had not let myself want anything for so long that suddenly I wanted everything. I was ravenous for life. I wanted to feel everything I had stifled and I wanted all the human contact I had denied myself. I wanted to ingest everything I could as a way of giving two fingers to an illness which had made me abstinent. I wanted to be the best recovery story ever.

Two years later it happened again. During the summer of my first year at university I was almost surprised at how quickly the weight dropped off and the old way of thinking came back to me. I was more amazed at how much worse it was the second time around. I was older, I had experienced life and I did not want to be different or ill or fragile. I wanted a life.

By December of that year I had battled my way back to recovery. I cannot tell what made me ill the first time or even the second. There are many schools of thought and having lived it I am no closer to choosing the most appropriate theory. I hope that one day someone will understand the connections that I felt with noise. How as a little girl noise was scary for me and how as I got older there were times when even my own thoughts screamed too loudly inside.

The only thing I am sure of is that this illness knows no cultural background and no specific trauma. It does not discriminate and it does not give up without a fight.

To win my battle I had parents, siblings, therapists and care workers on my side. I met and worked with some of the best people I have ever known but there were relationships that I had to sacrifice. I am only sad that this had to be but I get it. Anorexia must be so frightening to watch. It is inexplicable to most people how someone can starve themselves with such determination. Many friends and their parents kept away from me as if sensing the force of the illness and terrified it might be catching.

I know my family faced the same stigma. I have worked hard to feel less guilty about this and to come to terms with everything that they went through. People grieve and heal differently and I have to respect that; my brother likes to talk about it to everyone and my sister does not want to remember. I think for those that know me there were mixed reactions about me writing this article and re-living that traumatic time. For years I suffered flashbacks. I do not remember much of that time, but often moments would come back to me; a feeling of pain or fear, a memory would come crashing into my world without warning.

For me it is only now, aged 25, that I feel able to write this and able to close that chapter of my life, safe in the knowledge that it cannot hurt me again. There are still anxieties that I deal with, but mostly I just feel peaceful. I know the people around me might be scared of me getting sick again. Only time will help assuage those fears. For me I just know that the cloud has lifted. I am comfortable in my own skin. I am not frightened.

Chapter 3

A parent's perspective

*Fiona Simons**

The big black cloud

I have heard Eating Disorders (EDs) called many things during my close acquaintance with them, but the one that sticks in my mind came from a consultant of an in-patient unit. He described EDs as 'a big black cloud over the whole family'. What he meant, I now think, is not just that a family member is enveloped in and isolated by the cloud, but also that the family does not have and cannot find an umbrella strong enough to withstand the onslaught.

My beloved daughter, the eldest of two girls, has had a diagnosed eating disorder for some nine years. I recognised that her attitude to food was unusual when she was about 12, when I sought some help, but we all now accept that she was ill before then. She became afraid that she would die of a horrible disease, and that we would not notice, and started to ask a set of ritualised questions before eating. The set became longer, and, if interrupted, had to be repeated. She was also doing a lot of sport (that said, so were most of the family) but the advice I got was that, as long as she wasn't either losing weight or vomiting, she was not deemed to have a problem. We later learnt that the calorie counting that started at this stage was to cover up the anxiety that my daughter felt about her health, growing up, and innumerable other concerns that she was unable to discuss.

Referral

We moved house at this stage, after a period when my husband (father of both children) worked in the new town. I thought that once the period of disruption and the move were over, things would get better: this was probably a phase. My daughter's questions increased in quantity and frequency. In hindsight, I could have dealt with them differently, but we were referred by the school nurse, to whom I had admitted my concerns, to the local Child and Adolescent Mental Health Service (CAMHS) team as a consequence of the questions and my

* The author's name is a pseudonym

increasing frustration and inability to cope with them. We were thus in the right place when, shortly after the first meeting at CAMHS, my daughter started to lose weight. Some five months later, just before Christmas 2005, she was formally diagnosed by our General Practitioner (GP) as anorexic. She was 14 years old.

Next stage

For the next year, the team involved with my daughter's care, GP, dietician, outreach workers from CAMHS, specialist nurse therapist, family therapist and family fought hard: the only person not fighting was the only person who could make a difference: my beautiful, funny, talented daughter. She was convinced there was nothing wrong with her, we were making a fuss about nothing, and anything said or done to contradict her view was simply ignored. She continued to lose weight, despite being on a regime which amounted to house arrest. She was constantly watched, given no or very little autonomy (and certainly none approaching that of her peers). By this time, she looked less than beautiful, had lost touch with her peers in every respect apart from the academic, and had lost her sense of humour and of the ridiculous. She was rude, uncooperative, disconnected from us and impossible to talk to. According to her, our only aim was to make her fat.

That Easter, she was offered an in-patient bed. She was distraught, vowed that things would change, and against my judgment, under pressure from my (mostly absent) husband and from her, we agreed to carry on at home if she could put on some weight. She rallied a bit over the summer, then at the start of the academic year in which she would take her GCSEs (academic qualifications involving examinations usually taken by students aged 15/16 years), she lost weight quickly. As she was weighed weekly by one of either our GP or practice nurse, we were aware of the scale of the problem. Despite all the persuasion, the therapy, the overseeing, she refused to eat, continued to exercise. Her lovely thick hair was mostly in her hairbrush, she was pale, with purplish hands, if she bent over her backbone was raised so she resembled a stegosaurus and every day it seemed there was some new ritual which she had to obey. She was desperate to lose weight and held a number of illogical beliefs about food and calories, including that, should she ingest one extra calorie over the daily allowance she set herself and calculated obsessively, she would gain weight as if pumped up like a balloon.

In-patient

My daughter, a shadow of herself in size and personality, was admitted as an in-patient to an adolescent unit, not a specialist facility, immediately before Christmas 2006. She was not cooperative but gained some weight so by the time she was 16 her weight was better, but her head was not. There is a legal procedure which can be used in limited circumstances by which patients can be treated and/ or admitted against their will. At that stage, my daughter was well enough not to be forced to accept treatment under that procedure. She insisted on discharge, and came home. She tried to go elsewhere, in a quest for freedom to lose weight, and we considered allowing her to do so. However, it is hard for 16-year-olds with supportive families and EDs to find emergency accommodation, and, dreadful as we expected it to be, at least if she was at home we could monitor her, encourage her to access CAHMS and make sure they were aware of her behaviour. We would also be on hand in an emergency.

She was home for eight weeks. We had thought she was ill, difficult and impossible to reach before the first admission. Now, she was completely overcome by the illness. The horror of her behaviour, of the futility of our care and of the terror we felt were and are indescribable. She was re-admitted in July 2007, saying that she wanted to recover. We were cynical and believed she was merely trying to avoid being forced to accept treatment (she was concerned that it would be a matter of record and might affect, for example, applications for jobs or university) to repeat the process. Happily, we were wrong: she cooperated with staff and us, was discharged from the unit just before Christmas and from out- patient care about a year later. She also started a new school (which she was not well enough to attend for much of the first term) where she knew no-one, yet quickly showed she was able to understand other people and forge relationships, in contrast to the years before that when the only relationship which interested her was with the ED.

Family responsibilities and emotions

During the three years in which my daughter was acutely ill, we lost the essence of her, and feared that it would never return. I understood how ancient cultures used exorcism on the mentally ill, believing them to be possessed by evil. She was truly horrid to live with, interested only in anorexia, bad tempered, rude, disobedient, untrustworthy and untruthful. It was as though she was hidden behind a thick sheet of glass: we could see her, but not reach her in any meaningful way. We were told to love the child, hate the illness, but when the illness looks and sounds like the child, they are hard to separate. She was told, as were we, how dangerous her behaviour was, to help her to understand what she was doing to herself, and to help us appreciate how important it was that she should eat, and stop exercising. The problem was that we understood all too well, but we could neither tie her to a chair, nor force feed her. We understood what we had to do, were powerless to do it, and terrified of the consequences of not doing it.

As my daughter was at home, and as we were involved in her care, it felt as if it was our responsibility that she ate, and up to us to stop her exercising. We already felt like failures as parents. Clearly this was our fault; there was no-one else whose fault it could be, after all. No-one else's child behaved like this, so it must be something we had done wrong. Had we moved at the wrong time? Had our belief that sport was a good way of meeting people eclipsed our precious daughter's needs? Why hadn't we dealt with her early anxieties more appropriately? We could have headed all this off at the pass if only we had been better parents. Should I give up work? What more could we do? Why weren't we able to make her better? To add to all that, we compounded our failure by not imposing a food regime, and a limit on activity, on our daughter. I read the accounts of parents who just insisted that the child ate, the child did, and roses grew around the door and life was lovely again. I persuaded, cajoled, bribed, sat for hours, stayed calm, shouted, cried, insisted, but nothing worked. Clearly, I was inadequate as a parent, incapable of doing the most basic parental task of feeding my young and keeping them safe.

As a family, we felt increasingly isolated: other parents told me their woes and frankly I would gladly have swapped any of those woes for mine. If I told them what was going on (to which my daughter was opposed as many were parents of her friends) I was told that she'd eat when she was hungry (I wish) or, 'Let her come to me for a weekend, I'll get her eating in no time' (no you won't, but my goodness you know how to make me feel inadequate).

Our feelings, of anger, helplessness, worry, fear, isolation, did not improve our equilibrium as a family. My husband buried himself in his work and often was away from home, leaving me to manage at home, and work. I worked because I felt more competent there than I did at home, and for at least some of the time, EDs were not at the forefront of my mind, which amounted to a bit of respite. Our younger daughter became anxious and disconnected at school, and resentful of the time spent on and with her sister. I should have been keeping my younger daughter's nose to the grindstone, but after every day of appointments, telephone conversations, trying to get advice on days we had no appointments, dealing with endless questions, trying not to scream at my elder daughter that she just needed to bloody eat (and worse), spending hours in supermarkets watching my elder daughter examine plain fat free yogurt pots for calorie values, frankly as long as my younger daughter was undemanding, so was I of her. My worries about my elder daughter were much more pressing.

Looking back, we were helped by a sympathetic, knowledgeable GP, by CAMHS (in particular one man who first assessed us, gave me support and became our family therapist, seeing us regularly over five years) and then the in-patient unit. I would not have coped without friends, virtual and real, who understood what I was going through and empathised. There are things that might have helped us (and others) but there are also some things that those dealing with us appeared not to understand. It is both those things that I hope to highlight here.

What parents feel

Not that long ago, the cause of eating disorders was said to be parents. There are no doubt cases to which families contribute, but current thinking is that parental influence is not solely responsible for a child developing an ED. Certainly, it is hard to accept one element alone as the cause when there are so many contributing factors, one of which seems to be underlying genetic traits. Current research suggests that, if support is given to carers, they in turn can offer more support to sufferers, and outcomes will improve, showing that families have an important role to play. There is a difference, however, between logic, research, and how a parent feels. I have not yet come across a parent who does not blame him/herself at some point in the illness. In my case, I felt that if I was responsible for the illness, then surely there was something I could do (or stop doing) and everything would be alright. If I had no responsibility, I had also to accept that I could not change things, and in the early days, that felt like giving my child up to the illness. My child was not fighting so I had to, however futile it was. I knew in my head that the illness (it is an illness, after all) was not my fault, but it took a long time, and therapy, to accept that in my heart. Helping all parents to reach that point, and offering them therapy to help, should be part of the work of the professional team.

It is hard for us to be open with you, because we do not necessarily know what you do, or what you offer: we are referred to some mysterious place called CAMHS, and as we blame ourselves for the predicament we are in, we assume others, including you, will too. Whilst often you offer the first real expert help we have encountered, and seeing you is therefore A Good Thing, it takes us into unknown territory. Some of what you talk about, for example family therapy, sounds threatening to us.

In addition, when we first meet you, we have either been watching our child commit slow suicide in front of us and felt helpless, or have just discovered the magnitude of a problem our child had hidden, and feel neglectful. We may know an eating disorder has been diagnosed, but we may need time to come to terms with the fact that life is not as we expected it to be. Unless we have encountered an ED before, we are unlikely to understand the implications of the diagnosis. I thought that, once diagnosed, there would be a cure. We would see you, my daughter would get better. In my defence, that had been the context of my encounters with the medical profession until that point, as I guess it is for many. It later became apparent that things might not be that simple, and we might be in this for the long haul, which was profoundly depressing. I did not truly understand that an ED is a mental illness, and as I had had no real experience of mental illness, I did not know what to expect. Our team was careful to manage our expectations, not to give us false hope, and to avoid speculation as to what the time scale might be at any stage, which was frustrating at the time, but in retrospect I am glad that I did not know how long the long haul might be.

Hope, too, is a difficult issue. For me, the worst times were not the times I knew things were bad and expected them to stay that way or deteriorate. The worst times were when I began to hope that there was some progress in the right direction, only for those hopes to be dashed (as, after all, is the nature of the illness and of recovery). Losing hope is a desperate feeling, with which I learnt to cope by trying not to hope in the first place. I know I was seen as negative, and pessimistic, by the professional team, but I was the main carer, and my feelings needed to be accommodated too. I have heard carers tell each other that they need to look after themselves in order to have the strength to care for their loved one (as the airline advice goes, put your oxygen mask on before helping others with theirs) and professional teams need to understand that need, and do what they can to meet it. Is it possible for you to offer to supervise one meal a day, or even a week, for the parents? Can you give them time to get out and breathe air uncontaminated by the ED? This might be especially important for a single parent.

Walking on eggshells

One of the more pernicious aspects of an ED which is difficult to explain to those with no experience of it is the way in which the ED can control the entire family, as well as being a black cloud over and around it. The ED affects what one does and says, to the extent that it can control the vocabulary used by the family. 'Well' to a person with an ED, in terms of their looks, is synonymous with 'fat' and should be avoided. However, others do not understand that, and when they meet a sufferer, they think it rude to remark on how dreadful the sufferer looks. Families and professionals have learnt to comment on clothes, hairclips or makeup, but others say, untruthfully, 'You look well'. For some reason, what I or the professionals said a hundred times to my daughter was clearly wrong when compared to what a comparative stranger said once in a moment of awkwardness.

My daughter could not bear the thought that she was fat. She seemed pathologically afraid that she was or would become so (in passing, whilst I agree that the messages given out by the media are at best inconsistent so far as size and weight are concerned, my daughter did not want to look like a supermodel, or be a particular size). To be lazy, in her eyes, was the same as fat. Anything that could possibly infer that she was lazy therefore carried the implication that she was fat. So far, so logical, but carried to an ED driven conclusion, I could not ask her to help in the house. If, for example, she was asked to empty the dishwasher, she had not done it already, so I was accusing her of being lazy. I soon learnt that it was simpler, and quicker, to do the chore myself. In fact my daughter never did a chore without being asked, which confirmed in some people's minds the attention seeking nature of the illness, although I think she had so much ED noise in her head that there was no spare space for noticing the needs (or even sometimes the existence) of others.

The solution to an accusation of laziness was to exercise manically. The solution to a comment made thoughtlessly by me or by someone who did not know she was unwell/did not understand the effects of the illness was hours of ritualised questions. I remember one particular incident when I said to both girls in the midst of feeling that I was responsible for all things domestic, 'I am fed up with doing everything around here, you need to pull your weight'. What did I mean by that? What sort of weight was I referring to? I must mean she was heavy. If I thought she was heavy, why did I keep saying she was too thin? Why did I lie to her?

The whole family learned to think before they said anything, to examine every phrase for an ED interpretation, to treat every conversation as a game of chess and look two moves further on. It affected our spontaneity in words and deed, and in fact still does.

Objectivity

As part of the professional team, you do a wonderful, important job. It is, however, a job, and that gives you an objectivity that is impossible for us to have. For parents, this is our life. We wake up to it every morning, we go to sleep having dealt with it all day and we dread doing so again tomorrow. We face the worst thing a parent can face – the loss of a child – and that possibility is very real. My child was allocated an in-patient bed because the person in it before her died. My daughter believed that would not happen to her, but I had no such confidence. That, added to the constant reminders of how ill my daughter was, and of the consequences of her behaviour, increased my anxiety and my concern.

I recall one day not waking up to the usual sound of obsessive exercising in my daughter's bedroom. Like the mother of a baby who has slept all night for the first time, I dreaded going to her room. When I steeled myself to go in, it was empty. She arrived home, sweating and in exercise clothes, 30 minutes later and the first thing she did was to deny she had been out exercising. It is hard to argue with someone whose reality is not the same as yours, and sometimes I was convinced either I was mad, or my daughter was. We would go to the supermarket when she was banned from exercise because we had to shop, and she could not be left alone, as she would exercise. She would go and fetch an item, and disappear. I would look for her frantically, believing she had collapsed under a shelf, then I would spot her sprinting up and back down each aisle from one end of the shop to the other. And when we did meet up, she would deny having done so. What other shoppers must have thought, as we hissed at each other, I dread to think!

The concept of truth was stretched beyond recognition. My daughter would have handed in £5 found in the street, but she lied about many things all connected with the illness: her weight, what she had eaten, what she had done. This had important ramifications for us all: I tried always to be truthful, the approach counselled by the professionals. In the end, this was proved to be the best policy, because when the ED could rationally be shown to be untruthful, I had shown that I was always honest, so could be trusted. It would have been easier to lie myself, at times, but the team encouraged us to be straightforward and led by example, which was important to us as well as to my daughter. The issue for us, later, was how, and when, to trust someone who had shown themselves so consistently not to be trustworthy.

Positioning

As our family therapist put it, we were continually positioned by the ED so that, whatever we did, it was wrong. My wise mother used to say that a parent's place is in the wrong, but this was magnified by the illness. If I told my daughter off, or looked at her in the wrong tone of voice (as my mother would say to describe those moments when, whatever a parent does, or omits to do, they cause offence), I gave her permission to exercise/not eat. But if I did not tell her to eat, or not to exercise, I also gave her that permission. Either way, to my increasing despair and desperation, the result was star jumps performed aggressively in front of me, or running up and down stairs, in contravention of the professionals' advice, increasing the risk of a cardiac event. If I tried to stop her, she accused me of assault. In the supermarket, if I tired of waiting for her to examine the labels of foods, I was calling her fat, as I did not want her to eat the item. If I encouraged her to take an item, I was not persuasive enough, for the same reason. In any event, I was firmly positioned between the devil and the deep blue sea. It was important for us to understand that the illness so positioned us, not that this was, as we first thought, our fault, for not being quick or clever or simply good enough parents to recognise the issues and deal with them calmly.

Calm was a particular challenge for me. I was angry that this had happened to us, that the illness threatened my family, riled by the repetitive questions, and infuriated by the lying: I am not sure why that offended me so greatly, perhaps because it was so illogical, and thus hard to challenge, and it also went against all the moral values I was brought up with and had tried to transfer to my own children. That I was powerless increased my anger and frustration and it was hard not to take that out on the ED in the form of my daughter. Once the separation of child and illness was suggested, and it was pointed out to me that the ED thrived on conflict, I began to see that, if I lost my temper, the ED won that round. I was reluctant to hand it any victory, however small, and that knowledge helped me to stay calm. Again, you, the professionals, are more objective than us parents. You can use that objectivity sensitively, point out patterns we are too close to see, and suggest strategies that we might use to help ourselves as well as our children.

Strategies

We did of course discuss this and other strategies in family therapy and with CAMHS. One problem was that we had, what with holidays, absence and other commitments, not to mention the calls on therapists' time by other patients, a session (one hour) every two weeks, and then every week. In those sessions, if they were joint ones, we talked about the last week, the issues we had had, and then we were given some suggestions as to what to do. Often, this was in the last 10 minutes of a session. If the session was for my daughter alone, I was told what she had agreed as we were leaving. If we were given some strategies in that one hour, we often did not have time to fully discuss them, and I then had the rest of the week, some 167 hours, to fail to put into practice the thing discussed in that one hour.

It is perhaps also relevant that my daughter was getting older: once 16, the rules about what I could be told seemed to change. I was no less involved in her care, she was living with us and dependent on us, but there was more reluctance to involve me. I recognise it is hard for professionals if the child does not want information passed to parents, but where the parents are looking after, housing and caring for the child, they need the information and guidance to function appropriately in the relationship. It seems to me that parents cannot be relied upon to provide a safe place of residence and adequate care if those parents are not fully involved with the treatment and the strategies suggested by the professional team. One family I know were told, the child having agreed to stay at home and be constantly monitored, rather than go into a unit, that was the way forward. The effect on the parents, their jobs, their lives, seemed not to be considered: certainly they had not been consulted.

As to the strategies suggested, many involved food, and the effects of the illness on both us and our daughter. Food had once been a pleasurable experience: sitting round after a meal, chatting, putting the world to rights, but mealtimes were a battleground by the time we got to CAMHS. There we talked about planning meals, how to cope with a refusal to eat, what to do when there was nothing in the house my daughter would eat (cue trips to the supermarket), how to monitor consumption away from home, who would support which meals and how to challenge the myths put forward by the ED. I often needed to off-load, as well as discuss behavioural issues, so not all the sessions were about food. The dietician we saw was well regarded by my daughter (the rest of the team warranted only abuse) and she challenged my daughter's beliefs, talked about portion control and a healthy diet, but she could not prevent either the desperate attempts to lose more weight on my daughter's part, nor the obsessive weighing and calorie counting that was part of our lives. I tried to maintain eating meals together, but the decreasing list of things my daughter would eat made this increasingly challenging. That list also changed without warning, so planning was difficult. At some points my daughter was strict about when she ate, so not only were social occasions which involved food impossible, but those which occurred at a meal or snack time were too. Not only did my daughter become more isolated, so did the rest of us.

Doing one's best

As mentioned, these issues added up to a suggestion that my daughter be admitted as an in-patient some seven months before she was in fact admitted. In retrospect, was it a mistake to keep her at home? First, all any of us can ever do is make the best decision possible on the information available at any one time. There is no point in examining it later and wishing things had turned out differently. Parents need to understand that, and see that, whilst there may have been alternatives, what they did do was not wrong, it was just different.

Second, I am under no illusions that being admitted as an in-patient saved my daughter's life, but it was disruptive for us as a family. Patients can be resentful and difficult, and refuse to cooperate, increasing the distress levels of all concerned, and the transition from in- to out-patient, a gradual process requiring much flexibility, is challenging. So too is the disruption in terms of the family: do you make a round trip every night to visit? If you get there and your child refuses to speak to you, how do you cope? What do you do with younger children: make them visit too, or abandon them to friends or family, at a time when they feel they are already abandoned in favour of the ill sibling? Given these and other stresses, it was important for us to know that we had done all we could to keep my daughter out of hospital, so that, however hard it was to deal with the consequences, we understood that we had had no choice but to allow admission, and did not feel guilty. That lack of guilt is important for carers.

I hope it is apparent that we worked as a team with CAMHS, the unit and with all our supporters at home and school. That cooperation was vital, not least because, if the ED spots a way of driving a wedge between those involved in the sufferers' care, it will exploit it. I would only say this: please acknowledge that we know our children. We have known them a long time, and whilst you are experts on EDs, you are not an expert on my child: please try to trust me and listen to me when I tell you about him or her.

Adapting

Looking back, I can see that what I was able to do at the start of our dreadful journey was very different to that which I was capable of by the end. In the beginning, I thought that, if my daughter ate at all, that was better than eating nothing. The advice from the team was that I should ensure she ate what she had agreed to eat, not a different meal, or a different version of the same meal. If she refused, I was not to run about finding an acceptable alternative (those supermarket trips again!), because that was a downward spiral of concession on my part.

Initially, there were two issues. First, how was I to ensure she ate anything? Second, I found it impossible to go against my parental instincts, which were telling me that eating something was surely better than nothing. I therefore found it impossible to do what the professional team were advising. Later on in the journey, we were advised to stand back, tell my daughter that what she ate and did was her choice, not ours, and it was up to her to make responsible choices: if she did not, the consequences were known to her. I was not, prior to the first admission, able to follow that advice.

Some years further on, however, and in the face of my daughter's absolute determination to lose weight as fast as possible, we reconsidered our position. We felt that we had tried everything, and that there were no options available save to consider more carefully that those which the team were suggesting. Until then, we did not feel able to go against our instincts, but we reached a point where we understood that there were four of us in the family, and if my daughter was ready to destroy herself, the rest of us were not about to go with her. We told her how we felt, and got our lives back a little: we went out, we left her to her own devices. We understood that she did what she chose to do whether we approved or not, were in the house or not, and it was apparent that us caring so much and trying to stop her behaviours did no good to her or us. We carried on caring, but stopped taking responsibility. I recall for example ensuring that she had bus money in the beginning, so she could get the bus, and if she chose not to, she could not blame me for the decision to walk home. Later on, I reimbursed her only if I saw a ticket. Frustrating as it was for the professional team, we had to get to that place when we were ready (we got there faster than we would have without them, of that I am sure). In fact, I now see that time as a turning point and wonder whether, if we had taken a harder line earlier, it would have made a difference: but we made the best decision we could on the information available, which was all we could have done.

Continuity

Continuity of care is also important. We were lucky: the in-patient unit was close to home, and for over five years my daughter was seen by only two therapists and our family therapist saw us all through two admissions and two discharges. Others in our area and in other areas have not been so fortunate, but continuity of care should not be a matter of luck. The continuity we experienced enabled us to know and trust each other and thus to be honest: our therapist may have preferred less honesty, as we screeched at each other and indeed at him. The work he did was invaluable, and the skills my husband and I learnt have been useful and practical in any situation. Whilst sessions were painful, they were also constructive.

It is my view that, for any therapy to work, there has to be honesty, and for that, we have to trust you. If we do not, or if the relationships just do not gel, in a private setting, different therapies or therapists or both can be tried. That should be available in the public sector also (and would benefit you as well as us) but there is something particularly depressing about explaining ones situation yet again to someone new, wasting time getting to know each other, going over old ground, when the illness is running rampant.

Endgame

For us, the journey has been a long one. Many times I hoped we were at the beginning of the end, only to find we were not even near the end of the beginning, but my daughter has done well in exams despite the illness. She decided to go to university, where she works and plays hard, and her friends do not suspect her of having been unwell. There remain vestiges of the illness which are affecting and will continue to affect her long term health. We however are the lucky ones.

The illness has made us question our values and our priorities, although I wish we had done so without it. We have met some of our best friends through or as a result of it, and even had opportunities which would not otherwise have come our way. We have learnt about ourselves and each other, and we know who we can rely on and who we can trust to help. As a unit and individually, we have emerged stronger and our resilience has astounded us. That said, my only wish, every new year, is not to have to endure another year of a life polarised by the ED, and I have wished that far too many times.

The consultant was half right: EDs are a big black cloud over the family. The other half of the story, however, is that EDs are insidious killers, and they blight lives. We have been fortunate, so far, to survive as intact as we are, and I have no doubt that our professional team were instrumental in helping us achieve that. You may be the only people that understand some of what we go through, can acknowledge our pain, help us to feel less isolated and powerless, give us some options and support. As objective professionals, your perspective is not the same as ours, and that fundamental difference can be, I am sure, as frustrating for you as it is for us. Appreciating the reasons why your advice is hard for us to follow, and helping us to understand the reasoning behind the advice should help parents and professionals to work together as a team. The more we work as a team, parents and professionals together, the better the chances of recovery for the sufferer, but also the better the chance of the family surviving this dreadful illness intact.

Anything you can do to help parents feel understood is also valuable. Setting up and publicising parents and carer groups, or giving us the help and support to do so, helps us feel less isolated. I had wonderful support from the message board funded by **beat*** and the helpline that charity operates, but found out about it by accident. I tended to find that, if I asked, help was available, but until I asked, I did not know what was on offer. Could you, for example, prepare a pack of information to be given to parents referred to you, with helpful numbers, **beat** details and their helpline number, nearby carers groups, perhaps some references to books parents might find informative?

In the end, you go home (I hope) to a safe haven. Our houses have ceased to be safe, inhabited as they are by the illness. But with your help, and cooperation between us, there will be a haven for us in time. I look back and am grateful to those involved in my daughter's care, particularly those who were straightforward, firm but fair. We had some robust discussions, at times, but I still see and look forward to seeing some of them. I wonder, will families referred to you reflect on their involvement with your service and feel the same way?

---

* **beat** provides helplines, online support and a network of UK-wide self-help groups to help adults and young people in the UK beat their eating disorder: www.b-eat.co.uk

Part II

Assessment and course

Chapter 4

Overview of eating disorders in childhood and adolescence

Rachel Bryant-Waugh and Bryan Lask

Overview

In this chapter we provide an overview of the range of eating difficulties and disorders commonly encountered in child and adolescent clinical practice. We discuss presenting features, as well and diagnostic and classification issues. We reflect on developmental variations in clinical presentation, and at the end of the chapter we provide working definitions of the types of eating disorder and eating disturbance we have described

Introduction

Anorexia nervosa and bulimia nervosa most commonly affect adolescent girls and young adult women, with those between the ages of 15 and 35 representing the majority who receive treatment for eating disorders. Yet eating disorders are not restricted to this population; they also occur in boys and men (e.g. Muise, Stein and Arbess, 2003; Mangweth-Matzek, Rupp, Hausmann, Gusmerotti, Kemmler et al., 2010; Pinhas, Morris, Crosby and Katzman, 2011), in older women (e.g. Scholtz, Hill and Lacey, 2010) and in pre-pubertal children of both sexes (e.g. Swenne and Thurfjell, 2003; Lazaro, Moreno, Baos and Castro, 2005; Madden, Morris, Zurynski, Kohn and Elliot, 2009). Although there might be some variability in the detail of the clinical presentation related to age and gender, the core features are constant across the life span.

However, there are a number of other types of eating difficulty or disturbance that occur in childhood and adolescence that can be equally clinically significant, yet have been difficult to categorise using the existing diagnostic classification schemes of the World Health Organization's ICD 10 (1992) and the American Psychiatric Association's DSM-IV-TR (2000). This situation has contributed to considerable debate and confusion, with a multitude of different terms being used to describe what appear to be essentially similar presentations. The classification of childhood eating difficulties has in general been relatively neglected, although currently the main diagnostic systems are under revision (Rosen, 2010). The hope is that some of the better described clinical presentations described further in this chapter might be better captured by available diagnostic categories in the future.

In the meantime there continues to be considerable inconsistency in the literature about the nature of eating difficulties in children and the terminology used to describe them (see Chatoor and Surles, 2004). Some believe that eating disorders such as anorexia nervosa simply do not occur in children. Our own clinical experience suggests that the youngest patients with true anorexia nervosa are around eight years of age. Diagnostic criteria that include a requirement that amenorrhoea should be present have probably contributed to pre-menarcheal girls being excluded for consideration by some, as by definition they cannot fulfil one of the essential criteria. In contrast to this tendency to exclude children from being considered as having anorexia nervosa has been the use of the term 'infantile anorexia nervosa' to describe a specific form of infant feeding difficulty (e.g. Chatoor, Egan, Getson, Menvielle and O'Donnell, 1988). Infants clearly cannot fulfil the diagnostic criteria for anorexia nervosa of ICD 10 or DSM-IV-TR as they do not have the required cognitive capacity to develop the core psychopathology. The use of the term infantile anorexia nervosa (now replaced by 'infantile anorexia') has perhaps been unhelpful as it implies some developmental continuity for which there is at present no convincing evidence.

Other children may present with one of a range of problems described further in this chapter, and there remains a lack of consensus and clarity as to whether these are age-related precursors of the formal eating disorders or something else entirely. For example, some clinicians might describe childhood presentations not meeting full criteria for anorexia nervosa as eating disorder not otherwise specified (EDNOS) while others might consider them a different type of disorder entirely (e.g. a primary phobic disorder characterised by food avoidance). It is most likely that we are seeing a mixture of different types of clinically significant presentations, some which may be related to formal eating disorders and some not. There is much scope for further work in this area to achieve greater clarity around the classification of childhood onset eating disorders. Current proposals for diagnostic revision of DSM-IV-TR include a new category named Avoidant/ Restrictive Food Intake Disorder (ARFID). If a criteria set for this proposed diagnosis is included in DSM 5, it will hopefully help move the field forward (Bryant-Waugh, Markham, Kreipe and Walsh, 2010).

There are also real difficulties related to the assessment of eating difficulties in children, both in relation to assessing specific eating disorder psychopathology, but also in relation to elucidating the basis for other forms of clinical eating disturbances occurring in children. This is in part related to the general lack of psychometrically sound, standardised instruments appropriate for age and presentation, and in part related to the cognitive competencies of children (see Chapter 7 for some of the currently available assessment measures). This has meant that much of the published work on the subject has been based on clinical case reports. Whereas many of the children included in these case series have received formal diagnoses of an eating disorder, it has been difficult to demonstrate this on the basis of objective, reliable assessment because the necessary tools simply have not been available.

There has been much media interest in the occurrence of eating disorders in children over recent years. This interest has unfortunately helped to promote two myths. The first is that we are currently seeing some sort of 'epidemic' and the second is that eating disorders in children are a new phenomenon, with eating disorder sufferers becoming ever younger. Neither is true. The first point is dealt with in more detail in Chapter 5. Although it does seem true that there is a general increase in weight sensitivity and even dieting behaviour in children, these do not necessarily lead to full eating disorders, which remain relatively rare in the childhood population. It may well be that attempts to manipulate weight in childhood lead to a greater risk of developing an eating disorder later, but the rates of children with anorexia nervosa presenting under the age of 12 appear relatively stable (although again there are significant difficulties obtaining good epidemiological data).

The second myth can be easily dispelled by looking at some of the historical literature. Two of the earliest authors who are attributed as describing cases of anorexia nervosa in children were Collins (1894) and Marshall (1895). Collins wrote a case history of a 7-year-old girl who was emaciated and refusing food. Further details of the case history suggest that this was not simply related to physical illness, but that there was a psychological component to the girl's food avoidance. Marshall wrote about what he termed 'anorexia nervosa' in an 11-year-old girl, who eventually died from starvation. Since this time there have been many other reports in the literature. In the earlier publications, these were mostly individual case studies, but later case series began to be described. It is evident that in the eyes of the authors of such papers, for the most part child and adolescent mental health practitioners, the young age of the patient has never excluded a possible diagnosis of anorexia nervosa.

It is difficult to be certain that a similar concept of anorexia nervosa has been held throughout the period it has been described in the literature, and in fact it is likely that this is not the case. After all, the diagnostic criteria we are using at the start of the twenty-first century remain in a constant state of revision. Criteria included under the term anorexia nervosa in the past differ from current criteria. The case series described over 50 years ago by Warren (1968) seems likely to include children who would not now fulfil diagnostic criteria for anorexia nervosa, but instead presented with food fads, food refusal, or other more commonly occurring childhood eating difficulties. The fact remains, however, that children have for a very long time been known to suffer from alterations in eating patterns, which are recognised to have a psychological component and can lead to very serious physical complications. This situation is by no means new, and is not a twenty-first century phenomenon.

It is really only over the last two or three decades that children with eating disorders have come to be regarded as a subgroup of interest. The literature on all aspects of eating disorders specifically relating to this younger population remains small in relation to that relating to older adolescents and adults, yet continues to grow. This chapter aims to describe the different types of eating disorder and eating disturbance occurring in children aged 14 and under. We use the terms 'early onset' and 'childhood onset' to refer to eating disorders seen in clinical settings in children between the ages of 7 and 14 years.

Eating disorders and eating disturbances occurring in childhood

We have worked in child and adolescent mental health clinics specifically providing a service for children and their families where under-eating, food restriction, low weight and/or avoidance of weight gain are primary features. The types of problem most commonly seen in the age range from around 8 to 14 years in this context are the following:

- anorexia nervosa (and atypical or subclinical forms);
- bulimia nervosa (and atypical or subclinical forms);
- food avoidance emotional disorder;
- selective eating;
- restrictive eating;
- food refusal;
- specific fear or phobia leading to avoidance of eating (includes functional dysphagia);
- pervasive refusal syndrome;
- appetite loss secondary to depression.

The interrelationship between these different types of eating disturbance is not always clear, and there are certainly areas of overlap between some of them. They will be described in more detail in the following sections. It should be noted that there is a further set of types of eating disturbance not in the above list, and not further discussed here. These include presentations such as binge eating disorder, compulsive overeating, overeating associated with organic disease and pica (the deliberate ingestion of non-food substances). In addition, feeding disorder of infancy and early childhood and other feeding difficulties encountered in preschool children are also not covered here. The interested reader is referred to other volumes and publications regarding presentations not covered in this chapter (e.g. Cooper and Stein, 2006; Decaluwé, Braet and Fairburn, 2003; Marcus and Kalarchian, 2003).

The diagnosis of eating disorders in children

The diagnosis of an eating disorder in a child remains in many cases problematic. Diagnostic criteria are currently being revised, but at the time of writing those of ICD–10 (WHO, 1992) and DSM-IV-TR (American Psychiatric Association, 2000) are in most common use. Using the ICD–10 system the following eating disorder diagnoses are possible:

- anorexia nervosa (F50.0);
- atypical anorexia nervosa (F50.1);
- bulimia nervosa (F50.2);
- atypical bulimia nervosa (F50.3);
- overeating associated with other psychological disturbances (F50.4);
- vomiting associated with other psychological disturbances (F50.5);
- other eating disorders (F50.8);
- eating disorder, unspecified (F50.9).

The DSM-IV-TR eating disorder diagnoses are:

- 307.1 anorexia nervosa
    - restricting type
    - binge eating/purging type;
- 307.51 bulimia nervosa
    - purging type
    - non-purging type;
- 307.50 eating disorder not otherwise specified (EDNOS).

If we consider the different types of clinically significant eating disturbance already mentioned, it is evident that the terms used to describe these presentations do not always neatly translate into available diagnostic categories. For the purposes of research the use of clearly defined diagnostic criteria is essential to aid communication. Where diagnostic criteria are not strictly applied or different diagnostic or classificatory systems are used, the value of any results may be limited as it will be difficult to make comparisons with findings from other studies. For example, comparing results of outcome studies is only possible if the selection of individuals included in the different studies has been based on similar criteria for inclusion. However, for clinical purposes, it may be less essential to apply strict diagnostic criteria since, for a large group of children with significant eating difficulties, this will not be a particularly meaningful exercise as they simply do not fit (Nicholls, Chater and Lask, 2000).

We know that around half of all adults attending eating disorder clinics will receive a diagnosis of eating disorder not otherwise specified, more commonly known as EDNOS (Fairburn and Harrison, 2003; Turner and Bryant-Waugh, 2004). We also know that within this group a number of distinct subgroups can be identified (e.g. those with binge eating disorder; those not quite meeting diagnostic criteria for anorexia nervosa; and those not quite meeting diagnostic criteria for bulimia nervosa). If we were to use EDNOS for all types of clinically significant eating disturbance seen in children, the heterogeneity of the group would be so great that the term would be meaningless. To us, it seems more sensible to reserve EDNOS for children who present with the core cognitive features of anorexia and bulimia nervosa, but who may not meet full diagnostic criteria for these disorders. That is, in children who present with weight and/or shape concerns EDNOS can helpfully be considered. Presentations such as selective eating and food avoidance emotional disorder (see below) are clearly different, and in particular lack any evidence of concern about weight and shape. In our view they should not be included under the EDNOS umbrella. At present there are no satisfactory widely accepted diagnostic terms for such presentations. In the meantime, we suggest that the continued use of descriptive terms remains clinically worthwhile. The sections below describe in a little more detail the various types of disturbances commonly encountered.

Anorexia nervosa

Anorexia nervosa is characterised by determined attempts to lose weight or avoid weight gain. This can be achieved through avoiding or otherwise restricting normal food intake, self-induced vomiting, laxative abuse, excessive exercising, or more usually a combination of one or more of these. Weight and/or body mass index (BMI) drop to a level well below that necessary to allow the child to continue to grow and develop. Because children should be growing, failure to gain weight can be regarded as equivalent to weight loss in adults. Weight loss is a matter of considerable concern in childhood, and is particularly worrying in pre-pubertal children who have relatively low total body fat levels. As well as dietary restriction leading to weight loss, restriction of fluid intake is not uncommon in young patients with anorexia nervosa. In a relatively early paper Irwin (1981) highlighted this 'refusal to maintain hydration' which can rapidly lead to a state of dangerous dehydration.

Children with anorexia nervosa have characteristic thoughts about weight and/or shape, often believing they are fat when they are underweight, or displaying a pronounced fear of becoming overweight, which directly influence their eating behaviour and attempts to manage their weight. They tend to have a tremendous sense of dissatisfaction regarding their bodily appearance, which can initially become worse as treatment progresses and weight increases. Many children with anorexia nervosa suffer from a preoccupation with their weight, shape, food, and/or eating, to the extent that their concentration can be significantly impaired. They may be experts at calorie counting and are acutely aware of the calorie content of every mouthful they eat.

Such children may give a range of reasons for refusing food. The most common, in our experience, is a fear of fatness, but they may also give feelings of fullness, nausea, abdominal pain, appetite loss and difficulty in swallowing as reasons (Fosson, Knibbs, Bryant-Waugh and Lask, 1987). In order to fulfil a diagnosis of anorexia nervosa though, there must be some evidence of specific concerns around weight, shape or body composition.

In terms of strategies used by children to reduce their weight or avoid weight gain, aside from restriction of food intake, the most common by far are excessive exercising and self-induced vomiting. Laxative abuse is less common. Excessive exercising may have developed out of an increase in activity levels that has initially been encouraged. Daily exercise workouts, excessive swimming, jogging, or other routines, can become time-consuming features of the child's life. Exercising may be carried out in secret, often at night. Vomiting is a strategy used by many children, to such an extent that it is often prudent to assume that a child who is not gaining weight once treatment has started must be vomiting. Laxative abuse is probably less common in younger individuals due to limitations in access. However, laxative abuse does occur and potential electrolyte imbalances and mineral deficiencies need to be monitored.

In our experience, children may develop anorexia nervosa from around the age of 8 onwards. The clinical presentation of anorexia nervosa in childhood is very similar to that in adulthood (with the obvious exception of absence of menstruation in pre-menarcheal patients). The only slight exception to this is perhaps the fact that, in most boys with AN, shape appears to be much more of an issue than weight. These boys are more concerned to avoid becoming fat, unfit or unhealthy, and may not be so much set on losing weight as on preventing the development of a flabby physique. The end result is however very similar, with the avoidance of foods regarded as being fattening or unhealthy, usually excessive exercising, and subsequent significant weight loss.

There continues to be debate around which of the clinical features of anorexia nervosa should be included as prerequisites for diagnosis (see e.g. Hebebrand, Casper, Treasure and Schweiger, 2004), and which represent commonly occurring characteristics that may or may not be present. The finer detail of the physical, behavioural, cognitive and emotional aspects of the disorder are likely to differ between individuals, indicating that different children will require different priorities in treatment. In addition, anorexia nervosa will be associated with an accompanying depression in a significant number of children (see also the later subsection on appetite loss secondary to depression). In some cases, it may be associated with clear obsessive-compulsive symptomatology, and may come and go in intensity in an inverse relationship with the obsessive compulsive disorder. It has been shown that, in particular, boys with anorexia nervosa present with relatively high levels of obsessive-compulsive features (Shafran, Bryant-Waugh, Lask and Arscott, 1995).

Current proposals for revision to the diagnostic criteria for anorexia nervosa include dropping the amenorrhea requirement (Attia and Roberto, 2009) and relaxing the weight criterion (Walsh and Sysko, 2009).

Bulimia nervosa

Bulimia nervosa is an eating disorder characterised by episodes of overeating in which the person experiences a sense of loss of control, with accompanying attempts to avoid weight gain by self-induced vomiting, laxative abuse, diuretic abuse, dietary restriction, or excessive exercise. Weight and shape concern is a core feature, as in the case of anorexia nervosa, which is manifested by attempts to control weight and minimise the weight gain that might normally result from overeating. Self-induced vomiting is the most common method used to avoid weight gain in young patients with this disorder. Bulimia nervosa is often accompanied by other forms of self-harm such as wrist scratching, burning the skin with cigarettes, alcohol and drug abuse, overdosing, and other risk-taking behaviour. None of these additional features are essential to making the diagnosis as their presence is very variable between individuals.

Bulimia nervosa appears to be rare in childhood and early adolescence, with very few below the age of 14 presenting for treatment. It is of interest to note, however, that many bulimic women, who typically only present for treatment after many years of having the disorder, often report that their bulimia started in early adolescence. In our own experience, we have seen only very small numbers of children aged 13 and under who have received a full diagnosis of bulimia nervosa. Of these young patients with bulimia nervosa (one was only 7 years old), none has manifested the more dramatic forms of self-harming seen in older patients.

Food avoidance emotional disorder

Food avoidance emotional disorder (FAED) is a term that was first used by Higgs and colleagues to describe a group of children who have a primary emotional disorder where food avoidance is a prominent feature (Higgs, Goodyer and Birch, 1989). These authors originally described a group of children who did not fully meet diagnostic criteria for anorexia nervosa, but who did present with weight loss and food avoidance. They suggested that food avoidance emotional disorder may be an intermediate condition between anorexia nervosa and childhood emotional disorder (with no eating disorder). They also suggested it might have an overall more favourable prognosis. The characteristics of food avoidance emotional disorder were originally set out as follows (Higgs et al., 1989):

- a disorder of the emotions in which food avoidance is a prominent symptom in the presenting complaint;
- a history of food avoidance or difficulty (e.g. food fads or restrictions);
- a failure to meet the criteria for anorexia nervosa;
- the absence of organic brain disease, psychosis, illicit drug abuse, or prescribed drug related side effects.

Our experience of children who fall into the food avoidance emotional disorder category is that they are often extremely unwell physically, with very low weight and growth impairment. We do not consider that they by definition have a less serious or milder form of eating disorder than those with anorexia nervosa, although there is considerable variability within both groups in terms of prognosis and outcome. It is clear that children with food avoidance emotional disorder do not have the same preoccupation with weight and shape, nor do they have a distorted view of their own weight or shape. They do have mood disturbance, combined with weight loss and determined food avoidance. The mood disturbance tends to take the form of mild depression or more generalised anxiety, which is difficult to diagnose in its own right. Interestingly many of these children come from families who experience a significant level of non-specific illness, aches, pains and health-related impairment. Often such children will have missed the odd day of school here and there throughout their school career. It is interesting to speculate whether such children learn to express emotional difficulties physically through family modelling and reinforcement. There is no evidence for this but there is no doubt that it is extremely difficult for these children to eat normally.

Although organic brain disease is an exclusion criterion, we have noted that some children with food avoidance emotional disorders do have other physical illnesses or disorders. These children seem to develop food avoidance as part of their emotional response to physical ill health. In such cases the food avoidance is not a direct symptom of the child's illness, and might arguably be equally well conceptualised as a form of adjustment disorder.

Selective eating

This term has been used to describe children who limit their food intake to a very narrow range of preferred foods (see e.g., Nicholls, Christie, Randall and Lask, 2001). Typically they may only eat five or six different foods, often being particular about brands or where the food is bought. The diet is usually high in carbohydrates, often including bread, chips, or biscuits. A typical example might be a child who will eat only one particular brand of baked beans, white sliced bread from a certain supermarket, one brand of cheese and onion crisps, and chocolate biscuits, again of a particular make. Attempts to widen the repertoire of food are usually met with extreme resistance and distress, sometimes accompanied by gagging and retching.

This type of rigid restriction is not uncommon in children with autism, but equally it can occur in children who are not on the autism spectrum. Often there is a strong association with anxiety and/or sensory sensitivities. Many children will accept or refuse foods on the basis of sensory aspects, to include taste, texture, smell, appearance, colour, and temperature. They appear acutely sensitive to minor variations, to the extent that previously accepted foods might be dropped if the packaging changes.

Children with this form of extremely selective eating behaviour are often of appropriate weight and height for their age. In other words, their growth does not seem to be adversely affected by their eating habits. We see more boys than girls with this type of eating pattern. In these older children, parental requests for help and advice are usually precipitated by the impact that the selective eating patterns have on social functioning, and by increasing parental concern given the advancing age of the child. Some parents are worried that their child may not be getting the nutrients they need for good health, and worry about vitamin and mineral intake. In most instances, parents have been able to manage the child's extreme fussiness around food largely by making sure they have access to preferred foods. However, as the child becomes older and engages in more social activities with peers, the eating may present more of a problem. Typical events precipitating help seeking include an inability to take part in social events such as birthday parties or sleep-overs, impending school trips, or planned change of school. In the majority of cases, selective eaters are seen because of social rather than physical concerns, although there are often problematic emotional, behavioural and parental management issues as well.

These children are clearly distinguishable from those with anorexia nervosa and bulimia nervosa as they do not share a preoccupation with weight and/or shape or a distorted perception of their own body size. Their weight is usually within normal limits and they tend to have a longstanding history of selective food intake. They also differ from children with food avoidance emotional disorder as they do not have a problem consuming normal amounts of calories as long as they come from their preferred range of foods. They generally do not present with a prominent fear of gagging or choking (see functional dysphagia, discussed later), although they may do so if forced to eat foods outside their repertoire. In many children with selective eating, problems tend eventually to resolve although they may grow up to be adults who remain quite particular about food likes and dislikes. In a minority problems will persist and become associated with significant impairment to development and functioning.

We get many referrals of children below the age of 10 who are selective eaters, but otherwise growing and developing normally and in good general health. Invariably they are not at all motivated to change their eating behaviour, and any decision to intervene should be based on a risk assessment of whether the current eating pattern is having a negative impact on the child's health and well-being. If it is not, then it is usually better to let it run its own course. The individual may well seek help further down the line when they feel ready to address their difficulties. Our usual approach is to recommend some physical monitoring over the coming years to check the child is going through puberty normally, to recommend keeping options open for involvement with food (e.g. cooking), and to come back when they feel ready to work on making changes. As they grow older, peer group influence becomes stronger and the need to conform in adolescence will often result in a relaxation of the limits placed on dietary intake. Some will, however, persist in accepting only a very narrow range of foods, becoming adult selective eaters. As a rule of thumb, as long as the eating habits are not having an adverse effect on social, physical and emotional development, they should not form a focus for concern.

Restrictive eating

Restrictive eaters are those children who seem never to have eaten very large amounts, and who on the whole do not express a particular interest in or enjoyment of food. There is no evidence of mood disturbance and on the whole restrictive eaters are fine as long as they are not forced to eat more than is their natural inclination. Physically, they tend to be small and light, but within the normal range of variation. Again, as long as growth proceeds steadily along a constant percentile, there is usually no cause for real concern. Restrictive eaters will accept a normal range of types of food, but simply do not eat very much. They seem to have very small appetites.

These children may run into difficulties as they approach puberty with its additional energy requirements. Height and weight centiles should be monitored, and it may be necessary to encourage the child to take some particularly energy-rich sources of food to ensure sufficient intake over this period. These children do not present with body image distortion or preoccupation with weight or shape. Their eating pattern tends to be normal and they do not actively avoid food, or attempt to lose weight. They may present with weight loss around the time of puberty, but are usually willing to accept energy supplements or dietary advice to ensure continued growth.

Food refusal

Food refusal is a common phenomenon in younger children, and one which often causes much anxiety and distress. Preschool children quickly learn the effects of refusing food and some will use this as a strategy to get other things. In older children, food refusal can persist and is clearly distinguishable from the eating disorders and other types of eating disturbance. Food refusers tend to be less consistent in their avoidance of food. They will typically eat favourite foods without any problem at all, or will reserve the refusal for one or two particular people, or particular situations. Examples here include children who refuse to eat at school but eat normally at home, or the child of separated parents whose eating behaviour is resistant and problematic during the week when with the mother, but completely problem free when with the father at weekends. Such children are not preoccupied with weight and shape and tend not to have weight problems. As with most types of eating disturbance in childhood, there is some unhappiness or worry that is underlying the child's food refusal. Once this has been identified and worked upon, hopefully the refusal will lessen. Whereas food refusal is developmentally normal in toddlers, it is not in older children and usually represents a difficulty in the direct expression of existing concerns or uncertainties. In many cases it will not represent a serious threat to the child's general health and well-being, but it can interfere with the quality of relationships with the child.

Specific fear/phobia leading to avoidance of eating (includes functional dysphagia)

Children with functional dysphagia and other specific phobias (e.g. fear of vomiting, fear of going to the toilet) also display a marked avoidance of food, often of a certain type or texture. The characteristic feature of children with functional dysphagia is a fear of swallowing, or choking, which makes them anxious and resistant to eating normally. There is in many cases a clear precipitant in the form of an aversive event that has resulted in the fear of swallowing or choking. Examples might include: traumatic gastrointestinal investigations; a choking incident on a piece of food; or experience of abuse, which becomes associated with particular types or textures of food. Other children have had food poisoning and felt they lost control completely, or a bout of diarrhoea and vomiting where they may have vomited or soiled themselves in public, which has led to a fear of eating. Children with such fears and those with functional dysphagia do not have the weight and shape concerns of anorexia nervosa or bulimia nervosa. They can, however, present at extremely low weights and will experience real fear at the prospect of eating normally.

Pervasive refusal syndrome

The term 'pervasive refusal syndrome' was first used in 1991 to describe a small group of children who presented with a potentially life-threatening condition manifested by what appeared to be a profound and pervasive refusal to eat, drink, walk, talk, or care for themselves in any way over a period of several months (Lask, Britten, Kroll, Magagna and Tranter, 1991). The authors of this paper noted that children with this particular combination of symptoms and presenting features do not fit any existing diagnostic category, and suggested that the condition may be understood as an extreme form of post-traumatic stress disorder (PTSD). Since this first paper, others have been published (Lask, 2004; McGowan and Green, 1998; Nunn and Thompson, 1996; Thompson and Nunn, 1997), describing the condition, presenting case histories and offering a model for understanding the development and clinical phenomena of pervasive refusal syndrome. Thompson and Nunn (1997: 163) conclude that the term pervasive refusal syndrome 'remains a descriptive label for a group of children who present with a constellation of clinical features which is distinct from other related disorders'.

Children with pervasive refusal syndrome present as underweight and often dehydrated, seeming adamantly to refuse food and drink (as well as other normal everyday activities) and determinedly resisting any attempts at treatment. In this way their presentation may be confused with that of a child with acute anorexia nervosa. However, a diagnosis of anorexia nervosa would be inappropriate because, first, the child tends not to be communicating sufficiently to ascertain whether the cognitive criteria for anorexia nervosa are fulfilled, and, second, the apparent refusal extends across all areas of social and personal functioning, which is not the case in anorexia nervosa.

Pervasive refusal syndrome is a rare but potentially life-threatening disorder that invariably requires hospital admission. Treatment is rarely straightforward and often distressing for all concerned. It may be lengthy and intensive, but children can recover. It has been suggested that there may be a relationship between the length of illness prior to presentation and the degree of improvement while in treatment and the time taken to recover (Thompson and Nunn, 1997).

Recently Nunn, Lask and Owen (2012 submitted) have argued that pervasive refusal syndrome is a misnomer, in that what appears to be refusal is not refusal at all but a far more complex phenomenon. They suggest that in a constitutionally anxious and sensitive child, there is hyper-activation of the sympathetic nervous system as a result of intense stress or trauma, from which there is no escape. The parasympathetic nervous system reacts by itself becoming hyper-activated in an attempt to dampen down the sympathetic response. Consequently there is a deadlock of hyper-activation of both systems. Extreme sympathetic activity is manifested by emotional arousal and extreme parasympathetic activity by withdrawal and regression. Nunn et al. propose that the condition should be renamed as Pervasive Arousal-Withdrawal Syndrome to reflect more accurately the presenting and underlying features. This reconceptualization offers not only a less pejorative perspective, but also an intriguing psychophysiological explanation for this mystifying phenomenon. (It also opens up avenues for rational prescribing of psychotropic medication; e.g. adrenergic antagonists for the sympathetic arousal; anticholinergics for the parasympathetic arousal; GABA agonists for their non-specific inhibition of CNS over-activity.)

Appetite loss secondary to depression

Appetite loss secondary to depression is of course not an eating disorder in itself but a well-recognised symptom of clinical depression. Many depressed adults suffer from poor appetite and can lose quite substantial amounts of weight. For a number of reasons children with true 'anorexia' (that is, appetite loss, not anorexia nervosa) may be referred for treatment of an eating disorder. If there is a history of poor eating and weight loss, combined with a change in mood and behaviour, an eating disorder may be suspected. It is important to distinguish between a primary depressive disorder and a primary eating disorder, as the treatment required differs considerably. It is usually not difficult to tell the difference as the central features of anorexia nervosa, such as determined food avoidance, body image distortion and preoccupation with body weight and shape, are absent in depressed children. Some of the other features, including social withdrawal, may however be very similar.

There is undoubtedly a common association of childhood onset anorexia nervosa with depression. Over half of our own clinical population have been found to be moderately to severely depressed (Cooper, Watkins, Bryant-Waugh and Lask, 2002; Fosson et al., 1987). There is an extensive literature relating to the relationship between affective and eating disorders, with much debate around the nature of this relationship. Most of this literature pertains to the situation in older adolescents and adults, and it may not be appropriate to extrapolate findings and conclusions in relation to a younger population. DiNicola, Roberts and Oke (1989) have cautioned that in children the relationship between eating and mood disorder is more complex than in an older population, and suggest that the two types of disorder are even more likely to be intertwined.

Summary

This chapter gives an overview of the main types of eating disturbance occurring in children aged 8 to 14 years. The group of children with anorexia nervosa and related presentations is predominantly female, though a constant number of boys are seen. Children who present with disorders other than anorexia nervosa show a more even gender balance across this group as a whole, although there are some differences between the different types of eating disturbance in relation to the relative numbers of boys and girls.

Working definitions of the types of eating disorder and eating disturbance described in this chapter are as follows:

1   *Anorexia nervosa*

   - determined weight loss (e.g. through food avoidance, self-induced vomiting, excessive exercising, abuse of laxatives);
   - distorted cognitions regarding weight and/or shape;
   - intense preoccupation with weight and/or shape, food and/or eating.

2   *Bulimia nervosa*

   - recurrent binges and purges and/or food restriction;
   - sense of lack of control;
   - distorted cognitions regarding weight and/or shape.

3   *Food avoidance emotional disorder*

   - food avoidance;
   - weight loss;
   - mood disturbance;
   - no distorted cognitions regarding weight and/or shape;
   - no intense preoccupations regarding weight and/or shape;
   - no organic brain disease, psychosis, illicit drug use or prescribed drug related side effects.

4   *Selective eating*

- narrow range of foods (for at least two years);
- unwillingness to try new foods;
- no distorted cognitions regarding weight and/or shape;
- no intense morbid preoccupations regarding weight and/or shape;
- weight may be low, normal, or high.

5   *Restrictive eating*

- smaller than usual amounts for age eaten;
- diet is normal in terms of nutritional content, but not in amount;
- no abnormal cognitions regarding weight and/or shape;
- no intense preoccupations regarding weight and/or shape;
- weight and height tend to be low.

6   *Food refusal*

- tends to be episodic, intermittent, or situational;
- no distorted cognitions regarding weight and/or shape;
- no intense preoccupations with weight and/or shape.

7   *Functional dysphagia and other phobic conditions*

- food avoidance;
- specific fear underlying food avoidance, e.g. fear of swallowing, choking, vomiting;
- no distorted cognition regarding weight and/or shape;
- no intense preoccupation with weight and/or shape.

8   *Pervasive refusal syndrome*

- profound emotional arousal and withdrawal manifested by avoidance of eating, drinking, walking, talking, or self-care;
- determined resistance to efforts to help.

References

American Psychiatric Association (APA, 2000). *Diagnostic and Statistical Manual of Mental Disorders* (4th ed.). Text Revision. Washington, DC: American Psychiatric Association.

Attia, E., and Roberto, C. A. (2009). Should amenorrhea be a diagnostic criterion for anorexia nervosa? *International Journal of Eating Disorders, 42*, 581–589.

Bryant-Waugh, R., Markham, L., Kreipe, R. E., and Walsh, B. T. (2010). Feeding and Eating Disorders in Childhood. *International Journal of Eating Disorders, 43*, 97–111

Chatoor, I., Egan, J., Getson, P., Menvielle, E., and O'Donnell, R. (1988). Mother–infant interactions in infantile anorexia nervosa. *Journal of the American Academy of Child and Adolescent Psychiatry, 27*, 535–540.

Chatoor, I., and Surles, J. (2004). Eating disorders in mid-childhood. *Primary Psychiatry*, *11* (4), 34–39.

Collins, W. (1894). Anorexia nervosa. *The Lancet, I*, 202–203.

Cooper, P., Watkins, B., Bryant-Waugh, R., and Lask, B. (2002). The nosological status of early onset anorexia nervosa. *Psychological Medicine, 32*, 873–880.

Cooper, P., and Stein, A. (2006). *Childhood Feeding Problems and Adolescent Eating Disorders*. London: Routledge.

Decaluwé, V., Braet, C., and Fairburn, C. (2003). Binge eating in obese children and adolescents. *International Journal of Eating Disorders, 33*, 78–84.

DiNicola, V., Roberts, N., and Oke, L. (1989). Eating and mood disorders in young children. *Psychiatric Clinics of North America, 12*, 873–893.

Fairburn, C. G., and Harrison, P. J. (2003). Eating disorders. *The Lancet, 361*, 407–416.

Fosson, A., Knibbs, J., Bryant-Waugh, R., and Lask, B. (1987). Early onset anorexia nervosa. *Archives of Disease in Childhood, 621*, 114–118.

Hebebrand, J., Casper, R., Treasure, J., and Schweiger, U. (2004). The need to revise the diagnostic criteria for anorexia nervosa. *Journal of Neural Transmission, 111*, 827–840.

Higgs, J., Goodyer, I., and Birch, J. (1989). Anorexia nervosa and food avoidance emotional disorder. *Archives of Disease in Childhood, 64*, 346–351.

Irwin, M. (1981). Diagnosis of anorexia nervosa in children and the validity of DSM III. *American Journal of Psychiatry, 138*, 1382–1383.

Lask, B. (2004). Pervasive refusal syndrome. *Advances in Psychiatric Treatment, 10*, 153–159.

Lask, B., Britten, C., Kroll, L., Magagna, J., and Tranter, M. (1991). Children with pervasive refusal. *Archives of Disease in Childhood, 66*, 866–869.

Lazaro, L., Moreno, E., Baos, P., and Castro, J. (2005). Anorexia nervosa and obsessive compulsive disorder in a pre-pubertal patient with bone dysplasia: a case report. *International Journal of Eating Disorders, 37*, 275–277.

Madden, S., Morris, A., Zurynski, Y.A., Kohn, M., and Elliot, E. J. (2009). Burden of eating disorders in 5–13 year old children in Australia. *Medical Journal of Australia, 190*, 410–414.

Mangweth-Matzek, B., Rupp, C. I., Hausmann, A., Gusmerotti, S., Kemmler, G., and Biebl, W. (2010). Eating disorders in men: current features and childhood factors. *Eating and Weight Disorders, 15*, 15–22.

Marcus, M., and Kalarchian, M. (2003). Binge eating in children and adolescents. *International Journal of Eating Disorders, 34*, S47–S57.

Marshall, C. (1895). Fatal case in a girl of 11 years. *The Lancet, I*, 817.

McGowan, R., and Green, J. (1998). Pervasive refusal syndrome: A less severe variant with defined aetiology. *Clinical Child Psychology and Psychiatry, 3* (4), 583–589.

Muise, A. M., Stein, D. G., and Arbess, G. (2003). Eating disorders on adolescent boys: a review of the adolescent and young adult literature. *Journal of Adolescent Health, 33*, 427–435.

Nicholls, D., Chater, R., and Lask, B. (2000). Children into DSM don't go: A comparison of classification systems of eating disorders for children. *International Journal of Eating Disorders, 28* (3), 317–324.

Nicholls, D., Christie, D., Randall, L., and Lask, B. (2001). Selective eating: Symptom, disorder or normal variant. *Clinical Child Psychology and Psychiatry, 6* (2), 257–270.

Nunn, K. P., and Thompson, S. L. (1996). The pervasive refusal syndrome: Learned helplessness and hopelessness. *Clinical Child Psychology and Psychiatry, 1*, 121–132.

Nunn, K. P., Lask, B., and Owen, I. (2012 submitted). Pervasive Refusal Syndrome (PRS) 21 Years On – a re-conceptualisation and re-naming.

Pinhas, L., Morris, A., Crosby, R. D., and Katzman, D. K. (2011). Incidence and age specific presentation of restrictive eating disorders in children: a Canadian Paediatric Surveillance Program study. *Archives of Paediatric and Adolescent Medicine 165*, 895–899.

Rosen, D. S. (2010). Identification and management of eating disorders in children and adolescents. *Pediatrics, 126*, 1240–1253.

Scholtz, S., Hill, L. S., and Lacey, H. (2010). Eating disorders in older women: does late onset anorexia nervosa exist? *International Journal of Eating Disorders, 43*, 393–397.

Shafran, R., Bryant-Waugh, R., Lask, B., and Arscott, K. (1995). Obsessive-compulsive symptoms in children with eating disorders: A preliminary investigation. *Eating Disorders: The Journal of Treatment and Prevention, 3*, 304–310.

Swenne, I., and Thurfjell, B. (2003). Clinical onset and diagnosis of eating disorders in pre-menarcheal girls is preceded by inadequate weight gain and growth. *Acta Paediatrica, 92*, 1133–1137.

Thompson, S. L., and Nunn, K. P. (1997). The pervasive refusal syndrome: The RAHC experience. *Clinical Child Psychology and Psychiatry, 2*, 145–165.

Turner, H. M., and Bryant-Waugh, R. (2004). Eating Disorder Not Otherwise Specified (EDNOS): Profiles of those who present at a community eating disorder service. *European Eating Disorders Review, 12*, 18–26.

Walsh, B. T., and Sysko, R. (2009). Broad categories for the diagnosis of eating disorders: an alternative system for classification. *International Journal of Eating Disorders, 42*, 754–764.

Warren, W. (1968). A study of anorexia nervosa in young girls. *Journal of Child Psychology and Psychiatry, 9*, 27–40.

World Health Organization (WHO, 1992). *The ICD–10 Classification of Mental and Behavioural Disorders: Clinical Descriptions and Diagnostic Guidelines.* Geneva: WHO.

Chapter 5

Aetiology

Dasha Nicholls

Overview

The aetiology of eating disorders is complex and multi-factorial. Evidence continues to emerge for the well-established importance of social and cultural factors related to body image and peer/media influence. Alongside this a now substantial body of evidence is accumulating regarding the neurobiological (including genetic) and psychological vulnerabilities and sensitivities that increase risk for eating disorder onset. The quality of the evidence for these predisposing risk factors is variable, given the need for longitudinal, prospective data for what are relatively low incidence disorders. Much of the evidence therefore comes from study of risk behaviours rather than full syndrome disorders, or from clinical samples, which are subject to bias. The majority of treatment approaches for eating disorders continue to target maintaining factors, but new approaches targeting underlying psychological vulnerabilities are beginning to emerge.

Introduction

Aetiology is the study of causation, or origin. The word is derived from the Greek, aitiologia, meaning 'giving a reason for'. Of the many factors identified as being associated with the onset of eating disorders, from genetics to the media, none is in itself either necessary or sufficient to explain eating disorders of any kind. Instead, we understand eating disorders, like most mental health problems, to have complex biological, psychological and social aetiologies. This chapter focuses on our current understanding of the predisposing and precipitating factors for the eating disorders, and how these are thought to come together to 'cause' eating disorders.

However, causation and reasons are not necessarily the same thing and, importantly, recognising cause(s) does not necessarily suggest a solution. For example, if an episode of weight related bullying is identified as the trigger for the onset of an eating disorder, addressing the bullying may not in itself address the eating disorder. Many of our current treatments are aimed at perpetuating or maintaining factors, since these are often easier to influence than those that might be understood as causal. However, the search for potentially modifiable predisposing risk factors, with a view to prevention or early intervention, remains an important endeavour. It is usual therefore to think of aetiology in terms of predisposing (or risk factors), precipitating (or triggers), and perpetuating (maintaining factors).

Aetiological factors are often categorized in terms of factors specific to the child, the family, and the wider social system. Alternatively we talk about biological, psychological and social factors, and this is the approach chosen for this chapter. It is important to recognise that there may be overlap between these factors. For example, there is a very close relationship between temperament and personality, concepts usually understood in psychological terms, and neurodevelopmental profile, which is usually considered to be more biologically or genetically determined. And both are influenced by individual and cultural experience. So no attempt is made to separate nature from nurture, but instead to recognise the subtle interplay between these factors within any one individual. Equally, it behoves us to consider, given the high prevalence of many of the risk factors, why some people do *not* develop an eating disorder, i.e. what might mitigate risk and provide resilience or protection.

Understanding of the aetiology of eating disorders has been subject to definite 'fashions' over the century or so since their description with family and social models dominating the latter half of the twentieth century (Schmidt, 2003). It has even been suggested that the plausibility of socio-cultural theories held back scientific progress in seeking neurobiological aetiological factors (Bulik, 2004). Now, in the second decade of the twenty-first century, exciting advances in the fields of neuroscience and molecular genetics, are shaping our understanding of the underlying biological substrate necessary for the maintenance of disordered eating behaviours, especially in anorexia nervosa. Such has our knowledge in this area expanded there are now two whole books dedicated to the neuroscience of eating disorders (Lask and Frampton, 2011; Adan and Kaye, 2011). This is not to negate the importance of socio-cultural factors. As with the global obesity 'epidemic', understanding the biological make up of those most at risk does not explain the changing epidemiology of eating disorders, such as their emergence in non-western cultures. A comprehensive bio-psycho-social model that considers the necessary preconditions or biological substrate on which psychological and social risk factors have an impact will enable us to delineate who is and who is not at risk, and ultimately begin to explain why, within a family, one member rather than another can be affected.

This chapter focuses on the aetiology of anorexia nervosa, bulimia nervosa and related eating disorders. As yet no research has yet been undertaken on the other clinically significant eating problems described elsewhere in this book. Hopefully that will not always be the case. Despite clear overlap with the other eating disorders, restrictive anorexia nervosa would appear to 'breed true', with crossover to bulimic and purging presentations largely seen only in those with anorexia nervosa binge/purge type (Eddy et al., 2010). Similarly, those with bulimia nervosa are more likely to go on to develop sub-threshold bulimia nervosa or binge eating disorder than to develop anorexia nervosa. Whilst these developmental trends become clearer with time, most of the younger patients present with weight loss and extreme weight and shape concerns and it can be quite difficult to distinguish, at initial presentation, who will go on to develop binge/purge related disorders and who will remain restrictive eaters. The study and characterisation of risk factors may be one way of improving prediction of individual life course and therefore prognosis.

Understanding causality

In complex, multifactorial, bio-psychosocial disorders the cause includes a number of factors coming together in different ways. Some of these factors will be *correlates*, i.e. there is a statistically significant chance of their being associated with eating disorders. An example might be the association between eating disorders and depression, where a strong association is recognised, but cause and effect is not established. If correlates clearly precede the onset of the illness, they are known as *risk factors*, of which there are three types:

1   Variable risk factors – those that can change (e.g. age) or which can be influenced by intervention such as medication.
2   Causal risk factors – those that, if influenced, can be shown to change the outcome or onset of the disorder. For example, if anxiety were identified as a risk factor, and treating anxiety prevented the onset of an eating disorder, then anxiety could be clearly identified as a causal risk factor.
3   Fixed marker – those that cannot change (e.g. race or gender).

Consequently risk factors can really only be identified from longitudinal studies that establish the order of events, and causal risk factors can only be identified through trials of intervention, to demonstrate the effect of changing the risk factor. This scientific approach to understanding causality has become dominant in the past few decades (Kraemer et al., 1997), and as a result pressure has increased on theory-based understandings of eating disorders to demonstrate their 'truth' through the development of testable hypotheses. More recently, focus has shifted to identifying which factors, either variable or fixed, mediate or moderate outcome and response to treatment (Kraemer, Stice, Kazdin, Offord, and Kupfer, 2001).

Over 30 risk factors for eating disorders have been identified thus far, with varying degrees of significance depending on the type of study. For anorexia nervosa, these include obstetric complications (Favaro, Tenconi, and Santonastaso, 2006), childhood feeding (Nicholls and Viner, 2009) and sleeping problems, high levels of physical exercise, anxious parenting (Shoebridge and Gowers, 2000) and parental malaise (Nicholls and Viner, 2009), obsessive compulsive personality (OCP) traits, perfectionism and negative affect/self-evaluation (Pike et al., 2008). For bulimia nervosa, they include obstetric complications, dieting (Patton, Selzer, Coffey, Carlin, and Wolfe, 1999), childhood and parental obesity, alcoholism, pubertal timing, sexual abuse and negative self-evaluation (Fairburn, Welch,

Doll, Davies, and O'Connor, 1997). For binge eating disorder, they include child-hood obesity coupled with critical comments about shape, weight, or eating, family overeating/binge-eating, negative affect, stress related to work, school or other sources (Pike et al., 2006), parental mood and substance misuse disorders, perfectionism, separation from parents, and maternal problems with parenting (Striegel-Moore et al., 2005), possibly mediated by perceived stress in early adolescence (Striegel-Moore and Bulik, 2007).

A distinction is made in most studies between risk factors for anorexia nervosa and those for bulimia nervosa or other eating disorders. This distinction is some-what artificial, given the overlap between the two disorders in terms of psychopa-thology and over the course of an individual's lifetime. Shared risk factors for anorexia nervosa and bulimia nervosa include dieting (Patton et al., 1999; Stice, Marti, and Durant, 2011), media exposure (Becker et al., 2011), body image dissatisfaction and weight-related teasing, especially when combined with nega-tive affect (Stice et al., 2011), and psychosocial stress. Overall therefore, early environment contributes many of the potentially modifiable risk factors and the others are related to personality traits and affect/coping style.

Genetic and biological risk factors

Genetics

Evidence for the importance of heritance in the development of eating disorders comes from family, twin and adoption studies. In family studies, the frequency with which a disorder occurs in families of affected individuals is compared with the risk in families without an affected member. In the largest study of this kind, for the full syndrome of anorexia nervosa, the relative risks were 11.3 and 12.3 in female relatives of subjects with anorexia nervosa and bulimia nervosa, respec-tively. The relative risks for bulimia nervosa were 4.2 and 4.4 for female relatives of subjects with anorexia nervosa and bulimia nervosa, respectively (Strober, Freeman, Lampert, Diamond, and Kaye, 2000). This means that a female relative of someone with a clinical eating disorder is more than 4 times as likely to have bulimia nervosa and more than 11 times more likely to have anorexia nervosa than someone with no family history of eating disorders. The risk for subclinical eating problems may be even higher (Stein et al., 1999), and there is a large degree of overlap between anorexia nervosa and bulimia nervosa within families, suggesting that at least some of the genetic risk is common to both disorders (Walters and Kendler, 1995) and that there may be a continuum of genetic liability within families (Strober et al., 2000).

In twin studies the frequency of a disorder in identical (monozygotic) twins, who share all their genes, is compared with the frequency in non-identical (dizygotic) twins, who share no more genes than other siblings. This powerful study design assumes that both twins are exposed to similar environmental risk factors (the equivalent environment assumption – EEA), which may not always be the case.

This assumption, together with small numbers in many studies, makes for considerable variation in findings. anorexia nervosa has an estimated heritability of 58% to 76% (Holland, Sicotte, and Treasure, 1988; Klump, Kaye, and Strober, 2001) and bulimia nervosa an even wider range from 31% to 83% depending on the study (Bulik, Sullivan, Wade, and Kendler, 2000). In disentangling the relative contributions of gene and environment, it is usual to separate non-shared environmental factors (i.e. experiences specific to the individual) from shared environmental factors (i.e. experiences to which others are exposed too, such as media pressure). Family factors, such as parental illness or separation, are considered shared between siblings.

In addition to heritability for full eating disorder syndromes, there is considerable evidence for genetic contributions to individual symptoms, attitudes and behaviours, which together with environmental factors, increase risk for the disorders within individuals. For example, binge eating and self-induced vomiting have been shown to have heritabilities ranging from 46% to 70% in twin studies (Sullivan, Bulik, and Kendler, 1998), and personality traits conferring risk, such as perfectionism and interpersonal mistrust, are increased in the relatives of subjects with bulimia nervosa (Lilenfeld et al., 2000). Studies so far have been consistent in their finding that individual differences between twins and siblings in terms of weight and shape concerns and disordered eating behaviours (such as binge eating) can be explained by additive genetic influences and non-shared environmental influences, with very little contribution from shared environmental influences (e.g. Munn et al., 2010).

With the latter decades of the twentieth century came the technology necessary to begin identifying specific genes that may be involved in disease processes. Conditions such as eating disorders rarely have a simple genetic aetiology, although new genetic screening capabilities have increased the likelihood of detection of single gene variants that have a role in body weight and eating behaviour. For example, a region on the short arm of chromosome 16 has recently been found to cause a highly penetrant form of obesity, while its reciprocal duplication is associated with being underweight in both children and adults, and with a high frequency of selective and restrictive eating behaviours (Jacquemont et al., 2011). It is likely that many more genes will be implicated over time, each with small effect, as has occurred for obesity.

On the whole however, complex or multifactorial disorders arise where there is thought to be a complex interplay between genetic predisposition or vulnerability, and environmental factors, so called 'GxE interactions'. The mechanisms by which environmental factors influence genes are the focus of much interest. Epigenetic mechanisms are molecular changes (such as methylation) that regulate gene expression independent of the DNA sequence, coordinating gene expression during development (Campbell, Mill, Uher, and Schmidt, 2011). Some periods are more sensitive to epigenetic modification than others, e.g. the perinatal period. Thus the impact of perinatal stress, nutrition or infection (Favaro et al., 2011) may affect the expression of characteristics such as temperament or behaviours predisposing to eating disorders. It is also possible that epigenetic phenomena account for the differential expression of eating difficulties around puberty (Culbert, Racine, and Klump, 2011), when the female to male ratio increases rapidly. This hypothesis is supported by the finding that the relative role of genetic and environmental factors in risk for eating disorders is profoundly different in pre-pubertal compared to pubertal subjects (Klump, Perkins, Alexandra, McGue, and Iacono, 2007).

Candidate genes are genes suggested from pharmacological, physiological or genetic evidence, and their possible role in the disease process is explored by one of two methods: linkage analysis or association studies. Linkage studies often involve sibling pairs where one or both are affected. In *non-parametric linkage analysis*, marker alleles (gene variant) are identified as occurring more frequently than would be expected by chance in affected siblings, suggesting a link between the allele and the disease. A logarithm of the odds (LOD) score is based on the logarithm of the likelihood ratios for linkage versus non-linkage. A score of more than 3.3 is usually taken to suggest significant linkage. In *genome wide linkage studies*, quantitative trait loci (QTL) are chromosomal regions that may contain genes contributing to a quantitative trait which can be identified in sibling pairs with extreme scores of that trait.

A number of genome wide linkage studies have now been published, from the large multisite, international collaborative studies needed to obtain the necessary sample sizes. So far only modest evidence for linkage on chromosomes 1, 4, 11, 13, and 15 was found when all forms of eating pathology (i.e., anorexia nervosa, bulimia nervosa and eating disorders not otherwise specified) were included. However, when repeated on a subgroup with restrictive anorexia nervosa, when two family members were affected, the evidence for a susceptibility locus on chromosome 1p was much higher (LOD score 3.03) (Grice et al., 2002). For bulimia nervosa, on a sample of 308 families, a double peak was seen on linkage analysis, with the highest LOD score of 2.92 on chromosome 10. Where two family members showed evidence of self-induced vomiting the highest LOD score was 3.39, observed on chromosome 10. These results suggest a susceptibility locus for bulimia nervosa on chromosome 10p (Bulik et al., 2003). Linkage studies have also identified greater evidence of linkage for traits such as age at menarche and anxiety in relatives of bulimia nervosa subjects than for obsessionality and low BMI in relatives of anorexia nervosa subjects (Bacanu et al., 2005).

For association studies either case controls or family trios are used. In the former, the frequency of a genetic variant of a candidate gene (an allele) is compared in the affected and the control groups. If it is directly involved in the genetic susceptibility to a disease process, the allele will occur more frequently in the cases than controls. Candidate genes that have been studied are generally those associated with monoamine functioning or with weight control and energy balance. Despite looking at 5,151 single-nucleotide polymorphisms (SNPs) judged as likely candidate genetic variations conferring susceptibility to anorexia nervosa, using broad and narrow definitions of anorexia nervosa, and over 1,000 sufferers, Pinheiro et al. (2010) found no statistically significant associations for any individual SNP. When the analysis was repeated for association with specific behaviours or psychopathology (lowest illness-related attained body mass index; age at menarche; drive for thinness; body dissatisfaction; trait anxiety; concern over mistakes; and anticipatory worry and pessimism), again no statistically significant results emerged (Root et al., 2011). These results underline the limitations of the 'candidate gene approach' in eating disorders; whether Genome-Wide Association (GWA) studies or Copy Number Variation (CNV) analyses prove more productive remains to be seen.

Several studies have looked at serotonin genes, based on evidence of 5HT dysregulation in both anorexia nervosa and bulimia nervosa (Kaye et al., 2005). A meta-analysis of nine studies examining the 5-HT2a receptor gene found significant associations between anorexia nervosa and the −1438/A allele and AA genotype (Gorwood, Kipman, and Foulon, 2003). Although not all studies have replicated these findings, the evidence does suggest a role for the 5-HT2a receptor gene in the aetiology of anorexia nervosa. In addition a possible association between anorexia nervosa and ser23 allele of the 5-HT2c receptor gene has been suggested as a result of two studies (Westberg et al., 2002; Hu et al., 2003). Findings for other serotonin related genes have been less promising. Much is still to be uncovered about the mechanism by which these genes exert their influence (Scherag, Hebebrand, and Hinney, 2010). For example the role of the 5-HT2a receptor in anorexia nervosa may be to influence affect regulation (e.g., anxiety, depression) and personality traits (e.g., harm avoidance) that predispose an individual to the development of anorexia nervosa, rather than being linked to specific anorexia nervosa psychopathology.

Candidate genes from other neurotransmitter systems that have been examined include the dopamine and opioid systems, as well as those associated with weight and appetite regulation such as neuropeptide Y, leptin and ghrelin. Bloss et al. (2011) found that GABA (?-aminobutyric acid) SNPs were over-represented in a sample of women with anorexia nervosa, possibly mediated by trait anxiety, which they postulate may be a mechanism through which ED outcome may be influenced. Urwin et al. (2002) have demonstrated differences in noradrenergic gene profile between those with and without anorexia nervosa with odds ratios of up to eleven-fold. There is an increased likelihood of specific gene variants contributing to anorexia nervosa for interactions between the MAO long variant (located on the X chromosome) and genes on chromosomes 16 and 17 regulating both noradrenergic and serotonergic mechanisms (Urwin et al., 2003). Conversely the serotonergic genes studied had no independent capacity to predict differences between those with anorexia nervosa and healthy controls. Findings such as these provide possible avenues for exploring psychopharmacological interventions.

The interplay between biological mechanisms, possibly through epigenetic effects, is also a promising area for future research. For example, serotonin receptors are regulated by oestrogen, which in turn is known to be associated with the onset of eating disorders and to weight and appetite regulation. It has been suggested therefore that interactions between serotonin and oestrogens may influence genetic susceptibility to anorexia nervosa, accounting for increased heritability during puberty (Klump and Gobrogge, 2005). The hypotheses are that puberty may activate the genetic influence on anorexia nervosa by:

1   activating oestrogen genes that directly influence liability to anorexia nervosa;
2   increasing levels of oestrogens which then influence the transcription of the 5-HT2a receptor gene; or
3   some combination of the two.

In bulimia nervosa and related binge-purge syndromes, Steiger et al. have developed a model to help account for the way in which genetic and environmental influences, including negative childhood experiences (Steiger et al., 2010), modify serotonin responses, resulting in variations in symptomatology, personality traits and treatment response.

Ghrelin is a recently identified amino acid secreted from the stomach and proximal small intestine, whose role is to stimulate appetite and promote food intake in response to reduced stomach contents. It results in increases in food intake, reduced energy expenditure, and retention of body fat. Peripheral and central administration of ghrelin increases feeding and promotes weight gain, mediated via the hypothalamus. The last decade has highlighted the importance of this peptide for human metabolism and growth (Hillman, Tong, and Tschop, 2011). Studies of ghrelin secretion in patients with anorexia nervosa demonstrate a hypersecretory state, with increased basal total ghrelin concentrations of both the inactive and active forms, although there is some variation with severity and chronicity (Prince, Brooks, Stahl, and Treasure, 2009). Results so far suggest that any ghrelin insensitivity seen in anorexia nervosa may be more important in terms of understanding maintenance than causation. Findings regarding genetic differences between patients with eating disorders and controls with regard to ghrelin and the related gastric peptide neuropeptide Y have been contradictory (Kindler et al., 2011). Nevertheless, the possibility that genetic variation in the regulation of these peptides may influence the course of illness is a promising area for future enquiry (Ando et al., 2010).

Neurobiological factors

See Chapter 8 for a full review of the evidence.

Perinatal factors and infection

The importance of perinatal risk factors has been established, the commonest hypothesised risks including hypoxic-induced brain damage and inadequate pre and postnatal nutrition (Favaro et al., 2006). A few specific associations that have been identified include very preterm birth and cephalohematoma (Cnattingius,

Hultman, Dahl, and Sparen, 1999; Lindberg and Hjern, 2003), maternal anaemia, diabetes mellitus and pre-ecamplasia associated with anorexia nervosa, and retarded foetal growth (lower birth weight and length, decreased head circumference) in bulimia nervosa (Favaro et al., 2006). For both anorexia nervosa and bulimia nervosa, the increased risk associated with multiple rather than individual perinatal findings such as hyporeactivity, low birth weight, and placental infarctions, suggest a 'dose-response' effect (Favaro et al., 2006) although this finding was not replicated in a well powered study (Nicholls and Viner, 2009). The suggested mechanism is one of mild hypoxia affecting hippocampal and cortical brain development, mediated through harm avoidance (Favaro, Tenconi, and Santonastaso, 2008).

More recently, the same group has postulated a role for in vivo exposure to viral infection (Favaro et al., 2011). Both this finding, and the small number of cases in the literature of anorexia nervosa triggered by infection, a phenomenon known as pediatric autoimmune neuropsychiatric disorder associated with streptococcus (PANDAS) (Sokol, 2000; Sokol et al., 2002), may be examples of epigenetic effects in those with genetic vulnerability. PANDAS have already been linked to other childhood onset illnesses such as obsessive compulsive disorder and tic disorders. In those cases where strong evidence exists for a PANDAS association, antibiotics may be a useful adjunct to treatment. Larger studies are needed to determine whether the association is robust enough for streptococcal infection to be considered a routine part of screening, and will rely on the development of reliable detection methods (Vincenzi, O'Toole, and Lask, 2010).

The role of puberty

The sexual dimorphism of eating disorders is one of their most characteristic yet complex features. Puberty has long been recognized as a trigger for the onset of eating disorders (Crisp, 1977), and for many years prepubertal onset illness defied explanation. Theories accounting for the 10-fold increase in risk for females over males exist in biological, psychological, psychodynamic and socio-cultural domains. Puberty is associated with important physical and psychological changes due to the increase in sex steroids and growth hormone (GH). Both growth and reproduction require high levels of energy. Puberty is also associated with a greater increase in fat mass in girls than in boys, and with it increases leptin production, the peripheral hormone that provides feedback to the hypothalamus regulating weight and appetite (Mantzoros, 1999). There is a rapid development in our knowledge of how peptides produced in the digestive tract (in charge of energy intake), e.g. ghrelin, and in adipose tissue (in charge of energy storage), e.g. leptin, provide information regarding metabolic status to the central nervous system. Leptin- and ghrelin-driven enhanced appetite may be one of the factors associated with body dissatisfaction and dieting (O'Dea and Abraham, 1999), particularly in those already predisposed to obesity.

In addition to body weight and shape changes, major brain changes take place during adolescence (Blakemore, Burnett, and Dahl, 2010). Some precede and initiate puberty; others continue for up to a decade beyond. Some are directly associated with gonadal hormones, and sex differences in brain development during puberty may reflect the different effects of male and female gonadal hormones. Early studies focused on the hypothalamus and other regions directly involved in reproductive function. Recent studies, however, also demonstrate influences on the hippocampus, striatum, cerebellum, amygdala and cerebral cortex. Three known oestrogen receptors mediate the effects of gonadal hormones on cholinergic, noradrenergic, serotinergic and dopaminergic neurotransmitter systems. The functions affected include cognitive abilities, aggression, affect regulation, learning and memory. In animal studies an increased response to stress in females becomes evident in early adolescence, a process that is partially mediated by ovarian hormones (Arnsten and Shansky, 2004). In humans, there is also some evidence for pubertal changes in sex-specific responses to stressors with men showing greater HPA reactivity to achievement challenges and women to social rejection (Stroud, Salovey, and Epel, 2002).

The possibility that problems arise because of a mismatch between the emotional reactions and cognitive capacities of the younger adolescent has long interested clinicians, and led to a number of studies exploring the timing of puberty as a risk factor for eating disorders e.g. (Killen et al., 1992; Hayward et al., 1997). The findings are somewhat mixed. Some studies have found no association between the timing of puberty and subsequent eating pathology (Stice, Agras, and Hammer, 1999; The McKnight Investigators, 2003). In contrast Striegel-Moore et al. (2001) found early-onset menarche to be a risk factor for the development of body image and dieting concerns, the timing of menarche being largely determined by body weight. Kaltiala-Heino et al. (2001) found that bulimic-type eating pathology among girls was associated with early menarche. Jacobi (2005), reviewing the evidence, considers that puberty can be considered a non-specific fixed marker of anorexia nervosa and bulimia nervosa, but as yet there is no longitudinal basis for classifying puberty as a risk factor. However early puberty has been reported to be a predictor of chronic symptomatology (Graber et al., 1994, cited in Jacobi, 2005).

Psychological risk factors

Numerous psychological theories about the development of eating disorders exist, many forming the basis for treatment approaches such as cognitive behaviour therapy, cognitive analytic therapy and so on. Some are specific to constructs thought to be important in maintenance of disorder, such as the centrality of control (Fairburn, Shafran, and Cooper, 1999). Others are thought to be necessary preconditions, such as the temperamental trait of perfectionism (Bulik et al., 2003), which mediates the relationship between perceived criticism and dietary restraint (Sassaroli et al., 2011). The best characterised psychological factors or models relevant to eating disorders are psychodynamic theories, temperament, attachment, the processing of negative experiences particularly trauma and threat, low self-esteem, early feeding behaviour, and weight and shape concern and the related behaviour of dieting. Also reviewed here are findings from neuropsychological studies regarding predisposing neurodevelopmental traits reported in patients with eating disorders, and their hypothesised role in aetiology.

Psychodynamic theories

With the increasing dominance of neuroscience in our understanding of mental illness, the prominence of psychodynamic theory is declining in terms of our understanding of aetiology. Nonetheless, psychodynamic concepts remain central to much treatment practice and the integration of psychodynamic theory and neuroscience are embodied in new therapeutic modalities such as mentalisation based therapy (Fonagy and Target, 2007). Disturbed eating in a psychodynamic framework has a number of symbolic meanings, from suppressed rage, omnipotent control of parental figures, fear of intrusion, denial of self and needs, etc. Particularly influential has been the writing of Bruch in the 1970s, who wrote about eating disturbance as a 'solution or camouflage for the problems of living' (Bruch, quoted in Lask, 2000). Bruch understood anorexia nervosa in terms of a failure to develop a sense of self as independent and entitled to take initiative, instead adopting a compliant stance of the perfect child, with the consequence that she feels controlled and adopts safe predictable routines to determine her behaviour and control her environment. The hypothesis assumes that mothers think they know a girl's needs, whereas they seek to understand their male children differently. Bruch's ideas are central to the concept of 'infantile anorexia' (Chatoor, Hirsch, Ganiban, Persinger, and Hamburger, 1998), a feeding disorder of early infancy characterised by a lack of reciprocity, conflict and a struggle for control, at which food refusal is central. The relationship, if any, between 'infantile anorexia' and anorexia nervosa is not established.

Psychodynamic theories of bulimia and bingeing disorders similarly focus on aggression, increasingly using insights from work with borderline personality disorder, to inform treatment.

Temperament

Temperament is best understood as those innate characteristics unique to children that they bring to their actions, behaviours and relationships. Temperament is often understood as the precursor to personality, although the two constructs are distinct and the term 'personality' is best not used when referring to children and young adolescents, for the simple reason that personality is not yet fully developed. The assessment of personality and temperament in the context of eating disorders is complicated by the impact of the symptoms, including the direct effects of starvation, on personality and temperamental traits. While it is unlikely that temperamental characteristics per se lead to disordered eating, it has been argued that, in combination with other risk factors, certain temperamental characteristics may increase vulnerability (Martin et al., 2000), affect coping with stressful life events, or influence prognosis.

Current data support the likelihood that neuroticism and perfectionism are risk factors for EDs, while harm avoidance and low self-directedness, although consistent, cannot clearly be said to precede onset. Other temperamental traits associated with anorexia nervosa include low novelty seeking, high persistence, perfectionism and obsessional traits (Klump et al., 2000; Fassino et al., 2002). Women with bulimia nervosa show high novelty seeking (Fassino et al., 2002), while impulsivity characterises those with binge eating pathology. Most of these traits can also be found in the parents of eating-disordered offspring (Fassino, Amianto, and Abbate-Daga, 2009), but they may also be exacerbated by having, or having had, an eating disorder, as illustrated by the classic semi-starvation studies of the 1950s (Keys, Brozek, Henschel, and Taylor, 1950).

Attachment, threat and trauma

Attachment behaviour is defined as proximity seeking behaviour by a dependent organism (infant or child) when he or she senses discomfort of any sort, including pain, fear, cold or hunger (Glaser, 2000). It is not simply affection, but a biological drive necessary for survival. Attachment style is specific to a child, not to a parent. Anxious, insecure attachment styles are a consistent finding in adults with eating disorders (Ward, Ramsay, Turnbull, Benedettini, and Treasure, 2000; Illing, Tasca, Balfour, and Bissada, 2010). The contributions that both child and parent bring to the relationship are important, hence the need to consider the temperament of the child, as well as the parents' own attachment relationships with their parents/carers. In a study of adolescents with anorexia nervosa, 25% of parents experienced loss of a child through miscarriage or severe obstetric complications in the pregnancy *before* the child with subsequent anorexia nervosa was born, compared to 7.5% of control parents (Shoebridge and Gowers, 2000). Qualitative data suggested that the loss or trauma was still resonant for those mothers many years later. It would not be surprising if such experiences led to heightened anxiety in relation to early parenting and impact on the attachment relationship. Against this background the tendency to minimise emotional distress and failure to learn processing of difficult and negative emotions, particularly anger and loss, is a tentative but plausible model that would account for the so called 'alexithymia' (literally 'no words for feelings') frequently described in patients with anorexia nervosa (Corcos et al., 2000), although lacking substantial empirical support.

Retrospective studies have implicated parental over-control and abuse as possible aetiological factors for later EDs, which also manifest through disturbed attachment relationships. Nicholls and Viner (2009) did not find a relationship between authoritarian parenting style and later anorexia nervosa, nor with likelihood of being taken into public care during childhood. However separation from mother in the first five years, and persistent maternal malaise during the first five years, did show some association with later anorexia nervosa. As noted above, obstetric complications and birth trauma have been shown to be increased 3- to 4-fold in subjects with anorexia nervosa compared to controls, which may be a factor in postnatal adaptation.

This picture of insecure attachment found in anorexia nervosa differs from that of bulimia nervosa and associated bingeing disorders, in which associations with early negative childhood experiences, including trauma and abuse are much clearer. For example, an association between parental psychopathology in early childhood and binge eating behaviour in later life has been demonstrated, mediated through abuse experiences (Ericsson et al., 2011). Early abuse experiences, including emotional abuse, in turn appear to be mediated through personal ineffectiveness and affective instability, affecting self-esteem and affect regulation (Groleau et al., 2011). As outlined above, the impact of these events will differentially affect those more genetically susceptible (Steiger et al., 2011).

In a meta-analysis of 53 studies, Smolak and Murnen (2002) found a modest relationship between childhood sexual abuse and eating disorders, in the face of considerable methodological variation. A more recent meta-analysis of over 3 million psychiatric cases found a statistically significant association between childhood sexual abuse and lifetime diagnosis of an eating disorder (odds ratio 2.7, comparable to that for depression and slightly lower than for anxiety disorder) (Chen et al., 2010). Psychological mechanisms include rejection of sexuality through weight loss, a heightened sense of personal disgust, and a wish to disgust others (Waller and Kennerly, 2003). In recent years a significant body of evidence has developed suggesting that patients with bulimia nervosa process differently threats not related to weight, shape and food. Specifically, patients with bulimia nervosa have an attentional bias towards threats to self-esteem with less attention toward physical threats (McManus, Waller, and Chadwick, 1996), and that the threats may then fail to be adequately processed, but rather avoided (Meyer et al., 2005) or denied.

In a study of the association between general adversity and the onset of eating disorders, Schmidt et al. (1997) found that patients with anorexia nervosa and bulimia nervosa did not differ from community controls in terms of the proportion of patients with at least one severe life event or difficulty. However, more patients with anorexia nervosa or bulimia nervosa had experienced a major difficulty, and this was most commonly in the year before the onset of eating difficulties. These life events usually concerned close relationships with family and friends for both bulimia nervosa and anorexia nervosa, while specific to anorexia nervosa were events related to 'pudicity' (events and difficulties with the potential to evoke sexual shame or disgust, including premature, inappropriate or 'forbidden' sexuality, or sexual situations which posed a moral dilemma for the patient). This is in keeping with clinical experience in younger patients, as well as in the adults to whom the study relates.

Attachment security and parent-child relationships have been studied beyond infancy, but it can then be difficult to disentangle cause and effect, and associations are tentative. For example, Suisman et al. (2011) found that parental divorce was associated with development of body dissatisfaction, but not with other types of disordered eating behaviour. Spanos et al. (2010) examined parent-child conflict as a non-shared environmental risk factor for disordered eating in monozygotic female twins (234 pairs). They found that twin differences in disordered eating predicted later differences in parent-child conflict rather than the reverse, suggesting that parent-child conflict may be a consequence of, rather than a risk factor for, disordered eating. Similar findings underpin the important move away from parent blaming to a more subtle appreciation of the nature/nurture debate (le Grange, Lock, Loeb, and Nicholls, 2010). Nonetheless, family discord and negative experiences of parenting are reported retrospectively by a significant proportion of those with psychiatric disorders, in addition to which, and specific to anorexia nervosa, are family discord and higher parental demands (Pike et al., 2008).

Self-esteem/negative self-evaluation

Low self-esteem is an established risk factor for the development of bulimia nervosa (Fairburn et al., 1997), although it is unclear the extent to which this is directly related to overweight (a risk factor for a proportion but not all with bulimia nervosa) or specific to weight and shape concerns. For example, women high in perfectionism who consider themselves overweight exhibit bulimic symptoms only if they have low self-esteem (Polivy and Herman, 2002). The picture for anorexia nervosa is more complex. Whilst many with anorexia nervosa do have low self-esteem, this has not been supported by risk factor studies (Fairburn, Cooper, Doll, and Welch, 1999). This is especially true of children; indeed many children with anorexia nervosa give the impression of being quite confident. It is likely that in some, low self-esteem is specific to the body image (Geller et al., 1998) and social domains, but can be relatively intact, and therefore protective, in relation to abilities, intelligence etc. (Geller, Zaitsoff, and Srikameswaran, 2002). Social desirability is a specific area of poor self-evaluation but high importance in pre-pubertal onset anorexia nervosa (Arnow, Sanders, and Steiner, 1999).

Early feeding behaviour

The evidence for eating disturbances in childhood as a precursor to later disordered eating is mounting. Stice et al. (1999) found that inhibited eating, secretive eating, overeating, and vomiting became increasingly apparent over the early years up to age 5, and were associated with parental weight and shape concern, including maternal body dissatisfaction, internalization of the thin-ideal, dieting, bulimic symptoms, and both maternal and paternal body mass. Three other longitudinal studies have explored the relationship between early feeding problems and later eating disorders. The first, by Marchi and Cohen (1990) found an association between digestive problems and picky eating and later anorexia nervosa. In the second, Kotler et al. (2001) found eating conflicts, struggles with food, and unpleasant meals (but not picky eating) in early childhood were risk factors for the later development of anorexia nervosa but not of bulimia nervosa. Subsequently, Nicholls and Viner (2009) confirmed the association between maternally reported early feeding problems and later anorexia nervosa. It is possible that this association reflects perceived burden of the feeding problem, such as refusal or conflict, rather than nutritional status. In the latter study, children who later developed anorexia nervosa were reported as under-eating at age 10, but were not of significantly lower mean BMI z-score than controls. Further exploration is needed to better understand the mechanisms.

Weight and shape concern and dieting

Clinical eating disturbances present at any age, but specific behaviours associated with weight and shape concerns are seen clinically in children as young as 6 years old (Nicholls, Lynn, and Viner, 2011). These include young children expressing fears of becoming fat and body image concerns, and around 40% of 10- and 11-year-olds wanting to be thinner, with no differences by gender (Bernier, Kozyrskyj, Benoit, Becker, and Marchessault, 2010). About 25% of these children report receiving frequent weight-related advice, but it is the girls more than boys who are likely to act on it (Shapiro, Newcomb, and Loeb, 1997; Bernier et al., 2010). In addition to gender bias, dieting awareness is linked to negative self-evaluation (Hill and Pallin, 1998).

In a review of the development of weight and shape concerns in the aetiology of eating disorders, Gowers and Shore (2001) emphasised the multi factorial contributions to weight and shape concerns, including the risk that parents pass on their concerns to their children. Smolak et al. (1999) found that direct comments, particularly by mothers, were more influential in the development of weight concerns in school children than modelling. This is especially true if the mother has an eating disorder herself (Agras, Hammer, McNicholas, 1999; Field et al., 2008). Wade, Treloar and Martin (2008) found a retrospective correlation between both self-induced vomiting and objective binge eating and (among other factors) parental comments about weight, although clearly negative comments about weight can come from a number of other potentially influential sources with lasting impact. For boys, paternal negative comments are a predictor of binge onset (Field et al., 2008).

Dieting is well established as a risk factor for the development of bulimia nervosa (Fairburn et al., 1997; Stice et al., 2011) independent of body image dissatisfaction, particularly in those premorbidly overweight or genetically predisposed to obesity. Dieting or weight loss precedes binge eating in a large proportion of those who go on to develop bulimia nervosa (Brewerton, Dansky, Kilpatrick, and O'Neil, 2000), severe dieters having an eighteen-fold increased risk of developing eating disorders (bulimia nervosa or eating disorders not other-wise specified) compared to non-dieters (Patton et al., 1999). The role of dieting in the onset of anorexia nervosa is less clear, and it is possibly more important as a maintaining than a precipitating factor.

In terms of high risk groups for weight and shape concern and associated weight control behaviours, perhaps most has been written about athletes and dancers. Possible factors include heightened genetic vulnerability and environ-mental pressure, but even amongst dancers some will be at higher risk than others. Thomas, Peel and Heatherton (2005) have suggested that dancers who exhibit high levels of perfectionism and, perhaps consequently, place themselves in highly competitive environments, may exhibit a significantly increased risk for disordered eating in comparison to dancers who are less perfectionist and/or less competitive.

Socio-cultural theories

The socio-cultural perspective is perhaps the most popular public narrative for why eating disorders occur, identifying pressure to be thin as a major source of body image disturbance and eating disordered behaviour. A glance at any glossy magazine aimed at young women, and increasingly those aimed at men, reveals the preoccupation with physical attractiveness and stories of weight loss and gain guaranteed to increase body awareness and promote weight control behaviours. It is clear however, that the so called obesogenic environment, with its abundance of cheap, highly calorific foods, creates a context for body dissatisfaction and dieting that can herald the onset of eating disorder pathology. While the fashion and diet industries are targeted primarily at adults, exposure to idealised body images occurs at much younger ages. For example, dolls typically have body sizes in the severe malnutrition range of BMI 11.8 to 13.4 kg/m^2 (Wells and Nicholls, 2001). This highlights how extreme is deformation of the female body shape in commer-cial images. Field et al. (1999) have demonstrated a relationship in preadolescent and adolescent girls between unhappiness with their weight and shape and the frequency with which they read fashion magazines, and shown that frequent dieting and trying to look like persons in the media predict the onset of binge eating (Field et al., 2008).

The effect of media portrayal of body image on a population has been most clearly documented in the study by Becker et al. (2002) on the Island of Fiji, where changes in attitude to body weight and shape were examined following the introduction of television. The study found increases in overall scores on the Eating Attitudes Test and a higher incidence of self-induced vomiting to lose weight following prolonged television exposure, with subjects explicitly linking these thoughts and behaviours with their aesthetic ideals drawn from Western television influence. The effects of media are both through direct exposure, and indirectly through media influence in social networks, such as peer groups (Becker et al., 2011). The influence of the media may be different on boys from girls;

disordered eating behaviours in males is associated with exposure to health sections of TV and magazines, whereas for girls it is exposure to dieting, fashion and sport sections that predicts greater body dissatisfaction, internalisation and awareness of the thin-ideal and lower self-esteem (Calado, Lameiras, Sepulveda, Rodriguez, and Carrera, 2010).

The thin ideal to which these images aspire is a product of specific cultures. Nevertheless, eating disorders can no longer be thought of as 'culture bound syndromes', cases having now been documented across the globe, albeit with slightly different psychopathological characteristics (Nasser, 1997; Becker, Thomas, and Pike, 2009). A key factor is thought to be that of societies or cultures undergoing socioeconomic transition. Katzman and Lee (1997) have argued that eating disorders may be precipitated by problems with transition, dislocation and oppression that produce solutions in manipulations of weight, diet and food. Postulated mechanisms range from gender politics to economic influences. For example, it has been suggested that the changing commercialism of eastern Europe, coupled with reduced state benefits such as education, health care, employment, may result in changes to the marketing of beauty (Nasser and Katzman, 2003). Socio-cultural models of eating disorders have moved beyond western cultures and gender politics to worldwide cultural dynamics, cultures in transition and confused identities (Nasser and Katzman, 2003).

More controversial in terms of socio-cultural influence is the impact of attempts to counteract the obesity epidemic on the development of disordered eating. Healthy eating campaigns are targeting primary school children, together with mandatory weighing in some schools. In some instances deliberate attempts have been made to stigmatise overweight in an effort to encourage weight control behaviours. The research evidence for the impact of anti-obesity strategies on young people is scant at present; most obesity intervention studies monitor for development of eating disorders but this is by no means universal for public health strategies.

Aetiological models

Figure 5.1 offers a simplistic overview of the way that multiple factors come together to create a context for development of an eating disorder. This is not a scientific model, nor is it a theory that can be tested. In recent years the eating disorders field has risen to the challenge of offering hypotheses and conceptual models of aetiology, (e.g. Connan, Campbell, Katzman, Lightman, and Treasure, 2003; Nunn, Frampton, Gordon, and Lask, 2008; Hatch et al., 2010; Steiger, Bruce, and Groleau, 2011). The emphasis has been on anorexia nervosa, as the heterogeneity of bulimic and binge purge presentations lends itself less well to all-encompassing models. Eating disorders are often described as the 'final common pathway' of a number of possible risk factors, and as such have potentially multiple mechanisms. The desire is for models that can be empirically tested and that have potential treatment or prevention implications.

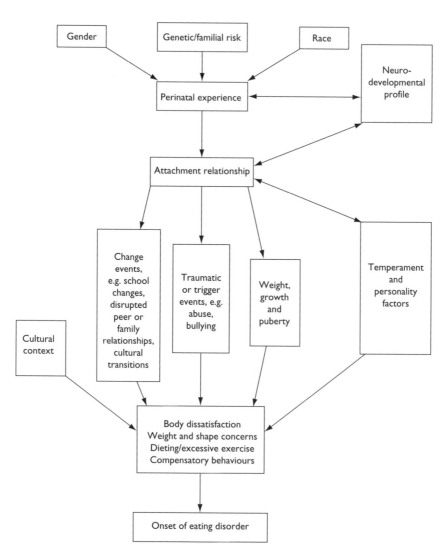

Figure 5.1 Simplified 'causal' pathway.

Conclusions

Eating disorders are complex in their aetiology, with biological, psychological and social factors all playing important parts in our understanding. The greatest growth in knowledge over the past two decades has been in our understanding of the genetic and neurobiological basis for eating disorders. Although as yet treatment is not based primarily on aetiology, better understanding the causation of eating disorders may in future have important implications for specific elements of treatment in vulnerable individuals, and improve our ability to detect and target those most at risk. Currently, whilst our knowledge of correlates and risk factors increases daily, it remains very difficult to demonstrate causality for many of the factors discussed above and consequently further research in this area remains a priority if potentially modifiable risks can be identified. As the capability of detecting genetic risk for disease increases, so will the need for emphasis on promoting wellbeing and mitigating risk in those with a high risk loading. Why the majority of adolescent girls and boys, coping with social, emotional and biological pressures do not develop an eating disorder needs to be better understood, and protective factors promoted. Whilst it is tempting to postulate what these might be, there has been little by way of research in this area.

Summary

- Cause and risk are not synonymous.
- Genetic factors are powerful influences in the development of eating disorders, through both direct and indirect mechanisms.
- Individual, non-shared, sensitivities and experiences are more important than shared family or environmental factors.
- Psychological, and increasingly neuropsychological, profiles that increase risk can be delineated but are not sufficiently specific to eating disorders to target for prevention.
- New, testable neurobiological models of aetiology are emerging.

References

Adan, R. A. H., and Kaye, W. H. (2011). *Behavioral Neurobiology of Eating Disorders*. Springer.

Agras, S., Hammer, L., and McNicholas, F. (1999). A prospective study of the influence of eating-disordered mothers on their children. *International Journal of Eating Disorders*, 25, 253–262.

Ando, T., Komaki, G., Nishimura, H., Naruo, T., Okabe, K., Kawai, K. et al. (2010). A ghrelin gene variant may predict crossover rate from restricting-type anorexia nervosa to other phenotypes of eating disorders: a retrospective survival analysis. *Psychiatric Genetics*, 20, 153–159.

Arnow, B., Sanders, M. J., and Steiner, H. (1999). Premenarcheal versus postmenarcheal anorexia nervosa: A comparative study. *Clinical Child Psychology and Psychiatry*, 4, 403–414.

Arnsten, A. F., and Shansky, R. M. (2004). Adolescence: vulnerable period for stress-induced prefrontal cortical function? Introduction to part IV. *Annals of the New York Academy of Sciences*, 1021, 143–147.

Bacanu, S. A., Bulik, C. M., Klump, K. L., Fichter, M. M., Halmi, K. A., Keel, P. et al. (2005). Linkage analysis of anorexia and bulimia nervosa cohorts using selected behavioral phenotypes as quantitative traits or covariates. *American Journal of Medical Genetics Part B, Neuropsychiatric Genetics, 139*, 61–68.

Becker, A. E., Burwell, R. A., Gilman, S. E., Herzog, D. B., and Hamburg, P. (2002). Eating behaviours and attitudes following prolonged exposure to television among ethnic Fijian adolescent girls. *British Journal of Psychiatry, 180*, 509–514.

Becker, A. E., Fay, K. E., Agnew-Blais, J., Khan, A. N., Striegel-Moore, R. H., and Gilman, S. E. (2011). Social network media exposure and adolescent eating pathology in Fiji. *British Journal of Psychiatry, 198*, 43–50.

Becker, A. E., Thomas, J. J., and Pike, K. M. (2009). Should non-fat-phobic anorexia nervosa be included in DSM-V? *International Journal of Eating Disorders, 42*, 620–635.

Bernier, C. D., Kozyrskyj, A. L., Benoit, C., Becker, A. B., and Marchessault, G. (2010). Body image and dieting attitudes among preadolescents. *Canadian Journal of Dietetic Practice and Research, 71*, 34–40.

Blakemore, S. J., Burnett, S., and Dahl, R. E. (2010). The role of puberty in the developing adolescent brain. *Human Brain Mapping, 31*, 926–933.

Bloss, C. S., Berrettini, W., Bergen, A. W., Magistretti, P., Duvvuri, V., Strober, M. et al. (2011). Genetic association of recovery from eating disorders: the role of GABA receptor SNPs. *Neuropsychopharmacology, 36*, 2222–2232.

Brewerton, T. D., Dansky, B. S., Kilpatrick, D. G., and O'Neil, P. M. (2000). Which comes first in the pathogenesis of bulimia nervosa: dieting or bingeing? *International Journal of Eating Disorders, 28*, 259–264.

Bulik, C. M. (2004). Role of genetics in anorexia nervosa, bulimia nervosa and binge eating disorder. In T.D.Brewerton (Ed.), *Clinical Handbook of Eating Disorders: An Integrated Approach* (pp. 165–182). New York: Marcel Dekker Inc.

Bulik, C. M., Devlin, B., Bacanu, S. A., Thornton, L., Klump, K. L., Fichter, M. M. et al. (2003). Significant linkage on chromosome 10p in families with bulimia nervosa. *American Journal of Human Genetics, 72*, 200–207.

Bulik, C. M., Sullivan, P. F., Wade, T. D., and Kendler, K. S. (2000). Twin studies of eating disorders: a review. *International Journal of Eating Disorders, 27*, 1–20.

Bulik, C. M., Tozzi, F., Anderson, C., Mazzeo, S. E., Aggen, S., and Sullivan, P. F. (2003). The relation between eating disorders and components of perfectionism. *American Journal of Psychiatry, 160*, 366–368.

Calado, M., Lameiras, M., Sepulveda, A. R., Rodriguez, Y., and Carrera, M. V. (2010). The mass media exposure and disordered eating behaviours in Spanish secondary students. *European Eating Disorders Review, 18*, 417–427.

Campbell, I. C., Mill, J., Uher, R., and Schmidt, U. (2011). Eating disorders, gene-environment interactions and epigenetics. *Neuroscience and Biobehavioural Review, 35*, 784–793.

Chatoor, I., Hirsch, R., Ganiban, J., Persinger, M., and Hamburger, E. (1998). Diagnosing infantile anorexia: the observation of mother-infant interactions. *Journal of the American Academy of Child and Adolescent Psychiatry, 37*, 959–967.

Chen, L. P., Murad, M. H., Paras, M. L., Colbenson, K. M., Sattler, A. L., Goranson, E. N. et al. (2010). Sexual abuse and lifetime diagnosis of psychiatric disorders: systematic review and meta-analysis. *Mayo Clinic Proceedings, 85*, 618–629.

Cnattingius, S., Hultman, C. M., Dahl, M., and Sparen, P. (1999). Very preterm birth, birth trauma, and the risk of anorexia nervosa among girls. *Archives of General Psychiatry, 56*, 634–638.

Connan, F., Campbell, I. C., Katzman, M., Lightman, S. L., and Treasure, J. (2003). A neurodevelopmental model for anorexia nervosa. *Physiology* and *Behaviour, 79*, 13–24.

Corcos, M., Guilbaud, O., Speranza, M., Paterniti, S., Loas, G., Stephan, P. et al. (2000). Alexithymia and depression in eating disorders. *Psychiatry Research, 93*, 263–266.

Crisp, A. H. (1977). Some psychobiological aspects of adolescent growth and their relevance for the fat/thin syndrome (anorexia nervosa). *International Journal of Obesity, 1*, 231–238.

Culbert, K. M., Racine, S. E., and Klump, K. L. (2011). The influence of gender and puberty on the heritability of disordered eating symptoms. *Current Topics in Behavioural Neurosciences, 6*, 177–185.

Eddy, K. T., Swanson, S. A., Crosby, R. D., Franko, D. L., Engel, S., and Herzog, D. B. (2010). How should DSM-V classify eating disorder not otherwise specified (EDNOS) presentations in women with lifetime anorexia or bulimia nervosa? *Psychological Medicine, 40*, 1735–1744.

Ericsson, N. S., Keel, P. K., Holland, L., Selby, E. A., Verona, E., Cougle, J. R. et al. (2011). Parental disorders, childhood abuse, and binge eating in a large community sample. *International Journal of Eating Disorders, 45* (3), 316–325.

Fairburn, C. G., Cooper, Z., Doll, H. A., and Welch, S. L. (1999). Risk factors for anorexia nervosa: three integrated case-control comparisons. *Archives of General Psychiatry, 56*, 468–476.

Fairburn, C. G., Shafran, R., and Cooper, Z. (1999). A cognitive behavioural theory of anorexia nervosa. *Behaviour Research and Therapy, 37*, 1–13.

Fairburn, C. G., Welch, S. L., Doll, H. A., Davies, B. A., and O'Connor, M. E. (1997). Risk factors for bulimia nervosa. A community-based case-control study. *Archives of General Psychiatry, 54*, 509–517.

Fassino, S., Abbate-Daga, G., Amianto, F., Leombruni, P., Boggio, S., and Rovera, G. G. (2002). Temperament and character profile of eating disorders: a controlled study with the Temperament and Character Inventory. *International Journal of Eating Disorders, 32*, 412–425.

Fassino, S., Amianto, F., and Abbate-Daga, G. (2009). The dynamic relationship of parental personality traits with the personality and psychopathology traits of anorectic and bulimic daughters. *Comprehensive Psychiatry, 50*, 232–239.

Favaro, A., Tenconi, E., Ceschin, L., Zanetti, T., Bosello, R., and Santonastaso, P. (2011). In utero exposure to virus infections and the risk of developing anorexia nervosa. *Psychological Medicine, 41*, 2193–2199.

Favaro, A., Tenconi, E., and Santonastaso, P. (2006). Perinatal factors and the risk of developing anorexia nervosa and bulimia nervosa. *Archives of General Psychiatry, 63*, 82–88.

Favaro, A., Tenconi, E., and Santonastaso, P. (2008). The relationship between obstetric complications and temperament in eating disorders: A mediation hypothesis. *Psychosomatic Medicine, 70*, 372–377.

Field, A. E., Cheung, L., Wolf, A. M., Herzog, D. B., Gortmaker, S. L., and Colditz, G. A. (1999). Exposure to the mass media and weight concerns among girls. *Pediatrics, 103*, E36.

Field, A. E., Javaras, K. M., Aneja, P., Kitos, N., Camargo, C. A., Jr., Taylor, C. B. et al. (2008). Family, peer, and media predictors of becoming eating disordered. *Archives of Pediatrics and Adolescent Medicine, 162*, 574–579.

Fonagy, P., and Target, M. (2007). The rooting of the mind in the body: new links between attachment theory and psychoanalytic thought. *Journal of the American Psychoanalytic Association*, *55*, 411–456.

Geller, J., Johnston, C., Madsen, K., Goldner, E. M., Remick, R. A., and Birmingham, C. L. (1998). Shape- and weight-based self-esteem and the eating disorders. *International Journal of Eating Disorders*, *24*, 285–298.

Geller, J., Zaitsoff, S. L., and Srikameswaran, S. (2002). Beyond shape and weight: exploring the relationship between nonbody determinants of self-esteem and eating disorder symptoms in adolescent females. *International Journal of Eating Disorders*, *32*, 344–351.

Glaser, D. (2000). Child abuse and neglect and the brain—a review. *Journal of Child Psychology and Psychiatry*, *41*, 97–116.

Gorwood, P., Kipman, A., and Foulon, C. (2003). The human genetics of anorexia nervosa. *European Journal of Pharmacology*, *480*, 163–170.

Gowers, S. G. and Shore, A. (2001). Development of weight and shape concerns in the aetiology of eating disorders. *British Journal of Psychiatry*, *179*, 236–242.

Grice, D. E., Halmi, K. A., Fichter, M. M., Strober, M., Woodside, D. B., Treasure, J. T. et al. (2002). Evidence for a susceptibility gene for anorexia nervosa on chromosome 1. *American Journal of Human Genetics*, *70*, 787–792.

Groleau, P., Steiger, H., Bruce, K., Israel, M., Sycz, L., Ouellette, A. S. et al. (2011). Childhood emotional abuse and eating symptoms in bulimic disorders: An examination of possible mediating variables. *International Journal of Eating Disorders*, *45* (3), 326–332.

Hatch, A., Madden, S., Kohn, M., Clarke, S., Touyz, S., and Williams, L. M. (2010). Anorexia nervosa: towards an integrative neuroscience model. *European Eating Disorders Review*, *18*, 165–179.

Hayward, C., Killen, J. D., Wilson, D. M., Hammer, L. D., Litt, I. F., Kraemer, H. C. et al. (1997). Psychiatric risk associated with early puberty in adolescent girls. *Journal of the American Academy of Child and Adolescent Psychiatry*, *36*, 255–262.

Hill, A. J. and Pallin, V. (1998). Dieting awareness and low self-worth: related issues in 8-year-old girls. *International Journal of Eating Disorders*, *24*, 405–413.

Hillman, J. B., Tong, J., and Tschop, M. (2011). Ghrelin biology and its role in weight-related disorders. *Discovery Medicine*, *11*, 521–528.

Holland, A. J., Sicotte, N., and Treasure, J. (1988). Anorexia nervosa: evidence for a genetic basis. *Journal of Psychosomatic Research*, *32*, 561–571.

Hu, X., Giotakis, O., Li, T., Karwautz, A., Treasure, J., and Collier, D. A. (2003). Association of the 5-HT2c gene with susceptibility and minimum body mass index in anorexia nervosa. *Neuroreport*, *14*, 781–783.

Illing, V., Tasca, G. A., Balfour, L., and Bissada, H. (2010). Attachment insecurity predicts eating disorder symptoms and treatment outcomes in a clinical sample of women. *Journal of Nervous and Mental Disease*, *198*, 653–659.

Jacobi, C. (2005). Psychosocial Risk Factors for Eating Disorders. In S.Wonderlich, J. Mitchell, M. de Zwann, and H. Steiger (Eds), *Eating Disorders Review: Part 1* (pp. 59–86). Abingdon, Oxon: Radcliffe Publishing.

Jacquemont, S., Reymond, A., Zufferey, F., Harewood, L., Walters, R. G., Kutalik, Z. et al. (2011). Mirror extreme BMI phenotypes associated with gene dosage at the chromosome 16p11.2 locus. *Nature*, *478*, 97–102.

Kaltiala-Heino, R., Rimpela, M., Rissanen, A., and Rantanen, P. (2001). Early puberty and early sexual activity are associated with bulimic-type eating pathology in middle adolescence. *Journal of Adolescent Health*, *28*, 346–352.

Katzman, M. A., and Lee, S. (1997). Beyond body image: the integration of feminist and transcultural theories in the understanding of self starvation. *International Journal of Eating Disorders*, 22, 385–394.

Kaye, W. H., Frank, G. K., Bailer, U. F., Henry, S. E., Meltzer, C. C., Price, J. C. et al. (2005). Serotonin alterations in anorexia and bulimia nervosa: new insights from imaging studies. *Physiological Behaviour*, 85, 73–81.

Keys, A., Brozek, J., Henschel, A., and Taylor, H. L. (1950). *The Biology of Human Starvation*. Minneapolis, MN: University of Minnesota Press.

Killen, J. D., Hayward, C., Litt, I. F., Hammer, L. D., Wilson, D. M., Miner, B. et al. (1992). Is puberty a risk factor for eating disorders? *American Journal of Disease in Childhood*, 146, 323–325.

Kindler, J., Bailer, U., de, Z. M., Fuchs, K., Leisch, F., Grun, B. et al. (2011). No association of the neuropeptide Y (Leu7Pro) and ghrelin gene (Arg51Gln, Leu72Met, Gln90Leu) single nucleotide polymorphisms with eating disorders. *Nordic Journal of Psychiatry*, 65, 203–207.

Klump, K. L., Bulik, C. M., Pollice, C., Halmi, K. A., Fichter, M. M., Berrettini, W. H. et al. (2000). Temperament and character in women with anorexia nervosa. *Journal of Nervous and Mental Disease*, 188, 559–567.

Klump, K. L., and Gobrogge, K. L. (2005). A review and primer of molecular genetic studies of anorexia nervosa. *International Journal of Eating Disorders*, 37 Suppl, S43–S48.

Klump, K. L., Kaye, W. H., and Strober, M. (2001). The evolving genetic foundations of eating disorders. *Psychiatric Clinics of North America*, 24, 215–225.

Klump, K. L., Perkins, P. S., Alexandra, B. S., McGue, M., and Iacono, W. G. (2007). Puberty moderates genetic influences on disordered eating. *Psychological Medicine*, 37, 627–634.

Kotler, L. A., Cohen, P., Davies, M., Pine, D. S., and Walsh, B. T. (2001). Longitudinal relationships between childhood, adolescent, and adult eating disorders. *Journal of the American Academy of Child and Adolescent Psychiatry*, 40, 1434–1440.

Kraemer, H. C., Kazdin, A. E., Offord, D. R., Kessler, R. C., Jensen, P. S., and Kupfer, D. J. (1997). Coming to terms with the terms of risk. *Archives of General Psychiatry*, 54, 337–343.

Kraemer, H. C., Stice, E., Kazdin, A., Offord, D., and Kupfer, D. (2001). How do risk factors work together? Mediators, moderators, and independent, overlapping, and proxy risk factors. *American Journal of Psychiatry*, 158, 848–856.

Lask, B. (2000). Aetiology. In B. Lask and R. Bryant-Waugh (Eds), *Anorexia Nervosa and Related Eating Disorders in Childhood and Adolescence* (2nd ed., pp. 63–80). Hove: Psychology Press.

Lask, B. and Frampton, I. (2011). *Eating Disorders and the Brain*. Chichester: John Wiley & Sons.

le Grange, D., Lock, J., Loeb, K., and Nicholls, D. (2010). Academy for Eating Disorders position paper: the role of the family in eating disorders. *International Journal of Eating Disorders*, 43, 1–5.

Lilenfeld, L. R., Stein, D., Bulik, C. M., Strober, M., Plotnicov, K., Pollice, C. et al. (2000). Personality traits among currently eating disordered, recovered and never ill first-degree female relatives of bulimic and control women. *Psychological Medicine*, 30, 1399–1410.

Lindberg, L., and Hjern, A. (2003). Risk factors for anorexia nervosa: a national cohort study. *International Journal of Eating Disorders*, *34*, 397–408.

Mantzoros, C. S. (1999). Leptin and the hypothalamus: neuroendocrine regulation of food intake. *Molecular Psychiatry*, *4*, 8–7.

Marchi, M., and Cohen, P. (1990). Early childhood eating behaviors and adolescent eating disorders. *Journal of the American Academy of Child and Adolescent Psychiatry*, *29*, 112–117.

Martin, G. C., Wertheim, E. H., Prior, M., Smart, D., Sanson, A., and Oberklaid, F. (2000). A longitudinal study of the role of childhood temperament in the later development of eating concerns. *International Journal of Eating Disorders*, *27*, 150–162.

McManus, F., Waller, G., and Chadwick, P. (1996). Biases in the processing of different forms of threat in bulimic and comparison women. *Journal of Nervous and Mental Disease*, *184*, 547–554.

Meyer, C., Serpell, L., Waller, G., Murphy, F., Treasure, J., and Leung, N. (2005). Cognitive avoidance in the strategic processing of ego threats among eating-disordered patients. *International Journal of Eating Disorders*, *38*, 30–36.

Munn, M. A., Stallings, M. C., Rhee, S. H., Sobik, L. E., Corley, R. P., Rhea, S. A. et al. (2010). Bivariate analysis of disordered eating characteristics in adolescence and young adulthood. *International Journal of Eating Disorders*, *43*, 751–761.

Nasser, M. (1997). The EAT speaks many languages: review of the use of the EAT in eating disorders research. *Eating and Weight Disorders*, *2*, 174–181.

Nasser, M., and Katzman, M. (2003). Sociocultural Theories of Eating Disorders: An Evolution in Thought. In J.Treasure, U. Schmidt, and E. van Furth (Eds), *Handbook of Eating Disorders* (2nd ed., pp. 139–150). Chichester: John Wiley & Sons Ltd.

Nicholls, D. E., Lynn, R., and Viner, R. M. (2011). Childhood eating disorders: British national surveillance study. *British Journal of Psychiatry*, *198*, 295–301.

Nicholls, D. E., and Viner, R. M. (2009). Childhood risk factors for lifetime anorexia nervosa by age 30 years in a national birth cohort. *Journal of the American Academy of Child and Adolescent Psychiatry*, *48*, 791–799.

Nunn, K., Frampton, I., Gordon, I., and Lask, B. (2008). The fault is not in her parents but in her insula—a neurobiological hypothesis of anorexia nervosa. *European Eating Disorders Review*, *16*, 355–360.

O'Dea, J. A., and Abraham, S. (1999). Onset of disordered eating attitudes and behaviors in early adolescence: interplay of pubertal status, gender, weight, and age. *Adolescence*, *34*, 671–679.

Patton, G. C., Selzer, R., Coffey, C., Carlin, J. B., and Wolfe, R. (1999). Onset of adolescent eating disorders: population based cohort study over 3 years. *British Medical Journal*, *318*, 765–768.

Pike, K. M., Hilbert, A., Wilfley, D. E., Fairburn, C. G., Dohm, F. A., Walsh, B. T. et al. (2008). Toward an understanding of risk factors for anorexia nervosa: a case-control study. *Psychological Medicine*, *38*, 1443–1453.

Pike, K. M., Wilfley, D., Hilbert, A., Fairburn, C. G., Dohm, F. A., and Striegel-Moore, R. H. (2006). Antecedent life events of binge-eating disorder. *Psychiatry Research*, *142*, 19–29.

Pinheiro, A. P., Bulik, C. M., Thornton, L. M., Sullivan, P. F., Root, T. L., Bloss, C. S. et al. (2010). Association study of 182 candidate genes in anorexia nervosa.

American Journal of Medical Genetics Part B, Neuropsychiatric Genetics, 153B, 1070–1080.

Polivy, J., and Herman, C. P. (2002). Causes of eating disorders. *Annual Review of Psychology, 53,* 187–213.

Prince, A. C., Brooks, S. J., Stahl, D., and Treasure, J. (2009). Systematic review and meta-analysis of the baseline concentrations and physiologic responses of gut hormones to food in eating disorders. *American Journal of Clinical Nutrition, 89,* 755–765.

Root, T. L., Szatkiewicz, J. P., Jonassaint, C. R., Thornton, L. M., Pinheiro, A. P., Strober, M. et al. (2011). Association of candidate genes with phenotypic traits relevant to anorexia nervosa. *European Eating Disorders Review, 19,* 487–493.

Sassaroli, S., Apparigliato, M., Bertelli, S., Boccalari, L., Fiore, F., Lamela, C. et al. (2011). Perfectionism as a mediator between perceived criticism and eating disorders. *Eating and Weight Disorders, 16,* e37–e44.

Scherag, S., Hebebrand, J., and Hinney, A. (2010). Eating disorders: the current status of molecular genetic research. *European Child and Adolescent Psychiatry, 19,* 211–226.

Schmidt, U. (2003). Aetiology of eating disorders in the 21 (st) century: new answers to old questions. *European Child and Adolescent Psychiatry, 12* (Suppl 1), I30–I37.

Schmidt, U., Tiller, J., Blanchard, M., Andrews, B., and Treasure, J. (1997). Is there a specific trauma precipitating anorexia nervosa? *Psychological Medicine, 27,* 523–530.

Shapiro, S., Newcomb, M., and Loeb, T. B. (1997). Fear of fat, disregulated-restrained eating, and body-esteem: prevalence and gender differences among eight- to ten-year-old children. *Journal of Clinical Child and Adolescent Psychology, 26,* 358–365.

Shoebridge, P. and Gowers, S. G. (2000). Parental high concern and adolescent-onset anorexia nervosa. A case- control study to investigate direction of causality. *British Journal of Psychiatry, 176,* 132–137.

Smolak, L., Levine, M. P., and Schermer, F. (1999). Parental input and weight concerns among elementary school children. *International Journal of Eating Disorders, 25,* 263–271.

Smolak, L., and Murnen, S. K. (2002). A meta-analytic examination of the relationship between child sexual abuse and eating disorders. *International Journal of Eating Disorders, 31,* 136–150.

Sokol, M. S. (2000). Infection-triggered anorexia nervosa in children: clinical description of four cases. *Journal of Child and Adolescent Psychopharmacology, 10,* 133–145.

Sokol, M. S., Ward, P. E., Tamiya, H., Kondo, D. G., Houston, D., and Zabriskie, J. B. (2002). D8/17 expression on B lymphocytes in anorexia nervosa. *American Journal of Psychiatry, 159,* 1430–1432.

Spanos, A., Klump, K. L., Burt, S. A., McGue, M., and Iacono, W. G. (2010). A longitudinal investigation of the relationship between disordered eating attitudes and behaviors and parent-child conflict: a monozygotic twin differences design. *Journal of Abnormal Psychology, 119,* 293–299.

Steiger, H., Bruce, K. R., and Groleau, P. (2011). Neural circuits, neurotransmitters, and behavior: serotonin and temperament in bulimic syndromes. *Current Topics in Behavioural Neurosciences, 6,* 125–138.

Steiger, H., Bruce, K., Gauvin, L., Groleau, P., Joober, R., Israel, M. et al. (2011). Contributions of the glucocorticoid receptor polymorphism (Bcl1) and childhood abuse to risk of bulimia nervosa. *Psychiatry Research, 187,* 193–197.

Steiger, H., Richardson, J., Schmitz, N., Israel, M., Bruce, K. R., and Gauvin, L. (2010). Trait-defined eating-disorder subtypes and history of childhood abuse. *International Journal of Eating Disorders*, *43*, 428–432.

Stein, D., Lilenfeld, L. R., Plotnicov, K., Pollice, C., Rao, R., Strober, M. et al. (1999). Familial aggregation of eating disorders: results from a controlled family study of bulimia nervosa. *International Journal of Eating Disorders*, *26*, 211–215.

Stice, E., Agras, W. S., and Hammer, L. D. (1999). Risk factors for the emergence of childhood eating disturbances: a five-year prospective study. *International Journal of Eating Disorders*, *25*, 375–387.

Stice, E., Marti, C. N., and Durant, S. (2011). Risk factors for onset of eating disorders: evidence of multiple risk pathways from an 8-year prospective study. *Behaviour Research and Therapy*, *49*, 622–627.

Striegel-Moore, R. H., and Bulik, C. M. (2007). Risk factors for eating disorders. *Journal of American Psychology*, *62*, 181–198.

Striegel-Moore, R. H., Fairburn, C. G., Wilfley, D. E., Pike, K. M., Dohm, F. A., and Kraemer, H. C. (2005). Toward an understanding of risk factors for binge-eating disorder in black and white women: a community-based case-control study. *Psychological Medicine*, *35*, 907–917.

Striegel-Moore, R. H., McMahon, R. P., Biro, F. M., Schreiber, G., Crawford, P. B., and Voorhees, C. (2001). Exploring the relationship between timing of menarche and eating disorder symptoms in Black and White adolescent girls. *International Journal of Eating Disorders*, *30*, 421–433.

Strober, M., Freeman, R., Lampert, C., Diamond, J., and Kaye, W. (2000). Controlled family study of anorexia nervosa and bulimia nervosa: evidence of shared liability and transmission of partial syndromes. *American Journal of Psychiatry*, *157*, 393–401.

Stroud, L. R., Salovey, P., and Epel, E. S. (2002). Sex differences in stress responses: social rejection versus achievement stress. *Biological Psychiatry*, *52*, 318–327.

Suisman, J. L., Burt, S. A., McGue, M., Iacono, W. G., and Klump, K. L. (2011). Parental divorce and disordered eating: an investigation of a gene-environment interaction. *International Journal of Eating Disorders*, *44*, 169–177.

Sullivan, P. F., Bulik, C. M., and Kendler, K. S. (1998). Genetic epidemiology of binging and vomiting. *British Journal of Psychiatry*, *173*, 75–79.

The McKnight Investigators (2003). Risk factors for the onset of eating disorders in adolescent girls: results of the McKnight longitudinal risk factor study. *American Journal of Psychiatry*, *160*, 248–254.

Thomas, J. J., Keel, P. K., and Heatherton, T. F. (2005). Disordered eating attitudes and behaviors in ballet students: examination of environmental and individual risk factors. *International Journal of Eating Disorders*, *38*, 263–268.

Urwin, R. E., Bennetts, B., Wilcken, B., Lampropoulos, B., Beumont, P., Clarke, S. et al. (2002). Anorexia nervosa (restrictive subtype) is associated with a polymorphism in the novel norepinephrine transporter gene promoter polymorphic region. *Molecular Psychiatry*, *7*, 652–657.

Urwin, R. E., Bennetts, B. H., Wilcken, B., Beumont, P. J., Russell, J. D., and Nunn, K. P. (2003). Investigation of epistasis between the serotonin transporter and norepinephrine transporter genes in anorexia nervosa. *Neuropsychopharmacology*, *28*, 1351–1355.

Vincenzi, B., O'Toole, J., and Lask, B. (2010). PANDAS and anorexia nervosa—a spotters' guide: suggestions for medical assessment. *European Eating Disorders Review*, *18*, 116–123.

Wade, T. D., Treloar, S., and Martin, N. G. (2008). Shared and unique risk factors between lifetime purging and objective binge eating: a twin study. *Psychological Medicine, 38,* 1455–1464.

Waller, G., and Kennerly, H. (2003). Cognitive-Behavioural Treatments. In J.Treasure, U. Schmidt, and E. van Furth (Eds), *Handbook of Eating Disorders* (2nd ed., pp. 233–252). Chichester: John Wiley & Sons Ltd.

Walters, E. E., and Kendler, K. S. (1995). Anorexia nervosa and anorexic-like syndromes in a population-based female twin sample. *American Journal of Psychiatry, 152,* 64–71.

Ward, A., Ramsay, R., Turnbull, S., Benedettini, M., and Treasure, J. (2000). Attachment patterns in eating disorders: past in the present. *International Journal of Eating Disorders, 28,* 370–376.

Wells, J. C., and Nicholls, D. (2001). The relationship between body size and body composition in women of different nutritional status. *European Eating Disorders Review, 9,* 416–442.

Westberg, L., Bah, J., Rastam, M., Gillberg, C., Wentz, E., Melke, J. et al. (2002). Association between a polymorphism of the 5-HT2C receptor and weight loss in teenage girls. *Neuropsychopharmacology, 26,* 789–793.

Chapter 6

Physical assessment

Debra Katzman and Cathleen Steinegger

Overview

This chapter focuses on the comprehensive assessment of a child or adolescent with an eating disorder. The important components of an interdisciplinary assessment are highlighted and include a complete and careful individual assessment, family assessment, nutritional assessment, and a thorough medical evaluation. Developmental aspects of the assessment of a child or adolescents with an eating disorder are emphasized.

Introduction

A complete assessment of a child or adolescent with an eating disorder is both similar to and different from the assessment of other psychological disorders. It does require a complete and careful psychological assessment. This may include a structured, semi-structured or free form interview and self-administered standardised questionnaires. Similarly, it usually includes a family assessment (see Chapter 13). However, unlike other areas of child and adolescent mental health, an eating disorder assessment requires a nutritional assessment, a thorough medical history and physical examination, and appropriate laboratory tests.

Assessments should be conducted by an interdisciplinary team (Golden et al., 2003) which would normally include two or more people, each of whom brings a different expertise to the process of assessment. The team may include, but is not limited to, a psychiatrist or psychologist, a paediatrician, a nurse, a dietitian, and a social worker. The composition of the interdisciplinary team will vary depending on resource availability and geographic location. A useful guide for the initial identification and management of eating disorders in children and adolescents for the primary care provider has recently been published (Rosen et al., 2010).

Another important potential difference in an eating disorder assessment is that the child with an eating disorder may not be a willing participant in the process. Most children struggling with medical or mental health issues usually experience distress and understand that it is related to or caused by their disorder. They usually want treatment to relieve their symptoms. Children with eating disorders may not perceive a problem and may not believe that there is any need to change. Often it is the parents who seek help. Therefore, assessing a child individually, without any input from an adult (either the parent or at the very least the referring health-care provider), may result in an inconclusive or misleading assessment. Beginning with a family assessment, or at a minimum having an initial meeting with the child and parents together, is often useful. Some children come to an assessment planning to avoid any discussion around eating. However, they often change their minds once the parents reveal explicitly the child's struggles and voice their concerns.

Preparation for the assessment

Creating a respectful relationship with the child is important to the success of the assessment. This is accomplished by working to develop an alliance with the child (see also Chapter 11). An alliance is developed in the initial stages of the assessment and is strengthened, as the process continues, by providing a safe, empathic, non-judgemental environment for the child. The team members providing the assessment should introduce themselves and their roles to both the child and parent. A description of what is to happen during the assessment and how long it will take should also be reviewed.

Confidentiality is particularly important for patients seeking psychological assessments, necessitating a discussion of who will be privy to the information disclosed during the assessment. Families may be less forthcoming if they believe that information may be released, for example, to an insurance company. The ethical and legal definitions of confidentiality will vary depending on the locality. Regardless, a clear discussion of the limits of confidentiality should be reviewed with the child and family at the beginning of the assessment. A child or adolescent who is informed and clear about these limitations has the choice of how much to reveal during the interview. Studies have shown that when adolescents are assured confidentiality they are more willing to disclose sensitive information and more likely to trust their clinician (Klostermann, Slap and Nebrig, 2005). The literature has also shown that parents respond to education about the issues of confidentiality and recognise the importance of allowing a child the opportunity to speak alone with their clinician (Hutchinson and Stafford, 2005).

For most children, the expectation that their parents will take part in their health-care decision making is developmentally appropriate. Even adolescents who are reluctant to include their parents can be encouraged to involve them in the process. A supportive and accepting interview style can help children realise that they are not alone in their struggles with behaviours and thoughts that were previously experienced as embarrassing or humiliating. They may also realise that they do not have to protect their parents from these symptoms. By the end of the interview, most patients will agree to have a discussion about their eating difficulties with their parents.

It is important to remember that children who present with eating disorders can range from 5 to 18 years old (see Chapter 4). It is therefore important that the interviewer be mindful of the child's age and developmental stage. For younger children, questions should be simple and straightforward. The child should be comfortable with the questions rather than intimidated. Some younger children may not yet have developed the ability for abstract thinking and may answer questions in a concrete way. It is developmentally normal for them to have difficulty understanding any symbolic connections between their eating disorder and their life situation. The older the child, the more complex the interview can be, but it remains important to remember that an older adolescent is not an adult. The frontal and prefrontal cortex of their brains, which are responsible for executive functions, are still developing (Miller, 2005).

The individual interview

The interviewer should approach this part of the assessment with the intention of getting 'the story' of the child's troubles, while following a logical order of questions to ensure that all the important topics are covered. The interview should begin with an open-ended question such as 'Tell me about why you and your family decided to come to the assessment today?' or simply, 'What brought you here today?' Answers can range from 'A car brought me here' to 'My parents dragged me here' to 'I have a problem with not eating and I need help'. How a child answers these first questions reveals much about her attitudes, motivations and developmental stage. Once the problem has been identified – even if the patient's perception is simply that her parents have labelled her eating as the problem – the next step is to obtain a complete history of the problem.

History of present illness

In an assessment of a child with symptoms of anorexia nervosa (AN) or bulimia nervosa (BN), it is important to track when and how the child's initial concerns about food, weight and shape arose, and to ascertain when these concerns translated into specific behaviours. The child should be asked to describe the initial stages of the disorder:

- Was she trying to lose weight and why?
- What were her initial attempts at weight control?
- Did this work?
- How did her symptoms progress?
- What came next?
- How much weight did she lose?
- Over what length of time?
- Has she binged and/or purged?
- When and how did this start?

- If she has binged, what is the frequency of bingeing, and what are the amounts and types of food she binges on?
- Are there any triggers that start or stop a binge, either emotional or environmental?
- What are the ways in which she purges?
- Is it through vomiting, or the uses of substances, such as laxatives, diuretics, emetics, insulin or amphetamines?
- How often does this occur and what are the triggers?
- Does she exercise, and if so, what kind of activities does she do, how often, and for how long? The specifics are important. For instance, an adolescent may tell the interviewer that she does 'just a few press-ups'. This requires further exploration as a few press-ups may translate into '500 press-ups a day'.
- Does the child participate in sport or dance training that requires long hours of practice or one that idealises an unrealistic body shape?

For a child with food avoidance emotional disorder (FAED), it is important to explore what was happening when the child started to decrease her intake and why this happened. Did she feel full more quickly? Did she lose interest in eating? Usually these children did not plan or want to lose weight, and are often as worried as their parents are about their weight loss (Nicholls, Chater and Lask, 2000).

Children may describe being selective eaters with a history of pickiness. Others may describe a fear of choking that limits what they can eat. All of these possible symptom clusters need to be considered in the assessment of a child with eating difficulties (Nicholls et al., 2000).

A detailed nutritional history is essential (see Chapter 12). This assessment is ideally suited to the dietitian on the team. However, if a dietitian is not available, the following information should be collected. To have the child describe a typical day of eating and drinking can be informative. Start by asking a child when is the first time she eats or drinks anything after awakening. What does she eat? How much? What does she drink? It is important to ask if the food or drink consumed is sugar or fat free. When is the next time in the course of the day that she eats or drinks? This should continue until a daily schedule of eating has been completed. It is also important to ask about night-time awakenings to eat, exercise, or purge. Are there any foods that are avoided and why? Does she count calories or fat grams? Does the child have food allergies? It is also important to ask about vegetarianism, as eating disorders are overrepresented in adolescent girls who are vegetarian (Neumark-Sztainer, Story, Resnick and Blum, 1997). While some families are vegetarian for religious or ethical reasons, children with eating disorders may become vegetarian as a way to avoid eating. It is important to track when the decision to become vegetarian occurred and if vegetarianism is a shared family value. Some children and adolescents may also use caffeine, diet pills or other appetite suppressants. They may use nutritional supplements or complementary and alternative medicines that they believe will help them to lose weight. These possibilities require exploration. Finally, it is important to understand the child's perceptions about her family's attitudes and behaviours about food, weight loss, and health. What are mealtimes like, do they have family meals, and are they peaceful or conflicted? Who prepares the meals?

The next area of focus should be weight and shape concerns. Not every child who presents with eating difficulties experiences these symptoms and some who do may avoid discussing them. It is therefore important to ask about these concerns in a variety of ways. Some children may admit to classic complaints of feeling fat, or being afraid of gaining weight. Others may express pleasure in their current state, but only reveal their distress when asked to return to a normal weight. Others may be happy to gain weight at first, but may want to stop while still underweight. For some, the issue is less related to weight and more to their shape or level of 'fitness'. A boy may be happy to gain weight as long as he believes it will be muscle and not fat. For some girls, their fears may be less about gaining weight and more about avoiding 'curves' that come with a mature female body and which they perceive to attract unwanted attention. Questions that can be useful in exploring these issues include:

- How do you feel about your body?
- What do you think about your body shape or weight?
- Is there anything about your body you would wish to change?
- What weight would you want to be at?

There may be a number of changes that the young person or the family has noticed during the course of development of the eating disorder. The child may be described as having undergone a personality change. It is not unusual for the child or adolescent to become socially isolated. This occurs for a variety of reasons. She may start to avoid social situations that involve food including holiday meals, parties, or even movies. As well, as the malnutrition progresses, the child may not have the energy to socialise, or she may be so obsessed by her eating that she would prefer to be in her room exercising, or planning and researching how, when and how much to eat. A comorbid depression may also contribute to increasing isolation.

Children and adolescents with eating disorders may also begin to have difficulties at school. They may see their grades drop or complain of having to work harder and longer to maintain their grades. This may be due to a number of factors including being distracted by intrusive and distorted thinking about eating and weight. Patients may also experience cognitive difficulties as a result of the eating disorder (see Chapter 8). A comorbid depression may contribute to difficulties with cognition or attention and concentration (Majer et al., 2004).

Another change may be an increase in mood lability – many patients state that they feel 'moody'. People with eating disorders may be described as more anxious, irritable, angry, sad, tearful, unpredictable, or rigid. Contributing to these perceptions is the fact that the child with an eating disorder may spend a lot of time planning or controlling when and how she will eat or purge, and any change in schedule that prevents her from following her plan is experienced as catastrophic. The direct effects of starvation also contribute to affect dysregulation, as do many other common comorbid diagnoses. Having said that, it is important to remember that during the active state of an eating disorder, particularly if the patient is starved, the effects of the eating disorder itself may mimic other psychiatric disorders, including mood disorders, anxiety disorders and obsessive compulsive disorder (OCD).

Past psychiatric history and comorbid psychiatric history

Up to two-thirds of patients with eating disorders will have another psychiatric disorder at some point in their lives (see Chapter 4). These can pre-date or co-occur with the development of eating problems. The interviewer should ask in detail about a past psychiatric history. During the review of symptoms, the interviewer should also ask specific questions about the more common comorbid diagnoses such as depression, generalised anxiety, other anxiety disorders, or OCD (Steinhausen, 2002). It is also important to find out if they have been treated in other mental health care programmes and if so information from these sources should be sought. This is also the time to ask if the patient is taking or has taken medication, the name of the medication, at what dose, for how long and if it has had any positive or negative effects. It is also important to rule out other psychiatric diagnoses that may lead to weight loss such as depression that can result in loss of appetite; psychotic disorders that result in delusional ideas such as 'all food has been poisoned by some conspiracy'; or OCD which may result in food avoidance due to worries about contaminants.

When completing an assessment of a child with an eating disorder, it is important to ask about self-harm and suicidal ideation or intent. Self-harm is a commonly recognised comorbid diagnosis in eating disorders, particularly in AN and BN (Ruuska, Kaltiala-Heino, Rantanen and Koivisto, 2005). It is also important to remember that almost half of the mortality associated with eating disorders relates to suicide, and that active plans for suicide should be taken seriously (Herzog, Greenwood and Dorer, 2000).

Family history

Parents are in the best position to provide a complete history of illness in the family. However, it is useful to ask the child if she is aware of any members of her family, no matter how distant, who have been unwell, and if so are they genetically related? It is important to match these questions to the child's age and developmental stage. A child's knowledge about family history can give the clinician important information about how the family operates with regards to sensitive information.

Social history and family relationships

Struggling with an eating disorder may be associated with difficulties in relationships both in the family and with peers. It is important to ask about the child's relationship with her parents and siblings. First, ask the child to describe who is in her family and her relationships with her family members, as well as comment on how the family functions as a whole. Were there stressors in the family that might be associated with the disorder? Are there family members who are weight conscious or dieting? Some children may have siblings who teased them about their weight or shape. It is important to ask whether there have been any changes in the family – either positive or negative – before or after the development of the eating disorder. For example, have the parents become more frustrated with the child and has this led to conflict? Or has the eating disorder brought the family together in some way?

How has the eating disorder affected the child's friendship network and vice versa? Again, it is important to ask the child about her social history: ask about close relationships and other friends. Children with eating disorders may have friends with eating problems, or they may start to socialise with others who have disordered eating. Friends may actually compete to see who can be the thinnest or may all purge together. It is important to explore whether these factors play a role in the child or adolescent's story (Paxton, Schutz, Wertheim and Muir, 1999). Potential stresses such as difficulties at school, academically or with peers, should be investigated. The clinician should ask about bullying or 'teasing' related to weight or other issues as a possible trigger or perpetuating factor (Haines, Neumark-Sztainer, Eisenberg and Hannan, 2006). The clinician should consider the benefit of communicating with the school, particularly if they have assessed or provided any special mental health or academic supports for the child.

It is important to ask questions about common adolescent behaviours such as smoking, drinking, alcohol, and abuse of street drugs or medications (Stock, Goldberg, Corbett and Katzman, 2002). A comorbid substance abuse problem can increase the patient's risk of mortality in long-term follow-up (Keel, Dorer and Eddy, 2003). As well, a sexual history including questions about sexual experience and sexual orientation should be gently covered with all adolescents. Finally the presence of abuse, whether physical, sexual or emotional, should be sensitively explored. While abuse does not 'cause' eating disorders, children with eating disorders are at least as likely to have histories of abuse as the general population and these may play a role in their illness and their treatment (Wentz, Gillberg, Gillberg, Råstam and Carina, 2005; Wonderlich, Brewerton, Jocic, Dansky and Abbott, 1997).

Developmental history

As with most psychological assessments, it is important to complete a developmental history. Depending on the age of the child, these questions may be more appropriate for the parents to address. However, it may be useful to ask the child if she was told about any details of her birth or early development. A developmental history should include a history of the pregnancy and birth history, developmental milestones and delays, and an academic history.

Finally, there should also be an exploration of the child's life outside the eating disorder through the course of the assessment. This may include questions about any religious affiliations, her value system, hobbies and wishes for the future.

Mental status examination

No psychological assessment is complete without a mental status examination. Findings may include an appearance that is cachectic, poor eye contact and speech that is slowed or low in volume. Mood may be sad or alexithymic. Affect may appear tearful, anxious, irritable, enraged or blunted, depending on the child or situation. Thought form may show slowing, ruminations, obsessionality, or, in cases of serious starvation, may be tangential or circumstantial. Thought content may include a constant food focus and/or weight and shape preoccupation. There may be current suicidal or self-harm ideation.

Body image distortion is common in patients with AN and BN, and children with food avoidance emotional disorder may describe vague abdominal sensations that affect their ability to eat. Cognition may be impaired due to starvation and comorbid psychiatric disorder, although it is generally normal. Disorientation raises the possibility of delirium (possibly secondary to refeeding syndrome). Capacity to consent to treatment should also be assessed as part of the mental status examination. An eating disorder may cloud judgement and, as a result, some children may not believe that they are ill, even in the face of obvious medical facts. Some may feel that death is preferable to gaining any weight. Others may not be able to bring themselves to eat under any circumstances. It is important to understand how much the patient actually understands her illness.

Medical assessment

The clinician has two primary objectives in the medical assessment of the child with a suspected eating disorder. The first is to use the medical history and physical examination to make the diagnosis. Medical conditions in children and adolescents that should be excluded when considering a diagnosis of an eating disorder include inflammatory bowel disease, hyperthyroidism, chronic infections, diabetes and malignancy. Brain tumours may co-occur (O'Brien, Hugo, Stapleton and Lask, 2001) or be disguised as an eating disorder (de Vile, Lask and Stanhope, 1995). The second goal of the assessment is to evaluate the child or adolescent for any medical complications that may be a result of the eating disorder.

Medical history

It is important to review the child and adolescent's current and past medical history. The child's family doctor or paediatrician can be helpful in providing information about the child's past medical history. Most importantly, the clinician should explore the onset and description of the current symptoms. Has the child ever had anything like this before? What makes it better/worse? Is there a pre-existing medical condition (e.g. inflammatory bowel diseases, diabetes mellitus) associated with weight loss, abnormal eating, gastrointestinal symptoms or meta-bolic issues? Have there been any hospitalisations for these symptoms now or in the past? What investigations have previously been done? What medical diag-nosis has been given to the child or adolescent to explain these symptoms? Is the child taking any medications including vitamins, mineral supplements or comple-mentary and alternative medicines? If yes, what kind of medication(s), at what dose and for how long? Does she have any allergies? A menstrual history should be elicited from all female children and adolescents. Has the child reached menarche? If so, what was the age of the adolescent's first menstrual period? Is the adolescent's menstrual period regular? What is the length of the adolescent's menstrual cycle? Have the cycles stopped? At what weight and date was the adolescent's last normal menstrual period? It is important to ask the mother about her own age of menarche. This can be useful in predicting the age of menarche in a girl who has not reached menarche. Questions about bone pain or fractures and the use of the contraceptive pill should also be raised.

Physical examination

A thorough physical examination is an essential component in the assessment of a child or adolescent with a suspected eating disorder. Care should be taken to ensure that the child or adolescent has privacy. The physical examination should be performed with the patient alone unless the patient requests otherwise. An adolescent may prefer having a third party present when the examining doctor is of the opposite sex of the patient. A third party may be viewed as a positive supporting role during the physical examination. Physical findings may help confirm the diagnosis and may also reveal signs of the physical consequences of the disorders (Table 6.1). On the other hand, the physical examination may be entirely normal even in the face of a serious disorder.

Children and adolescents with eating disorders often lose a large amount of weight in a very short period of time. Clinicians should assess physical growth using the child's weight and stature and plotting these measurements on the growth charts. A series of accurate weights and measurements of stature are important to assess a child's growth pattern. Deviations from normal growth are easy to visualize on the growth curve. Fall-off in either weight or height is an indication of nutritional insufficiency and requires immediate attention. Parental stature is often helpful as a guide to expected physical status. Patients should be

Table 6.1 Potential physical abnormalities

System	Anorexia Nervosa	Bulimia Nervosa
General	• Weight loss • Emaciation • Dehydration • Hypothermia • Short stature/delayed growth	• Weight fluctuations • Dehydration • Mood changes, irritability
Head, ears, eyes, nose and throat	• Dry, cracked lips and tongue • Breath smells of acetone (ketosis)	• Dry lips and tongue • Dental enamel erosion • Dental caries • Gingivitis • Parotid enlargement • Palatal erythema
Cardiac	• Arrhythmias • Hypotension • Orthostatic heart rate and blood pressure changes • Congestive heart failure • Mitral value prolapse • Acrocyanosis • Cool extremities • Delayed capillary refill • Oedema	• Arrhythmias • Hypotension • Oedema
Abdomen	• Scaphoid • Palpable evidence of constipation	• Epigastric tenderness
Dermatologic	• Pallor • Acrocyanosis (purple discolouration) • Yellow/orange discolouration (carotenaemia) • Lanugo hair • Thinning scalp hair • Dry skin • Brittle nails • Evidence of self-harm	• Russell's sign (calluses on dorsum of hand) • Periorbital petechiae • Evidence of self-harm
Extremities	• Muscular atrophy	
Neurological	• Diminished deep tendon reflexes • Reduced concentration, memory and thinking ability • Peripheral neuropathy • Nocturnal enuresis	• Reduced concentration, memory and thinking ability

weighed in a hospital gown after voiding. Body mass index (BMI) should be calculated (BMI = weight in kilograms divided by height in meters squared) and plotted on the growth curves. The percentage of ideal body weight (IBW, the average weight of children of the same age, height and gender) can also be determined. It should be noted that there are a variety of methods used to determine IBW. For instance, some clinicians express body weight as a percentage of an 'ideal weight for that stature' using various methods to determine ideal weight, including the median weight-for-age (Gomez, 2000), median weight-for-height (Golden, 1997), and median weight-for-height adjusted for age (Frisch, 1990; Hebebrand et al., 1996). However, there is no one accepted and consistent method used to calculate the IBW in children and adolescents. Vital signs, including oral temperature and orthostatic measurements of the heart rate and blood pressure will help determine if the young person is medically stable. Finally, sexual maturity rating (breast and pubic hair for girls, genital and pubic hair for boys) is a crucial part of the exam as pubertal delay is likely to occur as a consequence of malnutrition.

Laboratory examination

Laboratory findings in children and adolescents with eating disorders are often completely normal. However, certain tests can be helpful in ruling out other medical conditions. Initial laboratory tests might include a complete blood cell count, erythrocyte sedimentation rate, electrolyte measurements, glucose, renal and liver function tests, urinalysis and thyroid-stimulating hormone. Renal function is generally normal except in the case of dehydration when the blood urea, nitrogen and creatinine may be elevated. Although protein and albumin are typically normal, liver function tests have been reported to be minimally elevated (Sherman, Leslie, Goldberg, Rybczynski and St. Louis, 1994). Additional tests to be considered in girls who are amenorrhoeic include a urine pregnancy test, luteinising and follicle-stimulating hormone, and oestradiol levels. A baseline electrocardiograph is helpful in children and adolescents with bradycardia or electrolyte abnormalities.

Low bone mineral density (BMD) is an early and frequent complication of AN in children and adolescents. Dual-energy X-ray absorptiometry (DEXA) scans are often recommended after six months of amenorrhoea in patients with AN and in patients with BN who have a history of AN. Results should be interpreted using the Z-scores which compare the patient's bone density to age and gender matched controls. If the result is abnormal or the adolescent remains amenorrhoeic, it is recommended that the DEXA scan be repeated annually (Golden, 2003). Determination of a child's bone age should be considered if there is growth failure. A child's current height and bone age can be used to predict growth potential and final adult height.

Pelvic ultrasound has been shown to be a safe and reliable method for determining ovarian and uterine maturity in children and adolescent girls with

AN (Key, Mason, Allan and Lask, 2002; Lai, de Bruyn, Lask, Bryant-Waugh and Hankins, 1994). Children with AN and primary amenorrhoea show the prepubertal appearance of the uterus and ovaries, whereas young people with AN and secondary amenorrhea show marked regression in the size of the uterus and ovaries (Figures 6.1–6.4). In particular, the ovaries become quiescent and show no follicular activity. Successful sonographic examination and evaluation in young girls with AN requires accurate knowledge and assessment of both uterine and ovarian size and morphology, equipment that can produce images of high resolution and experience in the reading and interpreting this examination. Over the past decade, ultrasound has played an increasingly important role in determining when a healthy weight has been achieved (Adams, 1993; Key et al., 2002; Lai et al., 1994). Mason, Allan, Hugo and Lask (2006) have produced an algorithm to assist the clinician in the interpretation of pelvic ultrasound and to determine the next steps.

Medical complications

The complications of eating disorders may be seen in every organ system and are primarily due to weight control practices (e.g. purging) and malnutrition. With early identification and treatment, most complications in children and adolescents are fully reversible.

Metabolic abnormalities and the refeeding syndrome

Recurrent purging may result in serious fluid and electrolyte disturbances. Loss of hydrogen and chloride ions through vomiting may lead to hypochloremic metabolic alkalosis. Abuse of diuretics causes a similar metabolic situation. Bicarbonate loss in diarroea associated with laxative abuse results in hyperchloremic (non-anion gap) metabolic acidosis. Hypokalemia, which occurs in approximately five per cent of people with BN (Greenfeld, Mickley, Quinlan and Roloff, 1995; Wolfe, Metzger, Levine and Jimerson, 2001) may predispose to cardiac arrhythmias, muscle weakness, or confusion. Potassium chloride supplements and fluids may be necessary to correct these electrolyte abnormalities. Hyponatremia might occur with excessive water intake or the inappropriate secretion of antidiuretic hormone.

Glucose metabolism can be erratic in AN and low blood glucose measurements are not uncommon. Hypoglycaemia is observed secondary to lack of glucose precursors in the diet or low glycogen stores. Rebound hypoglycaemia may occur with refeeding following a hyper-insulinemic response. Bingeing and purging can cause glucose levels to fluctuate widely, which is a particular danger in patients with diabetes mellitus.

Elevated serum cholesterol can be seen in states of prolonged starvation. The proposed aetiologies for this finding include depressed triiodothyronine (T3) levels affecting cholesterol breakdown, low cholesterol-binding protein levels,

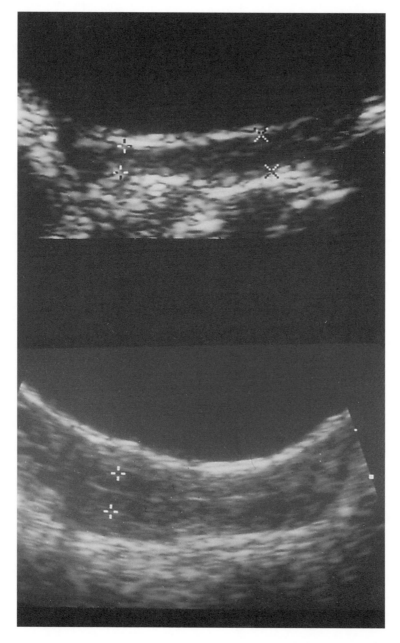

Figure 6.1 Patient aged 13 years with primary amenorrhoea: longitudinal sonogram of the uterus.

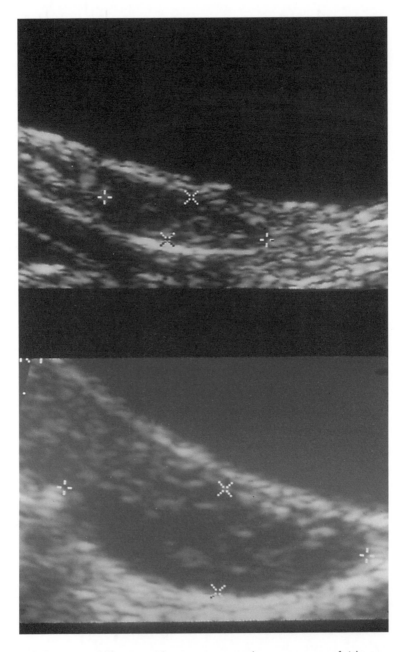

Figure 6.2 Patient aged 13 years with primary amenorrhoea: sonogram of right ovary.

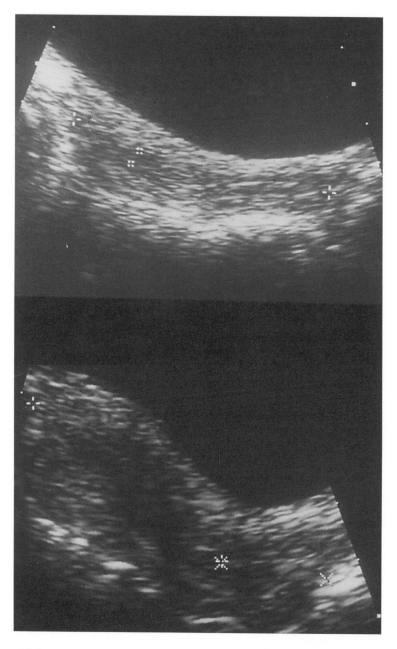

Figure 6.3 Patient aged 13 years with secondary amenorrhea: longitudinal sonogram of the uterus.

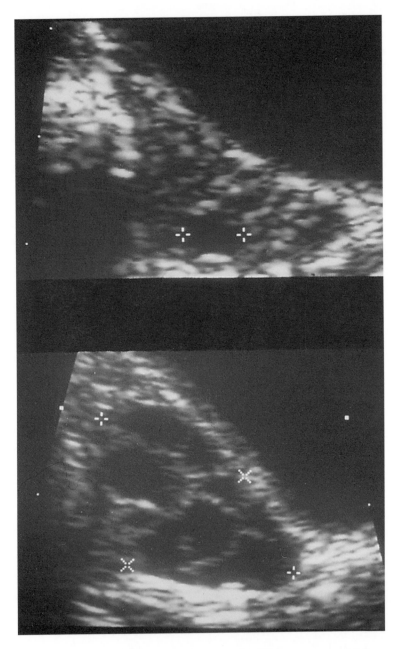

Figure 6.4 Patient aged 13 years with secondary amenorrhoea: sonogram of right ovary.

and fatty infiltration of the liver causing leakage of intrahepatic cholesterol into the peripheral circulation (Rome and Ammerman, 2003).

Refeeding syndrome refers to severe shifts in fluid and electrolyte levels in children and adolescents with an eating disorder who are undergoing nutritional rehabilitation. When the starving patient is given a high glucose meal, insulin release is stimulated which shifts metabolism from catabolic to anabolic. Phosphate moves into the cells to be incorporated into newly synthesised tissues and adenosine triphosphate (Solomon and Kirby, 1990). The resulting hypophosphatemia may cause cardiovascular, neurologic and haematologic complications. The syndrome can be prevented by slowly refeeding with close cardiac and metabolic monitoring. Supplemental phosphate may be indicated.

Haematologic status

Although the complete blood count may be normal in children and adolescents with eating disorders, pancytopenia has been reported (Palla and Litt, 1988). Anaemia and mild neutropenia are found in up to one-third of patients with AN. The mechanism is not fully understood, but many such patients display morphological signs of partial bone marrow atrophy (Hutter, Ganepola and Hofmann, 2009). Leukopenia has been observed secondary to increased margination of neutrophils but there does not seem to be an increased risk of infection in children and adolescents with eating disorder. The haemoglobin is typically normal and elevations may suggest dehydration. Anaemia requires further investigation. An iron-deficiency anaemia can be seen in children and adolescents who are vegan. Thrombocytopenia is very rare. The erythrocyte sedimentation rate tends to be low or normal; an elevated value should prompt further investigation for an underlying medical condition. These haematologic abnormalities resolve with nutritional rehabilitation.

Nutritional deficiencies

Overt nutritional deficiencies are rare in patients with eating disorder s. A role for essential fatty acid deficiency in the pathogenesis and symptomatology of AN has been postulated. In particular, omega-3 polyunsaturated fatty acids (PUFAs) have been found to be deficient in several medical and mental disease states (Ayton, 2004). PUFA deficiencies in AN have been described and the pattern reported is different from that seen with simple essential fatty acid deficiency or chronic malnutrition (Holman et al., 1995). Preliminary studies of PUFA supplementation have yielded promising, but inconclusive results (Ayton, Azaz and Horrobin, 2004).

Cardiovascular

The cardiac complications of eating disorders are among the earliest and most dramatic of all the physical effects of the disorders. One-third of deaths in adults with eating disorders are due to cardiac complications (Isner, Roberts, Heymsfield and Yager, 1985). Such data does not exist for adolescents.

Electrocardiographic abnormalities are common with AN and are reported in up to 75 per cent of hospitalised adolescent patients (Palla and Litt, 1988). Sinus bradycardia is reported to be present in 35–95 per cent of adolescents with AN (Mont et al., 2003; Olivares, Vazques, Fleta, Moreno, Perez-Gonzalez and Bueno, 2005; Palla and Litt, 1988) and correlates with disease severity as measured by BMI (Panagiotopoulos et al., 2000). Bradycardia corrects with refeeding and weight gain.

Prolongation of the QTc interval (normal interval <0.44 seconds) is inconsistently reported in adolescents with AN (Lupoglazoff et al., 2001; Mont et al., 2003; Panagiotopoulos, McCrindle, Hick and Katzman, 2000; Ulger, Gurses, Ozyurek, Arkan, Levent et al., 2006). Prolonged QTc has been associated with ventricular arrhythmias and sudden death in adults who lost weight rapidly using a liquid protein modified fast (Isner et al., 1985). In studies that report prolonged QTc in adolescents, there does not appear to be a correlation with disease severity and none of these studies report life-threatening arrhythmias. The absence of a prolonged QTc interval should not, however, be taken as a sign of stability.

As with the QTc interval, reports of increased QTc dispersion in adolescents with AN are inconsistent (Panagiotopoulos et al., 2000). When an increase in QTc dispersion has been reported in adolescents with AN, it appeared to correct with refeeding and was not associated with arrhythmias (Mont et al., 2003; Ulger et al., 2006).

Orthostatic heart rate changes (rate increase >20 bpm on standing) and blood pressure changes (>10 mmHg) are common in adolescents with eating disorders and place such teens at risk for syncope. Orthostasis may be due to dehydration, autonomic dysregulation, or atrophy of the peripheral muscles which results in decreased venous return to the heart. Evidence shows that normalisation of orthostatic pulse changes occurs after approximately three weeks of nutritional rehabilitation or when adolescents reach 80 per cent of their IBW (Shamim, Golden, Arden, Filiberto and Shenker, 2003). Resolution of orthostasis may be used as a one indicator of medical stability.

Echocardiographic changes seen in adolescents with AN include reduced left ventricular mass, reduced cardiac output and mitral valve prolapse. These findings are likely due to heart muscle wasting with malnutrition and improve with refeeding (Mont et al., 2003).

It is important to remember that prescribed medications, illicit drug use, or complementary and alternative medications may have adverse cardiac effects.

Endocrine status

Regular menstruation is an indicator of a normal hypothalamic-pituitary-ovarian axis. Amenorrhoea (absence of three consecutive menstrual periods after the establishment of regular menstruation) is a hallmark of AN. The amenorrhoea of AN is hypothalamic in origin and gonadotropin secretion resembles that of prepubertal females (Stoving, Hangaard and Hagen, 2001). The aetiology of amenorrhoea in AN is multifactorial and thought to be the result of hypothalamic dysfunction related to weight loss (with low body fat) and exacerbated by excessive exercise, abnormal eating behaviours and stress.

A main aim of refeeding is the initiation or restoration of regular periods. However, clinicians should be wary of using target weights to achieve this. Weight as a measure is remarkably unreliable and easily open to manipulation and setting a target weight may reinforce a patient's preoccupation with weight Furthermore, it must be frequently revised as children are in a state of continuous growth and development. One study found that menses returned at approximately 90 per cent of IBW or at least 2.05 kg above the weight at which menses was lost (Golden, Jacobson, Schebendach, Solanto, Hertz et al., 1997). Serum oestradiol levels of 110 pmol/L (30 pg/mL) were also closely associated with return of menses. In another study, young girls with eating disorders who reached menarche did so when they reached their prepubertal growth track (Swenne, 2005). The same group also found that if weight at return of menstruation was expressed in standard deviation scores (SDS), it could be predicted by a linear regression on weight SDS at loss of menstruation (Swenne, 2004). Key et al. (2002) used pelvic ultrasound in adolescent girls with AN to determine the optimal weight-to-height ratio to achieve maturity of the reproductive organs. They found that 88 per cent of the subjects required a weight-to-height ratio of 100 per cent (BMI = 20) to achieve reproductive maturity.

This work suggests that previous target weights had been set too low to ensure reproductive maturity and therefore return of menstruation. Furthermore, in contrast, some subjects achieved reproductive maturity at weights below the average range. Also it must be emphasised that the weight at which menstruation returns may not be the final weight required. Children and adolescents are in a state of growth and development and therefore further weight gain may be required for the maintenance of regular ovulatory cycles, the restoration of lean body mass and the continuation of physical health.

Amenorrhoea is an important risk factor for low BMD, which is an early and frequent complication in children and adolescents with AN. At least 50 per cent of peak bone mass is accrued during adolescence (Theintz et al., 1992). In adolescents with AN, both decreased bone formation and increased bone resorption are responsible for lowering BMD. Poor nutrition, low calcium and vitamin D intake, hypoestrogenemia, low levels of insulin-like growth factor I (IGF-I), increased cortisol levels, low body mass, and exercise all influence bone mineralisation.

Whether the loss of BMD is reversible with recovery is unknown. Follow-up studies have found that weight gain (even before the return of menstrual function) increases BMD (Bachrach, Katzman, Litt, Guido and Marcus, 1991; Hartman, Crisp, Rooney, Rackow, Atkinson et al., 2000; Rigotti, Neer and Skates, 1991). As such, the most important and effective treatment for low BMD in children and adolescents with AN is weight recovery. Calcium is a major component of bone, and vitamin D is crucial in calcium absorption. Although no association has been found between calcium intake and bone mass in adolescents with AN (Bachrach, Guido, Katzman, Litt and Marcus, 1990) it is recommended that adolescents take 1300 mg/day of calcium and 400 IU/day of vitamin D. A recent study showed that physiological estrogen replacement is effective in prospectively halting reductions in BMD in girls with AN (Misra et al. 2011). This is the first study to demonstrate benefits from physiological estrogen replacement in the form of a transdermal estrogen patch. Such treatment may be considered a therapeutic option in girls' refractory to weight gain and menstrual recovery despite ongoing multidisciplinary therapy.

The use of bisphosphonates has been considered to be another possible theraputic strategy to increase BMD in this population. Bisphosphonates have been given to adolescents girls with AN with no improvement in spine BMD after controlling for weight changes, although there was some beneficial effect at the femoral neck (Golden et al., 2005). Bisphosphonates have a very long half-life and are associated with marked reductions in bone turnover; both issues in the adolescent population. In teen-aged girls, there is concern for potential adverse effects on reproductive health, in particular teratogenic effects to the fetus. Use of bisphosphonate therapy in pediatric patients remains controversial because of inadequate long-term efficacy and safety data. Current data are inadequate to support the use of bisphosphonates in children and adolescents to treat reductions in bone mass/density alone (Bachrach and Ward, 2009).

Adequate nutrition is critical for achieving maximum height potential. Impaired linear growth and possibly permanent short stature may occur as a result of an eating disorder during critical periods of growth. Children and adolescents with AN can present with growth failure or stunting (Nussbaum, Baird, Sonnenblinck, Cowan and Shenker, 1985; Root and Powers, 1983). The onset of AN in relation to the onset of puberty may also influence linear growth. Adolescents who develop AN in early puberty and before menarche may present with growth retardation compared with those who develop the disorder when they are postmenarcheal. Weight restoration can induce resumption of growth. However, catch-up growth may not be complete and potential adult height may not be reached if skeletal maturation has advanced (Lantzouni, Frank, Golden and Shenker, 2002; Swenne, 2005).

Growth hormone (GH) levels in adolescents with AN are usually increased, despite low IGF-I levels, suggesting a state of GH resistance (Misra et al., 2003). IGF-I synthesis by the liver is inhibited during states of malnutrition, leading to decreased negative feedback on the hypothalamus. GH action is impaired despite these elevated GH levels. GH secretion in AN probably reflects altered neuroendocrine feedback regulation (Stoving et al., 1999).

'Euthyroid sick syndrome' or 'low T3 syndrome' characterised by markedly decreased triiodothyronine (T3), normal or subnormal thyroxine (T4), and normal thyrotropin (TSH) serum levels, is commonly found in AN (Stoving et al., 2001). Thyroid volume is often markedly reduced. Although commonly thought that the low T3 levels are due to decreased peripheral deiodination of T4 to T3, there is also evidence for hypothalamic-pituitary-thyroid axis dysfunction with poor response of T3 to TSH stimulation (Kiyohara, Tamai, Takaichi, Nakaqawa and Kumagai, 1989). Thyroid replacement therapy is not indicated and this condition will correct with refeeding.

Hypercortisolemia and abnormalities of the hypothalamic-pituitary-adrenal axis are common in AN. Most patients with AN have abnormal cortisol suppression during dexamethasone suppression testing (Munoz and Argente, 2002). Cortisol levels rapidly normalise with refeeding and weight gain.

Leptin is an adipocyte-secreted hormone involved in the regulation of food intake and energy expenditure. Additionally, leptin is thought to affect the hypothalamic-pituitary-gonadal axis by signalling sufficient energy stores for puberty and reproduction. Serum leptin levels correlate with fat mass and are low in AN. The mechanisms of action of this hormone are still largely unknown, but many studies demonstrate that its primary target is the hypothalamus (Rogol, 1998). Leptin may be important in mediating the neuroendocrine abnormalities of hypothalamic amenorrhoea. It may also play a role in treatment of bone loss associated with amenorrhoea (Welt et al., 2004). Low leptin levels have been related to increased activity in adolescents with AN (Holtkamp, Herpertz-Dahlmann and Mika, 2005). Abnormally high levels after refeeding have been associated with relapse (Holtkamp et al., 2005).

Infection

Some recent studies have suggested that AN may be part of the spectrum of the paediatric autoimmune neuropsychiatric disorders associated with streptococcus infection (PANDAS). PANDAS has been described in a subset of children with the sudden onset of OCD and/or tic disorders that occur weeks following a group A B-hemolytic streptococcal infection (GABHS). The hypothesis suggests that antibodies to GABHS may cross-react with neurons in the basal ganglia as part of a post-infectious process, possibly altering emotions and behaviour (Kurlan and Kaplan, 2004; Sokol, 2000). There is no laboratory test that can diagnose PANDAS, although a guide to assessing for it in AN has been proposed (Vincenzi, O'Toole and Lask, 2010). At present, the diagnosis of PANDAS is made clinically and includes five criteria:

- presence of OCD or tics;

- onset between three years of age and the beginning of puberty;
- abrupt onset or episodic course of symptom severity;
- association with GABHS infection (confirmed by culture and/or elevated antistreptococcal titers);
- associated neurological abnormalities (Swedo et al., 1988).

Gastrointestinal

Starvation, bingeing, and vomiting can all have a significant impact on the gastrointestinal system. Starvation may produce slowed gastrointestinal motility and constipation (Benini, Todesco, Dalle Grave, Deiorio, Salandini et al., 2004; Palla and Litt, 1988). In older adolescents and adults restriction of food intake has also be shown to cause delayed gastric emptying. These gastric symptoms will cause the child and adolescent to complain of early satiety, bloating and constipation, all of which inhibit further oral intake. One of the few studies of the gastrointestinal tract performed in children with eating disorders (Ravelli, Helps, Devane, Lask and Milla, 1993) demonstrated that gastric antral electrical dysrhythmias were not a feature of children with AN (age range 11.6 to 15.5). While eight of 14 patients complained of upper gastrointestinal symptoms, this study maintains that there is currently no evidence to support the promotion of gastric emptying with prokinetic drugs in children and young adolescents. Reassurance that symptoms will improve after several weeks of refeeding should be provided (Benini et al., 2004; Waldholtz and Andersen, 1990).

Binge eating has been reported to cause gastric dilation (Barada et al., 2006; De Caprio, Pasanisi, and Contaldo, 2000), gastric rupture, oesophageal rupture, and pancreatitis (Morris, Stephenson, Herring and Marti, 2004). Pancreatitis has also been reported and associated with refeeding in AN (Backett, 1985). Vomiting may be elicited by the use of a finger or foreign object (spoon, toothbrush, etc.) to stimulate the gag reflex. In some situations, this may progress to the point where mechanical stimulation is not necessary (Palla and Litt, 1988). Frequent vomiting commonly causes esophagitis and gastro-oesophageal reflux. Antacids, histamine-2 receptor blockers (e.g. ranitidine), or proton pump blockers may be necessary to relieve discomfort associated with acid reflux and esophagitis.

Renal

A variety of renal function abnormalities have been described in adult patients with AN including alterations in renal function, as manifested by elevated levels of blood urea nitrogen (BUN), decreased GFR, and low urinary specific gravity. One study in adolescents with AN reported that 22% of adolescents with AN had mildly elevated serum BUN levels (>20 mg/dL; maximum 27 mg/dL) with associated normal serum creatinine levels. In this same population, patients had hematuria, pyuria, and proteinuria (with a negative urine culture) that subsequently resolved with rehydration and refeeding (Palla and Litt, 1988).

Impaired osmoregulation has been reported in adolescents with AN. The evidence to date suggests that the pathophysiological mechanisms causing impaired osmoregulation in AN is multifactorial and includes abnormalities in osmoregulation of vasopressin intrinsic renal defects and the influence of antidepressants that are used in the treatment of this disorder (Kanbur, 2011).

Effects on the brain

The structural and functional brain abnormalities reported in children and adolescents with eating disorder are discussed in Chapter 8.

Conclusion

By virtue of the complexity of child and adolescent EDs, a comprehensive assessment typically takes longer than most paediatric mental health evaluations. The assessment of a child or adolescent with an ED may occur as a single assessment but commonly requires multiple evaluations over time. Additional interviews with the patient and parents, collecting collateral information from the primary health-care provider, the school system, the caseworker, or the therapist, will help to complete a comprehensive diagnostic assessment for these complex and life-threatening disorders.

Summary

- An interdisciplinary team should conduct the assessment of a child or adolescent with an eating disorder.
- When assessing a child or adolescent for an eating disorder, it is important to be mindful of the young person's age and developmental stage.
- Parents are essential to the assessment of a child or adolescent with an eating disorder.
- Medical assessment of the child with a suspected eating disorder will help in making a diagnosis, exclude other medical conditions and identify medical complications.
- Medical complications in paediatric eating disorders are seen in every organ system are primarily due to weight control practices and malnutrition, and are reversible with early identification and treatment.

Acknowledgement

Acknowledgement is made to Dr. Leora Pinhas for her written contributions to this chapter. Dr. Pinhas' written contributions have been reprinted as part of the chapter with her permission.

References

Adams, J. (1993). 'The role of pelvic ultrasound in the management of paediatric endocrine disorders'. In C.G.D. Brook (Ed.), *Clinical paediatric endocrinology* (pp. 675–691). Oxford: Blackwell.

Ayton, A. K. (2004). Dietary polyunsaturated fatty acids and anorexia nervosa: Is there a link? *Nutritional Neuroscience, 7* (1), 1–12.

Ayton, A. K., Azaz, A., and Horrobin, D. F. (2004). A pilot open case series of ethyl-EPA supplementation in the treatment of anorexia nervosa. *Prostaglandins, Leukotrienes, and Essential Fatty Acids, 71* (4), 205–209.

Bachrach, L. K., and Ward L. M. (2009). Clinical Review: bisphosphonate use in Childhood Osteoporosis. *Journal of Clinical Endocrinology* and *Metabolism, 94* (2), 400–409.

Bachrach, L. K., Guido, D., Katzman, D., Litt, I. F., and Marcus, R. (1990). Decreased bone density in adolescent girls with anorexia nervosa. *Pediatrics, 86* (3), 440–447.

Bachrach, L., Katzman, D. K., Litt, L., Guido, D., and Marcus, R. (1991). Recovery from osteopenia in adolescent girls with anorexia nervosa. *Journal of Clinical Endocrinology and Metabolism, 72* (3), 602–606.

Backett, S. A. (1985). Acute pancreatitis and gastric dilatation in a patient with anorexia nervosa. *Postgraduate Medical Journal, 61* (711), 39–40.

Barada, K. A., Azar, C. R., Al-Kutoubi, A. O., Harb, R. S., Hazimeh, Y. M., Abbas, J.S. et al. (2006). Massive gastric dilatation after a single binge in an anorectic woman. *International Journal of Eating Disorders, 39* (2), 166–169.

Benini, L., Todesco, T., Dalle Grave, R., Deiorio, F., Salandini, L., and Vantini, I. (2004). Gastric emptying in patients with restricting and binge/purging subtypes of anorexia nervosa. *American Journal of Gastroenterology, 99* (8), 1448–1454.

De Caprio, C., Pasanisi, F., and Contaldo, F. (2000). Gastrointestinal complications in a patient with eating disorders. *Eating and Weight Disorders, 5* (4), 228–230.

de Vile, C., Lask, B., and Stanhope, R. (1995). Occult intracranial tumours masquerading as anorexia nervosa. *British Medical Journal, 311*, 1359–1360.

Frisch, R. E. (1990). The right weight: body fat, menarche and ovulation. *Baillieres Clinical Obstetrics and Gynaecology, 4*, 419–439.

Golden, N.H. (2003). Osteopenia and osteoporosis in anorexia nervosa. *Adolescent Medicine: State of the Art Reviews, 14* (1), 97–108.

Golden, N. H., Iglesias, E. A., Jacobson, M. S., Carey, D., Meyer, W., Schebendach, J., et al. (2005). Alendronate for the treatment of osteopenia in anorexia nervosa: A randomized, double-blind, placebo-controlled trial. *Journal of Clinical Endocrinology and Metabolism, 90* (6), 3179–3185.

Golden, N. H., Jacobson, M. S., Schebendach, J., Solanto, M. V., Hertz, S. M., and Shenker, I. R. (1997). Resumption of menses in anorexia nervosa. *Archives of Pediatric and Adolescent Medicine, 151* (1), 16–21.

Golden, N. H., Katzman, D. K., Kreipe, R. E., Stevens, S. L., Sawyer, S. M., Rees, J. et al. (2003). Society for Adolescent Medicine. Eating disorders in adolescents: Position paper of the Society for Adolescent Medicine. *Journal of Adolescent Health, 33*, 496–503.

Gomez, F., Galvan, R. R., Frenk, S., Munoz, J. C., Chavez, R., and Vazquez J. (2000). Mortality in second and third degree malnutrition. *Bulletin World Health Organization, 78* (10), 1275–80.

Greenfeld, D., Mickley, D., Quinlan, D. M., and Roloff, P. (1995). Hypokalemia in outpatients with eating disorders. *American Journal of Psychiatry, 152* (1), 60–63.

Haines, J., Neumark-Sztainer, D., Eisenberg, M. E., and Hannan, P. J. (2006). Weight teasing and disordered eating behaviors in adolescents: Longitudinal findings from Project EAT (Eating Among Teens). *Pediatrics, 117* (2), 209–215.

Hartman, D., Crisp, A., Rooney, B., Rackow, C., Atkinson, R., and Patel, S. (2000). Bone density of women who have recovered from anorexia nervosa. *International Journal of Eating Disorders, 28* (1), 107–112.

Hebebrand J., Himmelmann, G. W., Heseker, H., Schafer, H., and Remschmidt, H. (1996). Use of percentiles for the BMI in anorexia nervosa: diagnostic, epidemiological, and therapeutic considerations. *International Journal of Eating Disorders, 19,* 359–369.

Herzog, D. B., Greenwood, D. N., and Dorer, D. J. (2000). Mortality in eating disorders: A descriptive study. *International Journal of Eating Disorders, 28* (1), 20–26.

Holman, R. T., Adams, C. E., Nelson, R. A., Grater, S. J., Jaskiewicz, J. A., Johnson, S. B. et al. (1995). Patients with anorexia nervosa demonstrate deficiencies of selected essential fatty acids, compensatory changes in nonessential fatty acids and decreased fluidity of plasma lipids. *Journal of Nutrition, 125,* 901–907.

Holtkamp, K., Herpertz-Dahlmann, B., and Mika, C. (2005). Changing parental opinions about teen privacy through education. *Pediatrics, 116* (4), 966–971.

Hutchinson, J. W., and Stafford, E. M. (2005). Changing parental opinions about teen privacy through education. *Pediatrics, 116* (4), 966–971.

Hutter, G., Ganepola, S., and Hofmann, W. K. (2009). The hematology of anorexia nervosa. *International Journal of Eating Disorders, 42* (4), 293–300.

Isner, J. M., Roberts, W. C., Heymsfield, S. B., and Yager, J. (1985). Anorexia nervosa and sudden death. *Annals of Internal Medicine, 102* (1), 49–52.

Kanbur N., Pinhas, L., Lorenzo, A., Farhat, W., Licht, C., and Katzman. D. K. (2011). Nocturnal enuresis in adolescents with anorexia nervosa: prevalence, potential causes, and pathophysiology. *International Journal of Eating Disorders, 44* (4), 349–55.

Keel, P. K., Dorer, D. J., and Eddy, K. T. (2003). Predictors of mortality in eating disorders. *Archives of General Psychiatry, 60* (2), 179–183.

Key, A., Mason, H., Allan, R., and Lask, B. (2002). Restoration of ovarian and uterine maturity in adolescents with anorexia nervosa. *International Journal of Eating Disorders, 32* (3), 319–325.

Kiyohara, K., Tamai, H., Takaichi, Y., Nakaqawa, T., and Kumagai, L.F. (1989). Decreased thyroidal triiodothyronine secretion in patients with anorexia nervosa: Influence of weight recovery. *American Journal of Clinical Nutrition, 50* (4), 767–772.

Klostermann, B. K., Slap, G. B., and Nebrig, D. M. (2005). Earning trust and losing it: Adolescents' views on trusting physicians. *Journal of Families Practice, 54* (8), 679–687.

Kurlan, R., and Kaplan, E. L. (2004). The pediatric autoimmune neuropsychiatric disorders associated with streptococcal infection (PANDAS) etiology for tics and obsessive-compulsive symptoms: Hypothesis or entity? Practical considerations for the clinician. *Pediatrics, 113* (4), 883–886.

Lai, K. Y., de Bruyn, R., Lask, B., Bryant-Waugh, R., and Hankins, M. (1994). Use of pelvic ultrasound to monitor ovarian and uterine maturity in childhood onset anorexia nervosa. *Archives of Disease in Childhood, 71,* 228–231.

Lantzouni, E., Frank, G. R., Golden, N., and Shenker, R. I. (2002). Reversibility of growth stunting in early onset anorexia nervosa: A prospective study. *Journal of Adolescent Health, 31* (2), 162–165.

Lupoglazoff, J. M., Berkane, N., Denjoy, I., Maillard, G., Leheuzey, M. F., Mouren-Simeoni, M. C. et al. (2001). Cardiac consequences of adolescent anorexia nervosa. *Archives Mal Coeur Vaiss, 94* (5), 494–498.

Majer, M., Ising, M., Kunzel, H., Binder, E. B., Holsboer, F., Modell, S. et al. (2004). Impaired divided attention predicts delayed response and risk to relapse in subjects with depressive disorders. *Psychological Medicine, 34* (8), 1453–1463.

Mason, H., Allan, R., Hugo, P., and Lask, B. (2006, September). Pelvic ultrasonography in anorexia nervosa: What the clinician should ask the radiologist and how to use the information provided. Retrieved October 26, 2006. *European Eating Disorders Review.* DOI 10.1002/erv.719.

Miller, K. J. (2005). Executive functions. *Pediatric Annals, 34* (4), 310–317.

Misra, M., Katzman, D. K., Miller, K. K., Mendes, N., Snelgrove, D., Russell, M. et al. (2011) Physiologic Estrogen Replacement Increases Bone Density in Adolescent Girls with Anorexia Nervosa. *Journal of Bone Mineral Research.* [Epub ahead of print]

Misra, M., Miller, K. K., Bjornson, J., Hackman, A., Aggarwal, A., Chung, J. et al. (2003). Alterations in growth hormone secretory dynamics in adolescent girls with anorexia nervosa and effects on bone metabolism. *Journal of Clinical Endocrinology and Metabolism, 88* (12), 5615–5623.

Mont, L., Castro, J., Herreros, B., Pare, C., Azqueta, M., Magrina, J. et al. (2003). Reversibility of cardiac abnormalities in adolescents with anorexia nervosa after weight recovery. *Journal of the American Academy of Child* and *Adolescent Psychiatry, 42* (7), 808–813.

Morris, L. G., Stephenson, K. E., Herring, S., and Marti, J. L. (2004). Recurrent acute pancreatitis in anorexia and bulimia. *Journal of the Pancreas, 5* (4), 231–234.

Munoz, M. T., and Argente, J. (2002). Anorexia nervosa in female adolescents: endocrine and bone mineral density disturbances. *European Journal of Endocrinology, 147* (3), 275–286.

Neumark-Sztainer, D., Story, M., Resnick, M. D., and Blum, R. W. (1997). Adolescent vegetarians. A behavioral profile of a school-based population in Minnesota. *Archives of Pediatric and Adolescent Medicine, 151* (8), 833–838.

Nicholls, D., Chater, R., and Lask, B. (2000). Children into DSM don't go: A comparison of classification systems for eating disorders in childhood and early adolescence. *International Journal of Eating Disorders, 28* (3), 317–324.

Nussbaum, M., Baird, D., Sonnenblinck, M., Cowan, K., and Shenker, I. R. (1985). Short stature in anorexia nervosa patients. *Journal of Adolescent Health Care, 6* (16), 453–455.

O'Brien A., Hugo, P., Stapleton, S., and Lask, B. (2001). Anorexia nervosa saved my life – coincidental anorexia nervosa and cerebral meningioma. *International Journal of Eating Disorders, 30,* 246–249.

Olivares, J. L., Vazques, M., Fleta, J., Moreno, L. A., Perez-Gonzalez, J. M., and Bueno, M. (2005). Cardiac findings in adolescents with anorexia nervosa at diagnosis and after weight restoration. *European Journal of Pediatrics, 164* (6), 383–386.

Palla, B., and Litt, I. F. (1988). Medical complications of eating disorders in adolescents. *Pediatrics, 81* (5), 613–623.

Panagiotopoulos, C., McCrindle, B. W., Hick, K., and Katzman, D. K. (2000).

Electrocardiographic findings in adolescents with eating disorders. *Pediatrics, 105* (5), 1100–1105.

Paxton, S. J., Schutz, H. K., Wertheim, E. H., and Muir, S. L. (1999). Friendship clique and peer influences on body image concerns, dietary restraint, extreme weight-loss behaviors, and binge eating in adolescent girls. *Journal of Abnormal Psychology, 108* (2), 255–266.

Ravelli, A. M., Helps, B. A., Devane, S. P., Lask, B. D., and Milla, P. J. (1993). Normal gastric antral myoelectrical activity in early onset anorexia nervosa. *Archives of Diseases of Childhood, 69* (3), 342–346.

Rigotti, N. A., Neer, R. M., and Skates, S. J. (1991). The clinical course of osteoporosis in anorexia nervosa: A longitudinal study of cortical bone mass. *Journal of the American Medical Association, 265* (9), 1133–1138.

Rogol, A. D. (1998) Leptin and puberty. *Journal of Clinical Endocrinology* and *Metabolism, 83* (4), 1089–1090.

Rome, E. S., and Ammerman, S. (2003). Medical complications of eating disorders: An update. *Journal of Adolescent Health, 33* (6), 418–426.

Root, A. W., and Powers, P. S. (1983). Anorexia nervosa presenting as growth retardation in adolescents. *Journal of Adolescent Health Care, 4* (1), 25–30.

Rosen, D. S. and the Committee on Adolescence (2010). Identification and management of eating disorders in children and adolescents. *Pediatrics, 126* (6), 1240–1253.

Ruuska, J., Kaltiala-Heino, R., Rantanen, P., and Koivisto, A. M. (2005). Psychopathological distress predicts suicidal ideation and self-harm in adolescent eating disorder outpatients. *European Child and Adolescent Psychiatry, 14* (5), 276–281.

Shamim, T., Golden, N. H., Arden, M., Filiberto, L., and Shenker, I. R. (2003). Resolution of vital sign instability: An objective measure of medical stability in anorexia nervosa. *Journal of Adolescent Health, 32* (1), 73–77.

Sherman, P., Leslie, K., Goldberg, E., Rybczynski, J., and St. Louis, P. (1994). Hypercarotenemia and transaminitis in female adolescents with eating disorders: A prospective, controlled study. *Journal of Adolescent Health, 15* (3), 205–209.

Sokol, M. S. (2000). Infection-triggered anorexia nervosa in children: Clinical description of four cases. *Journal of Child and Adolescent Psychopharmacology, 10* (2), 133–145.

Solomon, S. M., and Kirby, D. F. (1990). The refeeding syndrome: A review. *Journal of Parenteral and Enteral Nutrition, 14* (1), 90–97.

Steinhausen, H. C. (2002). The outcome of anorexia nervosa in the 20th century. *American Journal of Psychiatry, 159* (8), 1284–1293.

Stock, S. L., Goldberg, E., Corbett, S., and Katzman, D. K. (2002). Substance use in female adolescents with eating disorders. *Journal of Adolescent Health, 31* (2), 176–182.

Stoving, R. K., Hangaard, J., and Hagen, C. (2001). Update on endocrine disturbances in anorexia nervosa. *Journal of Pediatric Endocrinology* and *Metabolism, 14* (5), 459–480.

Stoving, R. K., Veldhuis, J. D., Flyvbjerg, A., Vinten, J., Hangaard, J., Koldkjaer, O. G. et al. (1999). Jointly amplified basal and pulsatile growth hormone (GH) secretion and increased process irregularity in women with anorexia nervosa: Indirect evidence for disruption of feedback regulation within the GH-insulin-like growth factor I axis. *Journal of Clinical Endocrinology and Metabolism, 84* (6), 2056–2063.

Swedo, S. E., Leonard, H. L., Garvey, M., Mittleman, B., Allen, A. J., Perlmutter, S. et al. (1988). Pediatric autoimmune neuropsychiatric disorders associated with streptococcal infections: Clinical description of the first 50 cases. *American Journal of Psychiatry, 155* (2), 624–627.

Swenne, I. (2004). Weight requirements for return of menstruations in teenage girls with eating disorders, weight loss and secondary amenorrhoea. *Acta Paediatrica*, *93* (11), 1449–1455.

Swenne, I. (2005). Weight requirements for catch-up growth in girls with eating disorders and onset of weight loss before menarche. *International Journal of Eating Disorders*, *38* (4), 340–345.

Theintz, G., Buchs, B., Rizzoli, R., Slosman, D., Clavien, H., Sizonenko, C. et al. (1992). Longitudinal monitoring of bone mass accumulation in healthy adolescents: Evidence for a marked reduction after 16 years of age at the levels of lumbar spine and femoral neck in female subjects. *Journal of Clinical Endocrinology and Metabolism*, *75* (4), 1060–1065.

Ulger, Z., Gurses, D., Ozyurek, A. R., Arkan, C., Levent, E., and Aydogdu, S. (2006). Follow-up of cardiac abnormalities in female adolescents with anorexia nervosa after refeeding. *Acta Cardiologica*, *61* (1), 43–49.

Vincenzi B., O'Toole J., and Lask B. (2010) PANDAS and Anorexia Nervosa—A Spotters' Guide: Suggestions for Medical Assessment. *European Eating Disorders Review*, *18*, 116–123.

Waldholtz, B. D., and Andersen, A. E. (1990). Gastrointestinal symptoms in anorexia nervosa. A prospective study. *Gastroenterology*, *98* (16), 1415–1419.

Welt, C. K., Chan, J. L., Bullen, J., Murphy, R., Smith, P., DePaoli, A. M. et al. (2004). Recombinant human leptin in women with hypothalamic amenorrhea. *New England Journal of Medicine*, *351* (10), 987–997.

Wentz, E., Gillberg, I. C., Gillberg, C., Råstam, M., and Carina, G. (2005). Fertility and history of sexual abuse at 10-year follow-up of adolescent-onset anorexia nervosa. *International Journal of Eating Disorders*, *37* (4), 294–298.

Wolfe, B. E., Metzger, E. D., Levine, J. M., and Jimerson, D. C. (2001). Laboratory screening for electrolyte abnormalities and anemia in bulimia nervosa: A controlled study. *International Journal of Eating Disorders*, *30* (3), 288–293.

Wonderlich, S. A., Brewerton, T. D., Jocic, Z., Dansky, B. S., and Abbott, D. W. (1997). Relationship of childhood sexual abuse and eating disorders. *Journal of the American Academy of Child and Adolescent Psychiatry*, *36* (8), 1107–1115.

Chapter 7

Psychological assessment

Jenny Nicholson

Overview

This chapter focuses on the psychological assessment of the young person with an eating disorder from a child-centred, developmentally sensitive perspective. It will outline the importance of assessment within a developmental framework and identify a range of the factors important to consider in relation to the process of the assessment. A number of psychological assessment domains are explored with a view to building a comprehensive formulation for guiding management and intervention strategies. Finally, a selection of quantitative assessment measures, which may provide a useful addition to qualitative assessment, are presented.

Introduction

If formulation is the piecing together of the puzzle of eating disorders into a coherent and meaningful picture of the difficulties, then assessment can be thought of as the process of identifying the pieces to ensure the puzzle is complete. It is the foundation upon which the clinical understanding of psychopathology is built. As such, a thorough, comprehensive and individualized assessment of each young person presenting with an eating disorder is essential if an accurate formulation is to be developed and lead to successful treatment planning.

Assessment is arguably one of the most complex parts of working with this patient group, requiring the development of an understanding of the complex interplay between multiple external factors and internal processes which are culminating in the primary symptom of eating disturbance. Assessing children and adolescents has additional challenges, including the need to adopt and integrate multiple perspectives, whilst having to work creatively to engage a younger client group in a way that enables an insight into their internal world. In the field of eating disorders, these challenges are exacerbated by the extremely high-risk nature of the disorder leading to understandably high levels of anxiety both within family and professional systems as well as the presence of the psychological phenomenon sometimes referred to as 'ego-syntonicity' (Vitousek, Watson and Wilson, 1998). The majority of mental health symptoms are experienced as being primarily aversive, or 'ego-dystonic'; the resulting distress providing a desire to seek alleviation and thus providing a motivation for change. Eating disorders however are often experienced as rewarding or comforting in that they act to reduce anxiety and guilt (Reiger and Touyz, 2006) and are thus 'ego-syntonic'. In approaching assessment it can be helpful to keep this ego-syntonicity in mind, as the resulting lack of motivation to change, or fear of removal of the symptom, can lead to an immediate conflict of aims between the young person and the adults around them. This needs to be taken into account if collaboration is going to be effectively achieved.

When completed effectively, the assessment process itself can be a powerful intervention; helping to create a collaborative understanding of the difficulties, laying the foundations of good engagement, and in the forming of a shared motivation around the goals and aims of any intervention. It is therefore important, before embarking upon an assessment, to consider not only the specific psychological domains of interest but also the process by which they will be assessed in order to facilitate this.

In addition, before undertaking an assessment, it is important to clarify its purpose; the nature of the assessment will vary considerably in relation to this. For example, the screening assessment required by a primary care professional will be very different from that for research or clinical purposes. Furthermore, the perspective of the child and family regarding the purpose of their participation in the assessment may be somewhat different. It can therefore be helpful to initiate all assessments with a clarification of the hopes and expectations of the individuals being assessed.

Assessment within a developmental context

In any assessment of children and adolescents it is important that a developmental perspective is adopted. This is even more pertinent in the field of eating disorders where the impact of the disorder on all domains of development can be catastrophic, and where the developmental considerations impact so heavily upon the presentation, course and importantly, on the risk factors to be considered.

This requires understanding the individual's eating difficulties in the context of their stage of physical, cognitive, linguistic, emotional and social development, and conceptualizing the difficulties as being a departure from the norm of this development. Furthermore, given how beholden to their systemic context children and adolescents are, it is important to take into account the familial and educational systems. This needs to be considered both in terms of how these systems influence the development and maintenance of difficulties, and how they may themselves be affected.

In adopting a developmentally sensitive assessment of young people with eating disorders it should be recognized that the current formal categorization of eating disorders lacks developmental sensitivity (Bravender, Bryant-Waugh, Herzog, et al., 2007). For example, whilst there is no doubt that the core features of anorexia nervosa occur in children (Fosson, Knibbs, Bryant-Waugh and Lask, 1987), there is evidence to suggest that the expression of the difficulties may be different in the younger age group. One simple but important example of this is the increased likelihood of younger children to generalize their restriction to fluid as well as food, significantly increasing their physical risk. Other examples include some differences in psychological correlates, such as a lower 'drive for thinness' and a smaller range of purging behaviours (Arnow, Sanders and Steiner, 1999).

As in any developmentally sensitive assessment, an estimation should be made of the child's level of neuro-cognitive development; the younger the child, the less well developed will be their verbal capacity, abstract reasoning ability and emotional awareness. This will have an impact on their ability to express themselves, or endorse certain diagnostic criteria as they are currently defined. Expressing, for example, a fear of weight gain, a distortion of body image, or an over-emphasis of body weight on self-evaluation, requires a level of abstract reasoning which simply may not be present in younger adolescents (Bravender et al., 2007).

Emotional development is hard to classify or quantify, however psychological mindedness, the ability to identify feelings, distinguish between feelings and bodily sensations and describe emotions, are all undoubtedly processes that develop with age (Taylor, Bayby and Parker, 1997). All of these processes are then filtered through the child's developing beliefs about emotional expression, which are of course in turn, influenced by parental beliefs and family culture around emotional expression. It is widely recognized that individuals with eating disorders often find it difficult to express their internal world and associated emotional state, especially distress, verbally. Historically this has been understood as a deficiency in understanding, processing, or describing emotions, labeled 'alexithymia' (Cochrane, Brewerton, Wilson and Hodges, 1993). More recently theories propose that rather than a deficiency model of emotional expression, the difficulty seen in emotional expression in eating disorders could be a result of learning and beliefs about how one should express oneself (Davies, Swan, Schmidt and Tchanturia, 2011; Hambrook, Oldershaw, Rimes, et al., 2011). Whatever the underlying route of the differences seen in emotional expression in individuals with eating disorders, it could be predicted that the younger the individual, the less well developed will be their skills in verbal emotional communication. With this in mind, it can be helpful to have a conceptualization of the eating disturbance as having come to serve a function, at least in part, of communicating distress.

Systemic factors which may impact on the expression of eating disorders in childhood as opposed to older adolescents and adults, and which therefore need to be considered in assessment, include the restrictions placed on children by their context. These make it far harder to express certain features of an eating disorder. For example not having access to money to buy food for binges, or not having the freedom to engage in behaviours such as compensatory fasting. Therefore, it can be helpful to keep in mind intent as well as actual behaviours during assessment (Bryant-Waugh, Cooper, Taylor and Lask, 1996).

The process of assessment

Before deciding upon the exact information that is needed to build a psychological picture of the young person, it is helpful to consider some of the practicalities around the process of information gathering itself.

Beginning the assessment

Whilst the receipt of a referral to a mental health service may mark the beginning of the assessment process, it is often a long way into what has already been a highly anxiety provoking journey for parents, many of whom will have had to battle to get their child's difficulties recognized. For the young person, this period is usually one of great distress characterized by low mood and high anxiety; often experiencing high levels of agitation, distressing compulsive behaviours, increasing battles with adults around intake, and potentially becoming increasingly socially isolated and possibly more physically compromised the more time that passes. Not surprisingly therefore one is often faced with assessing a very distressed and frightened individual, who may respond by retreating into withdrawal or hiding behind angry protestations. Within this context, and given the high-risk nature of eating disorders, beginning the process of assessment and evaluation of risk should not wait until the point of initial meeting. Contacting the child and family on receipt of referral has some benefit. It allows for screening of immediate health risks, ascertainment of the urgency of the assessment, ensures that the relevant individuals are invited to assessment and allows the gaining of consent to access any relevant previous reports or medical records, prior to first appointment. This will enable an informed judgment regarding the urgency of the assessment and the most appropriate time to meet with the child and family face-to-face, and avoid situations arising in which young people at high risk are left without input.

Who to involve in the assessment

Family members

Whilst this chapter focuses upon the individual psychological assessment of the young person with an eating disorder, it is rarely appropriate to assess a child or adolescent without the involvement of their family or caregivers (National Institute of Health and Clinical Excellence, NICE, 2004). This is due to the physical health risks involved, the potential of the young person to minimize the extent of their difficulties, and the significant impact the difficulties are likely to be having on all family members. Involving parents or caregivers from the outset is also helpful as it is likely that a component of the intervention will be supporting the young person in relinquishing some of the control that they have taken over food and eating, and thus supporting the primary care givers in taking back responsibility around mealtime management.

Professionals

A comprehensive assessment should be multi-disciplinary, ideally involving at least two suitably qualified professionals who can between them ensure assessment of both the physical and psychological aspects of the eating disorder. The nature of professionals involved is likely to be a pragmatic decision based on service structure and available resource, however even when resource is limited multi-disciplinary input should be offered at a team level, through supervision and case discussion.

Developing collaborative relationships

The manner in which an assessment is undertaken sets the tone for future engagement in therapy, and therefore should be viewed as much more than a simple information gathering exercise. The development of collaborative working relationships between clinician, child and family are essential when working with eating disorders; disorders in which relationships with others as well as with food, may have become characterized by an imbalance of control and power and which consequently often lack the important element of collaboration.

The assessment may be the first opportunity the young person has been given to view their eating difficulty as a 'problem' in its own right rather than just a behaviour they are performing that the adults around them find unacceptable. Externalising the eating disorder in this way allows for the acknowledgment that although it may have perceived benefits, there are also associated negative aspects and consequences related to the eating disorder. This can enable the expression of ambivalence, even in individuals with very little insight or motivation for change. Collaboration can then be sought in terms of the clinician facilitating the adults to support the part of the child that desires change – a very different position from that of the young person fighting against adults trying to get them to eat.

Central to the development of an effective, collaborative, therapeutic relationship is the stance adopted by the clinician. The young person is being asked to share a great deal of information, much of which may be highly sensitive and personal. It may be the first time experiences have been openly asked about and discussed, and this may be quite alien from usual family culture. Adopting a stance that is child-centred, curious, empathic and warm, and that conveys a position of positive regard is most likely to facilitate a collaborative engagement in which the therapist can be viewed as a potentially helpful collaborator in supporting the young person.

A clinician's understanding of the aetiology of eating disorders may impact somewhat on their therapeutic stance. It is therefore helpful to be explicit about the multi-factorial bio-psycho-social aetiology of eating disorders (as outlined in Chapter 5), in order that a genuinely non-blaming stance can be adopted.

Format of assessment

Psychological assessment of the child necessarily needs to be in the context of a broader parent based systemic assessment.

How the information is to be collected

The clinical interview with the young person is likely to provide the mainstay of the psychological assessment, and as such it is important that the optimal environment (both physical and relational) for allowing this is created. This requires the clinician to be mindful of both the generic development factors present when assessing any young person, and also the additional challenges posed by the distress associated with the eating disorder.

Engagement therefore needs to take into account not only the child's developmental cognitive, linguistic and emotional abilities, but also the impact of their level of distress, anxiety, fearfulness and potentially physically compromised state. This may mean providing alternative ways of engaging, or alternatives to direct verbal communication such as through play, games or art, or having specific child focused assessment techniques that use drawing and writing.

In order to create as holistic a psychological picture as is possible, one needs to understand both the young person as an individual and the nature of the difficulties they are experiencing. Whilst this assessment will necessarily entail a clinical interview, supplementing interview techniques with standardized measures can provide useful additional information including providing a quantitative element to the assessment. This quantitative aspect of the assessment may be in both symptom and child domains (e.g. temperament/personality/behaviour). However it is important to keep in mind that there is some lack of clarity in the literature as to whether measurement of the same construct within different modalities provides the same results. For example, whether measuring eating disorder symptoms using the Eating Disorder Examination interview (EDE: Fairburn and Cooper, 1993) elicits the same responses as the Eating Disorder Examination Questionnaire (EDE-Q: Fairburn and Beglin, 1994) (Passi, Bryson and Lock 2003, Pretorius, Waller, Gowers and Schmidt, 2009). There are a number of hypotheses as to why interviewing children and adolescents might elicit slightly different information from questionnaire measures, including that there may be less of a pressure felt to respond in a 'socially appropriate' manner when there isn't the need to relate to an interviewer, but also that instructions and explanation of difficult concepts such as 'bingeing' may be easier in person (Passi et al., 2003).

Consent and confidentiality

Consent and confidentiality are always complex issues when working in child and adolescent mental health, where it is usually necessary to involve those with parental responsibility in assessment and resulting decisions around treatment planning. In eating disorders this is compounded by one of the defining features of the disorder being a minimization of the severity of the impact of the symptoms. This can lead to a lack of acknowledgement of the need for intervention, often resulting from the ego-syntonic features previously discussed. It can also result in a conflict between parental consent for assessment and intervention and child or adolescent refusal of consent. The ethical issues around consent are outlined more fully in Chapter 17.

Given the central role of engagement, collaboration and motivation in working with eating disorders a very clear delineation of the boundaries of confidentiality needs to be given from the outset. For adolescents it can be particularly important to be clear about what information is likely to be shared with parents and what information would fall outside the boundaries of confidentiality, as a perception that confidence has been breached will be extremely detrimental to engagement.

Domains to include in the assessment

In thinking about psychological evaluation of the young person with an eating disorder, it is obviously important to develop a detailed understanding of the exact nature of the eating difficulties. It is however also important to develop a holistic picture of the young person; an understanding of the individual aside from their difficulties. This provides information as to what function the problem may have come to serve, what individual factors may be acting to maintain the difficulties, what the individuals strengths and weaknesses are that need to be accounted for and utilized in therapy, and what developmental course the young person would be following if they did not have the difficulty. This can ultimately provide a picture of the developmental course to which they should return once the difficulties have been resolved.

Eating disorder symptom factors

An overview of the young person's perception of the difficulties should initially be sought in an open ended way. Standard enquiries may include 'Your parents have bought you here as they are worried about how things have been recently. Can you tell me what's been going on from your point of view?' or 'It sounds as if you've been having a really hard time of it recently; can you tell me a bit about what's been going on?' This allows the young person to present whatever they consider to be the most pressing difficulties, which may of course have nothing to do with eating!

Table 7.1 Example of a timeline of symptom development

Healthy eating talk at school	G'ma died	Argument with best friend	Secondary transfer
March 2010	*May 2010*	*July 2010*	*Sept 2010*
Stopped eating crisps and sweets	*Sad and didn't feel hungry*	*Didn't have anyone to eat lunch with*	*Fainted in PE so mum took to GP*

Once this understanding of what the young person is struggling with has been developed, more direct attention can be paid to the core features associated with food, eating, fear of weight gain and the influence of weight and shape on self-perception.

In assessing the nature and impact of the symptoms it is important to understand them in the context of their development; one way of doing this is to plot a time-line of the difficulties in light of other life events (Table 7.1).

Eating

Restriction of nutritional intake is the key feature in the majority of childhood eating disorders, and assessment of current nutritional intake is important to establish the level of restriction, to identify areas of nutritional need, to establish the behavioural impact of the eating disorder and to enable accurate risk assessment. A brief picture of difficulties around eating can be gained from asking the child to describe what a usual day's intake would be, starting from first thing in the morning. However a food diary, completed by either the young person or their parent prior to attending, can allow for a more complete dietary analysis. The process of dietetic assessment is more fully explored in Chapter 12.

A description of nutritional intake can highlight problems in the range or types of food a young person eats, as found in selective eating difficulties, as well as difficulties with over or under eating. In exploring the child's nutritional intake, it is important to enquire about any fears or anxieties associated with eating. These may range from a fear of swallowing or choking as in certain food related phobias, to a fear of new foods (neo-phobia) as in young people with selective eating difficulties, to a general feeling of fullness and lack of appetite as in children with food avoidance emotional disorder (FAED) (Nicholls, Chater and Lask, 2000). It is important that an open mind is kept to the reasons for food avoidance or nutritional restriction. Examples of questions that might be asked include 'What would happen if you tried to eat something different from usual?', 'Do you have any worries about changing what you currently eat?', 'What would happen if you were asked to eat more?'

Some eating behaviours that may be associated with the eating disorder (for example the cutting, shredding, mashing or smearing of food; drawing out the amount of time meals are taking; excessive chewing, rumination, hiding or dropping of food etc.) may be more accurately noted by parents.

Problems with over eating, or bingeing should be asked about separately, as they may not be captured in asking about a 'usual' day's intake.

Weight control behaviours

Extreme weight control strategies such as self-induced vomiting, purging, excessive exercise and use of appetite suppressants or diuretics commonly characterize adult eating disorders. In the general adolescent population these behaviours increase with age, particularly associated with developmental transitions (Neumark-Sztainer, Wall, Eisenberg, Story and Hannan, 2006), thus whilst these features may be less common in the younger eating disordered population (Bravender et al., 2007) it is important to be vigilant to the possibility of their presence.

Body image

Disturbance of body image is one of the central features of many eating disorders, and assessment of possible distortions in body image, as well as the presence of over-valuing the significance of weight and shape in self-evaluation is an important part of the assessment of the young person with an eating disorder. It has significance not only in terms of diagnosis but also clinically; distortions in body image have been shown to have an impact on the aetiology, maintenance and prognosis of eating disorders (Stice, 2002; Keel, Dorer, Franko, Jackson and Herzog, 2005).

Assessment of eating disorder symptoms should be done in the context of a physical assessment having already been undertaken in order that the impact of the symptoms on weight, height, growth and development is already known.

There are a number of advantages to supplementing qualitative descriptions of the core symptoms of eating disorders with the use of structured standardized symptom measures. Structured measures provide a thorough, standardized enquiry, ensuring that symptoms are not overlooked or minimized. They can allow the endorsement of symptoms that otherwise might not be mentioned for fear of embarrassment or shame, and can also provide an element of normalization or psychoeducation around the presence of certain symptoms. The measures can also be used to assess change over time, including the efficacy of any interventions. A number of the structured symptom measures are diagnostic, allowing for a more concrete assertion of the confirmation, or otherwise, of various eating disorder diagnoses. A description of some of the more useful symptom measures can be found at the end of this chapter.

Psychological functioning

General mental health functioning

In addition to assessing the presence of the core symptoms of eating disorders, the assessment of a child or adolescent should include some thinking about psychological functioning outside of the eating disorder symptom domain. Co-morbid mental health symptoms are very common in children and adolescents with eating disorders, and in particular attention should be paid to symptoms of anxiety, depression, obsessive-compulsive disorder and neurodevelopment difficulties such as the autistic spectrum disorders (Herpertz-Dahlmann, 2009). It can be helpful to have a framework for approaching an assessment of mental health and functioning, such as that provided by a standard 'mental state examination' (Table 7.2).

The young person should be asked about their mood, and visual analogue scales can help to illustrate this. Fluctuations in mood should be enquired about including times when things feel better or worse, and what helps when they are feeling low. As self-harm and suicidality are commonly associated with low mood in eating disorder (Ruuska, Kaltiala-Heino, Rantanen and Koivisto, 2005), the presence of suicidal thoughts or self-harm needs to be asked about directly. Questions such as 'when you are feeling as low as you have indicated here, do you ever have thoughts about not wanting to carry on or about trying to end it?'; 'When it feels like that, have you had thoughts about how you might carry it through?' and 'When you are feeling like this have you done anything to try and hurt yourself?'

Similarly, anxiety can be assessed using visual analogue scales, and enquiry should be mindful of what helps the young person to manage their anxiety, including any neutralizing strategies or compulsions.

Table 7.2 Framework of a basic Mental State Examination

Domain	Possible examples
Appearance	Visible emaciation, lanugo hair
Rapport	Withdrawn, lack of reciprocity and engagement
Behaviour	Fidgeting, repetitive movements, 'perching' rather than sitting, withdrawn, poor eye contact
Speech	Whispering or selectively mute
Mood and affect	Evidence of low mood, anhedonia, anxiety
Thought process	Perseveration of ideas around food/calories/eating concerns
Thought content	Overvaluing of weight/shape in self evaluation
Perception	Evidence of dissociation
Insight	Lack of acknowledgment of severity of medical impact of low weight

Low self-esteem has long been understood to play a role in the development and maintenance of mental health difficulties, and there is some evidence specifically suggesting that low self-esteem might make adolescents more vulnerable to the development of eating disorder symptoms (Button, Sounga-Barke, Davies and Thompson, 1996). It is important, therefore, to keep in mind through the assessment what impression the young person is giving about their opinion of themselves and their self-worth. Are they able to acknowledge their strengths, positive attributes, and what others see in them to be valued? How would they describe themselves to someone who has never met them before? Are they able to take a compliment or accept praise? As self-esteem can also be protective, and bolstered in order to support recovery, it is helpful to have a measure of it from the outset.

Development

As already discussed, it is important that all assessment is completed through the lens of a developmental model, which will include the need to hold in mind all domains of development. Whilst a full picture of development can most helpfully be gained by completing a neuro-developmental assessment with input from the child's parents, an estimation of cognitive, social and emotional development can be gained through direct assessment.

Psychometric assessment

There are a number of neuropsychological deficit models of eating disorders, and therefore screening for cognitive difficulties could potentially be indicated for all young people presenting with eating disorders. Assessment can also allow for an exploration of the relationship between cognitive level, psychosocial development and the development of the eating difficulty (Lena, Fiocca and Leyenaar, 2004). It can also help to identify any unmet educational need, and indicate the level at which therapeutic interventions and psychoeducation should be pitched. In the absence of formal psychometric assessment an estimation of cognitive functioning and ability can be gained from a detailed educational history. This needs to take account of the high levels of academic motivation that are often present, which can sometimes result in cognitive deficits being masked by hard work and high levels of perfectionism.

School/education

Education and the school environment are key aspects of the lives of most children and adolescents; taking up the majority of their waking week, providing learning and social opportunities and adding important structure to the day. Unsurprisingly therefore difficulties within the educational environment can have a significant impact on the precipitation and perpetuation of eating difficulties, and a full educational history is important in understanding these factors.

Social development

Social development can be accessed through enquiry about friendships and relationships at school; whether friendships are maintained outside of the school context; what after-school social activities or engagements the child is involved with; and whether they have a same age peer group (an older or younger peer group may be more forgiving of social difficulties or less challenging).

It is important to explore a young person's social network in terms of possible stressors, such as episodes of bullying, that may have occurred (Haines, Neumark-Sztainer, Eisenberg and Hannan, 2006), as well as the impact that the eating disorder may be having upon relationships. Working within a developmental model, it is important that appropriate social relationships are maintained or developed in order that treatment aims can facilitate a return to age appropriate social functioning.

Attachment

Although a formal assessment of attachment style is probably not indicated at initial assessment (unless a primary attachment disorder is suspected) it can be helpful to keep in mind that the child's primary attachment relationships, and resulting style of attachment, will have a significant impact on their clinical presentation. Attachment style will also impact on their ability to utilize psychological therapies, and their relationship to those around them including clinicians. In adult eating disordered populations anxious and insecure attachment styles are commonly found (Ward, Ramsay, Turnball, Benedettini, and Treasure, 2000).

Motivation to change

Whilst the egosyntonic nature of eating disordered symptoms can result in young people lacking a motivation to change specific symptoms, it is rare that there are no aspects they would want to change. Motivation is not a static trait and is relational in nature; it arises in the context of an interpersonal process (Miller and Rollinick, 1991). Identifying factors where there is a desire for things to be different is an important part of harnessing motivation to change for use within therapeutic interventions. Commonly these factors might include a desire for better relationships with parents or siblings, a reduction in arguments around food, or an improvement in mood or anxiety levels. Assessing motivation can be thought about within the three domains of: desire for change; readiness for change; and beliefs about ability to make change.

Risk

Risk is an assessment domain in its own right, and a vein that must be running through the entire assessment. There are a number of unique risk factors which should be particularly kept in mind through the assessment.

Physical Health

Unique to the assessment of eating disorders in psychiatric services is the need to prioritize medical risk. This is particularly important due to the increased likelihood of dietery restriction generalizing to fluids in the younger age group, and the possible long-term detrimental effects of starvation on growth, development and pubertal status. These issues are outlined fully in Chapter 6.

Psychosocial Risk

There has been some evidence to suggest that childhood abusive experiences may be a contributing precipitating risk factor in the development of an eating disorder (for a review, see Steiger and Bruce, 2007). Whilst this is not to imply that the presence of abuse should be assumed in young people presenting with eating disorders, it is important that abusive experiences are enquired about directly, in a sensitive and age-appropriate manner. Attention should be paid to the possibility that young people are at greater risk of physical harm in the context of an eating disorder, given the level of heightened conflict and distress that occurs around mealtimes and the potential this may have to lead to physical conflict.

The risk that the young person poses to others should also be assessed, including to other vulnerable individuals in the family such as the potential detrimental impact of the eating disorder or associated behaviours on siblings.

A comprehensive assessment of psychosocial risk should also take into account parental mental health and resource. In instances of parental vulnerability the increased burden of care resulting from the presence of the eating disorder may result in what would under normal circumstances be considered 'good enough' parenting, being inadequate for the needs of a child with an eating disorder.

Suicidality, self-harm, substance misuse and sexual activity

Depression and low mood are commonly associated with eating disorders in childhood and adolescence, and it is therefore important to assess the level of risk posed by self-harming behaviours, which studies have found to be highly prevalent in eating disorders (Ruuska et al., 2005). Successful suicide has been estimated to account for around half of the mortality associated with eating disorders, and suicidality should always be taken very seriously (Herzog, Greenwood and Dorer, 2000).

The presence of other risky adolescent behaviours such as alcohol and drug use and promiscuous sexual activity should be assessed, and the level of risk associated with the behaviours evaluated. Self-harm and alcohol use have been found to be negatively associated with outcome (Steinhausen, 1999).

Risk to development

Throughout the assessment, consideration should be given not just to the impact of the eating disorder on the various developmental domains, but to the damage that is being done to the likelihood of getting back on course with the developmental trajectory that would have been followed if the eating disorder had not arisen. This requires assessment of the impact of the duration of the symptoms and careful assessment of protective factors.

Formulation

Pulling the strands of the assessment together into a comprehensive and functional formulation enables the young person to develop a psychological understanding of their difficulties and the maintenance factors, and gives a rationale for intervention. This should be the ultimate goal of psychological assessment in the clinical setting.

Formulation requires the assessment of multiple psychological domains, which are then considered within a framework that considers their impact on the triggering, development and maintenance of the difficulties. Attention should also be given to the presence of resilience factors. This model of formulation is sometimes called the '5P' model as it takes into account the events and psychological processes that are relevant in five key areas. These are; factors 'Predisposing' the individual to difficulties; factors 'Precipitating' the onset of the problem; the nature of the 'Presenting' problem; factors that 'Perpetuate' or maintain the problem; and factors 'Protective' of the individual (Figure 7.1). By considering these factors within the biological, psychological, social and systemic domains it should be possible to build a comprehensive multi-factorial picture of the young person and their difficulties, reflecting the complex multi-factorial nature of the

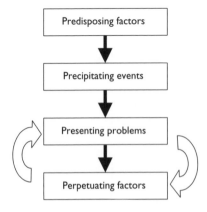

Figure 7.1 Format for basic formulation.

aetiology of eating disorders (as outlined in Chapter 5). Once this basic under-standing has been developed, it may be that a more sophisticated or more detailed, model specific therapeutic formulation can be constructed within its framework (see Chapter 14). Furthermore, as assessment and formulation are a dynamic process, the picture is likely to be constantly evolving, with the development of relationships and increased understanding.

Assessment instruments and interviews

Structured quantitative measures are commonly used in the assessment of eating disorders, and can helpfully add to the assessment and formulation process in clinical practice. They can also be useful in evaluating outcome, providing valu-able information for screening populations, and act as an essential objective measure within the research field. Whilst there are many well standardized measures available for the screening, assessment and diagnosis of eating disorder psychopathology in adults, there are relatively few comparative measures for use with children and adolescents. The measures outlined below are those which have been specifically designed or adapted for use with a younger population.

Structured interviews

Although there are a number of comprehensive structured interview measures available for use with adults, the only one which has been adapted for use with children and adolescents is the Eating Disorder Examination (EDE: Fairburn and Cooper, 1993). Considered the 'gold standard' in the assessment of adult eating disorders (Wilson, 1993), the EDE provides frequency or severity ratings for behaviours and attitudes relating to the key diagnostic features of anorexia nervosa and bulimia nervosa. It is made up of the four subscales of 'restraint', 'eating concern', 'shape concern', and 'weight concern', and is diagnostic for both anorexia nervosa and bulimia nervosa based on DSM-IV criteria.

The Child Eating Disorder Examination (ChEDE: Bryant-Waugh et al., 1996) is modified to allow for the diagnosis of anorexia nervosa and bulimia nervosa in children and adolescents according to the DSM-IV criteria. The adaptations are primarily focused on making it more understandable and easier to complete for the younger group. This was achieved through the rewording of a number of the questions as well as by the instructions given guiding completion. In particular, the items assessing the constructs of importance of weight and shape have been adapted to make them more understandable. The interview takes around an hour to complete, and the semi-structured format allows for exploration and clarifica-tion of responses, thus also providing a wealth of qualitative information. As well as being diagnostic, the measure can be used to evaluate therapeutic outcome and change in symptoms over time. Basic data about the psychometric properties of the ChEDE have been collected, suggesting that it has reasonable discriminant validity (Frampton, 1996) as well as a high level of internal consistency and good inter-rater reliability (Watkins, Frampton, Lask and Bryant-Waugh, 2005). The EDE has been translated into a number of European languages, and studies suggest that these translated versions also have reasonable psychometric properties (Frampton, Wisting, Overas, Midtsund and Lask, 2011).

Eating disorder symptom questionnaires

The Eating Disorder Examination Questionnaire

The Eating Disorder Examination Questionnaire (EDE-Q: Fairburn and Beglin, 1994) is a 38-item questionnaire measure derived from the Eating Disorder Examination interview (EDE: Fairburn and Cooper, 1993), the adult measure of eating disorder psychopathology. It measures behavioural and cognitive symptoms in the domains of 'restraint', 'eating concern', 'weight concern' and 'shape concern', deriving subscale scores of severity in each. Although developed for use in adults, normative data have been established with girls aged 12–14 years (Carter, Stewart and Fairburn, 2001).

The Eating Disorder Inventory for Children

There are various versions of the Eating Disorder Inventory for Children (EDI-C: Franko, Streigel-Moore, Barton et al., 2004) adapted from the different versions of the Eating Disorder Inventory (EDI: Garner, Olmsted and Polivy, 1983; Garner, 1991, 2004). The EDI is a 64-item questionnaire measure assessing attitudes towards weight, body shape and eating, as well as five psychological characteristics common to adult disorders. This results in the eight subscales of 'drive for thinness', 'bulimia', 'body dissatisfaction'; 'ineffectiveness', 'perfection', 'interpersonal distrust', 'interoceptive awareness' and 'maturity fears'. A study with a large sample of non-clinical adolescents (Franko et al., 2004) suggests that this may not be an appropriate factor structure with adolescents.

The EDI-2 (Garner, 1991) has also been adapted for use with adolescents with questions being reworded to make them more age appropriate. This version has been found to have good internal consistency and good discriminant validity in adolescent females (Thurfjell, Edlund, Arinell, Hagglof and Engstrom, 2003).

The EDI-3 is designed for use with adults and adolescents down to 13 years old. It is a 91 item scale – comprising 12 scales organized into three eating-disorder-specific scales, and nine general psychological scales that are thought to be relevant to eating disorders. It yields the six composite scores of 'eating disorder risk' 'ineffectiveness', 'interpersonal problems', 'affective problems', 'over-control' and 'general psychological maladjustment'. A recent, large-scale study into the psychometric properties confirmed the factor structure, found good discriminant validity and found that the measure had excellent sensitivity and specificity (Clausen, Rosenvinge, Friborg and Rokkedal, 2011).

The Development and Well-Being Assessment (DAWBA)

The Development and Well-Being Assessment (DAWBA) (Goodman, Ford, Richards, Gatward and Meltzer, 2000), is a package of questionnaires, interviews and rating scales designed to generate ICD-10 and DSM-IV psychiatric diagnoses in 5- to 16-year-olds. It includes a section on eating disorders comprising a 28-item computer administered interview, which can be administered electronically or in person by a non-clinician. In a validation study the DAWBA was found to identify all cases of eating disorder in a sample of 174 7- to 17-year-olds and to have excellent specificity and test-retest validity (Moya, Fleitlich-Bilyk, Goodman, et al., 2005).

Screening measures

Screening measures are usually designed to be used with large populations of individuals to identify those at high risk. As such they are generally simple, easy to use, quick to administer and inexpensive and may be useful for those in primary care or for research purposes.

The Children's Eating Attitudes Test (ChEAT: Maloney et al., 1988) is a modified version of the adult screening measure the 'Eating Attitudes Test' (EAT: Garner et al., 1982). It is a 26-item questionnaire examining perceived body image, obsessions/preoccupation with food and dieting practices. Normative data is available for children aged 8–13 years, although it is recommended that administration instructions are given orally for younger children, increasing the administration time and reducing its effectiveness as a screening tool.

The Kids' Eating Disorder Survey (KEDS: Childress, Brewerton, Hodges and Jarrell, 1993) is a simple, 14-item questionnaire measure, designed for use with children aged 10–13 years. Its simple format and good psychometric properties make it a useful screening tool for children and young adolescents.

Summary

- The assessment process should be much more than a simple information gathering exercise and is most effectively completed if the child can be engaged in a collaborative therapeutic manner.
- Assessment should occur within a developmental framework considering holistically all aspects of a young person's physical, cognitive, linguistic, emotional and social development.
- There is likely to be a high level of anxiety and distress for the young person and their family at assessment; it is helpful to keep in mind the role of the eating disorder in managing anxiety and guilt, as well as the role it may have come to serve in communicating distress.

- Individual psychological assessment should occur in the context of a parental or family led systemic assessment and include a comprehensive risk assessment.
- To develop a comprehensive collaborative formulation, taking account of the multi-factorial bio-psycho-social aetiology of eating disorders; symptom, child and systemic factors must be assessed.
- Quantitative measures can usefully add to the assessment process as well as providing opportunity for outcome measurement and symptom change over time.

References

Arnow, B., Sanders, M. J., and Steiner, H. (1999). Premenarcheal versus postmenarcheal anorexia nervosa: A comparative study. *Clinical Child Psychology and Psychiatry*, *4*, 403–414.

Bravender, T., Bryant-Waugh, R., Herzog, D., Katzman, D., Kreipe, R. D., Lask, B. et al. (2007). Classification of child and adolescent eating disturbances. Workgroup for Classification of Eating Disorders in Children and Adolescents (WCEDCA). *International Journal of Eating Disorders*, *40*, S117–S122.

Bryant-Waugh, R., Cooper, P., Taylor, C., and Lask, B. (1996). The use of the Eating Disorder Examination with children: A pilot study. *International Journal of Eating Disorders*, *19*, 391–397.

Button, E. J., Sonuga-Barke, E. J. S., Davies, J., and Thompson, M. (1996). A prospective study of self esteem in the prediction of eating problems in adolescent girls: questionnaire findings. *British Journal of Clinical Psychology*, *35* (2), 193–209.

Carter, J. C., Stewart, D. A., and Fairburn, C. G. (2001). Eating Disorder Examination Questionnaire: Norms for young adolescent girls. *Behaviour Research and Therapy*, *39*, 625–632.

Childress, A. C., Brewerton, T. D., Hodges, E. L., and Jarrell, M. P. (1993). The Kids' Eating Disorders Survey (KEDS): A study of middle school students. *Journal of the American Academy of Child Adolescent Psychiatry*, *32*, 843–850.

Clausen, L., Friborg, O., Rokkedal, K., and Rosenvinge, J. H. (2011). Validating the Eating Disorder Inventory-3 (EDI-3): a comparison between 561 female eating disorders patients and 878 females from the general population. *Journal of Psychopathology and Behavioral Assessment*, *33*, 101–110.

Cochrane, C., Brewerton, T., Wilson, D., and Hodges, E. (1993). Alexithymia in the eating disorders. *International Journal of Eating Disorders*, *14*, 219–222.

Davies, H., Swan, N., Schmidt, U., and Tchanturia, K. (2011). An Experimental Investigation of Verbal Expression of Emotion in Anorexia and Bulimia Nervosa. *European Eating Disorders Review*. doi: 10.1002/erv.1157.

Fairburn C. G., and Cooper, Z. (1993). The Eating Disorder Examination (12th edn). In: C. G. Fairburn and G. T. Wilson (Eds), *Binge Eating: Nature, Assessment* and *Treatment* (pp. 317–360). New York: Guilford Press, 1993.

Fairburn, C., and Beglin, S. (1994). Assessment of eating disorders: Interview or self report questionnaire? *International Journal of Eating Disorders*, *16*, 363–370.

Fairburn, C., and Cooper, Z. (1993). The Eating Disorder Examination (12th edn). In C.G. Fairburn and G.T. Wilson (Eds), *Binge Eating: Nature, Assessment* and *Treatment* (pp. 317–360). New York: Guilford Press.

Fosson, A., Knibbs, J., Bryant-Waugh, R., and Lask, B. (1987). Early Onset Anorexia Nervosa. *Archives of Disease in Childhood, 62,* 114–118.

Frampton, I., Wisting, L., Overas, M., Midtsund, M., and Lask, B. (2011). Reliability and validity of the Norwegian translation of the Child Eating Disorder Examination (ChEDE). *Scandinavian Journal of Psychology, 52,* 196–199.

Franko, D. L., Striegel-Moore, R. H., Barton, B. A., Schumann, B. C., Garner, D. M., Daniels, S. R. et al. (2004) Measuring eating concerns in Black and White adolescent girls. *International Journal of Eating Disorders. 35,* 179–189.

Garner, D. M. (1991). *Eating Disorders Inventory 2: Professional manual.* Odessa, FL: Psychological Assessment Resources.

Garner, D. M. (2004). *Eating Disorders Inventory 3: Professional manual.* Odessa, FL: Psychological Assessment Resources.

Garner, D., Olmsted, M., and Polivy, J. (1983). Development and validation of a multi-dimensional eating disorder inventory for anorexia nervosa and bulimia. *International Journal of Eating Disorders, 2,* 15–34.

Garner, D. M., Olmsted, M. P., Bohr, Y., and Garfinkel, P. E. (1982). The Eating Attitudes Test: Psychometric features and clinical correlates. *Psychological Medicine, 12,* 871–878.

Goodman, R., Ford, T., Richards, H., Gatward, R., and Meltzer, H. (2000). The Development and Well-Being Assessment: Description and initial validation of an integrated assessment of child and adolescent psychopathology. *Journal of Child Psychology and Psychiatry, 41,* 645–655.

Haines, J., Neumark-Sztainer, D., Eisenberg, M. E., and Hannan, P. J. (2006). Weight-teasing and disordered eating behaviors in adolescents: Longitudinal findings from Project EAT (Eating Among Teens). *Pediatrics, 117,* e209–e215.

Hambrook, D., Oldershaw, A., Rimes, K., Schmidt, U., Tchanturia, K., Treasure, J. et al. (2011), Emotional expression, self-silencing, and distress tolerance in anorexia nervosa and chronic fatigue syndrome. *British Journal of Clinical Psychology, 50,* 310–325.

Herpertz-Dahlmann, B. (2009). Adolescent eating disorders: definitions, symptomatology, epidemiology and comorbidity. *Child and Adolescent Psychiatric Clinics of North America, 18* (1), 31–47.

Herzog, D. B., Greenwood, D. N., Dorer, D. J., Flores, A. T., Ekeblad, E. R., Richards, A. et al. (2000), Mortality in eating disorders: A descriptive study. *International Journal of Eating Disorders, 28,* 20–26.

Lena, S. M., Fiocca, A. J., and Leyenaar, J. K. (2004). The Role of Cognitive Deficits in the Development of Eating Disorders. *Neuropsychology Review. 14* (2), 99–113.

Maloney, M. J., McGuire, J. B., and Daniels, S. R. (1988). Reliability testing of a children's version of the Eating Attitude Test. *Journal of the American Academy of Child and Adolescent Psychiatry, 27,* 541–543.

Miller, W. R., and Rollnick, S. (1991). *Motivational Interviewing: Preparing People to Change Addictive Behavior.* New York: Guilford Press.

Moya, T., Fleitlich-Bilyk, B., Goodman, R., Nogueira, F. C., Focchi, P., Nicoletti, M. et al. (2005). The eating disorders section of the Development and Well-Being Assessment (DAWBA): development and validation. *Revista Brasileira de Psiquiatria, 27,* 25–31.

National Institute for Health and Clinical Excellence (NICE, 2004). *Eating disorders: core interventions in the treatment and management of anorexia nervosa, bulimia nervosa and related eating disorders: A national practice guideline.* Clinical guideline 9. National Institute for Health and Clinical Excellence.

Neumark-Sztainer, D., Wall, M. M., Eisenberg, M. E., Story, M., and Hannan, P. J. (2006). Overweight status and weight control behaviors in adolescents: Longitudinal and secular trends from 1999–2004. *Preventive Medicine. 43*, 52–59.

Nicholls, D., Chater, R., and Lask, B. (2000). Children into DSM don't go: a comparison of classification systems of eating disorders for children. *International Journal of Eating Disorders, 28*, 317–324.

Passi, V. A., Bryson, S. W., and Lock, J. (2003). Assessment of eating disorders in adolescents with anorexia nervosa: Self-report questionnaire versus interview. *International Journal of Eating Disorders, 33*, 45–54.

Pretorius, N., Waller, G., Gowers, S. G., and Schmidt, U. (2009). Validity of the EDE-Q for adolescents with bulimia. *Journal of Eating and Weight Disorders, 14*, 243–248.

Rieger, E., and Touyz, S. W. (2006). An investigation of the factorial structure of motivation to recover in anorexia nervosa. *European Eating Disorders Review, 14*, 269–275.

Ruuska, J., Kaltiala-Heino, R., Rantanen, P., and Koivisto A. M. (2005). Psychopathological distress predicts suicidal ideation and self-harm in adolescent eating disorder outpatients. *European Journal of Child and Adolescent Psychiatry, 14* (5), 276–281.

Steiger, H., and Bruce, K. R. (2007). Phenotypes, endophenotypes, and genotypes in bulimia-spectrum eating disorders. *Canadian Journal of Psychiatry, 52*, 220–227.

Steinhausen, H. C. (1999). Eating disorders. In H. C. Steinhausen and F. Verhulst (Eds), *Risks and Outcomes in Developmental Psychopathology* (pp. 210–330). Oxford: Oxford University Press.

Stice, E. (2002). Risk and maintenance factors for eating pathology: A meta-analytic review. *Psychological Bulletin. 128*, 825–848.

Taylor, G. J., Bagby, R. M., and Parker, J. D. (1997). *Disorders of Affect Regulation: Alexithymia in Medical and Psychiatric Illness.* Cambridge: Cambridge University Press.

Thurfjell, B., Edlund, B., Arinell, H., Hagglof, B., and Engstrom, I. (2003). Psychometric Properties of Eating Disorder Inventory for Children (EDI-C) in Swedish girls with and without a known eating disorder. *Eating and Weight Disorders, 8*, 296–303.

Vitousek, K., Watson, S., and Wilson, G. T. (1998). Enhancing motivation for change in treatment-resistant eating disorders. *Clinical Psychology Review, 18*, 391–420.

Ward, A., Ramsay, R., Turnbull, S., Benedettini, M., and Treasure, J. (2000). Attachment patterns in eating disorders: Past in the present. *International Journal of Eating Disorders, 28*, 370–376.

Watkins, B., Frampton, I., Lask, B. and Bryant-Waugh, R. (2005), Reliability and validity of the child version of the eating disorder examination: A preliminary investigation. *International Journal of Eating Disorders, 38*, 183–187.

Wilson, G. T. (1993). Assessment of binge eating. In C. G. Fairburn and G. T. Wilson (Eds), *Binge eating: Nature, assessment, and treatment* (pp. 227–249). New York: Guilford.

Chapter 8

Eating disorders and the brain

Ian Frampton and Mark Rose

Overview

This chapter outlines contemporary knowledge about the relationship between eating disorders and the brain. It considers how inadequate nutrition affects the brain and how brain dysfunction may contribute to the pathogenesis of eating disorders. It reviews evidence from neuroimaging and neuropsychology and demonstrates how such knowledge can be applied in clinical practice.

Introduction

It is obvious that the brain must be involved in the core features of eating disorders – in behavioural features such as restricted food intake, bingeing or purging; in cognitive features such as overvalued ideas about weight and shape; and in emotional features such as extreme anxiety or fear of weight gain. However, recent neuroscience research suggests that neurobiological mechanisms may also play a more fundamental role in the aetiology and maintenance of eating disorders. In this chapter we consider the role of the brain; other components of aetiology are considered in Chapter 5.

A brain perspective suggests that the characteristic restrictive eating behaviours or bingeing and intrusive thoughts about weight and shape make eating disorders appropriate candidates for neuroscience modelling. Such models aim to account for how the surface features of a disorder relate to underlying information abnormalities. For example overvalued ideas about weight and shape and restrictive eating behaviours have obvious information processing parallels (in *flexible thinking* or *behavioural inhibition* for example). Modelling them in neuropsychological terms may help our understanding and treatment.

Developmental issues

A developmental perspective is fundamental to any consideration of child and adolescent eating disorders. From a neuroscience perspective, studying and ultimately helping children with eating disorders requires us to take account of the child's developing brain and cognitive skills, and how these might be affected by, as well as effect, starvation. Developmental neuropsychology is fundamentally not just about applying adult neuropsychology to little people but has a distinct basis in developmental psychology and developmental cognitive neuroscience (Johnson, 2005).

Nevertheless, because of the paucity of neuroscience research focusing solely on the early onset group, it will be necessary to draw cautiously on the adult neuroscience literature, remaining mindful of the potential pitfalls of applying adult findings to children. Thus theoretical models aiming to account for the generation and maintenance of overvalued ideas about weight and shape and of restrictive eating should be able to explain how normal ways of thinking and behaving relate to the development of the disorder. Equally, taking a developmental perspective might challenge the adult-oriented assumption, derived mainly from cognitive models of psychopathology, that restrictive eating is a *consequence* of concerns about weight and shape.

Developmentally, behaviours tend to occur first in infancy and childhood, and are followed by more complex cognitive processes. So we cannot immediately discount the possibility that children might give up eating first, and *then* adopt beliefs about fear of fatness or weight gain as secondary sense-making phenomena to account for their behaviour. Developmental models should be able to account for either possibility. In the case of childhood obsessive compulsive disorder, Rosenberg et al. (1997) have argued that studies of childhood onset are critical in determining whether neurodevelopmental abnormalities contribute to the genesis of the disorder, or are a consequence of it. For this review, we draw therefore on studies of both adult and childhood onset eating disorders, taking into account, where helpful, what we know about related and co-morbid disorders such as obsessive compulsive disorder and depression. The main focus in this chapter is on early onset anorexia nervosa as most studies have focussed on this condition, and far less information is available on the other eating disorders in childhood and adolescence.

Theoretical basis

Models implicating neurobiological deficits should begin from a theory that generates testable hypotheses. One possibility is that the characteristic behavioural, cognitive and emotional features of early onset anorexia nervosa could arise as a *consequence* of underlying neurobiological abnormalities. The second is that eating disorder symptoms, such as maintained low weight, could themselves be the *cause* of disruption in neural mechanisms. Subsequently this might lead to interference with mental functioning, and hence to secondary neuropsychological deficits.

In addition, theory underpinning neurobiological models of early onset anorexia nervosa should be able to account for the developmental and natural history of the disorder. Early onset anorexia nervosa itself may be a final common pathway emerging from a variety of predisposing and precipitating factors, and models should encompass such complexity. Finally, an adequate theoretical neuroscience model of early onset anorexia nervosa must predict the direction of the relationship between the neurobiological abnormalities that have been empirically reported, the consistently-found neuropsychological functioning deficits and the core cognitive, behavioural and emotional features of eating disorders.

Figure 8.1 shows a basic conceptual model, which predicts that neuro-psychological functioning mediates between underlying neurobiological abnormalities (revealed by the neuroimaging studies reviewed below) and the core psychological features of eating disorders, with independent effects on behaviour, cognition and emotion (an attractive proposition for a neuroscientist, since these phenomena have different temporal and spatial realisation in the brain). This model also has the benefit of accounting for the relative lack of effectiveness of the current psychological treatments for early onset anorexia nervosa. Since these interventions are all targeted at the 'CBT triangle' of emotions, cognitions and behaviours, they are unlikely to address an underlying deficit in neurobiological functioning.

In the remainder of this chapter, we explore the brain structures that are important in eating and review how recent advances in neuroimaging technologies have helped us to become much clearer about the neurobiological abnormalities in anorexia nervosa. We go on to review the evidence for neuropsychological deficits in at least a subset of patients with early onset anorexia nervosa, and the implications of these findings for understanding the aetiology and/or maintenance of the condition. Finally, we conclude with a summary overview of the published neurobiological models of eating disorders and point to potential future directions for research and treatment.

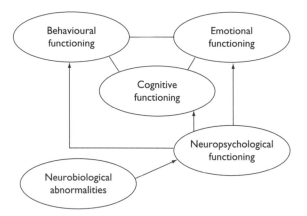

Figure 8.1 Conceptual model for the role of neuropsychological functioning in mediating between underlying neurobiological abnormalities and psychological functioning in eating disorders.

The brain in eating

To answer the question 'What part of the brain is involved in eating?', it would be a lot easier to begin by specifying those parts of the brain that are not implicated. This would be a very short list indeed. Eating meets a primary need to sustain life. As such it falls under the control of a vast number of brain structures, from instinctive behaviours that drive automatic responses, through to the highest-level cognitive representations of how to behave in complex social situations, such as not snaffling all the canapés at the departmental Christmas party.

From the outset it is important to clarify that we are grossly oversimplifying the situation in ascribing specific functions to individual parts of the brain. Recent advances in the neurosciences have helped us to understand how performance of even the simplest task requires the integrated functioning of a vast number of structures *and the connections between them*, all operating as a neural network. These so-called connectionist models of cognitive functioning place at least as much emphasis on the connections between structures as on the structures themselves. This has led to the development of disconnection theories of a range of psychiatric disorders including schizophrenia (Ng et al., 2001) and anorexia nervosa (Nunn et al., 2008, 2011, 2012).

Having presented this caveat, Table 8.1 below summaries the principal neural structures potentially involved in anorexia nervosa, based on Nunn et al. (2008). Many of the structures proposed by Nunn and colleagues are consistent with alternative models developed by Connan et al. (2003) Southgate et al. (2005), Steinglass and Walsh (2006), Marsh et al. (2009), Kaye et al. (2009), Hatch et al. (2010), which are reviewed in more detail below.

Table 8.1 Proposed relationship between eating disorder characteristics, neural structure and function, after Nunn et al. (2008)

Eating disorder characteristic	Key neural structure	Proposed function
Core psychopathology		
Morbid preoccupation with weight and shape	Somatosensory cortex	Body size evaluation
	Amygdala	Threat detection
	Frontal cortex	Information processing
Distorted body image	Somatosensory cortex	Body size evaluation
	Hippocampus	Contextual memory
	Frontal cortex	Information processing
Restricted food intake	Hypothalamus	Appetite and satiety
	Striatum	Reward value of eating
	Frontal cortex	Goal directed behaviour
Associated features		
Low self esteem, shame and disgust	Insular cortex	Disgust
	Limbic system	Linking bodily experience to feelings and thoughts
	Frontal cortex	Information processing

Drive for thinness	Striatum	Reward
	Frontal cortex	Goal directed behaviour
Common co-morbid features		
Obsessions and	Striatum	Compulsive behaviours
compulsions	Frontal cortex	Obsessional thoughts
Anxiety	Amygdala	Threat detection
	Hippocampus	Contextual memory
Depression	Hippocampus	Contextual memory
	Frontal cortex	Information processing
Impaired visuo-spatial skills	Parietal cortex	Visual association processing
	Hippocampus	Long term visual memory
Impaired executive functions	Frontal cortex	Cognitive inhibition
Empathy impairment	Limbic system	Linking bodily experience to feelings and thoughts
	Frontal cortex	Information processing
Anosognosia	Somatosensory cortex	Body evaluation
	Frontal cortex	Information processing
Raised pain threshold	Thalamus	Pain processing
	Insular cortex	Pain processing
	Somatosensory cortex	Body evaluation

Neuroimaging studies in early onset anorexia nervosa

Having identified which brain structures are predicted to be important in eating and its disorders, the obvious next stage is to use neuroimaging technology to look at their *structure* and *function* both in states of malnutrition and after weight restoration treatment. Taking this theory-driven approach has enabled researchers to address, in part, the fundamental question about whether any abnormalities are more likely to be secondary to the disorder, or pre-existing and therefore potentially causal. From a methodological perspective, the low incidence of early onset anorexia nervosa presents a challenge in eating disorder research in proving that abnormalities in brain functioning *cause* the disorder. We would need to design a prospective study to investigate a very large number of children at a young age before eating disorder psychopathology starts to emerge, to look for both structural and functional abnormalities that predict the subsequent emergence of anorexia nervosa or other eating disorder.

Structural scanning

The technology to scan the detailed internal structure of the brain has been available for several years. Computed tomography (CT) scans use digital geometry processing to generate a three-dimensional image of the brain from a large series of two-dimensional X-ray images. More recently, magnetic resonance imaging (MRI), using the safe application of a fast-switching electromagnetic field together with radio frequency (RF) waves, has been used to create very detailed maps of the microstructure of the brain, with higher levels of spatial resolution than CT.

Structural brain imaging studies in anorexia nervosa have consistently identified structural changes such as brain shrinkage (seen as enlargement of the fluid-filled ventricles and reduction of the cortical gyri) that do not fully resolve following treatment both in mixed populations of adults and adolescents (Plazidou et al., 1990), and in early onset anorexia nervosa (Lambe et al., 1997; Katzman et al., 1996, 1997; McCormick et al., 2008; Castro-Fornieles et al., 2009). These studies suggest that the observed structural changes may be due to neuronal damage secondary to malnutrition, with possible regeneration of myelin accounting for the partial reversibility (Artman et al., 1985; Swayze et al., 1996; Giordano et al., 2001).

In summary, grey matter reductions in anorexia nervosa do not seem to return to pre-illness levels in the short term, though it is encouraging that white matter changes do appear to resolve. It does seem to be the case from these studies that absolute lowest weight rather than illness duration is the most important factor in determining structural brain outcome following refeeding, which may have important implications for refeeding regimens. However, longer-term outcome studies will be needed to explore the effect of starvation on brain structure over the lifespan. A detailed review of structural neuroimaging studies in childhood and adult eating disorders can be found in Fuglset and Frampton (2011).

Functional imaging studies

Why image brain function? Clearly, the ability to look into the internal working of the brain has considerable potential for researchers interested in the neuro-science of eating disorders. It is central to current thinking in neuroscience that the brain is built up of complex interconnected systems such that any given brain region may support more than one function, and each function may be supported by multiple brain regions. Furthermore, the effects of a brain lesion can change over time, such that injured regions heal and may once again be able to support cognitive processes, or other regions may take over the function originally served by the damaged area. Particularly in children, such neuroplastic factors mean that damage occurring in early development may not become apparent until later in life. Functional imaging techniques enable us to identify specific brain regions that are operating differently in patients compared with controls; such specific regional differences are theoretically considered more likely to be directly linked to eating disorder psychopathology than to the generalised effects of starvation on the whole brain.

Single photon emission computed tomography (SPECT), is a nuclear medicine imaging technique using gamma rays. This technique, one of the first developed for functional imaging, enables visualization of brain function by measuring the rate of blood flow (or perfusion) in different parts of the brain – regional cerebral blood flow (rCBF). Rastam et al. (2001) reported on the use of SPECT on 21 adult patients seven years after adolescent onset of anorexia nervosa. They found reduced blood flow in the temporal or associated regions in 14 patients (66%) with no correlation between reduction in blood flow and current BMI, lowest ever BMI, any residual eating disorder psychopathology, or IQ, suggesting that this may be an underlying 'trait' marker of the disorder rather than a result of the acute effects of starvation.

Very few neuroimaging studies using SPECT have been conducted on children with early onset anorexia nervosa, and none with bulimia nervosa, partly because of the relative rarity of these disorders in this age group, and partly because of the ethical issues raised by using this technique with children. Gordon et al. (1997) demonstrated hypoperfusion in at least one brain region, primarily temporal, in 13 of 15 patients with early onset anorexia nervosa. These findings were replicated by the same group in a new sample in which 11 of 15 patients with anorexia nervosa showed similar degrees of hypoperfusion, again primarily in the temporal region (Chowdhury et al., 2003). This abnormality appears not to reverse with long-term weight restoration four years after successful treatment (Frampton et al., 2011).

As well as producing high-resolution images of brain *structure*, MRI technology also enables us to explore how different parts of the brain *function* together. As if structural MRI were not computationally complex enough, even more sophisticated functioning imaging techniques have been developed to overlay the resulting images with a representation of the amount of functional activity occurring at each brain location at a given point in time. These techniques rely on the rapid reduction in blood oxygenation levels in areas of the brain that are functionally active. As blood passing through the network of arteries and capillaries in the brain comes into contact with oxygen-demanding active tissue, it gives up its oxygen contained in oxyhaemoglobin to be metabolised. Detection of these changes in blood oxygen levels is made possible by modelling the characteristic changes in the time series of MR images consistent with the BOLD (blood oxygen level detection) effect in a series of images acquired while the research participant completes a functional task (such as watching some still or moving images, responding to questions or playing a computer game) in the scanner.

Functional imaging studies have shown that patients with anorexia nervosa process pictures of food differently from controls, both when hungry and satiated (Santel et al., 2006), and that this may be linked to reduced reward value of food and to experiencing food images as disgusting (Uher et al., 2004) and threatening (Ellison et al., 1998). Taste stimuli are also processed differently by current and former patients (Wagner et al., 2008), who also have a different response to their own body image than to images of others (Sachdev et al., 2008). Studies of risk and reward processing in anorexia nervosa and bulimia nervosa (Kaye et al., 2005) suggest that both disorders are characterised by difficulties in evaluating the emotional significance of a stimulus.

The studies conducted over the last 10 years have reliably linked these functional findings to specific brain structures, including the attentional, emotional, visual spatial, reward and response motivation systems. As neuroscience progresses, we should be able to refine our understanding of the relationship between these structural systems and their functional implications in eating disorders. A detailed review of functional neuroimaging studies in childhood and adult eating disorders can be found in Fuglset and Frampton (2011).

Neurotransmitter imaging

As well as exploring brain structure and functioning using CT and MRI, neuroimaging technologies have also been developed to look at neurotransmitter activity in anorexia nervosa using Positron Emission Tomography (PET), a technique in which radioactive *ligands* that can be detected by a scanner, are injected into the bloodstream. PET imaging techniques have been extremely helpful in our understanding of the role of neurotransmitters in eating disorders, both in the low weight state during acute illness and as long term trait markers, following weight recovery.

Studies using PET have established that altered serotonin and dopamine functioning are central to anorexia nervosa and bulimia nervosa. Individuals who are vulnerable to developing an eating disorder appear to have increased synaptic serotonin concentration and an imbalance in postsynaptic serotonin receptor activity, which together might contribute to increased satiety and an anxious, harm-avoidant temperament (Kaye et al., 2009). This predisposing vulnerability could be triggered by the challenges of adolescence to precipitate an eating disorder. An altered reward response to food and dieting modulated by the dopamine system could then perpetuate the eating disorder (Frank et al., 2005). Since eating disorders have a complex aetiology, in which genetic, biological, psychological and sociocultural factors seem to contribute, PET scanning has uniquely contributed to our understanding of the neurochemistry (see Kaye et al., 2011 for an overview of neurotransmitter imaging in eating disorders).

Neuropsychological factors

Neuropsychological testing was initially developed to assess the behavioural and cognitive effect of brain lesions or trauma, but in recent years it has been used extensively in psychiatric populations to inform diagnosis and to aid treatment planning. Neuropsychological impairments have been consistently documented in many disorders such as schizophrenia, obsessive-compulsive disorder and bipolar disorder.

Comprehensive reviews of neuropsychological functioning in eating disorders have been conducted by Duchesne et al. (2004), and Lena et al. (2004). Four domain-specific reviews have been published on central coherence (Lopez et al., 2008a), intelligence (Lopez et al., 2010) and set-shifting (Tchanturia et al., 2005 and Roberts et al., 2007). Rather than list findings from the literature here, we present the latest research developments since 2004, which cover three main areas with consistent findings: central coherence, executive functioning, and visuospatial processing and memory.

I. Central coherence

Central coherence is the ability to achieve a balance between efficiency and attention to detail. Typically, an individual processes incoming information on a gestalt level which enables them to see the 'bigger picture' or general gist. This sort of processing style is known as strong, or high central coherence. On the other hand, weak central coherence refers to a processing bias towards featural or local information, usually at the expense of the overall gestalt (Happe and Frith, 2006). It is becoming increasingly clear that central coherence weaknesses are common in anorexia nervosa, whether that is because of a global processing weakness or a bias toward local processing strength.

Lena et al. (2004) noted that several studies reported tendencies that would now be described as weak central coherence, including a focus on detail at the expense of the bigger picture. Lopez et al. (2008a) reviewed central coherence and concluded from their meta-analysis that there were clear global processing weaknesses across the eating disorder spectrum, but in terms of superiority local processing, the evidence was weaker.

Four studies since 2004 show support for both aspects. Tokley and Kemps' investigation (2007) into preoccupation with detail suggests that patients with anorexia nervosa were both significantly weaker on abstract thinking in the Object Assembly Test and more field independent on the Embedded Figures Test. Lopez et al. (2009) investigated weight-recovered individuals with a history of anorexia nervosa and found comparatively mixed results that broadly supported the central coherence theory. Of the tests measuring local processing benefit, they found significant differences on the Embedded Figures Test but not on Block Design, and on measures of global processing deficit, they found significant differences on Rey Recall and Sentence Completion Tasks, but not on the Homograph Reading Task. Tenconi et al. (2010) studied a group of 153 out-patients with anorexia nervosa and found significant impairment compared to healthy controls on a variety of central coherence measures. However some of the results changed substantially when medication and anxiety were controlled. They also found significant weaknesses in a group of healthy sisters of patients with anorexia nervosa on a number of central coherence measures. Harrison et al. (2011) studied current and recovered patients to see if local processing findings were replicable and additionally to explore global integration using the Fragmented Pictures Task. Findings suggest that both groups had enhanced performance on the detail processing task. Only the acute phase of anorexia nervosa was associated with difficulties in global integration.

Support for weak central coherence in anorexia nervosa comes from two studies since 2004. Lopez et al. (2008b) found significant results on the Rey Copy and Embedded Figures Test which support the idea that weak central coherence may underlie anorexia nervosa. Southgate et al. (2008) found a positive bias in patients with anorexia nervosa towards local detail processing on the Matching Familiar Figures Test. Broadly speaking, recent research has supported both the global-deficit and local-benefit aspects of the central coherence theory, the implication being that an imbalance between global and detail functioning may be a factor that perpetuates the psychopathology of anorexia nervosa.

2. Executive functioning

Executive functioning skills encompass a broad range of independent cognitive abilities including planning, organising, cognitive flexibility, inhibition, and self-monitoring (Stuss, et al., 1994). These are the skills necessary for purposeful, goal directed human activity (Shallice, 1988) including the meaningful organisation of incoming stimuli, the planning and development of strategies for the attainment of future goals, flexible problem solving, and the utilization of feedback for the appropriate assessment and/or modification of behaviour.

Evidence from ethology suggests that most species, in an uncertain world when it is not clear where the next meal might be coming from, will be prompted by the presence of food to eat it, Patients with anorexia nervosa have an enhanced ability to inhibit such behaviours. On the other hand, there is also evidence that individuals with anorexia nervosa have *impaired* cognitive inhibition, in the sense that they are prone to overvalued ideas of the importance of body weight and shape to self-concept (Shafran and Somers, 1998).

A number of studies have found set-shifting deficits (the tendency to adopt concrete and rigid approaches to problems) in anorexia nervosa. Two reviews have been carried out on set-shifting. Tchanturia et al. (2005) found that set-shifting difficulties were evident in individuals with acute anorexia nervosa, in long-term recovered patients, as well as in the healthy sisters of those with anorexia nervosa, concluding that set-shifting difficulties were therefore not purely a function of the acute illness state but may also be part of an endophenotype. A review by Roberts et al. (2007) found a consistent deficit for all states of illness and for most of the measures used. They also noted that, from limited data, it appeared that the deficit remained after weight restoration in anorexia nervosa, supporting the notion that set-shifting difficulties could be an endophenotype.

3. Visuo-spatial processing and visual memory

Visuo-spatial processing relates to perception of location, size and organisation of stimuli in the visual field. Visuo-spatial skills are required to perceive and manipulate objects in two and three dimensions (Rauch and Savage, 1997). The idea that visuo-spatial deficits might contribute to anorexia nervosa is plausible, given the core feature of distorted body image.

The findings in visuo-spatial processing have been more consistent than in other domains. Lena et al. (2004) reported that patients with anorexia nervosa consistently displayed significant weaknesses compared to controls, where the studies used appropriately sized samples. They also reported a general consensus that these deficits remained after refeeding and weight gain. Duchesne et al. (2004) noted that, while the majority of studies found deficits in visuo-spatial and perceptive functions, the correlation between these deficits and body-image disturbance required further investigation.

Since 2004, four studies have addressed this area. Lask et al. (2005) investigated brain blood flow in early-onset anorexia nervosa and compared this to neuropsychological test results. Patients with anorexia nervosa showed a significant correlation between unilateral hypoperfusion in the temporal lobe and deficits in visuo-spatial ability. Key et al. (2006) found below average results for their anorexia nervosa group compared to normative data on the Rey Complex Figure Task. Kemps et al. (2006) found that their anorexia nervosa group were significantly poorer at the single memory task compared to both dieting and non-dieting controls. Mikos et al. (2008) found no significant difference between admission and follow-up scores in patients with anorexia nervosa.

Six studies have investigated visuo-spatial memory. Both Lask et al. (2005) and Key et al. (2006) found consistent deficits in memory functions associated with temporal lobe hypoperfusion. Fowler et al. (2006), using the CANTAB battery found significant differences in Spatial Recognition Memory. Connan et al. (2006), using the Doors and People Test, found no significant difference between controls and patients, despite significant reduction in hippocampal volume in the anorexia nervosa group. However, depression was not controlled for which has been implicated in reduced hippocampal volume. Mikos et al. (2008), using tests of immediate and delayed memory, found no significant increase between admission and follow-up, suggesting memory was not a nutrition-dependent factor. However no control data were provided. Sherman et al. (2006) used the Rey Copy and Recall found that the anorexia nervosa group compared to healthy controls were significantly worse at immediate and delayed recall.

Assessment of neuropsychological functioning

The neuropsychological literature of anorexia nervosa still suffers from a number of flaws. A significant part of the problem lies in the methodological inconsistencies between research studies. Different tests are used to investigate the same domains, with variance between the sensitivity and domain-specificity of the tests. The samples studied are also diverse, with subtype, chronicity and duration of illness often undifferentiated. Further, not all studies included control groups, thus it is uncertain if the results were anorexia nervosa -specific, eating-disorder specific or state-specific as a result of, for example, malnutrition. Confounders such as medication use and co-morbidity are another crucial issue.

The Ravello Profile (Rose et al., 2011; Stedal et al., 2012) has been developed to address these difficulties and to support large-scale international collaborative research between clinicians and researchers by using the same standardised neuropsychological assessment battery. Advantages of this approach include exploration of how psychological features such as eating disorder psychopathology, depression, anxiety and obsessive-compulsive features correlate with neuropsychological profiles. Longitudinal studies exploring neuropsychological functioning across time will help clarify how underlying neurobiological risk factors might render some individuals vulnerable to develop an eating disorder in the context of specific social factors. From a classification perspective, we know that the current diagnostic systems lack validity in identifying specific subtypes within the eating disorders (Milos, et al., 2005). The establishment of neuro-psychologically-based subgroups might help to develop our treatment as well as informing nosological approaches.

The research to date suggests that neuropsychological deficits certainly *could* precede the onset of anorexia nervosa in some individuals, based on the fact that although many neuropsychological abilities appear to improve with refeeding some deficits – namely visuospatial/sensory and set-shifting and inhibitory abilities – do not (Steinglass and Glasofer, 2011). It is worth considering that other groups that have experienced extreme weight loss, hypoglycaemia and/or inadequate nutritional uptake, such as extreme dieters, prisoners of war and people with diabetes, frequently do recover function once they are no longer malnourished. Additionally, these groups show different patterns of deficits to those found in anorexia nervosa. Although prisoners of war, extreme dieters and those with diabetes show similar impairments in executive functioning, it seems that the consistent deficit in the visuospatial domain is unique to people who have experienced starvation due to anorexia nervosa. Impaired executive functioning and visuospatial skills has also been demonstrated in a variety of pervasive developmental disorders, as well as obsessive compulsive disorder and attention deficit/ hyperactivity disorders, in children. Such a similar pattern of impairments between early onset anorexia nervosa and well-defined developmental disorders suggests that early onset anorexia nervosa may too follow some form of neurodevelopmental course, at least in a subset of cases.

A second possibility is that neuropsychological deficits do not precede the illness and are simply the end result of having experienced malnutrition at a specific point in development. Studies into malnutrition were conducted with adult participants; for early onset anorexia nervosa, it may be that experiencing malnutrition during a critical period of hormonal and neurological development, perhaps alongside body shape changes, might lead to these observed impairments.

There is mounting evidence that the frontal lobes of the brain go through significant stages of synaptic reorganisation and proliferation during childhood, with a final prominent cycle occurring during adolescence. During these peak periods of synaptic proliferation some cognitive abilities are temporarily impaired. For example, longitudinal studies have shown that 13-year-olds are worse at detecting facial emotion in other people than they were a year previously (Turkstra et al., 2008). A similar study, investigating unfamiliar face recognition in late childhood and adolescence, found that these skills seemed to be impaired between the ages of 11 and 14 years of age, after which improvement occurs.

Thus, as the frontal areas continue developing into adolescence, young people who already have a predisposing bias towards enhanced behavioural inhibition, may now be at risk of developing an opposite bias, i.e. reduced cognitive inhibition, and so find it difficult to inhibit socially imposed beliefs regarding weight and shape. If this were the case, the individual would be 'flooded' with conscious negative ideas relating to the self and the body. Those with enhanced behavioural inhibition might attempt to 'neutralise' these thoughts via altering their eating behaviours, which if successful could lead to a self-maintaining cycle of thinking and behaviour, as seen in anorexia nervosa.

If this pattern of impaired cognitive and enhanced behavioural inhibition exists during the final cycle of synaptic reorganisation and proliferation then it is conceivable that these biases might become a stable part of that person's neuropsychological functioning into adulthood. Equally, this model could account for the fact that adolescence is a risk period for a range of neurodevelopmental disorders that implicate executive dysfunction, including obsessive compulsive disorder and early psychosis.

There is clearly more work needed to help us understand the role of adolescence in neuropsychological development (and vice versa), both within clinical and normally developing populations. Future work including prospective studies are needed to clarify whether an individual, who goes on to develop anorexia nervosa, is neuropsychologically predisposed from early life to developing specific cognitive and behavioural biases, or as suggested above these become 'hard-wired' if encountered during later critical stages of brain development in adolescence when networks supporting advanced cognitive functions are becoming established.

Neuroscience Models

Attempts to explore the role of the brain has led several research groups to develop and publish models to help explain how they understand the role of neural factors in the development and maintenance of eating disorders. Seven neuroscience-based conceptual models that endeavour to explain the pathogenesis and maintenance of eating disorders have been selected. These are presented in date order of publication and cover a wide range of perspectives from genes through to thoughts and behaviours.

Connan et al.'s (2003) model focuses on pre- and peri-natal factors and childhood stages of development. The authors propose there is an interaction between genes, early life experience, and biopsychosocial environment at puberty, which may make an individual susceptible to developing anorexia nervosa via alteration of appetite and emotional regulation systems. At the heart of this model is the proposal of poor regulation of the stress response due to modification of the hypothalamic-pituitary-adrenal (HPA) axis. Southgate et al. (2005) have developed this model to incorporate factors that may be involved in the development and maintenance of eating disorders such as disruption in brain development and immaturity in emotional and complex inhibitory and reflective processing.

Steinglass and Walsh (2006) have suggested how knowledge about the cognitive and neurobiological basis of habitual behaviours in obsessive compulsive disorder may contribute to our understanding of anorexia nervosa. Given the similarity of many of the clinical features of obsessive compulsive disorder and anorexia nervosa (repetitive and stereotyped behaviours and preoccupations with thoughts and ideas), the high degree of co-morbidity between these two disorders, case reports of anorexia nervosa and obsessive compulsive disorder developing after an infection (autoimmune anorexia nervosa), and evidence of serotonin dysfunction in both anorexia nervosa and obsessive compulsive disorder, they suggest it is plausible that both of these conditions share an similar neurobiological foundation. Their model distinguishes between implicit learning and stimulus-response learning. Implicit learning refers to the learning processes that occur outside of consciousness which are distinct from conscious (or declarative) learning. Implicit learning dysfunction in obsessive compulsive disorder manifests itself as thoughts and behaviours that should be implicitly processed but intrude into consciousness as obsessions and compulsions. This model of implicit learning failure can also be applied to anorexia nervosa and may contribute to the explicit, routine and repetitive behaviours frequently associated with the disorder and reinforced by set-shifting difficulties which may make it difficult for a patient to change or stop established routines.

Nunn et al. (2008; 2011) propose that dysfunction with a single brain region can account for the aetiology and maintenance of anorexia nervosa. Research has suggested that abnormal functioning exists in several cortical structures in anorexia nervosa: frontal, somatosensory and parietal cortices; and sub-cortical structures: amygdala, hippocampus, hypothalamus and the striatum. Rather than there being damage to each of these, Nunn and colleagues argue it is more likely that there is damage or dysfunction within the part of the brain that connects between these structures: the insular cortex or insula. This means that the insula is unable to perform its function of integrating information from cognitive, affective and physiological systems. They suggest that the clinical phenomena of anorexia nervosa may be explained by the rate limiting dysfunction in the insula which reduces its capacity to integrate information from cognitive, affective and physiological systems. This underlying risk factor may interact with risk factors such as socio-cultural pressures, gender, life events including puberty and psychosocial stressors, to precipitate the illness during adolescence.

Marsh et al. (2009) have noted that self-regulation encompasses cognitive and inhibitory control, the ability to organize thoughts, emotions and behaviour to attain goals. In eating disorders, bulimia nervosa is characterised by binge episodes and impulsive acts whilst the core feature of anorexia nervosa is extreme dietary restriction and intrusive thoughts about weight and shape. Evidence has shown that frontal-striatal circuits are used in these self-regulatory processes. Anatomical and function disturbance in these circuits may contribute to a failure of inhibitory control, leading to the intrusive expression of various thoughts about weight or shape. These thoughts elicit compensatory or maladaptive behaviours to reduce the anxiety associated with the original intrusive thoughts. This eventually manifests itself in a variety of ways such as compulsions, rigid and ritualistic behaviour and purging.

Kaye et al. (2009) have noted that despite anorexia nervosa being characterised as an eating disorder, it still remains to be found if it is a primary disturbance of the appetitive pathways or whether it is secondary to psychological phenomena such as anxiety. The authors suggest that the neural correlates of these cognitive and affective processes may provide clues to the pathophysiology of anorexia nervosa. Their model focuses on four main areas:

1   *Premorbid traits*, including temperament and personality traits such as perfectionism and harm avoidance that may have a genetic basis;
2   *Neurobiology* of the limbic brain circuit (which determines the emotional significance of stimuli) and the cognitive circuit (which is involved in selective attention, planning and regulation of affective states);
3   *Neurotransmitter* function of the serotonin (5-HT) and dopamine (DA) systems, which may confer additional risk and sustain symptoms of anorexia nervosa;
4   *Neurocircuitry of Appetite*, which is governed by a complex interaction of psychobiological factors including the reward properties of food, homeostatic needs and flexible approaches to eating.

Hatch et al. (2010) have called attention to the non-conscious aspects of brain functioning including responses to emotional cues. Their model incorporates multiple scales of functioning – from gene to brain structure, function and finally behaviour. Concepts normally considered as dichotomous (cognition/emotion; conscious/non-conscious; and cortical/sub-cortical) have been re-arranged along a dynamic time continuum consisting of three phases: During the **Emotion Phase** (less than 200 milliseconds after a new stimulus), adaptive action responses are automatically made that are outside of consciousness. The **Thinking**

and Feeling Phase (more than 200 ms after a new stimulus) is distinguished by subjective experiences and conscious awareness. In this phase cognitive deficits that predispose an individual to a rigid and detail-bound thinking style may combine with reduced reward signals from food cues to trigger the avoidance of food. Finally the **Self-regulation Phase** (seconds and longer) is characterized by the management of thinking and feeling to maximise reward and minimise danger.

Treatment Implications

Taking a neuroscience perspective may encourage the development of novel treatment strategies in anorexia nervosa. The theoretical and functional models presented above, if proven, may point to novel pharmacological treatment to modulate the activity of serotonin, dopamine and noradrenergic neurotransmitter systems.

From a neuropsychological intervention perspective, the elucidation of set shifting and inhibition deficits in anorexia nervosa has led to the development of novel *cognitive remediation* therapy. This approach, grounded in neuropsychological theory, adapted from work with adults with acquired brain injury and initially applied in the context of early psychosis (Wykes, 1998) has been extended by Tchanturia et al. (2006) to apply to eating disorders. In a series of structured sessions, patients are invited to work on cognitive tasks to improve their ability to shift cognitive perspective (for example, by looking at visual illusions that contain two embedded images and to shift between them). Through repeated practice and reflection on the process, patients are encouraged to adopt more flexible thinking styles in their everyday life.

Results from early trials of this intervention have been promising (Davies and Tchanturia, 2005), with participants reporting a high degree of satisfaction and enjoyment with the tasks. In particular, taking the focus away from endless discussion over food and eating creates the possibility for making therapeutic progress in other areas. Patients report that they are making connections between the tasks and their everyday experiences, and the results of controlled trials in schizophrenia are positive (Wykes, 1998). Cognitive remediation approaches have recently been developed for young people with anorexia nervosa (see Wood, et al., 2011, Lindvall and Lask, 2011 and Chapter 16).

As well as guiding cognitive remediation therapy, neuropsychological assessment can also help identify young people who fit the classic anorexia nervosa profile of being academic overachievers. Research has shown that young people with anorexia nervosa typically have worked diligently in school to achieve good grades and make impressive academic progress, beyond the level predicted by their cognitive ability. Bruch (1973) originally described a tendency for concrete thinking with a perfectionist and compulsive attitude towards scholastic achievement. Subsequent studies have confirmed average-range IQ using global measures of intellectual functioning, contrasted with over-achievement in attainment measures particularly in reading and spelling (Lopez et al., 2010). It is therefore helpful to identify those children presenting with eating disorders who have been striving to produce good grades beyond their predicted ability level, and to encourage a more realistic level of expectation from teachers, parents and young people themselves.

Turning to psychotherapeutic treatments, neuroscience may be valuable in helping to account for why to date no effective first line approach for anorexia nervosa has been identified. If, as many of the neuroscience models predict, the underlying basis for the disorder is neurobiological (for example, the rate-limiting disconnection of neural networks proposed in the insula hypothesis (Nunn et al., 2008, 2011), then intervening at a cognitive-behavioural level is unlikely to be effective. Recently developed models such as that of Hatch et al. (2010) also predict that therapies targeted at conscious thought processes (cognitive therapy and psychotherapy) are less likely to be effective if the fundamental underlying problem lies in 'lower level' pre-linguistic emotion processing networks.

On the other hand, neuroscience models of eating disorders do predict alternative psychotherapeutic treatments that should be effective. For example, Hatch and colleagues (2010) suggest that novel 'emotion processing' psychological treatments will need to be developed. The emphasis on emotion processing deficits highlighted in the models of Connan (2003) and Southgate (2005) implies that psychological approaches to improving emotion recognition and expression may be appropriate for use with this client group. Such 'mindfulness' approaches to enhancing and regulating subjective emotional experience have been developed in a range of other psychiatric disorders, and may be applicable to anorexia nervosa. Mindfulness-based treatments that specifically address awareness of the emotional state of the body are predicted to be effective by the insula hypothesis (Nunn et al., 2008, 2011). This is a promising suggestion since it has been shown that Buddhist meditators have significantly more grey matter than expected in their right insula, an area involved in interoceptive awareness (Lazar et al., 2005).

If advances in neuroscience identify specific neural circuits that are impaired in eating disorders, it should be possible to develop targeted treatments designed to improve their functioning. For example Caria et al. (2007) recently demonstrated that it is possible to learn to control local brain activity with operant training by using real time fMRI-based neurofeedback. In their study, a group of healthy participants were provided with continuously updated information about the level of activation of their right anterior insula cortex by visual feedback while in the scanner. All participants were able to successfully regulate neural activation in this region within three sessions of four minutes each. This extraordinary study is the first to investigate the volitional control of emotionally relevant brain region by using rtfMRI training and confirms that self-regulation of local brain activity with rtfMRI is possible, with potentially profound treatment implications.

Finally, neuroscience approaches to the understanding and treatment of eating disorders could profoundly affect how patients and their families understand and manage their illness. Although psychosocial factors such as the Western ideal for thinness remain important precipitating factors in triggering an eating disorder, neuroscience may help us to understand why some girls and young women are more vulnerable than others to the influence of these universal pressures. Understanding more about the potential neurobiological basis for eating disorders may help to reduce stigma and guilt for sufferers and their families, despite the risk of the 'neuro-essentialist' reduction of complex behaviours to simplistic neurobiology (see Singh and Wengaard, 2011 for an overview of these ethical issues).

Conclusion

Neuropsychological models may be very helpful in developing our understanding of anorexia nervosa. Restricted behaviours and disinhibited thoughts have obvious information processing parallels, and a strong neuropsychological theory would posit core processing deficits (in perseveration or cognitive inhibition, for example), which can account for the psychopathology of eating disorders. Weaker models might make comparisons between neuropsychological deficits and the phenomenology of anorexia nervosa, without suggesting that they are somehow causal.

The development of neuropsychological models of anorexia nervosa has tended to follow trends in neuropsychology research, beginning with a focus on visual-spatial deficits and more recently encompassing executive dysfunction and central coherence. Early experimental studies were flawed by design weaknesses including use of non-clinical control groups, failure to control for multiple comparisons, poor selection of clinical cases and lack of underlying theory guiding experimentation. More recent studies have addressed some of these weaknesses and links with other areas of neuroscience research including struc-tural and functional neuroimaging has strengthened theory and experimental design.

One of the key areas where neuropsychological models may become increas-ingly helpful is in the delineation of subgroups within early onset anorexia nervosa. Neuropsychology may be helpful in defining subgroups of patients, based on common neuropsychological profiles, who will be predicted to have more complex and enduring problems. Functional neuroimaging tasks that include measures of specific neuropsychological functions may be particularly useful for detecting characteristics that distinguish early onset anorexia nervosa subgroups (Lask et al., 2005). From a developmental neuropsychology perspective, early identification and intervention during childhood and adolescence, when these cognitive skills would normally be maturing, may provide new opportunities to prevent young people with early onset anorexia nervosa facing a chronic and debilitating disorder.

Summary

- Restricting food intake or binge-purging has a significant effect on brain structure and function.
- Novel neuroimaging techniques allow us to understand more about the acute and long-term effects of eating disorders on the brain.
- Recent neuroscience theories also propose a potential role for brain factors in making some people more vulnerable than others to developing an eating disorder.
- These insights could have profound implications for the way we understand and treat eating disorders.

References

Artmann, H., Grau, H., Adelmann, M., and Schleiffer, R. (1985). Reversible and non-reversible enlargement of cerebrospinal fluid spaces in anorexia nervosa. *Neuroradiology*, *27* (4), 304–312.

Bruch, H. (1973). *Eating Disorders: Obesity, Anorexia and the Person Within*. New York: Basic Books.

Caria, A., Veit, R., Sitaram, R., Lotze, M., Weiskopf, N., Grodd, W., et al. (2007). Regulation of anterior insular cortex activity using real-time fMRI. *Neuroimage*, *35* (3), 1238–1246.

Castro-Fornieles, J., Bargalló, N., Lázaro, L., Andrés, S., Falcon, C., Plana, M., et al. (2009). A cross-sectional and follow-up voxel-based morphometric MRI study in adolescent anorexia nervosa. *Journal of Psychiatric Research*, *43* (3), 331–340.

Chowdhury, U., Gordon, I., Lask, B., Watkins, B., Watt, H., and Christie, D. (2003). Early-onset anorexia nervosa: is there evidence of limbic system imbalance? *International Journal of Eating Disorders*, *33* (4), 388–396.

Connan, F., Campbell, I. C., Katzman, D., Lightman, S. L., and Treasure, J. (2003). A neurodevelopmental model for anorexia nervosa. *Physiology and Behaviour*, *79*, 13–24.

Connan, F., Murphy, F., Connor, S., Rich, P., Murphy, T., Bara-Carill, N., et al. (2006). Hippocampal volume and cognitive function in anorexia nervosa. *Psychiatry Research: Neuroimaging*, *146*, 117–125.

Davies, H., and Tchanturia, K. (2005). Cognitive remediation therapy as an intervention for acute anorexia nervosa. *European Eating Disorders Review*, *13*, 311–316.

Duchesne, M., Mattos, P., Fontenelle, L., Veiga, H., Rizo, L., and Appolinario, J. (2004). Neuropsychology of eating disorders: A systematic review of the literature. *Revista Brasileira de Psiquiatria*, *26* (2), 107–117.

Ellison, Z., Foong, J., Howard, R., Bullmore, E., Williams, S., and Treasure, J. (1998). Functional anatomy of calorie fear in anorexia nervosa. *The Lancet*, *352* (9135), 1192.

Fowler, L., Blackwell, A., Jaffa, A., Palmer, R., Robbins, T. W., Sahakian, B. J., et al. (2006). Profile of neurocognitive impairments associated with female in-patients with AN. *Psychological Medicine*, *36*, 517–527.

Frampton, I., Watkins, B., Gordon, I., and Lask, B. (2011). Do abnormalities in regional cerebral blood flow in anorexia nervosa resolve after weight restoration? *European Eating Disorders Review, 19,* 55–58.

Frank, G., Bailer, U., Henry, S., Drevets, W., Meltzer, C., Price, J., et al. (2005). Increased Dopamine D2/D3 Receptor Binding After Recovery from Anorexia Nervosa Measured by Positron Emission Tomography and [11C]Raclopride. *Biological Psychiatry, 58* (11), 908–912.

Fuglset, T., and Frampton, I. (2011). Neuroimaging. In B. Lask and I. Frampton (Eds), *Eating Disorders and the Brain.* Chichester: Wiley.

Giordano, G., Renzetti, P., Parodi, R., Foppiani, L., Zandrino, F., Giordano, G., et al. (2001). Volume measurement with magnetic resonance imaging of hippocampus-amygdala formation in patients with anorexia nervosa. *Journal of Endocrinological Investigation, 24* (7), 510–514.

Gordon, I., Lask, B., Bryant-Waugh, R., Christie, D., and Timimi, S. (1997). Childhood-onset anorexia nervosa: towards identifying a biological substrate. *International Journal of Eating Disorders, 22* (2), 159–165.

Happe, F., and Frith, U. (2006). The weak coherence account: Detail-focused cognitive style in autism spectrum disorders. *Journal of Autism and Developmental Disorders, 36,* 5–25.

Harrison, A., Tchanturia, K., and Treasure, J. (2011). Measuring state trait properties of detail processing and global integration ability in eating disorders. *World Journal of Biological Psychiatry, 12* (6), 462–472.

Hatch, A., Madden, S., Kohn, M., Clarke, S., Touyz, S., and Williams, L. M. (2010). Anorexia Nervosa: towards an integrative neuroscience model. *European Eating Disorders Review, 18* (3), 165–179.

Johnson, M. (2005). *Developmental Cognitive Neuroscience* (2nd ed.). Oxford: Oxford University Press.

Katzman, D., Lambe, E., Mikulis, D., Ridgley, J., Goldbloom, D., and Zipursky, R. (1996). Cerebral gray matter and white matter volume deficits in adolescent girls with anorexia nervosa. *Journal of Pediatrics, 129* (6), 794–803.

Katzman, D., Zipursky, R., Lambe, E., and Mikulis, D. (1997). A longitudinal magnetic resonance imaging study of brain changes in adolescents with anorexia nervosa. *Archives of Pediatrics and Adolescent Medicine, 151* (8), 793–797.

Kaye, W., Frank, G., Bailer, U., Henry, S., Meltzer, C., Price, J., et al. (2005). Serotonin alterations in anorexia and bulimia nervosa: New insights from imaging studies. *Physiology and Behavior, 85,* 73–81.

Kaye, W. H., Fudge, J. L., and Paulus, M. (2009). New insights into symptoms and neurocircuit function of anorexia nervosa. *Nature Reviews: Neuroscience, 10,* 573–584.

Kaye, W., Wagner, A., Fudge, J., and Paulus, M. (2011). Neurocircuity of eating disorders. *Current Topics in Behavioural Neurosciences, 6,* 37–57.

Kemps, E., Tiggemann, M., Wade, T., Ben-Tovim, D., and Breyer, R. (2006). Selective working memory deficits in AN. *European Eating Disorders Review, 14,* 97–103.

Key, A., O'Brian, A., Gordon, I., Christie, D., and Lask, B. (2006). Assessment of neurobiology in adults with AN. *European Eating Disorders Review, 14,* 308–314.

Lambe, E., Katzman, D., Mikulis, D., Kennedy, S., and Zipursky, R. (1997). Cerebral gray matter volume deficits after weight recovery from anorexia nervosa. *Archives of General Psychiatry, 54* (6), 537–542.

Lask, B., Gordon, I., Christie, D., Frampton, I., Chowdhury, U., and Watkins, B. (2005). Functional neuroimaging in early-onset Anorexia Nervosa. *International Journal of Eating Disorders, 37*, 49–51.

Lazar, S., Kerr, C., Wasserman, R., Gray, J., Greve, D., Treadway, M., et al. (2005). Meditation experience is associated with increased cortical thickness. *Neuroreport, 16* (17), 1893–1897.

Lena, S. M., Fiocco, A. M., and Leyenaar, J. K. (2004). The role of cognitive deficits in the development of eating disorders. *Neuropsychological Review, 14* (2), 99–113.

Lindvall, C., and Lask, B. (2011). Implications for treatment. In B. Lask and I. Frampton (Eds), *Eating Disorders and the Brain*. Chichester: Wiley.

Lopez, C., Stahl, D., and Tchanturia, K. (2010). Estimated intelligence quotient in anorexia nervosa: a systematic review and meta-analysis of the literature. *Annals of General Psychiatry, 9*, 40.

Lopez, C., Tchanturia, K., Stahl, D., and Treasure, J. (2008a). Central coherence in eating disorders: a systematic review. *Psychological Medicine, 38* (10), 1393–1404.

Lopez, C., Tchanturia, K., Stahl, D., Booth, R., Holliday, J., and Treasure, J. (2008b). An examination of the concept of central coherence in women with AN. *International Journal of Eating Disorders, 41* (2), 143–152.

Lopez, C., Tchanturia, K., Stahl, D., and Treasure, J. (2009). Weak central coherence in eating disorders: a step towards looking for an endophenotype of eating disorders. *Journal of Clinical and Experimental Neuropsychology, 31* (1), 117–125.

Marsh, R., Maia, T. V., and Peterson, B. S. (2009). Functional Disturbances Within Frontostriatal Circuits Across Multiple Childhood Psychopathologies. *American Journal of Psychiatry, 166*, 664–674.

McCormick, L., Keel, P., Brumm, M., Bowers, W., Swayze, V., Andersen, A., et al. (2008). Implications of starvation induced change in right dorsal anterior cingulate volume in anorexia nervosa. *International Journal of Eating Disorders, 41* (7), 602–610.

Mikos, A. E., McDowell, B. D., Moser, D. J., Bayless, J. D., Bowers, W. A., Anderson, A. E., et al. (2008). Stability of neuropsychological performance in AN. *Annuals of Clinical Psychiatry, 20* (1), 9–13.

Milos, G., Spindler, A., Schnyder, U., and Fairburn, C. G. (2005). Instability of eating disorder diagnoses: prospective study. *British Journal of Psychiatry, 187*, 573–578.

Ng, V., Bullmore, E., de Zubicaray, G., Cooper, A., Suckling, J., and Williams, S. (2001). Identifying rate-limiting nodes in large-scale cortical networks for visuospatial processing: an illustration using fMRI. *Journal of Cognitive Neuroscience, 13* (4), 537–545.

Nunn, K., Frampton, I., Fuglset, T., Törzsök-Sonnevend, M., and Lask, B. (2011). Anorexia nervosa and the insula. *Medical Hypotheses, 76* (3), 353–357.

Nunn, K., Frampton, I., Gordon, I., and Lask, B. (2008). The fault is not in her parents but in her insula – a neurobiological hypothesis of AN. *European Eating Disorders Review, 16*, 355–360.

Nunn, K., Frampton, I., and Lask, B. (2012). Anorexia nervosa – A noradrenergic dysregulation hypothesis. *Medical Hypotheses, 78* (5), 580–584.

Palazidou, E., Robinson, P., and Lishman, W. (1990). Neuroradiological and neuropsychological assessment in anorexia nervosa. *Psychological Medicine, 20* (3), 521–527.

Rastam, M., Bjure, J., Vestergren, E., Uvebrant, P., Gillberg, I., Wentz, E., et al. (2001). Regional cerebral blood flow in weight-restored anorexia nervosa: a preliminary study. *Developmental Medicine and Child Neurology, 43* (4), 239–242.

Rauch, S., and Savage, C. (1997). Neuroimaging and neuropsychology of the striatum. Bridging basic science and clinical practice. *Psychiatric Clinics of North America, 20* (4), 741–768.

Roberts, M. E., Tchanturia, K., Stahl, D., Southgate, L., and Treasure, J. (2007). A systematic review and meta-analysis of set-shifting ability in eating disorders. *Psychological Medicine, 37*, 1075–1084.

Rose, M., Davis, J., Frampton, I., and Lask, B. (2011). The Ravello Profile – development of a global standard neuropsychological assessment for young people with anorexia nervosa. *Clinical Child Psychology and Psychiatry, 16* (2), 195–202.

Rosenberg, D., Averbach, D., and O'Hearn, K. (1997). Oculomotor response inhibition abnormalities in pediatric obsessive-compulsive disorder. *Archives of General Psychiatry, 54* (9), 831–838.

Sachdev, P., Mondraty, N., Wen, W., and Gulliford, K. (2008). Brains of anorexia nervosa patients process self-images differently from non-self-images: an fMRI study. *Neuropsychologia, 46* (8), 2161–2168.

Santel, S., Baving, L., Krauel, K., Munte, T., and Rotte, M. (2006). Hunger and satiety in anorexia nervosa: fMRI during cognitive processing of food pictures. *Brain Research, 1114* (1), 138–148.

Shafran, R., and Somers, J. (1998). Treating adolescent obsessive-compulsive disorder: applications of the cognitive theory. *Behaviour Research and Therapy, 36* (1), 93–97.

Shallice, T. (1988). *From Neuropsychology to Mental Structure.* Cambridge: Cambridge University Press.

Sherman, B. J., Savage, C. R., Eddy, K. T., Blais, M. A., Deckersbach, T., Jackson, S. C., et al. (2006). Strategic memory in adults with AN: are there similarities to obsessive compulsive spectrum disorders? *International Journal of Eating Disorders, 39* (6), 468–476.

Singh, I., and Wengaard, A. (2011). Neurobiological models: implications for patients and families. In B. Lask and I. Frampton (Eds), *Eating Disorders and the Brain.* Chichester: Wiley.

Southgate, L., Tchanturia, K., and Treasure, J. (2005). Building a model of the aetiology of eating disorders by translating experimental neuroscience into clinical practice. *Journal of Mental Health, 14*, 553–566.

Southgate, L., Tchanturia, K., and Treasure, J. (2008). Information processing bias in anorexia nervosa. *Psychiatry Research, 160* (2), 221–227.

Stedal, K., Rose, M., Frampton, L., Landrø, N., and Lask, B. (2012). The Neuropsychological Profile of Children, Adolescents and Young Adults with Anorexia Nervosa. *Archives of Clinical Neuropsychology, 27* (3), 329–337.

Steinglass, J., and Glasofer, D. (2011). Neuropsychology. In B. Lask and I. Frampton (Eds), *Eating Disorders and the Brain.* Chichester: Wiley.

Steinglass, J., and Walsh, T. (2006). Habit learning and AN: a cognitive neuroscience hypothesis. *International Journal of Eating Disorders, 39*, 267–275.

Stuss, D., Eskes, G., and Foster, J. (1994). Experimental neuropsychological studies of frontal lobe functions. In F. Boller and J. Grafman (Eds), *Handbook of Neuropsychology* (pp. 149–185). Amsterdam: Elsevier.

Swayze, V., Andersen, A., Arndt, S., Rajarethinam, R., Fleming, F., Sato, Y., et al. (1996). Reversibility of brain tissue loss in anorexia nervosa assessed with a computerized Talairach 3-D proportional grid. *Psychological Medicine*, *26* (2), 381–390.

Tchanturia, K., Campbell, I., Morris, R., and Treasure, J. (2005). Neuropsychological studies in AN. *International Journal of Eating Disorders*, *37*, S72–S76.

Tchanturia, K., Whitney, J., and Treasure, J. (2006). Can cognitive exercises help treat anorexia nervosa? *Eating and Weight Disorders*, *11* (4), 112–116.

Tenconi, E., Santonastaso, P., Degortes, D., Bosello, R., Titton, F., Mapelli, D., et al. (2010). Set-shifting abilities, central coherence, and handedness in anorexia nervosa patients, their unaffected siblings and healthy controls: exploring putative endophenotypes. *World Journal of Biological Psychiatry*, *11* (6), 813–823.

Tokley, M., and Kemps, E. (2007). Preoccupation with detail contributes to poor abstraction in women with anorexia nervosa. *Journal of Clinical and Experimental Neuropsychology*, *29* (7), 734–741.

Turkstra, L., Williams, W., Tonks, J., and Frampton, I. (2008). Measuring social cognition in adolescents: implications for students with TBI returning to school. *NeuroRehabilitation*, *23* (6), 501–509.

Uher, R., Murphy, T., Brammer, M., Dalgleish, T., Phillips, M., Ng, V., et al. (2004). Medial prefrontal cortex activity associated with symptom provocation in eating disorders. *American Journal of Psychiatry*, *161* (7), 1238–1246.

Wagner, A., Aizenstein, H., Mazurkewicz, L., Fudge, J., Frank, G., Putnam, K., et al. (2008). Altered insula response to taste stimuli in individuals recovered from restricting-type anorexia nervosa. *Neuropsychopharmacology*, *33* (3), 513–523.

Wood, L., Al-Khairulla, H., and Lask, B. (2011). Group cognitive remediation therapy for adolescents with anorexia nervosa. *Clinical Child Psychology and Psychiatry*, *16* (2), 225–231.

Wykes, T. (1998). What are we changing with neurocognitive rehabilitation? Illustrations from two single cases of changes in neuropsychological performance and brain systems as measured by SPECT. *Schizophrenia Research*, *34*, 77–86.

Chapter 9

Outcome

Simon Gowers

Overview

The outcome of child and adolescent eating disorders is variable and there is much controversy regarding its measurement. Assessment should take into account progress towards a normal physical and psychosocial developmental trajectory alongside cognitive and behavioural aspects. The literature on positive predictors of outcome is rather inconsistent, but tends to support good family support, motivation, a short history and healthy personality development as well as absence of purging behaviour.

Introduction

The course of an eating disorder is extremely variable and may range from a brief, mild episode leading to full recovery, to an illness with a chronic course lasting many years, sometimes leading to a fatal outcome. In childhood and adolescence this is especially so; most adults with a long and chronic history will have started off as young people in the early stages of their illness, but without the benefit of hindsight it can be difficult to predict how the condition will progress (Steinhausen et al., 2003).

In considering outcomes there are a number of ways in which children and young people are different from adults, chiefly because they are at a different developmental stage. In adult-onset anorexia nervosa, recovery generally implies restoration to a premorbid state of physical health, i.e. return of weight and hormonal functioning against a background of completed growth. In pubescent girls, treatment imposed weight gain may precipitate growth and the menarche, with all that that implies experientially. A recovering adult might anticipate return to a previous level of social functioning and occupation, whereas a young person's recovery will mean climbing back onto the developmental treadmill. In short, a positive outcome for a child or adolescent will involve a greater degree of facing the uncertainty of a physical and social identity that hasn't been experienced before. In a number of respects this will mean 'growing up', and facing the attendant anxieties which may have played a part in the original development of the condition. A related issue concerns the need to ensure that the 'recovered' child or adolescent doesn't 'stand still'. That is to say a 13-year-old restored to a normal weight might be considered recovered *to date*, but their health will decline if they are unable to keep pace with the 'moving goalposts' of physical and social development.

This chapter addresses what is known of the long term outcome of eating disorders and attempts to clarify the variables which predict outcome in a given case. Despite numerous outcome studies to date, research difficulties abound and there are few areas of certainty. As those with severe eating disorders inevitably attract medical attention, it is difficult to distinguish the natural history of the conditions from the outcome of treatment. Ethical issues preclude the use of 'no treatment' control groups in research in this area and whilst waiting list controls can often provide some measure of comparison, these are generally of short duration. Therefore, in this chapter an attempt will also be made to identify factors which predict response to treatment and to review prognostic factors indicating good or poor outcomes.

Making clear statements about outcomes is difficult, because of a number of research methodological issues and the consequent shortcomings of many of the treatment trials.

For a clinical series (cohort) to provide useful outcome information, it should have the following features:

- *Adequate size.*
- *Specified diagnostic criteria.*
- *Representativeness,* i.e. the series should not be selected from the larger eligible population in a way that might distort the outcome findings. Furthermore the size of the total population of subjects under consideration should be specified.
- *Specified follow-up rate.* Missing data should be accounted for, i.e. it should be clear if participants were not traced or refused follow-up; this is particularly crucial in any estimate of mortality.
- *Specified and adequate follow up period.*
- *Outcomes measured using reliable and valid measures.*

For a clinical trial reporting outcomes of a particular intervention, there ought to be:

- *Recruitment details,* e.g. population based or referrals to a specialist centre.
- *A control group or control intervention.*
- *A fully described intervention* (ideally with a manual to assist replication) and a check of adherence to the treatment protocol.
- *Outcome assessment, rated blind to treatment received.*
- *Adequate power* to detect a difference between groups, if one exists, based on the main outcome measure.
- *Sub-group analysis* of those with differential outcome, but only if numbers permit.

Addressing the above poses particular problems in children and adolescents in comparison with adults:

Diagnostic issues

Although both DSMIV (American Psychiatric Association, 1994) and ICD10 (World Health Organisation, 1993) include detailed criteria for the diagnosis of anorexia nervosa and bulimia nervosa, many individuals presenting to clinics fail to fit these diagnostic categories. Young people with atypical disorders or *Eating Disorders Not Otherwise Specified (EDNOS)* make up more than 50 per cent of those presenting to services with clinically significant disorders (Nicholls, Chater and Lask, 2000).

The diagnosis of anorexia nervosa in particular can be difficult to make in younger cases owing to a degree of overlap with feeding disorders of childhood which may also be characterized by restrictive eating patterns and low weight. The DSM5 working group has highlighted a number of diagnostic challenges in assessing children's cognition. For example, they may not verbally endorse fear of fatness despite determined food refusal (of a quantitative and/or qualitative nature) that results in severe weight loss. Sometimes this is a developmental issue, the child not having the cognition or communication skills to describe their thoughts and fears. Sometimes the characteristic preoccupation with fatness can be difficult to elicit, either because it does not appear to be present or because the child is scared to reveal their motives for dietary restraint. In addition it can be difficult to estimate a child's degree of underweight, particularly when stunting has slowed growth in height (see Chapter 6).

Outcome measures

When choosing an outcome measure, it is helpful to consider the following:

Whose perspective is relevant?

A researcher or clinician may not necessarily have the same perspective on outcomes as the young person or their parents, with the former possibly rating clinical measures such as weight gain and hormonal restoration as of major importance, whilst family members may focus on educational or psychosocial adjustment.

What is the important measure?

Recovery and remission rates differ in the literature depending on how it is defined and there is a lack of consensus about its measurement. (Couturier and Lock, 2006a, 2006b). Combining results from outcome research is hampered by the range of measures used. Many of these may be valid, but care must be exercised in combining results from studies which use different outcomes. For example an intervention may predict a good outcome in one area (weight gain) and a poor outcome in another (psychological adjustment).

Many studies report either outcome in one area only (e.g. weight gain or change in self-report scores of abnormal eating cognitions) or a crude outcome such as death.

Remission is an important outcome; many parents will want to know the likelihood of their son or daughter making a full recovery from a particular intervention, in a specified time. A categorical outcome based on a range of physical and psychosocial variables as used in the Maudsley studies (e.g. Eisler et al., 1997, 2000) may be very helpful. Within this a good outcome of anorexia nervosa implies weight restoration, return of normal hormonal functioning, absence of dieting / purging behaviour and satisfactory psychosocial adjustment. A poor outcome would imply that the subject still fulfilled diagnostic criteria for anorexia nervosa, whether or not there was some improvement, with an intermediate outcome indicating something in between. This would frequently mean weight gain without normalisation of eating or hormonal status.

Relapse. This might be defined as return to full criteria symptomatology for at least one week following a full recovery (Herzog et al., 1999).

Mortality. This is clearly an important outcome and research should distinguish death from an eating disorder, incidental cause, or suicide.

Physical measures. Weight should be expressed with reference to age and height e.g. as percentage weight for height or BMI percentile. Endocrine functioning should take into account premorbid pubertal status.

Psychosocial adjustment. This is an under-rated component of recovery and may well predict weight maintenance or loss after treatment, as well as success in, for example, return to education.

Global outcomes. These enable a composite assessment of recovery in a number of domains. Global quantitative measures such as the Eating Disorder Examination, modified for children (Bryant-Waugh et al., 1996) and the Morgan Russell Outcome Assessment Scale (Morgan and Hayward, 1988) enable statistical analysis of change over time.

Outcomes

Anorexia Nervosa

Outcome can be defined as the long-term result of a pathological process. There has been a recent increase in the outcome literature for anorexia nervosa, including those with adolescent and pre-pubertal onset.

Hsu (1996) outlined the following quality criteria for outcome studies of anorexia nervosa:

- explicitly stated diagnostic criteria;
- greater than 25 subjects;
- minimum follow up four years from onset of illness;
- failure to trace rate less than 10 per cent;
- use of direct interview in greater than 50 per cent;
- use of multiple well defined outcome measures.

Studies following the course of anorexia nervosa in young people often start from the point when they are discharged from treatment, with repeated follow-up assessments, and investigate a range of outcomes – global outcome, change in eating disorder, physical health, mental health, mortality and psychosocial functioning. Some studies have followed young people with anorexia nervosa for up to 30 years, e.g. Steinhausen (2002)

Global Outcome

Global outcome is generally reported as good, intermediate/fair or poor, with good outcome generally equating to full recovery. Steinhausen (2002) systematically reviewed and analysed 119 outcome studies of anorexia nervosa, dividing them into two age groups: those aged less than 17 years at onset and those above 17 years. Overall he found a good outcome in 46.9%, intermediate outcome in 33.5% and a poor outcome in 20.8% (based on a combined series of 5,590 subjects). Outcome was slightly better for normalisation of core symptoms such as menstruation, weight and eating behaviour, than good outcome overall. There was a trend towards better outcome in younger patients.

Recent outcome studies following up adolescents with anorexia nervosa (e.g. Helverskov et al., 2010), confirm this trend, and good outcomes of between 49% and 75.8%, intermediate outcome between 10.5% and 41%, and poor outcome between 8% and 14%, have been reported after ten or more years follow-up (Wentz et al., 2009; Herpertz-Dahlmann et al., 2001; Saccomani et al., 1998).

Bryant-Waugh et al. (1988) reported on the long-term follow-up of 30 younger children with anorexia nervosa whose initial treatment had been completed more than two years previously. The mean age of onset was 11.7 years and mean length of follow-up was 7.2 years. Outcome measures comprised nutritional state, menstrual function, mental state, psychosexual state and psychosocial adjustment. They reported a good outcome in 62%, an intermediate outcome in 13% and a poor outcome in 25%. Just over a quarter of subjects had required further inpatient treatment. The subjects tended to rate their own progress more favourably than objective measurement.

Rates of recovery usually increase with a longer duration of follow-up. Steinhausen's systematic review found that the number of adolescent-onset cases recovering, increased from 46% of those followed up for less than four years to 76% of those followed up for longer than 10 years. Nilsson and Hägglöf (2005) meanwhile reporting on a series of 68 adolescent females with anorexia nervosa followed up at 8 and 16 years and found that recovery increased from 68% to 85%. Strober et al. (1997) suggested that mean time to recovery ranged between 57 and 79 months and that full recovery was uncommon in the first three years. However, they found that relapse after full recovery was uncommon. It should be noted though that as well as improving outcomes with longer follow-up, most studies have found an increase in reported deaths over time (see below).

Overall, good outcome is achieved in over a half of young people with adolescent onset anorexia nervosa and the literature suggests that further improvements occur with time. Although adolescent onset series report better outcomes than adult onset series, the very young particularly pre-pubertal cases) appear to have poor outcomes (Russell, 1992).

Change in eating disorder

Although many young people with anorexia nervosa make progress over time, a number appear to progress through other eating disorders on the way to recovery. In the long-term follow-up of adolescents diagnosed with anorexia nervosa between 3% and 6% continue to have anorexia nervosa, between 4% and 9.5% progress to bulimia nervosa and between 18% and 23% develop EDNOS (Råstam et al., 2003; Herpertz-Dahlmann et al., 2001; Strober et al., 1997). Råstam et al. (2003) reported that half of their subjects had a lifetime diagnosis of bulimia nervosa. Strober et al. (1997) reported that almost a third of young people with restricting anorexia nervosa developed binge eating during follow-up, though this reduced to none after five years.

In their two year follow-up of 23 young people with anorexia nervosa Fichter and Quadflieg (1996) found that 30.2% had anorexia nervosa, 21.7% had bulimia nervosa, 47.8% were below any diagnostic threshold but only 18% had no eating disorder.

This recent literature on the progress of adolescent anorexia nervosa to another eating disorder suggests that this is particularly common in the first few years, with further improvements in the longer-term. Nilsson and Hägglöf (2005), for example found that between 8 and 16 year follow up of 68 subjects, rates of anorexia nervosa were steady at 3%, while EDNOS decreased from 24% to 10% and bulimia nervosa reduced from 6% to 1%.

Physical Health

Physical outcomes, details of weight and menstrual status are less commonly reported in the literature than global outcomes.

Adolescent onset eating disorders may confer a number of physical risks for the future, even if a reasonable degree of recovery is achieved. For example, peak bone mass achieved as a young adult determines bone density and fracture risk later in life. Lucas et al. (1999) in a retrospective population-based cohort study found that young women with anorexia nervosa were at increased risk of any fracture later in life. Zipfel et al. (2001) in a prospective study of bone mineral density (BMD) found significantly reduced BMD in chronic binge/purging anorexia nervosa at 3.6 year follow-up, increasing the risk of osteopenia and osteoporosis.

Nilsson and Hägglöf (2005) meanwhile found tooth enamel damage remained after normalisation of eating behaviour. They also reported height increases up to eight years following inpatient treatment of adolescent anorexia nervosa and median BMI increase at both 8 and 16 years.

In the longer term, eating disorders may have an impact on those who become pregnant, the literature suggesting that both anorexia nervosa and bulimia nervosa may affect the developing foetus. Kouba et al. (2005) found that women with previous or active eating disorders gave birth to a higher number of infants with low body weight, small head circumference and microcephaly and they were often small for gestational age. They also found that 22% of women had a relapse of their eating disorder during pregnancy.

Mental Health

Young people with anorexia nervosa have been found to have a number of psychiatric difficulties or personality disorders at follow-up. It is important to distinguish between those present at the time of diagnosis, which may influence outcome, from those that may be an outcome of having anorexia nervosa.

Steinhausen (2002) found a large proportion of additional psychiatric disorders including anxiety disorders, phobias, affective disorders, substance misuse disorders, OCD and personality disorders at follow-up.

Herpertz-Dahlmann et al. (2001) reported that at the 10 year follow-up a half of their adolescent subjects had an Axis I psychiatric disorder and almost a quarter had a personality disorder. However, long-term recovered subjects were no more likely than controls to have a current psychiatric diagnosis or personality disorder. Råstam et al. (2003) found that almost all young people with anorexia nervosa had a lifetime diagnosis of an affective disorder, but this was present in only 10% at the 10 year follow-up.

Nilsson and Hägglöf (2005) also found that mental health problems decreased with follow-up of 16 years. However 15% of subjects still considered their mental health to be bad or very bad.

Mortality

The majority of outcome studies for anorexia nervosa report crude mortality rates, though standard mortality rates (SMR – observed mortality divided by expected mortality) are easier to interpret. Mortality in adolescent anorexia nervosa is said to be higher than in other psychiatric disorders, as high as 15% in some studies (Herzog et al., 1992)

In the series reviewed by Steinhausen (2002) the mean crude mortality rate was reported as 5%. This was lower in adolescent onset anorexia nervosa compared with the adult condition and he concluded more deaths were expected with increasing age at onset and also with length of follow up.

Bryant-Waugh et al. (1988) found 2 deaths in their series of childhood onset anorexia nervosa. A boy aged 14 died from an unrelated asthma attack and a girl aged 12 died from complications of a ruptured oesophagus. Nilsson and Hägglöf (2005) found one death in their sample of 76 subjects. This death occurred due to cardiac failure following intravenous nutrition, at the age of 23 years. Wentz et al. (2009) meanwhile found no deaths after 18 years in their sample of 51 adolescents.

Nielsen et al. (1998) reviewed ten eating disordered populations and found that the standardised mortality rate was raised in anorexia nervosa, particularly for subjects presenting aged 20–29 years, in which it was three times higher than expected. The SMR was 3.1 in childhood onset anorexia nervosa and 3.2 in adolescent onset anorexia nervosa. The highest mortality was in the first year after presentation in females and in the first two years after presentation in males. In females the risk of death was 2% in the first year, with an annual risk of death of 0.59% thereafter. In males the risk of death was 5% in the first two years and then 0%. They found that the length of follow-up had an inverse effect on SMR, but this was significantly increased for at least 15 years after presentation. A lower weight at presentation was associated with higher SMR overall, though this was not found in children with anorexia nervosa. More deaths were found to be due to suicide and other/unknown causes and fewer due to the eating disorder than previously reported.

Psychosocial functioning

Halvorsen, Andersen and Heyerdahl (2004) found fairly good social functioning at between 3 and 14 year follow-up, but only 48% of their series reported being satisfied with life compared to 83% of a control population. Wentz et al. (2009) found one in four of their followed up cases were unable to work owing to psychiatric problems.

Hsu et al. (1979) found disturbed family relationships in 40% of patients at follow-up. In their 16 year follow-up study Nilsson and Hägglöf (2005) found most former patients had a satisfactory family and work situation, however interpersonal relationships were variable, 28% having slightly unsatisfactory social contacts, and 8% having moderate or severely unsatisfactory social contacts. According to self-evaluation avoidance of sexual behaviour was moderate in 13% and severe in 2% (Nilsson, 2007). This group also reported a significant difference in sexuality, number of children and social contacts in subjects recovered at 16 years compared to those who still had an eating disorder.

Bulimia Nervosa

There are few long-term outcome studies in bulimia nervosa focusing on children and adolescents. Many adults with bulimia nervosa report symptoms starting in adolescence. Outcome studies in the literature are mainly prospective and exclusively of females.

Global Outcomes

Steinhausen (1999) reviewed 24 studies of bulimia nervosa, with a total of 1383 patients. The mean age of onset ranged from 14 years and 4 months to 22 years and 2 months. Full recovery was reported in 47.5%, intermediate outcome in 26% and poor outcome in 26%, after a mean follow-up of 2.5 years.

Quadflieg and Fichter's (2003) literature review found a steady rate of recovery with increasing length of follow-up. Good outcome was observed in 28% to 78% after 6 months to 1 year, 38% to 69% after 1.5 to 2 years, 13% to 77% after 3 to 6 years and 47% to 73% after 9 to 11 years. Between two thirds and three quarter of women with bulimia nervosa show at least partial recovery after 10 year follow-up. Relapse rates vary considerably between studies, but with lower relapse rates with longer follow-up. Poor outcome was observed in 3% to 67% after 6 months to 1 year, 5% to 50% after 1.5 to 2 years, 19% to 87% after 3 to 6 years and 9% to 30% after 9 to 11 years. One quarter of women may still have bulimia nervosa after 10 year follow-up.

Change in Eating Disorder

Progression from bulimia nervosa to anorexia nervosa is much less common than the reverse. Quadflieg and Fichter (2003) reported that there is some evidence to suggest cross-over from bulimia nervosa to EDNOS. However, interpretation is difficult as this finding could reflect partial recovery or the development of sub-syndromal disorders.

Physical Health

Zipfel et al. (2001) found bone mineral density (BMD) to be within the normal range for recovered and chronic bulimia nervosa at 3.6 year follow-up, suggesting no increased risk of osteopenia or osteoporosis.

Mental Health

Patton et al. (2003) found higher rates of depression and alcohol consumption in adolescents with bulimia partial syndrome, suggesting that this condition might be better viewed as a variant of early onset affective disorder.

Mortality

Steinhausen (1999) found an average crude mortality rate of 0.7%, with a range of 0% to 6% in different studies. Nielsen et al. (1998) found no firm evidence that

SMR was raised in bulimia nervosa. Quadflieg and Fichter (2003) reported that it was difficult to identify a cause of death directly attributable to the specific eating habits of bulimia nervosa.

Psychosocial Functioning

Quadflieg and Fichter (2003) found that improvements in social functioning were observed over time, and subjects with a good global outcome showed a better social outcome. Social outcome (based on leisure activity and having confidantes) was reported as good in 52.1%, intermediate in 22.4% and poor in 25.5%, at 6 year follow-up. Outcome in terms of sexual adjustment was reported less favourably, with good outcome in 40%, intermediate outcome in 17.6% and poor outcome in 42.4% of subjects, after 6 year follow-up.

Eating Disorder not otherwise specified

Eating disorder not otherwise specified (EDNOS) covers a range of eating difficulties, not fulfilling criteria for either Anorexia Nervosa or Bulimia Nervosa. There is disagreement in the literature as to the progression of these diagnoses to others and there is little on the natural course and outcome. Patton et al. (2003) performed a prospective, community based study, following up 982 female participants over six years. They found that 8.8% reported an eating disorder across the six-year period. Out of 55 subjects with any eating disorder in adolescence, 11% had persisting eating difficulties into young adulthood. They concluded that the life-time experience of sub-syndromal eating disorders is quite common in young women, but in many is self-limiting.

Outcome of treatment

Anorexia nervosa

Anorexia nervosa in children and adolescents is a very visible disorder in which weight loss and food avoidance are readily evident to family members, peers and school teachers. It is difficult therefore for the young person to escape detection and attempts to direct them towards treatment. As a result there are no large series of untreated young people from which to ascertain the natural history of the condition. For similar reasons, it is difficult to gauge the impact of treatment; that is the extent to which treatment improves the outcome over and above no treatment. One attempt however, a medium sized (n = 90) randomised controlled trial of three treatments versus no treatment, in a mixed age (14–30) series (Crisp et al. 1991), showed better outcomes for the three treated groups compared to the no treatment group.

In this section the main evidence for the effectiveness of different treatments is reviewed.

Physical treatments

Food supplements, nasogastric and parenteral feeding

Food supplements and dietary alternatives to food are generally given either in cases of severe physical concern or in situations of non-compliance with normal eating. The UK National Institute for Clinical Excellence (NICE) guideline (NCCMH, 2004) found that there was limited evidence that nasogastric feeding, but not total parenteral nutrition (TPN), produced greater weight gain than standard care. There was little or no evidence of the acceptability of naso-gastric feeding to patients or its impact on core eating disorder psychopathology. TPN was associated with high levels of adverse effects. The guideline concluded that feeding against the will of the patient should be a treatment of last resort in anorexia nervosa and that TPN should not be given unless there was evidence of gastrointestinal dysfunction which precluded enteral feeding. One small trial of zinc supplementation to an in-patient treatment regime in subjects aged over 15, suggested that rates of daily weight gain were greater in the zinc supplementation group despite nearly all subjects having zinc levels in the normal range before embarking on treatment (Birmingham et al., 1994). However the NICE guideline concluded there was insufficient evidence to support its use and this finding requires replication.

Pharmacological agents

Randomised controlled trials have examined a range of drugs in low weight anorexia nervosa, though almost exclusively in adults. However, a survey amongst UK specialist eating disorder services for children and adolescents (Gowers et al., 2010) found psychotropic drugs to be used in about 25% of cases.

Antidepressants

Antidepressants have been used to promote eating and weight gain and also to relieve depressive symptoms when these are present comorbidly. The use of selective serotonin reuptake inhibitor antidepressants (SSRI's) in children and adolescents is difficult to evaluate currently whilst major reservations exist about their use in childhood depression (Whittington et al., 2004).

Three RCT's of SSRI's (two with fluoxetine, Attia et al., 1998; Kaye et al., 2001; and one with citalopram, Fassino et al., 2002) failed to find advantages of active drug over placebo or no treatment for weight gain, maintenance or eating behaviour, though the citalopram study reported a trend towards a greater improvement in mood symptoms in the group receiving the active drug. A trial of the tricyclic antidepressant amitriptyline meanwhile in 48 early onset cases (mean age 16.6 years) failed to find an advantage relative to placebo (Biederman et al., 1985).

Major tranquillizers/neuroleptic drugs

These are sometimes used to reduce extreme anxiety or because of their noted potential to increase appetite. A systematic review found no convincing evidence of any beneficial effect of these drugs in anorexia nervosa, whilst concerns were expressed about their potential to prolong the electrocardiographic QT interval, which is often already increased in anorexia nervosa (Treasure and Schmidt, 2004). This may add to the risk of severe cardiac complications already conferred by emaciation. However Gowers et al.'s (2010) survey found that Olanzapine in particular was quite commonly prescribed to support in-patient care, apparently without major side effects and with perceived clinically assessed benefit in two thirds of cases.

Psychological therapies

Given that the physical manifestations of anorexia nervosa are largely viewed as secondary to the psychological disorder, it would seem logical that those receiving psychological therapies would have better outcomes than those without. In practice the evidence to support psychological therapies is limited. On the basis of a meta-analysis of three studies, however, the NICE guideline concluded that there was limited evidence that a range of psychological treatments with more therapeutic contact was superior to 'treatment as usual' with a lower rate of contact, both in terms of weight gain and proportion of patients recovered (NCCMH, 2004).

The psychotherapy trials in the literature are notable for their small size and hence lack of power and also the presence of confounding treatments. A number have compared individual treatments to family based treatments, but most would view it as difficult or inappropriate to deliver a treatment to a young person without providing at least some family intervention alongside. Thus in one randomised study comparing individual therapy with family therapy, those receiving the individual therapy option also received parental counselling (Robin et al.1999). Some trials are also difficult to interpret, as a variable number of subjects have received in-patient treatment alongside the therapy under investigation.

Although there have been a few small (adult) trials of cognitive behaviour therapy (CBT), cognitive analytic therapy (CAT), interpersonal therapy (IPT) and focal psychodynamic therapy, in general there is insufficient evidence to conclude advantages of any specialist psychotherapy over another (NCCMH, 2004).

Despite the clear role of abnormal specific and non-specific abnormal cognitions in anorexia nervosa, there are few studies of individual CBT based treatments (Gowers and Bryant-Waugh, 2004; Gowers, 2006). The published studies (Channon et al., 1989; Serfaty, 1998; Pike et al., 2003) suggest that CBT may be moderately effective but possibly no more so than other therapies. One relatively large RCT (Gowers et al., 2010), found no advantages for a specialist out-patient

CBT programme over generic child mental health service treatment (which may have included some CBT elements but generally included more family interventions), at one or two years.

The most impressive findings relate to family therapies in this age group, but some caution should be used in interpreting the findings. Firstly the studies tend to be very small. Secondly different studies employ a different entry point (i.e. subjects may enter the trial at low weight as in Lock et al., 2005; or after in-patient weight restoration as in the Maudsley study, Eisler et al., 1997). Finally despite the relatively good body of evidence suggesting the benefit of family interventions, uncertainty exists about which families benefit and the optimal style of treatment. Eisler et al. (2000) for example showed that the outcomes were very poor for conjoint family therapy in the presence of high maternal expressed emotion; it may be that such families do better when the family intervention is delivered as parental guidance, without the child being present.

Multi-family day therapy aims to help family members learn by identifying with members of other families with the same condition, by analogy. It is generally delivered within a day hospital programme, in which up to 10 families with an adolescent with anorexia attend a mixture of whole family group discussions, parallel meetings of parents and adolescents and creative activities. Preparation of lunch and communal eating is a central part of the programme. This treatment is at an early stage of evaluation but preliminary findings suggest a high degree of acceptability and promising outcomes particularly in terms of a reduced need for hospitalisation (Scholz and Asen, 2001).

Service issues

Medical in-patient admission is necessary and unavoidable in cases of severe physical compromise or where initiation of feeding cannot be achieved on an out-patient basis. However, the role of in-patient management in improving recovery from anorexia nervosa as opposed to achieving physical stability is unclear. To date two RCT's (Crisp et al., 1991; Gowers et al., 2010) have failed to show a benefit for in-patient management over out-patient treatment at two year follow up, the latter in an adolescent-only series. This showed that the one year outcomes of those who were initially assigned out-patient management but later transferred to in-patient management on clinical grounds were especially poor, this naturalistic outcome replicating a finding from a cohort study in which only 3/21 young people with anorexia treated as in-patients had fully recovered four years later (Gowers et al., 2000). The outcome of compulsory treatment is controversial; however a recent study of adolescents suggested those treated under the UK Mental Health Act, had outcomes no worse than a matched group of informal patients even though they had a number of worse prognostic indicators at admission (Ayton, et al., 2009).

Increasingly, day programmes are being developed in an effort to reduce costs, but more importantly to avoid potentially negative consequences of in-patient admission. Significant therapeutic factors may include the importance of mobi-lising resources within the family and the multi-family day unit approach (Scholz and Asen, 2001) is yielding promising early findings in this regard.

Bulimia nervosa

Bulimia nervosa, being easier to hide from parental or medical attention is a condition which frequently goes untreated for several years, before often in young adulthood, the sufferer seeks help as they realise the condition is interfering with health, or social functioning. Anecdotally we know from adult series of bulimia that the mean length of history before presentation is often 7–10 years (Fairburn and Harrison, 2003), suggesting that outcome without treatment has, in these cases been poor. What we don't know here, is how many young people have made a full recovery without treatment and therefore don't later present to adult services.

Physical treatments

Selective serotonin re-uptake inhibitors (SSRI's) have been shown in adults to improve symptoms of bulimia and also improve mood, though long term follow-up data are scarce, suggesting possibly that beneficial effects are obtained only while on the drugs. One systematic review found no differences in outcome between antidepressants and CBT (Bacaltchuk and Hay, 2003)

Psychological therapies

There is now quite a substantial body of literature to suggest that a course of cognitive behaviour therapy specifically designed for bulimia (Fairburn et al., 1993) reduces bulimic symptoms and improves non-specific symptoms of depression compared to waiting list controls (Hay and Bacaltchuk, 2003). A further RCT (Agras et al., 2000) found CBT was more effective than interpersonal therapy (IPT) in producing abstinence by the end of treatment, but the differences were lost by 8 and 12 month follow up. More recently a 'transdiagnostic' development of this therapy suggests some efficacy in anorexia nervosa, at least where physical complications are less marked (Fairburn et al., 2009). To date however the treatment evidence base for adolescents with the condition is very limited.

Service issues

All the current evidence based treatments for bulimia nervosa are delivered on an out-patient basis, with in-patient management being reserved for extreme severity, comorbidity or suicidal risk. The outcome of in-patient management has not been fully evaluated.

Self help

Manualised CBT based self-help programmes may help overcome the sensitivities of young people to discussing embarrassing behaviours and enable them to work on their problems in their own time. Pure and 'guided' forms have been tested in adults with early promising results when self help was combined with fluoxetine (Mitchell et al., 2001). A multi-centre internet based self-help programme is currently under investigation in the UK.

'Transdiagnostic' approaches

Fairburn and Harrison (2003) have argued that existing classification systems are unsatisfactory and that there are more features in common between the eating disorder categories than differences. They therefore propose a 'transdiagnostic' approach to treatment, based on the established CBT for bulimia programme.

Prognosis

Prognosis is defined as the means to make a forecast or prediction about the probable course and the final outcome of a disease. A number of outcome studies of early onset anorexia nervosa have looked at prognostic predictors, i.e. variables present at the onset of the disorder influencing outcome. So far, the literature has shown few consistent findings. Motivation to change and degree of psychological concern with weight and shape may be amongst the most important in predicting outcome.

Anorexia Nervosa

Age of onset

An older age of onset (above 20 years) is often reported as having a poorer outcome (Hsu et al., 1979). A number of more recent reports have found a better prognosis with younger age of onset (Deter et al., 2005; Ratnasuriya et al., 1991). Franko et al. (2004) suggested suicidality was more common in those with a later onset. However, Strober et al. (1997) found age of onset to have no significant effect and Steinhausen (2002) concluded that findings were ambiguous on the basis of his large systematic review. It may be that the early onset cases comprise two groups with different outcomes defined by their pubertal status (see below).

Gender and socio-economic status

There is no conclusive evidence that gender has a significant effect on outcome of anorexia nervosa. Neither does socioeconomic status appear to have a significant impact (Steinhausen, 1999). Berkman, Lohr and Bulik (2007) drew attention to the lack of knowledge regarding disparities in outcomes based on gender, race or ethnicity and suggest these variables should be reported in future studies and differences between groups analysed.

Physical status

Outcome for pre-pubertal onset anorexia nervosa has been reported as poorer than adolescent onset anorexia nervosa. Bryant-Waugh et al. (1998) found a poor prognosis in their study and a young age of onset was positively correlated with low weight at follow-up. The outcome seems to be particularly poor in the group that have premorbid developmental abnormalities (Steinhausen, 1999). Low BMI at presentation is often reported as predicting a poorer outcome (Gowers and Bryant-Waugh, 2004; Casper and Jabine, 1996; Hsu et al., 1979). Steinhausen (2002) found the literature on this to be unclear. Bryant-Waugh et al. (1988) meanwhile found low BMI did not influence prognosis in their early onset anorexia nervosa study.

Eating Disorder Symptoms

Various symptoms associated with anorexia nervosa have been reported to affect outcome and a shorter duration of symptoms at presentation seems favourable (Steinhausen, 2002; Ratnasuriya et al., 1991, Hsu et al., 1979). However, this finding was not found in the Great Ormond St Hospital early onset series (Bryant-Waugh et al., 1988).

The bulimic sub-type, i.e. vomiting, bulimia and purgative abuse has been consistently found to predict a poor outcome (Steinhausen, 2002; Hsu et al., 1979, Gowers and Bryant-Waugh., 2004). Strober et al. (1997) found binge-eating was not a predictor of long term chronicity. Steinhausen (2002) reported that hyperactivity and dieting were not significant predictors of outcome. However, excessive exercise has been reported to predict a poor outcome (Casper and Jabine, 1996; Strober et al., 1997).

Unsurprisingly, chronicity in anorexia nervosa predicts an unfavourable prognosis (Steinhausen, 2002) and good outcome at five years predicts a good long term outcome (Ratnasuriya et al., 1991).

Life events

Life event research is often hampered by the poor quality of self-report life event questionnaires. North et al. (1997) however, using a standardised semi-structured interview, found that a severe negative life event occurring in the year before onset predicted a good outcome two years later, on the hypothesised basis that overcoming the life event reduced the need for the eating disorder as a coping strategy.

Co-morbidity

Outcome is often reported as less favourable in the presence of other psychiatric disorders, suicidal behaviour, personality disorder or substance abuse.

Comorbid mood disorders are well documented but the relationship between these and outcome is unclear. North and Gowers (1999) found greater improvement in eating disorder symptomatology at two years in adolescents with anorexia nervosa who had comorbid depression at presentation compared to those without comorbidity. Bryant-Waugh et al. (1988) however found that depressive features during the initial illness in pre-pubertal anorexia nervosa conferred a poor prognosis. Saccomani et al. (1998) reported that mood and personality disorders predicted a poor outcome and that anxiety disorders had no prognostic value.

Steinhausen (2002) found that 25% of patients with anorexia nervosa had anxiety disorders and 25% had mood disorders, at follow-up. He also found that OCD had no effect on outcome.

Different personality disorders may affect prognosis. Steinhausen (2002) found that a histrionic personality predicted a favourable outcome, whereas an obsessive-compulsive personality predicted an unfavourable outcome. Saccomani et al. (1998) found that borderline personality disorder showed a tendency towards chronicity and poorer outcome.

Family Functioning

Poor childhood social adjustment predicts poor outcome and disturbed relationships with or between parents predicted poor outcome in one study (Hsu et al., 1979). Conversely, a good parent child relationship appears to be associated with a favourable outcome (Steinhausen, 2002).

North et al. (1997) found that poor family functioning (based on the McMaster model) as rated by either a clinician or the young person predicted a poor outcome at one and two years, whilst the parent's assessment of their family's functioning had no predictive power.

Bryant-Waugh et al. (1988) found a number of family structures which predicted a poor outcome in pre-pubertal onset anorexia nervosa: one parent families, families in which one/both parents had been married before and families with several generations living together.

Bulimia Nervosa

There is little on prognostic factors for bulimia nervosa in the literature and NICE (NCCMH, 2004) provide no prognostic indicators for adolescents.

Age of onset

It is unclear whether age of onset predicts outcome in bulimia nervosa (Steinhausen, 1999).

Eating Disorder Symptoms

Although not conclusive, Quadflieg and Fichter (2003) found that a short duration of symptoms at presentation may predict a better outcome. They also found that more severe symptoms at presentation predicted a poorer outcome. An earlier history of anorexia nervosa did not affect outcome per se, though low body weight was considered a negative predictor. Vomiting and laxative abuse are reported to predict a poor outcome (Steinhausen, 1999). Frequency of vomiting seems to be a better predictor then binge frequency (Quadflieg and Fichter, 2003). Steinhausen (1999) reported that frequency of bulimic episodes did not affect outcome.

Co-morbidity

Quadflieg and Fichter (2003) found the evidence that comorbid Axis I psychiatric diagnoses influenced the outcome of bulimia nervosa contradictory. However they concluded that certain comorbid personality disorders (i.e. borderline and Cluster B personality disorders) predicted an unfavourable outcome.

Steinhausen (1999) concluded that the presence of substance misuse or obesity did not predict outcome.

Quadflieg and Fichter (2003) reported low self-esteem as a predictor of poor outcome. This seemed particularly influential when combined with high perfectionism and self-perceived overweight. They also suggested that patients with additional impulsive behaviours had a poorer outcome than those without them. Self-harm and alcohol abuse predict a negative outcome (Steinhausen, 1999).

Family Functioning

It is unclear whether family features are predictive of outcome in bulimia nervosa. Quadflieg and Fichter (2003) reported ambiguous findings for those with a family history of depression or alcohol abuse. They reported that a stable relationship did not predict outcome, but that an unstable relationship predicted a poor outcome.

Socioeconomic Status

There is no conclusive evidence that socioeconomic status has a significant effect on outcome of bulimia nervosa (Quadflieg and Fichter, 2003).

Conclusion

Recent years have shown an increase in understanding of the outcomes of eating disorders, treated in a range of services. Much of the outcome data are from adult patients, though increasingly information is emerging from series of children and adolescents, some from meta-analysis of smaller case series. Less is known of the outcomes of the very youngest patients. The outcome of adolescent bulimia nervosa is less well understood than that of anorexia nervosa. The impact of treatment and the relative merits of different approaches is less clear. In particular psychological therapies have not been tested in adequately powered randomised controlled trials. Prognostic factors suggest that lack of family and social supports and emerging abnormal personality development adversely affect recovery. Further research may help us identify at the earliest stage, which patients may benefit from the most intensive therapies, including hospital admission, so that we can target interventions effectively.

Summary

- Although the outcome of adolescent eating disorders is very variable, the majority are reported to make a good recovery at long term outcome.
- Comparing outcome rates between studies is complicated by differences in definition of remission and recovery.
- Abnormal personality development and major psychiatric comorbidity confers a poorer prognosis.

Acknowledgement

Thanks to Dr Frances Doherty who was co-author on a previous edition of this chapter.

References

Agras, W. S., Walsh, B. T., Fairburn, C. G., Wilson, G. T., and Kraemer, H. C. (2000). A multicenter comparison of cognitive-behavioral therapy and interpersonal psychotherapy for bulimia nervosa. *Archives of General Psychiatry, 57*, 459–466.

American Psychiatric Association (1994). *Diagnostic and Statistical Manual of Mental Disorders* (4th ed.) (DSM-IV). Arlington, VA: APA.

Attia, E., Haiman, C., Walsh, B. T., and Flater, S. R. (1998). Does fluoxetine augment the inpatient treatment of anorexia nervosa? *American Journal of Psychiatry, 155*, 548–551.

Ayton, A., Keen, C., and Lask, B. (2009). Pros and cons of using the Mental Health Act for severe eating disorders in adolescents. *European Eating Disorders Review, 17* (1), 14–23.

Bacaltchuk, J., and Hay, P. (2003). *Antidepressants versus psychological treatments and their combination for people with bulimia nervosa.* Cochrane Review. Cochrane Library Issue 1, Oxford.

Berkman, N., Lohr, K., and Bulik, C. M. (2007). Outcomes of eating disorders: A systematic review of the literature. *International Journal of Eating Disorders*, *40*, 293–309.

Biederman, J., Herzog, D. B., Rivinus, T. M., Harper, G. P., Ferber, R. A., Rosenbaum, J. F., et al. (1985). Amitriptyline in the treatment of anorexia nervosa; a double blind, placebo controlled trial. *Journal of Clinical Psychopharmacology*, *5*, 10–16.

Birmingham, C. L., Goldner, E. M., and Bakan, R. (1994). Controlled trial of zinc supplementation in anorexia nervosa. *International Journal of Eating Disorders*, *15*, 251–255.

Bryant-Waugh, R., Cooper, P., Taylor, C., and Lask B. (1996). The use of the Eating Disorder Examination with children: A Pilot Study. *International Journal of Eating Disorders*, *19*, 391–398.

Bryant-Waugh, R., Knibbs, J., Fosson, A., Kaminski, Z., and Lask, B. (1988). Long term follow up of patients with early onset anorexia nervosa. *Archives of Disease in Childhood*, *63*, 5–9.

Casper, R. C., and Jabine, L. N. (1996). An eight year follow-up: Outcome of adolescent compared to adult onset anorexia nervosa. *Journal of Youth and Adolescence*, *25* (4), 499–517.

Channon, S., de Silva, P., Hemsley, D., and Perkins, R. (1989). A controlled trial of cognitive behavioural and behavioural treatment of anorexia nervosa. *Behaviour Research and Therapy*, *27*, 529–535.

Couturier, J., and Lock, J. (2006a). What is remission in adolescent anorexia nervosa? A review of various conceptualizations and quantitative analysis. *Journal of Eating Disorders*, *39* (3), 175–183.

Couturier, J., and Lock, J. (2006b). What is recovery in adolescent anorexia nervosa? *International Journal of Eating Disorders*, *39* (7), 550–555.

Crisp, A. H., Norton, K. W. R., Gowers, S. G., Halek, C., Levett G., Yeldham D., et al. (1991). A controlled study of the effect of therapies aimed at adolescent and family psychopathology in Anorexia Nervosa. *British Journal of Psychiatry*, *159*, 325–333

Deter, H. C., Schellberg, D., Köpp, W., Friederich, H. C., and Herzog, W. (2005). Predictability of a favourable outcome in anorexia nervosa. *European Psychiatry*, *20* (2), 165–172.

Eisler, I., Dare, C., Hodes, M., Russell, G. F. M., Dodge, E., and le Grange, D. (2000). Family therapy for adolescent anorexia nervosa: the results of a controlled comparison of two family interventions. (In Process Citation). *Journal of Child Psychology* and *Psychiatry*, *41*, 727–736.

Eisler, I., Dare, C., Russell, G. F. M., Szmukler, G., le Grange, D., and Dodge, E. (1997). Family and individual therapy in anorexia nervosa. A 5-year follow-up. *Archives of General Psychiatry*, *54*, 1025–1030.

Fairburn, C. G., Cooper, Z., Doll, H. A., O'Connor, M. E., Bohn, K., Hawker D. M, et al. (2009). Transdiagnostic Cognitive-Behavioral Therapy for patients with eating disorders: A two-site trial with 60-week follow-up. *American Journal of Psychiatry*, *166* (3), 311–319.

Fairburn, C. G., Marcus, M. D., and Wilson, G. T. (1993). Cognitive-behavioral therapy for binge eating and bulimia nervosa: A comprehensive treatment manual. In C. G. Fairburn, and G. T. Wilson (Eds), *Binge Eating: Nature, Assessment and Treatment*. New York: Guilford Press, 361–404.

Fairburn, C. G., and Harrison, P. J. (2003). Eating Disorders. *The Lancet*, *361*, 407–416

Fassino, S., Leombruni, P., Daga, G., Brustolin, A., Migliaretti, G., Cavallo F., et al. (2002). Efficacy of citalopram in anorexia nervosa: A pilot study. *European Neuropsychopharmacology*, *12*, 453–459.

Fichter, M. M., and Quadflieg, N. (1996). Course and two year outcome in anorexic and bulimic adolescents. *Journal of Youth* and *Adolescence*, *25* (4), 545–563.

Franko, D. L., Keel, P. K., Dorer, D. J., Blais, M. A., Delinsky, S. S., Eddy, K. T., et al. (2004). What predicts suicide attempts in women with eating disorders? *Psychological Medicine*, *34*, 843–853.

Gowers, S. G. (2006) Evidence based research in CBT with adolescent eating disorders. *Child and Adolescent Mental Health*, *11* (1), 9–12.

Gowers, S., and Bryant-Waugh, R. (2004). Management of child and adolescent eating disorders: the current evidence base and future directions. *Journal of Child Psychology and Psychiatry*, *45* (1), 63–83.

Gowers, S. G., Clark, A. F., Roberts, C., Byford, S., Barrett B., Griffiths A., et al. (2010). HTA Project: 97/42/02 – A randomized controlled multi-centre treatment trial of adolescent anorexia nervosa, including assessment of cost effectiveness and patient acceptability. *Health Technology Assessment*, *14* (15), 1–98.

Gowers, S., Claxton, M., Rowlands, L., Inbasagaran, A., Wood, D., Yi, I., et al. (2010). Drug prescribing in child and adolescent eating disorder services. *Child* and *Adolescent Mental Health 15*, 18–22.

Gowers, S. G., Weetman, J., Shore, A., Hossain, F., and Elvins, R. (2000). The impact of hospitalisation on the outcome of adolescent anorexia nervosa. *British Journal of Psychiatry*, *176*, 138–141.

Hay, P., and Balcaltchuk, J. (2004). Bulimia nervosa. In *Clinical Evidence – Mental Health* (pp. 33–46). London: BMJ books.

Halvorsen, I., Andersen, A., and Heyerdahl, S. (2004). Good outcome of adolescent onset anorexia nervosa after systematic treatment: Intermediate to long-term follow-up of a representative county-sample. *European Child* and *Adolescent Psychiatry*, *10*, 295–306.

Helverskov, J. L., Clausen, L., Mors, O., Frydenberg, M., Thomsen, P., and Rokkedal, K. (2010). Trans-diagnostic outcome of eating disorders: A 30-month follow-up study of 629 patients. *European Eating Disorders Review*, *18* (6), 453–463.

Herpertz-Dahlmann, B., Müller, B., Herpertz, S., Heussen, N., Hebebrand, J., and Remschmidt, H. (2001). Prospective 10-year follow-up in adolescent anorexia nervosa – course, outcome, psychiatric morbidity and psychosocial adaptation. *Journal of Child Psychology and Psychiatry*, *42* (5), 603–612.

Herzog, D. B., Dorer, D. J., Keel, P. K., Selwyn, S. E., Ekeblad, E. R., Flores A. T., et al. (1999). Recovery and relapse in anorexia and bulimia nervosa: A 7.5-year follow-up study. *Journal of the American Academy of Child and Adolescent Psychiatry*, *38*, 829–837.

Herzog, W., Rathner, G., and Vandereycken, W. (1992). Long-term course of anorexia nervosa. A review of the literature. In W. Herzog, J. Detre and W. Vandereycken (Eds), *The Course of Eating Disorders* (pp. 15–29). Berlin: Springer Verlag.

Hsu, L. K., Crisp, A. H., Harding, B. (1979). Outcome of anorexia nervosa. *The Lancet*, *313* (8107), 61–65.

Hsu, L. K. G. (1996). Outcome of early onset anorexia nervosa: What do we know? *Journal of Youth and Adolescence*, *25* (4), 563–569.

Kaye, W. H., Nagata, T., Weltzin, T. E., Hsu, G., Sokol, M. S., Conaha, C. M., et al.

(2001). Double-blind placebo controlled administration of fluoxeting in restricting- and restricting-purging-type anorexia nervosa. *Biological Psychiatry, 49,* 644–652.

Kouba, S., Hällström, T., Lindholm, C., and Hirschberg, A. L. (2005). Pregnancy and neonatal outcomes in women with eating disorders. *Obstetrics and Gynaecology, 105* (2), 255–260.

Lock, J., Agras, W., Bryson, S., and Kraemer, H. (2005). A comparison of short and long term family therapy for adolescent anorexia nervosa. *Journal of the American Academy of Child and Adolescent Psychiatry, 44,* 632–639.

Lucas, A. R., Melton, L. J., Crowson, C. S., and O'Fallon, W. M. (1999). Long-term fracture risk among women with anorexia nervosa: A population based cohort study. *Mayo Clinic Proceedings, 74,* 972–977.

Mitchell, J. E., Fletcher, L., Hanson, K., Mussell, M. P., Seim, H., Crosby, R. et al. (2001). The relative efficacy of fluoxetine and manual based self help in the treatment of out-patients with buklimia nervosa. *Journal of Clinical Psychopharmacology, 21,* 298–304.

Morgan, H. G., and Hayward, A. E. (1988). Clinical assessment of anorexia nervosa. The Morgan-Russell Assessment Schedule. *British Journal of Psychiatry, 152,* 367–372.

National Commissioning Centre for Mental Health (NCCMH) (2004). *Eating disorders: Core interventions in the treatment and management of anorexia nervosa, bulimia nervosa and related eating disorders; a national clinical practice guideline.* London: National Institute for Clinical Excellence/British Psychological Society.

Nicholls, D., Chater, R., and Lask, B. (2000). Children into DSM don't go. A comparison of classification systems for eating disorders in children and early adolescence. *International Journal of Eating Disorders, 28,* 317–324.

Nielsen, S., Moller-Madsen, S., Isager, T., Jorgensen, J., Pagsberg, K., and Theander, S. (1998). Standardized mortality in eating disorders – a quantitative summary of previously published and new evidence. *Journal of Psychosomatic Research, 44,* 413–434.

Nilsson, K. (2007). *Recovery from adolescent onset anorexia nervosa; a longitudinal study.* Umeå, Sweden: Print and Media.

Nilsson, K., and Hägglöf, B. (2005). Long-term follow-up of adolescent anorexia nervosa in Northern Sweden. *European Eating Disorders Review, 13,* 89–100.

North, C., and Gowers, S. (1999). Anorexia nervosa, psychopathology and outcome. *International Journal of Eating Disorders, 26,* 386–391.

North, C., Gowers, S., and Bryam, V. (1997). Family functioning and life events in the outcome of adolescent anorexia nervosa. *British Journal of Psychiatry, 171,* 545–549.

Patton, G. C., Coffey, C., and Sawyer, S. M. (2003). The outcome of adolescent eating disorders: findings from the Victorian Adolescent Health Cohort Study. *European Child and Adolescent Psychiatry, 12,* 25–29.

Pike, K. M., Walsh, B. T., Vitousek, K., Wilson, G. T., and Bauer, J. (2003). Cognitive behavioral therapy in the post-hospital treatment of anorexia nervosa. *American Journal of Psychiatry, 160,* 2046–2049.

Quadflieg, N., and Fichter, M. (2003). The course and outcome of bulimia nervosa. *European Child and Adolescent Psychiatry, 12,* 99–109.

Råstam, M., Gillberg, C., and Wentz, E. (2003). Outcome of teenage-onset anorexia nervosa in a Swedish community-based sample. *European Child and Adolescent Psychiatry, 12,* 78–90.

Ratnasuriya, R. H., Eisler, I., Szmukler, G. I., and Russell, G. F. (1991). Anorexia nervosa: Outcome and prognostic factors after 20 years. *British Journal of Psychiatry*, *158*, 495–502.

Robin, A. L., Siegel, P. T., Moye A. W., Gilroy M., Dennis A. B., and Sikand, A. (1999). A controlled comparison of family versus individual therapy for adolescents with anorexia nervosa. *Journal of the American Academy of Child and Adolescent Psychiatry*, *38*, 1482–1489.

Russell, G. F. M (1992). Anorexia nervosa of early onset and its impact on puberty. In P. Cooper (ed.), *Feeding Problems and Eating Disorders in Children and Adolescents* (pp. 85–112). Chur, Switzerland: Harwood Academic.

Saccomani, L., Savoini, M., Cirrincione, M., Vercellino, F., and Ravera, G. (1998). Long-term outcome of children and adolescents with anorexia nervosa: Study of comorbidity. *Journal of Psychosomatic Research*, *44* (5), 565–571.

Scholz, M., and Asen, E. (2001). Multiple family therapy with eating disordered adolescents. *European Eating Disorders Review*, *9*, 33–42.

Serfaty, M. A. (1998). Cognitive therapy versus dietary counseling in the out-patient treatment of anorexia nervosa. *European Eating Disorders Review*, *7*, 334–350.

Steinhausen, H. C. (1999). Eating disorders. In H.C. Steinhausen and F. Verhulst (Eds), *Risks and Outcomes in Developmental Psychopathology*, pp. 210–230. Oxford: Oxford University Press.

Steinhausen, H. C. (2002). The outcome of anorexia nervosa in the twentieth century. *American Journal of Psychiatry*, *159* (8), 1284–1293.

Steinhausen, H. C., Boyadjieva, S., Griogoroiu-Serbanescu, M., and Neumarker, K. J. (2003). The outcome of adolescent eating disorders: Findings from an international collaborative study. *European Child* and *Adolescent Psychiatry*, *12*, 91–98.

Strober, M., Freeman, R., and Morrell, W. (1997). The long-term course of severe anorexia nervosa in adolescents: survival analysis of recovery, relapse, and outcome predictors over 10–15 years in a prospective study. *International Journal of Eating Disorders*, *22*, 339–360.

Treasure, J., and Schmidt, U. (2004). *Anorexia nervosa: Clinical Evidence*, pp. 1–12. London: BMJ Books.

Wentz, E., Gillberg, I. C., Anckarsater, H., Gillberg, C., and Rastam, M. (2009). Adolescent-onset anorexia nervosa: 18-year outcome. *British Journal of Psychiatry*, *194* (2), 168–174.

Whittington, C. J., Kendall, T., Fonagy, P., Cottrell, D., Cotgrove, A., and Boddington, E. (2004). Selective serotonin reuptake inhibitors in childhood depression – a systematic review of published versus unpublished data. *The Lancet*, *363*, 1341–1345.

World Health Organization (1993). *The ICD-10 classification of mental and behavioural disorders*. Geneva: WHO.

Zipfel, S., Seibel, M. J., Lowe, B., Beumont, P. J., Kasperk, C., and Herzog, W. (2001). Osteoporosis in eating disorders: A follow-up study of patients with anorexia and bulimia. *Journal of Clinical Endocrinology and Metabolism*, *86*, 5227–5233.

Part III

Management

Chapter 10

Overview of management

Bryan Lask and Rachel Bryant-Waugh

Overview

In this chapter we offer an overview of the management of early onset eating disorders. We emphasise the importance of a comprehensive approach that focuses on biological, social and psychological factors within the context of a well-coordinated multi-disciplinary team. Of equal importance is the involvement of, and close collaboration with parents, from the start, and the creation of a therapeutic alliance with the child. The details of specific therapeutic approaches are discussed in subsequent chapters.

Introduction

The treatment of eating disorders in childhood and adolescence presents many challenges. People with anorexia nervosa are terrified by the thought of eating and weight gain, overwhelmed with self-disgust and often suffering from co-morbid depression and/or obsessive compulsive disorder. In addition they may have specific cognitive impairments (see Chapter 8). Their inadequate diet frequently gives rise to serious physical complications, which in turn may exacerbate the psychological problems. As part of this vicious cycle these problems may be compounded by the fact that many do not accept that they are ill and have not chosen to enter treatment. Similarly with the other early onset eating disorders there are significant psychological problems, and commonly cognitive and physical complications. The disorders have a complex pathogenesis and the potential for a poor outcome.

Clearly, therefore, a rapidly initiated treatment programme is indicated. In all but the mildest cases this will need to be both intensive and comprehensive. This chapter offers an overview of such a programme as provided in our own work contexts, and in subsequent chapters some of the more specific treatments are described in depth. It is acknowledged that resources vary between services, but it should be possible to provide the key components of the programme with relatively few staff.

There is no one treatment of choice and typically combinations of treatment are needed (NICE, 2004). In practice, though far from desirable, the choice of specific therapies is determined as much by availability as by need. However, regardless of what disciplines and therapies are available, good teamwork is essential. It is also vital that the parents should be involved, the principle being that the clinician's task is to help the parents help their child to overcome the eating disorder. A therapeutic alliance is integral to a successful outcome. Individual treatments such as motivational enhancement therapy, cognitive behavioural therapy, psychodynamic psychotherapy and cognitive remediation therapy may all have a part to play and input from dieticians, physiotherapists and teachers add to the chances of a good outcome.

Teamwork

The management of any childhood disorder requires collaboration between the child, parents and all the clinicians involved. The tendency of some early onset eating disorders to be associated with both resistance to treatment and severely compromised physical health makes such collaboration far harder than in most other forms of illness. At presentation it is not at all uncommon for the child/adolescent to appear to be in charge, with the parents trying to ensure their child is eating adequately and at the same time trying to avoid upsetting her. Commonly they end up achieving neither. The parents are frequently bewildered by the change in their daughter's behaviour and apparent self-destructiveness and overwhelmed by frustration and anxiety. It is all too easy for clinicians then to take control. Whilst in some ways this may be necessary, the danger is that in so doing the parents feel marginalised and even more disempowered.

In such circumstances it is essential to address the issues of leadership, roles and responsibilities, between the parents themselves, between the parents and the clinical team, and within the clinical team. On an outpatient basis the parents should be in charge as they spend up to 24 hours per day with their child. When she is well enough to share some responsibility she should be encouraged to do so, with the aim of her eventually taking age- and culturally appropriate responsibility for her eating. Throughout, the clinicians should be available as consultants, counsellors and advisers, their prime tasks being to support the parents in their efforts to help their daughter overcome her illness and to offer specific input such as nutritional counselling and various forms of therapy (see below). The specifics of working with the parents are discussed further below and in Chapter 13.

The situation differs in residential settings. Far more people become involved in the child's care and the potential for miscommunication, confusion and splitting is enormous. Indeed, these phenomena are likely to be the norm in early onset anorexia nervosa. At the core of the illness is confusion and contradiction, both of which are likely to be experienced, not only by the patient but also by her parents and the clinical team. It is almost inevitable therefore that splitting will occur as different people experience and identify with different aspects of the child.

In these circumstances the question of leadership is vital and it needs to be clear who is in charge. That person should have a good knowledge of early onset eating disorders, be able to work effectively with colleagues to adopt a comprehensive approach to assessment and treatment, and be willing to work collaboratively with the parents (see Chapter 13). Once assessment is complete a treatment plan should be constructed, with the aims, content, roles and responsibilities of all involved clearly outlined. Each of these components plays an important part in the recovery process, but, if not clearly defined, can obstruct recovery. The aims should be formulated on the basis of the comprehensive assessment and should incorporate far more than just the restoration of weight. These aims therefore include (i) refeeding and restoration of overall physical health; (ii) enhancement of motivation to maintain healthy weight and cessation of compensatory behaviours; (iii) establishment of a shared understanding of underlying problems; (iv) resumption of normal and age-appropriate behaviour

Each person on the team, including the parents, needs to be clear regarding their roles since confusion and overlapping of roles commonly occurs. All too often team members reach beyond their remit. For example, several people on a team might participate in some form of individual work involving exploration and discussion of the child's feelings and behaviour. This cannot be helpful to the child or to the recovery process. Role clarification needs to be achieved at the start of the treatment process if the intensification of confusion and splitting is to be avoided.

A linked theme is that of responsibility. The potential for severe harm that accompanies some of the eating disorders places an enormous burden upon parents and clinicians. Clinicians often feel challenged by the potential of failing their patients and even at times impotent in the face of treatment resistance. In consequence they redouble their efforts. The problem with this is that the child may react by intensifying her resistance and the parents react by relinquishing any residual responsibility. This process is quite the opposite to what should be achieved – a collaborative approach to overcoming the illness with shared responsibility for so doing.

The necessary consideration of the involvement of the wider community – the illness network (Lask and Fosson, 1989) – makes matters even more complex. Within the family are the grandparents, who can be particularly influential, as well as siblings, aunts and uncles. Additionally there is often involvement of other clinicians not on the immediate team, such as the family doctor, community-based mental health professionals, and many others such as teachers. Each of these people may have contact with, and influence upon, the child. In consequence they all need to be taken into account, to some degree, when constructing a treatment plan.

The content of the treatment plan will differ from case to case and is discussed further below. Once it has been agreed, it is useful to document the decisions so that there is less potential for misunderstanding, confusion and splitting. Everyone, including the parents and child, should, as much as possible, contribute to drawing up the treatment plan and therefore have access to its documentation.

Another key ingredient to a successful treatment programme is that of consistency. Consistency can be considered at two levels: consistency between individuals and consistency over time. For example, the parents need to be consistent between each other in their approach to their child's management. It won't help the child if the father takes one approach, perhaps a coercive one, and the mother adopts the opposite. Even if they adopt a similar approach, there is a danger that they will not persevere with the approach and resort to a change before it has had a chance to have an effect. Parents commonly say they 'have tried everything'. But change can take a long time and will be compromised by frequent changes in the treatment plan. It is far more likely to occur in the context of a consistent approach to management. Therefore consistency between carers and consistency over time are both necessary. This applies equally to consistency between the parents and the clinical team and within the clinical team. With so many people involved this becomes a difficult aim to achieve and yet an important one. Much recovery is hampered by inconsistency.

It is wise to hold regular reviews to ascertain what progress has been made. For those who are very unwell this may need to occur frequently, although the treatment plan should not necessarily be changed simply because of lack of progress. Changes to the plan should be made only if there is obvious deterioration or a failure to progress after a number of weeks. It should also be noted that when initiating refeeding it is not always possible to start with a weight-restoring diet. For example, if a child has previously been consuming only 600 calories daily then she will only be able to tolerate gradual increments (see below and Chapter 12) of approximately 200–300 calories every three days. This means that it will take at least two weeks before weight gain can occur.

The management of early onset eating disorders can be complex, frustrating and challenging. Although commonly the least experienced at managing eating disorders, parents or junior nurses are in the front line. In consequence it is important to ensure sufficient support for those in such positions in the form of frequent counselling for parents and regular supervision for staff. Regular opportunities for continuing education should be integral to any eating disorders treatment programme.

Collaboration with parents

'Our job is to help you as parents to help your daughter fight and overcome her eating disorder': This is the mantra we offer to parents of children with eating disorders. Successful treatment is dependent upon the creation of a good working relationship with the parents and their child. It is the clinician's task to help the parents help their daughter to fight her eating disorder rather than fighting her. All too often parents and clinicians enter a struggle with the child instead of with the eating disorder. It is essential therefore to help the parents understand that their child has an illness that dictates her thoughts, feelings and behaviour. She is not choosing to behave this way, even though it may appear that she is. We use the analogy of another illness, e.g. pneumonia in which there is fever, cough, difficulty with breathing and extreme fatigue. These are features of the illness and not chosen by the person with pneumonia. We would not get angry with someone with pneumonia, nor tell them to breathe properly, stop coughing and behave normally. Parents commonly find this conceptualisation helpful in beginning to understand the very dramatic change in their previously normal child. We develop this theme of 'externalisation' further in Chapter 11.

The next requirement for the establishment of a successful collaboration with parents is the provision of information. Explanation and education form an essential part of the management of the eating disorders. Parents and child need a clear statement about the diagnosis, the course and complications of the condition, possible perpetuating factors and proposed treatment. Parents are understandably eager to understand the cause of their child's illness, but this rarely proves fruitful. Given the multifactorial aetiology of the eating disorders (see Chapter 5), we are extremely unlikely to understand the detailed pathogenesis of one particular person's eating disorder. It generally proves more useful to focus on those factors that may be maintaining the problem and to find ways of overcoming them.

Parental understanding of the seriousness or otherwise of their child's problem is very variable. For example, in anorexia nervosa some parents are stunned to discover how ill their child has become. In other instances they have had considerable difficulty convincing clinicians to take their child's eating difficulties seriously. In contrast, parents of 'selective eaters' (see Chapter 4) are often convinced that their child has suffered, or will suffer, irreversible damage because of their limited range of foods. These worries may occur despite the fact that their child is obviously in very good health.

We find it helpful to adopt a clear method of conveying our understanding of the situation. This varies depending upon the diagnosis and its implications. In anorexia nervosa, having completed the initial assessment, we might make a statement such as:

'As you are probably aware Alison has anorexia nervosa. You have probably read and heard quite a bit about this illness, but we think it might be helpful to explain it to you in some detail. It is hard to take everything in at once so we will provide you with information in writing and we will be happy to answer any questions at any time.

'Anorexia nervosa is a mean and mysterious disorder, which plays a lot of tricks and can be difficult to overcome. It makes Alison think she is fat when actually she is very thin, it makes her feel guilty when she eats, and it makes her see herself as a bad and useless person. It can even make her feel like it's her friend. It really can dominate her thoughts, feelings and behaviour.

'No one fully understands how it occurs but certainly there is no single cause and many different factors come together to create it. Parents sometimes wonder if it is something they have done wrong but there is no evidence that parents cause anorexia nervosa. It is actually more useful to try and identify what keeps it going, for this is usually something that we can tackle together. As parents you are in a strong position to help your daughter overcome it and that is why we will work closely with you to help you.

'Meanwhile, it is important to acknowledge that it is a serious illness and at least one-third of young people with anorexia nervosa don't make a full recovery. It can delay growth, impair development and fertility, and lead to osteoporosis and many other complications. Some people become desperately ill. Occasionally patients die from this illness. That is why we take it so seriously and why we must all work closely together to help her fight the illness.

'Fortunately we do know some of the factors that contribute to recovery. The children who do well are those whose parents are able to work well *together*, and are able to work *with us* to ensure their child's health. It is often a long hard struggle because the anorexia nervosa makes people so desperate to avoid gaining weight that they often resort to a wide range of methods to stay dangerously thin. These include, avoiding food, inducing vomiting, taking laxatives, and excessive exercising. You may think your daughter hasn't or wouldn't do these things but most people with anorexia nervosa from time to time use other methods beside food avoidance. So it will be necessary for a while for you to take responsibility for your daughter's health care, including what she eats. You will need to ensure that she doesn't vomit after meals, or use laxatives, or take excessive exercise. However, if you as parents can resolve to work together, and with us, to ensure her health, then we will all be doing everything we can to ensure a full recovery.

'When you leave here today it is very likely that she will tell you that we have got it all wrong and that we don't understand. She may promise to eat properly and beg you to give her a chance. It is important for you to understand that this is likely to be the 'anorexia' speaking. It really is like 'the enemy within' and it will fight all your efforts to overcome it. You will need to be strong and determined; at least as strong and as determined as the 'anorexia'. We will all have to fight together if we are to win.'

This sort of statement can be adjusted to suit the circumstances, and may be addressed predominantly to the parents or shared equally between child and parents. Using the child's name, rather than 'your daughter' probably has a greater impact. The analogy of a battle against a vicious and deceitful enemy is deliberately chosen for two reasons. First, this is so often just how it feels to all concerned. Second, it is useful to 'externalise' the problem so that the child does not feel even more persecuted (see Chapter 11). So often the parents believe that their daughter has deliberately chosen to behave this way, and respond accordingly by getting into fights with her. This is hardly helpful to a young person who is already in distress. It feels better to all concerned 'if we can all work together to fight the illness'.

The message we communicate to parents of children with selective eating is obviously quite different. In a child whose selectivity is not associated with significant risk, it might sound something like this:

'We are pleased to be able to tell you that your son's condition is nothing more serious than what is commonly called selective eating. This is a condition with which we are very familiar and is far more common than is generally realised and fortunately in most cases far less serious than you have probably feared. It can be understood as an extension of that normal phase you see in toddlers known as food faddiness. Most toddlers go through such a phase but usually grow out of it. Selective eaters seem to take much longer to grow out of it but fortunately most of them do so in their teenage years.

'As you can see your son is thriving. He is of normal weight and height for his age and shows no evidence of ill health. It is amazing how children can thrive on such a *narrow* range of foods, but clearly your son is having perfectly adequate *amounts* of food which are giving him all the necessary nutrients.

'The important thing to do here is just let him get on and eat what he likes rather than trying to make him eat foods he doesn't like. If you do try to make him eat foods he insists he does not like, this is likely to make the situation worse rather than better. I expect you have already discovered that for yourselves. He won't come to any harm and when he is ready he will gradually start trying other foods. No treatment is necessary at present but when he says he would like some help, we would be happy to offer it.'

Again the message can be adjusted to fit the circumstances. In those rare instances when selective eating does impair growth, is associated with significant nutritional deficiencies or has a serious negative impact on family or social functioning, we might offer a treatment programme including parental counselling and/or family work (Chapter 13) and cognitive behavioural therapy (Chapter 14).

Most parents seem to find this approach very helpful and appear grateful to us for being so clear and direct. Often they state that they have not previously been given any clear explanation of what is wrong. Understandably they also seem to value the opportunity to share the responsibility for their child's care.

We give all parents written information about eating disorders and recommend other reading. The handouts proved so useful that we published a Parent's Guide to Eating Disorders (Bryant-Waugh and Lask, 2004). At the next meeting we ensure sufficient time to answer further questions and discuss areas of concern or uncertainty. In our experience it has proved invaluable to provide this information and to allow considerable time for questions and concerns to be raised early in our contact with families. Otherwise unresolved anxieties can interfere with the process of treatment. Once the parents feel fully informed we can then move on to ensure that the adults take responsibility for tackling the eating disorder.

Important aspects of the eating disorders include: (i) their potential for severe damage to health; (ii) the anxiety this engenders; (iii) the child's frequent lack of insight; (iv) battles around control.

It is possible, therefore (as is commonly the case in anorexia nervosa), that the child or teenager may be seriously ill, have little insight into her condition and yet she fights vigorously to retain control over what she eats. Unsurprisingly, this exacerbates parental anxiety and the parents may find it hard even to think clearly, let alone to act firmly and consistently. In consequence one of the first clinical tasks, be it that of the physician, nurse, psychologist or family therapist, is to contain parental anxiety. The temptation to deal first with other matters such as exploring family history or offering management advice should be avoided.

Containing parental anxiety is done first by acknowledging the anxiety and encouraging expression and exploration of their concerns. Assurance is offered that we will provide as much support for the child and parents as is necessary and that we will be focusing on ensuring restoration of health. This process of containment gradually allows parents to think more clearly and to consider their options more calmly. The provision of information, as outlined above, runs in parallel with and assists this process.

People with anorexia nervosa often feel they have little control over their lives, and that the only two areas in which they can have control are their food intake and their weight. An understandable reaction is to over-control food intake, with a resultant sense of achievement. This ability to control food intake and body shape and size is so satisfying that it can develop an addictive quality. However, its health and life-threatening nature demands intervention.

For this reason it is vital that the adults responsible for the young person's welfare take charge. In the case of anorexia nervosa this will often seem to be against the child's apparent wishes. Giving a clear message that parents/adults should be taking charge can be even harder for the child as this is so commonly a change of approach. Previously the parents may have 'colluded' with their daughter's weight loss, either by not having noticed just how much weight she had lost, or by not intervening firmly enough once the weight loss had become obvious. Understandably parents may have considered that the weight loss was due to physical ill health and seek alternative explanations to self-starvation. Also, even when the weight loss becomes apparent, parents are often loath to take a firm approach for fear of upsetting their daughter. Commonly young people with anorexia nervosa become very angry when any attempt is made to discuss their eating habits and their weight. It is clear then that a key feature of management is that the adults responsible for the child's welfare take firm control. A clear statement to this effect should be made to the parents at an early stage, for example:

'You can see that Alison is very ill, having lost nearly a third of her body weight. You can also see that that she does not accept that she is ill. If this is allowed to continue unchecked, she will get worse and could even die. Therefore, as from this moment it is *not* appropriate for Alison to continue taking responsibility for her health and diet. She has shown you that she cannot do that safely. You must make a decision as to how you want to proceed from here, but it would be unwise to be influenced by Alison's protests. These protests are coming from the anorexia nervosa.'

At this stage it is likely that Alison will indeed be protesting, but if not she will almost certainly start to do so once discussion turns to her required food intake, for this is likely to be substantially greater than her current intake. The child may challenge the right of clinicians to dictate such terms or the right of her parents to take control, or she may start crying or screaming. Whatever the topic of discussion at the time the protest commences, it is important to demonstrate the battle for control to the parents, and to help them recognise the need for them to help their daughter to fight the eating disorder rather than to fight everyone else. This does not mean that the parents should take control over all aspects of their daughter's life, but specifically those concerning her health. It is important that she retains control in other areas of less immediate importance, such as the choice of clothing, hobbies, or friends.

This is a useful time to reiterate the importance of the parents working together, offering mutual support and agreeing a consistent plan of management. It is not at all unusual for parents to be in conflict over various issues, but particularly in relation to how to handle the eating disorder. One parent may feel unsupported or that the other is too strict or too lax. Frequently, the child is sided with one parent against the other. Clearly, the parents cannot be helpful to their daughter for as long as they are in disagreement.

Issues over which the parents may disagree, and therefore need help to resolve, include how to help their daughter to eat, whether or not they wish to accept treatment, and whether or not their child should be admitted to hospital. The clinician's role here is not to take sides but rather to offer advice, and to help the parents to reach agreement, preferably without being influenced by their daughter's protests.

It is sometimes difficult to feel sympathetic towards a child who has what initially appears to be a self-inflicted problem, who denies that she is ill and angrily rejects all attempts to help. Nonetheless, it is obviously important to acknowledge her distress, and a statement along the following lines may be helpful:

'Alison, I know that just now you are feeling very angry with me because of what I have said to your parents, and angry with them for listening to me. You may not believe me but I do understand not only how angry you are, but also that you may be worried about what has happened to you, and whether everything will get completely out of control. If your parents wish, I will help them to get you well again. We are not going to let you die and nor will we let you get overweight. If you have any questions I will do my best to answer them.'

Often at this point the child renews her protests or turns to her parents for support. It is helpful to note whether the parents are able to adopt a firmer and more united stance when this happens. If necessary the clinician can demonstrate how their daughter continues to control the situation by her protests or distress, and reiterate the need for her parents to take responsibility and not give way on life-threatening matters. It is always helpful to frame this as parents joining with their daughter in the fight against the illness rather than against her.

As treatment proceeds successfully there should be a gradual return of responsibility to the child so that ultimately she is taking full responsibility for her eating and health. The timing is crucial in that giving too much responsibility too soon almost always delays recovery. The emphasis is on 'gradual', with a degree of trial and error in the process.

It is important to emphasise that not all children with eating disorders will need such a vigorous approach. Indeed, selective eaters for example (see Chapter 4) are rarely physically ill and the parents may need help to allay their anxieties and to accept that their child is not ill (see earlier). Some children with food avoidance emotional disorder (see Chapter 4) lose as much weight as those with anorexia nervosa and their parents will need to adopt a similar approach. Others, however, are less ill and may benefit more from their parents adopting an approach that is less focused on eating and more on their underlying sadness or anxiety.

Similarly children with functional dysphagia (Chapter 4) need an approach that tackles their dread of vomiting, choking, or suffocating. Coercion to eat will have the most dramatic adverse effects. Parental responsibility here is to ensure their child receives the appropriate help needed to overcome the fears and is encouraged to progress at the right pace.

Bulimia nervosa requires yet another approach, in that most young people with this disorder accept that they have a problem and want help. Often, however, their parents have taken to monitoring all their activities in an attempt to stop them from bingeing or vomiting. Although it is perfectly reasonable for parents to try to help, it is usually more helpful if they do so by agreeing a plan, both between each other and with their daughter. People with bulimia nervosa are usually far more able to accept help than those with anorexia nervosa, and are able to explore with their parents strategies to help them resist the urge to binge and purge.

Motivation

It is important to consider the child's motivation, as their stage of ability and willingness (readiness) to change will determine to some extent the treatment. A child in 'pre-contemplation', without insight and with determined resistance to change, requires a totally different approach to management from that required by a child in 'action' or 'maintenance' who is eager for help. The more motivated the child, the more responsibility she should have for her treatment programme. Assessment and enhancement of motivation are discussed in depth in Chapter 11.

Re-feeding

The implementation or restoration of healthy eating patterns is one of the main goals of treatment for nearly all the eating disorders. However, this should be distinguished from refeeding, i.e. ensuring adequate nutrition and hydration. This is only indicated when there is evidence of nutritional deficiency such as electrolyte deficiency, dehydration, circulatory failure, or growth delay, as might be found in anorexia nervosa, functional dysphagia, food avoidance emotional disorder, and pervasive refusal syndrome (all discussed further in Chapter 4). Young people with bulimia nervosa are generally at normal weight and the main risks are of electrolyte imbalance and complications of recurrent vomiting. Selective eaters rarely show evidence of physical complications and early restoration of healthy eating patterns is not necessary. Indeed, it tends to occur spontaneously during the teenage years and there is usually no need for treatment unless the child specifically requests it or there is evidence of significant risk.

This distinction between refeeding and regularising eating patterns is of considerable importance. Refeeding must take priority when physical well-being is at risk. How, when or what a young person eats and drinks is far less important than that she eats and drinks sufficiently to restore physical health. Selective eaters are a good example of the fact that a seemingly inadequate and unhealthy diet can actually be perfectly adequate and healthy.

When indicated, refeeding may be achieved orally, by feeding through nasogastric or more rarely gastrostomy tubes. The decision on how to proceed is made on the urgency of the situation. When a child is severely dehydrated or has electrolyte deficiency, a delay of more than a few hours can be dangerous. In consequence, it is reasonable to spend some time encouraging and helping the child to eat and drink, but if there is no immediate success further delay in instituting artificial feeding is not advisable. Fortunately, most children do not require artificial feeds and respond over time to encouragement to resume sufficient nutritional intake.

Whether this is best achieved by a graded refeeding programme (see below and Chapter 12) or trying to impose a normal diet immediately is debatable. In fact, it really does not matter at this stage how, when, or where calories are consumed, so long as the intake is adequate. In general, however, children whose weight loss is not too severe, whose illness is of recent onset, and who are being treated on an outpatient basis, should be encouraged to resume a normal eating pattern and diet as soon as possible. For children whose weight loss is substantial or long lasting, it may be easier and safer for them to resume eating if offered a *graded* refeeding programme.

Graded refeeding

The full details of such a programme are described in Chapter 12. When dietary intake has been very low it is best to start with a slight increase on the current calorie total. Initially this may mean fewer than 1000 calories daily for a few days. Once the child is used to having slightly more there can be further increments of 200–300 calories every two to three days. How the diet is constituted can be determined by discussion between child, parents and a dietician. Although it is important to try to include foods that the child likes and are appealingly presented, it is also important that the adults take ultimate responsibility for determining the diet. (A useful tip is that a small portion served on a large plate is more likely to be consumed than the same portion served on a small plate!)

The dietician is an invaluable member of the clinical team. Her role is to act as a consultant to the parents and other members of the clinical team. She can be particularly helpful in a number of ways including:

- planning an intake acceptable to the child;
- increasing the intake gradually as food becomes less 'scary';
- recommending substitutions as necessary;

- emphasising the essential nutrients;
- advising regarding supplements such as high calorie drinks.

We do not believe that the dietician should offer individual support and counselling to this younger age group. The potential for splitting is far too high and we have seen time and again children who mislead the dietician with regard to what they are actually eating and then mislead their parents or the clinicians with regard to what the dietician has said. It is far better for the dietician to be a consultant to the parents and team advising on the meal plan (see Chapter 12).

Nasogastric and gastrostomy feeding

When the child's physical state demands immediate refeeding and if this cannot be achieved orally, a nasogastric feeding programme should be implemented. Such a programme is carefully co-ordinated with liaison between medical and nursing staff and the dietician. The aim should be to ensure the child is receiving an adequate diet and preferably in the region of 2000–3000 calories daily. It is usually helpful to tell the child exactly what the planned intake will be and to say that any amount taken by mouth will be deducted from the 24-hour total nasogastric feed (see Chapter 12).

Nasogastric feeding of young people with eating disorders does cause some concern with regard to the infringement of rights and the mistaken view that this is 'force-feeding'. If a child has a life-threatening illness and is unable to consume sufficient nutrition, there is general agreement within paediatric practice that artificial feeding by nasogastric tube is perfectly acceptable and no one would consider such action as infringing the child's rights. However, because anorexia nervosa and some of the other eating disorders present with the child refusing to eat sufficiently, anxieties then arise about overruling the child's wishes. Such views are based on an underlying misunderstanding of the psychopathology, which renders the child just as unable to eat adequate amounts as a child with any illness that impairs the appetite. If the child's life or long-term health is put at risk by the diminished intake, then whatever the underlying illness, remedial action has to be taken (see Chapter 17 for a fuller discussion of the ethical issues).

The intended course of action should always be discussed with the child and her parents and their agreement sought. Surprisingly, it is very rare for a child to refuse. It seems that most children in these circumstances are relieved that the responsibility for eating is taken away from them, at least temporarily. As much as possible they should always be given choices about who passes the tube, where and with whom present. If a child does strongly object to nasogastric feeding, in a few extreme cases she can be offered the alternative of intravenous feeds (see later), although there are risks related to this that also need to be taken into account.

There is some debate as to whether or not nasogastric feeds should be administered at night. The advantage of night feeding is purported to be that the child can lead as normal a life as possible during the day without being perceived as being different from others. This potential advantage is often outweighed by the possibility of her interfering with the feeds during the night. Further, whether or not repeated passing of the tube each evening is useful is unclear. Some children find it aversive and quickly opt to eat adequate amounts by mouth, whereas others very quickly adapt to it and pass their own tubes. Other disadvantages of overnight feeds include the discomfort associated with being fed while lying in bed and the fact that it is physiologically unnatural to be fed overnight. On balance, it is likely that daytime bolus feeding is more likely to hasten a normal eating pattern than overnight feeding. Occasionally, children can seem to become dependent on the tube and make no effort to eat normally:

Hannah, 12, was admitted to hospital having lost 52 per cent of her weight over a 12-month period. Her physical state was such that artificial feeding was essential. She refused to eat or drink anything by mouth for a further 18 months. All efforts to withdraw nasogastric feeding failed. Eventually, Hannah started eating normally after living with a foster family for six months.

Such circumstances are unusual and possibly in her case related more to her fear of returning to her family than to dependency on the tube. There is no evidence that long-term dependency on tube feeding does occur. In general, however, nasogastric tube feeding should be seen as a life-saving measure, preferably to be used for time-limited periods.

In extreme circumstances gastrostomy feeding may need to be considered. The indications for such an approach would be the same as those for nasogastric feeds but with the added complication that the patient is actively resisting the feeds to the point of fighting against them and withdrawing the tube herself. Gastrostomy feeds are easier to administer under such circumstances and it is much harder for the patient to withdraw the tube which is much more easily secured.

Finally, an audit of child and parent responses to nasogastric tube feeding has shown that in retrospect the vast majority of children who had been tube-fed and their parents were grateful that such action had been taken and had few regrets (Neiderman, Richardson, Farley, and Lask, 2001). The fact that the treatment was perceived as lifesaving far out-ruled any concerns about its intrusiveness. Their main criticism related to the manner in which the topic was raised, noting that all too often it had been presented punitively. Neiderman, Zardy, Tattersall, and Lask (2000) have described the successful use of gastrostomy feeding in these extreme circumstances.

Intravenous feeding

Intravenous feeding may on very rare occasions be used as an alternative to nasogastric feeds. All necessary nutrients are fed directly into a vein via an indwelling needle or catheter. The advantages are rapid rehydration and electrolyte replacement. The disadvantages are that it can only be implemented on a medical or paediatric ward and for short periods. Intravenous feeding is best reserved for the very rare times when immediate fluid or electrolyte replacement are required and the child can tolerate neither oral, nasogastric nor gastrostomy feeds.

Weight and target weights

In most of the early onset eating disorders, achieving and maintaining a healthy weight is invariably a matter of concern to parents, but it is only those young people with anorexia nervosa and bulimia nervosa who are unduly preoccupied with their weight. The others have unusual eating patterns for other reasons and are rarely concerned about their weight.

Thus, when considering what constitutes a healthy weight range the reactions are likely to differ depending upon the type of eating disorder. In anorexia nervosa there is such a preoccupation with and dread of weight gain that the clinician's reaction may reflect this. The temptation is either to distract the child from this theme, to fix a very specific target weight, or to become embroiled in endless discussions and negotiations about the target. Clinicians are often as preoccupied with a correct weight as are their patients.

We do not find any of these approaches in the least bit helpful. Attempting to determine a specific target is at best arbitrary as the 'ideal' for any individual will fall within a range dependent upon a number of factors including age, gender, height and genetic make-up. It is completely unclear how to determine which end of this range is the 'correct' one, thus it is impossible to know prospectively what is right for any one individual. Furthermore weighing is an inexact science; individual weight varies by up to one kilogram within any 24-hour period, and can be dependent upon accuracy of scales, time of day, relation to recent food intake and bowel and bladder activity. It can be manipulated by water-loading, concealing of objects to increase apparent weight, and posture on the scales.

Even if a target is set, on the basis of population norms for age, gender, and height population, regardless of its arbitrariness, this will then lead to considerable challenging and manipulation by the young person concerned. She may disagree with the target set and ensure that she stays below that point. Inpatients who want to avoid going home are even more likely to do this. Conversely she may wish to show that she has gained weight even though she has not, and does so by water-loading or concealing weights in her clothing or on her body. Some inpatients will achieve the target as quickly as they can so that they can be discharged home where they will lose the weight as quickly as they can.

For all these reasons we prefer to avoid completely the concept of a target weight. It is certainly possible to give the young person an idea of what constitutes a healthy weight range for someone of her age and height, but it is important to emphasise that we do not know if this will be right for her. Furthermore, we avoid getting into debates about this.

Pelvic ultrasound scanning (see Chapter 6) can be very helpful in determining a healthy weight. Once the ovaries and uterus have reached the appropriate size, shape and appearance for age, we know that they are mature and that the weight is satisfactory. In consequence we carry out regular pelvic ultrasound scans and discuss the findings with the individual concerned. Most girls reach ovarian and uterine maturity at between 95 and 100 per cent weight–height ratios. However, some achieve maturity at much lower weights, whereas a few need to be higher. For example, one pair of 13 year old twins, both had a weight–height ratio of 130 per cent at the start of their illness. Menstruation ceased when the ratio dropped to 115 per cent and by the time they had reached 105 per cent both were very ill. With refeeding, menstruation resumed at 115 per cent.

If clinicians, like the patients, feel obliged to focus on weight and targets, it is more helpful to use the concept of anticipated weight gain. This can be done by plotting on a graph the anticipated weights on a monthly basis. This is illustrated in Figure 10.1 which shows that the current weight is 27 kg (weight–height ratio 75 per cent) and the estimated healthy weight range is between 34 and 36 kg (weight for height ratio 95–100 per cent). As weight recovery takes time (approximately 2 to 3 kg per month), and during the childhood and teenage years weight and height should be increasing as time goes by, the estimated weight range should take these factors into account. Therefore, in the case example in Figure 10.1, the projected weight after one month is 29.5 kg, after two months 32.3 kg, and after three months 35 kg. Thereafter, the projected weight will be between the two lines representing 95 and 100 per cent weight–height ratio. This can be quite confusing for a young person who is already very frightened by the prospect of weight gain and it is helpful to let her have a copy of the graph. This

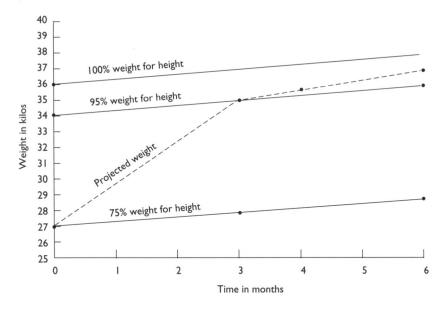

Figure 10.1 A sample growth chart (Lask, 1993, reprinted with permission).

is obviously particularly important for boys, for whom pelvic ultrasound is inapplicable.

Pelvic ultrasound examination can be repeated at approximately three-monthly intervals, and once maturity is shown on ultrasound no further weight gain is required. Menstruation usually commences or returns within three months of maturity being attained, but can take up to a year.

Family approaches

Working with the family, and especially the parents, is a sine qua non of the management of any child or adolescent with an eating disorder. The importance of collaborative work with the parents has been emphasised earlier in this chapter and family work generally is discussed in detail in Chapter 13.

Cognitive and behavioural therapy

The cognitive and behavioural therapy (CBT) approach to therapy is commonly used in the treatment of early onset eating disorders. It seems to be particularly helpful in bulimia nervosa, selective eating and functional dysphagia, but may also be used in the other eating disorders. A full account of these techniques is provided in Chapter 14.

Individual psychotherapy

Psychodynamically oriented psychotherapy has for some time been in common use in the treatment of early onset eating disorders. Its effectiveness has often been taken for granted in the absence of any evidence. Nonetheless in those instances where psychopathology is deeply entrenched it surely has a part to play. A full account of its application is provided in Chapter 15.

Cognitive remediation therapy

Cognitive remediation therapy (CRT) differs from other approaches through its emphasis on the process of thoughts and perceptions rather than their content. It is based upon the existence of the cognitive weaknesses commonly found in anorexia nervosa (see Chapter 8) and the remediation of these by application of games, puzzles and other fun activities. CRT is discussed fully in Chapter 16.

Group work

Group work is commonly used in inpatient units for the management of eating disorders. These include groups for children, teenagers and parents and can take the form of discussions, psycho-education, art, drama, dance, body awareness, and social skills training. There has been no evaluation of such approaches other than of multifamily groups (see Chapter 13). One of the main concerns is that such groups are commonly led by clinicians with little or no understanding or experience of group dynamics and group therapy. On inpatient units such groups may be led by 'whoever is available'. This is a worrying trend in that the subtlety and complexity of group phenomena are often neglected in such circumstances, which can hardly be to the benefit of the patients. Behr and Hearst (2005, 203–19) have offered a helpful guide to managing the complexities of groups for children and adolescents, and the techniques for leading such groups.

Physical activity and exercise

Physical activity and exercise play a major part in weight control in anorexia nervosa and sometimes in bulimia nervosa. Levels of activity may vary from marked inactivity (possibly relating to lowered mood) to damaging overactivity. Clinicians are often preoccupied with attempting to reduce overactivity as a means of trying to help reduce excessive calorie expenditure. However, little is known about how best to assess and manage pathological activity. Decisions are sometimes made in the absence of objective assessments and without consideration of the patient's physical and psychological need for exercise. In particular it is often not acknowledged that physical activity is necessary for: (i) general health; (ii) the prevention of osteoporosis, for which many adolescents with eating disorders are at risk, and (iii) in alleviating anxiety and depression. Therefore it is wise to support a healthy degree of activity, even in those whose nutritional state is inadequate. The amount should be determined by physical status. Only in the most physically compromised should physical activity be completely curtailed. This whole problematic area is comprehensively covered in a special issue of *European Eating Disorders Review* (Meyer, 2011).

Medication

In the current state of knowledge, medication has but a small part to play in the management of eating disorders.

Appetite stimulants, vitamins and food supplements

It is debatable whether there are any true appetite stimulants, but in any event they would have little part to play given that, with the possible exception of food avoidance emotional disorder, there is rarely a true loss of appetite. Nor is there is any evidence that vitamin or mineral supplements enhance appetite. Deficiencies of these substances are usually rapidly remedied by the implementation of a normal diet. What little evidence exists suggests that supplementation is no more effective than a refeeding programme in overcoming the deficiencies (e.g. Lask, Fosson, Thomas, and Rolfe, 1993). However, Ayton (2004) has shown in an open trial that omega-3 polyunsaturated fatty acids (PUFAs) supplementation has led to symptomatic improvement.

Anxiolytics and atypical antipsychotics

Anxiolytics and atypical antipsychotics have a very limited role. There have been a number of open and uncontrolled trials of such medications in anorexia nervosa but with sparse evidence as yet of any effect upon the core psychopathology. The same applies for bulimia nervosa. Nor is there any convincing evidence of their value in other eating disorders despite the fact that anxiety, phobias and obsessionality often accompany such conditions. Anxiolytics, particularly alprazolam, may be of some help in functional dysphagia. Both anxiolytics, such as hydroxyzine, and atypical antipsychotics, such as risperidol, olanzepine and amisulpiride may be helpful when used for short periods for those children suffering from extreme anxiety or distress associated with the eating disorder.

Antidepressants

Antidepressants do have a slightly more useful role in early onset eating disorders associated with depression. In many cases of depression accompanying anorexia nervosa, the depression lifts with adequate nutrition. However, in some instances the accompanying depression, associated with psychomotor retardation, feelings of guilt and worthlessness and biological changes such as poor sleep and diurnal mood variation, does not respond to nutritional rehabilitation. In these circumstances some of the selective serotonin reuptake inhibitors (SSRIs) such as fluoxetine do seem to have value. In addition the SSRIs have been shown to reduce the urge to binge in adults with bulimia nervosa (American Psychological Association, 1994), although this is yet to be shown in the younger population. In any event there is increasing restriction on the use of SSRIs in the under-18s because of an alleged increase in suicidal behaviour. Some of the newer generation of antidepressants, such as venlafaxine and mirtazepine, which contain a strong anxiolytic element, may be of more value. However their use in the younger population is also restricted.

Caution should always be taken when using psychotropic medication in the younger population. It is wise to check for normal cardiovascular, hepatic and renal functioning, and to start with low doses building up slowly through weekly increments. Cessation of any such medication should be conducted gradually. A comprehensive overview of the use and abuse of medication in childhood and adolescence has been provided by Lask, Taylor, and Nunn (2003).

Treatment of low bone density and delayed growth

There are major concerns regarding the possibility of irreversibility of osteopenia and osteoporosis. The value of calcium and vitamin D supplementation has yet to be established (see Chapter 6) although various centres do use them. The recommended dose is 1500 mg calcium daily and 400 IU of vitamin D. The best treatment is adequate nutrition and weight-bearing exercise. Oestrogen supplementation has until recently not been shown to be of value in child or adolescent eating disorders and incautious use may impair growth. Furthermore the associated monthly withdrawal bleeds are often misinterpreted as the resumption of menstruation. However Misra et al. (2011) have recently demonstrated that the use of transdermal administration of oestrogen supplementation in post-pubertal girls with osteopenia does increase bone-density (see Chapter 6). Bisphosphonates, shown to be useful in post-menopausal osteoporosis, should not be used in females of child-bearing age because of their teratogenic potential.

In longstanding eating disorders with markedly delayed growth and/or puberty, growth hormone or oestrogens may be indicated (testosterone for boys) but generally hormonal treatment should be avoided in the younger population. The treatment of these disorders of the musculo-skeletal system should be left to specialists and not managed by physicians or psychiatrists who lack the relevant expertise.

Finally, it is worth cautioning against the use of laxatives when constipation is troublesome. This is best overcome by a combination of adequate diet and exercise. In particularly resistant constipation, laxatives may be inadequate and suppositories may be required. If they are to be used then adequate doses should be given and withdrawal must be gradual, as 'rebound' constipation is common.

Schooling considerations

Whatever the type of eating disorder and its severity, there will be a need to consider the child's schooling. It is always helpful to have information available from the school about the child's abilities, performance, peer relationships and eating behaviour. Schools may find it useful to know how to handle mealtimes, and of course schooling must be provided within the context of any hospital admission. It is also important to acknowledge that despite the fact that people with anorexia nervosa appear to be highly intelligent, in fact very commonly they have specific cognitive deficits (see Chapter 8) that make some of their school work harder for them than for others. This is rarely recognised and in practice means that such youngsters have to work even harder to achieve. Their determination, diligence and perfectionism give pleasure to the adults around them but often come at considerable cost.

Consideration of hospitalisation

An early and important decision that needs to be made involves whether or not the child or teenager needs hospitalisation. A range of factors needs to be considered in making this decision, including the child's physical and mental state, the parents' anxieties and the availability of appropriate resources. In general, we give serious consideration to the possibility of hospitalisation under any of the following circumstances:

192 Eating Disorders in Childhood and Adolescence

1   There is a rapid deterioration in physical status (see Chapter 6) as manifested by:

- severe weight loss;
- dehydration;
- circulatory failure, as shown by low blood pressure, slow or irregular pulse rate, low temperature or poor peripheral circulation;
- electrolyte deficiency;
- persistent vomiting or vomiting blood.

2   Marked depression, suicidal ideation or intent.
3   Other major psychiatric disturbance.
4   Failed outpatient treatment.

In practice, this means that those young people most likely to need hospital admission are those with anorexia nervosa and pervasive refusal syndrome (which cannot be treated on an outpatient basis). Less commonly, admission may be necessary for those with bulimia nervosa, food avoidance emotional disorder and functional dysphagia. Selective eaters very rarely require admission.

The clinician's task is to advise the parents so that they can make an informed decision. It is perfectly reasonable to attempt a brief trial of outpatient treatment even for those who are seriously ill, but this should be very closely monitored. For those whose physical health is seriously compromised, progress should be reviewed on a day-by-day basis. If there is no immediate improvement the trial should be terminated and hospitalisation arranged.

It is also necessary to consider what resources are available. For urgent medical treatment such as rehydration or electrolyte replacement, admission to a paediatric unit is clearly appropriate. However, for the more long-term treatment of underlying emotional problems the emphasis in such a unit on immediate physical care makes admission less appropriate. In these circumstances if outpatient care has proved insufficient, admission to a unit that has some experience and expertise in the management of eating disorders in this age group should be considered. Ideally, there should be specialist units for young people with eating disorders, which can offer all aspects of the treatment required. However, there are few such units. A possible compromise involves a short admission to a paediatric unit for medical emergencies as required, linked with intensive outpatient treatment for the psychological issues. Day-care programmes have been shown to be of value for adults (Freeman, 1991) and their use for the younger population warrants consideration if the practicalities can be overcome. Whatever programme is being considered, it must be remembered that such patients need highly skilled age-appropriate mental health treatment allied with close medical supervision.

Stages of recovery

It is helpful to be aware of issues relating to both the pace and nature of change. The complexity and severity of eating disorders in young people, combined with the common resistance to change, are such that change is usually very slow. Furthermore, change is often accompanied by what initially appears to be deterioration. In anorexia nervosa particularly, but also with food avoidance emotional disorder, pervasive refusal syndrome, and sometimes other emotional disorders such as obsessive compulsive disorder, we have noticed specific patterns of behaviour which predominate at certain times. These are illustrated in Figure 10.2 and are usefully categorised as three stages. Stage 1 is that of the presenting problem, when the eating disorder is the predominant feature. The young person with anorexia nervosa tends to be preoccupied with weight and food intake almost to the exclusion of other considerations. With the possible exception of school-work, she shows no interest in anything else. She is unable to recognise that she has any problem other than that 'stupid adults are trying to make me fat'. A similar picture can be painted for other eating disorders. Once treatment is initiated, and usually within a few weeks, a slow improvement in the presenting problem occurs and will continue, providing the next stage of behaviour is tolerated.

This Stage 2 is one of increasing assertiveness and expression of very powerful, negative feelings, with an apparent absence of concern for those to whom the feelings are directed – most commonly the parents, but also clinicians. The young person behaves in a manner that is totally uncharacteristic and causes great distress to her parents. Indeed the parents may blame the clinician for 'turning their child into a monster'. This stage has now become so familiar to us as a necessary step to recovery that we not only predict it but also positively welcome it. We advise the parents in advance along the following lines:

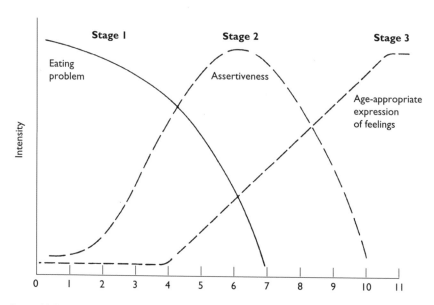

Figure 10.2 Stages of illness and recovery (Lask, 1993, reprinted with permission).

'If your daughter is to make a full recovery she will most likely go through a phase that you will probably find extremely difficult. This is a very trying phase indeed. She will be horrible to you and probably to us as well. You will be angry with us, and feel that we have made her worse. However, we will be pleased because this will mean that she is getting better. It is as if she has been unable to express these feelings and they have built up inside her almost to the point when she cannot eat. Once treatment starts, however, these feelings will come pouring out, almost like a volcano exploding. We will of course do our best to support you during this stage and it will come to an end. However, if you block her feelings, if you don't let her express them, or you punish her, she will withdraw and lock them inside again. You may then feel better but her eating problems won't resolve. Of course, you will need to set limits such as no breaking things or physical violence, but if you can tolerate the rest you will be helping her to recover.'

As Stage 2 behaviour diminishes it is gradually replaced by a more age-appropriate expression of feelings. For example, the young person may express her anger directly at the person concerned, but within a few minutes is able to discuss it all in a relatively calm and rational manner. Once this behaviour predominates over eating problems and excessive negativism, Stage 3 has been achieved and the child is well on the way to complete recovery.

As can be seen from Figure 10.2, there is considerable overlap between these stages, leading to some confusion and much distress, especially when Stages 1 and 2 overlap in the first few months. However, it can be seen that this overlap is part of a process and so long as it can be tolerated there will be movement forward to recovery.

Some children (especially those who have been severely traumatised either by neglect or abuse) are likely to go through a stage of regression, before they enter Stage 2. They may behave like a child much younger than their years and even adopt quite infantile behaviour, such as drinking from a baby's bottle or wetting the bed. Again, tolerance of this with sympathetic understanding and support aids recovery.

Conclusion

The management of all but the mildest cases of early onset eating disorders requires a comprehensive approach. This includes focusing on biological, social and psychological factors and requires a multidisciplinary team. The team might include nurses, psychologists, psychiatrists, family therapists, psychotherapists, social workers, dieticians and physiotherapists or occupational therapists. Between them they can provide a comprehensive (physical, social and psycho-logical) assessment and an integrated treatment, which might include parental counselling and/or family therapy, motivational enhancement therapy, cognitive behavioural therapy, psychodynamic psychotherapy, medication, meal plans, meal support, exercise activities. Teachers should be consulted and advised with regard to school-related issues and they are essential for an inpatient programme.

Social work input is necessary when neglect or abuse is suspected, or on the rare occasions when parents decline or in other ways resist treatment for their sick child. On such occasions the social worker can advise on the need for, and if necessary, organise a network meeting or case conference. It is important to share information and exchange views in such worrying circumstances before making decisions about management.

Such comprehensive teams are more likely to be available within an inpatient service, but the majority of children and adolescents with eating disorders are likely to be treated as outpatients. However, every effort should be made to ensure that the core components of the treatment programme are available, whatever the context. Generally it should be possible to provide these with even a relatively small team. It is our experience that early onset eating disorders become even more problematic as a result of the failure to acknowledge the need for and/or to implement appropriate treatment.

Finally, just as important as the professional discipline, is that there are clinicians available who have experience and expertise in treatment of eating disorders. Patients and parents emphasise the importance of having confidence in the clinician, which is so often connected to the clinician's experience. In clinics that lack a well-staffed multidisciplinary team the vital ingredient then becomes experience.

Summary

- The treatment of early onset eating disorders is both complex and challenging and a comprehensive approach to both assessment and treatment is essential.
- The formation of a therapeutic alliance with the parents and their daughter should be at the forefront of treatment.
- Teamwork, characterised by clarity of roles and responsibilities, consistency within the team, consistency between the team and the parents, and consistency over time, are all likely to enhance the outcome.
- Treatment that is relatively straightforward and focused is more likely to be of value than prolonged exploration of possible underlying causes.
- Change is likely to be slow and patience and empathy are necessary.

References

American Psychological Association (APA, 1994). *Diagnostic and Statistical Manual of Mental Disorders* (4th ed.). Washington, DC: APA.

Ayton, A. K. (2004). Dietary polyunsaturated fatty acids and anorexia nervosa: Is there a link? *Nutritional Neuroscience*, 7 (1), 1–12.

Behr, H., and Hearst, L. (2005). *Group-analytic Psychotherapy* (pp. 203–219). Chichester: John Wiley.

Bryant-Waugh, R., and Lask, B. (2004). *Eating Disorders in Childhood and Adolescence: A Parent's Guide*. Hove, UK: Psychology Press.

Freeman, C. (1991). Day treatment for anorexia nervosa. *British Journal of Bulimia and Anorexia Nervosa*, *6*, 3–8.

Lask, B., and Fosson, A. (1989). *Childhood Illness – the Psychosomatic Approach: Children Talking with their Bodies*. Chichester: John Wiley.

Lask, B., Taylor, S., and Nunn, K. (2003). *Practical Child Psychiatry: The Clinician's Guide*. London: BMJ Books.

Lask, B., Fosson, A., Thomas, S., and Rolfe, U. (1993). Zinc deficiency and childhood onset anorexia nervosa. *Journal of Clinical Psychiatry*, *54*, 63–66.

Meyer, C. (2011). Special Edition on Compulsive Exercise. *European Eating Disorders Review*, *19*, 169–287.

Misra, M., Katzman, D. K., Miller, K. K., Mendes, N., Snelgrove, D., Russell, M., et al. (2011). Physiologic Estrogen Replacement Increases Bone Density in Adolescent Girls with Anorexia Nervosa. *Journal of Bone Mineral Research*. 2011 Jun 22. [Epub ahead of print)

National Institute for Health and Clinical Excellence (NICE, 2004). *Eating Disorders: Core interventions in the treatment and management of anorexia nervosa, bulimia nervosa and related eating disorders: A National Clinical Practice Guideline*. London: NICE.

Neiderman, M., Richardson, J., Farley, A., and Lask, B. (2001). Naso-gastric feeding in early-onset eating disorders. *International Journal of Eating Disorders*, *29*, 441–448.

Neiderman M., Zardy, M., Tattersall, M., and Lask, B. (2000). Enteric feeding in early-onset anorexia nervosa. *International Journal of Eating Disorders*, *28*, 470–475.

Chapter 11

Therapeutic engagement*

Bryan Lask and Trine Wiig Hage

Overview

Children and adolescents suffering from an eating disorder, anorexia nervosa in particular, can be difficult to help, due to their lack of awareness of illness, fear of weight gain and consequent resistance to treatment. Working with this group can be challenging for everyone involved. Good therapeutic engagement is essential. The aim of this chapter is to examine the main components required to achieve this. These components include the establishment of a therapeutic alliance; externalisation; good communication and a focus on motivation. Each component is examined separately with the use of clinical illustrations.

Introduction

'Our aim is to help you to fight your eating disorder and overcome it.'

This is our therapeutic mantra, the essence of which permeates the entire treatment process. The aim is to help the patient to engage in her recovery, with help from her parents and the clinical team. Successful treatment is dependent upon successful therapeutic engagement, the essence of which is working *with*, not *against* the patient. All too often parents and clinicians enter a struggle with the *child* instead of with the *eating disorder*. It is the clinician's task to assist the parents in helping their daughter to fight her eating disorder, *not* to fight her. This theme is developed further below (see externalisation).

Those young patients with eating disorders such as bulimia nervosa (BN) and food avoidance emotional disorder (FAED), and some older children with selective eating, are generally more likely to want treatment and may therefore be easier to engage in a therapeutic alliance. However it is not always possible early in the treatment process to effect a therapeutic alliance with younger patients with

---

* Much of the dialogue with patients in the latter half of this chapter, and occasional segments of the text, appeared in Chapter 10 of the 3rd edition of this book, and are reproduced with the co-authors' permissions.

anorexia nervosa (AN) or others that have no wish to change their eating habits. Their fear and denial are often too strong. However, by ensuring a good working relationship with, and between, the parents, and by the implementation of appropriate treatment for the child, it is usually possible to form a good alliance over time.

In this chapter we examine the main themes that we believe constitute a firm foundation for a successful outcome for a young person with an eating disorder: the therapeutic alliance; externalisation; good communication; and enhancing motivation.

Therapeutic alliance

Creating a good therapeutic alliance is essential in the management of eating disorders. Along with the use of externalisation, the provision of relevant information, good quality communication and a focus on motivation (all discussed below), the key components from the clinician's perspective are:

- *Warmth* – a situation-appropriate friendliness that should serve toward putting the patient and her parents at ease.
- *Empathy* – the understanding of another's feelings and the ability to convey that understanding.
- *Respect* – showing regard and consideration for the patient and her views and feelings; this includes listening to her story without 'correcting' it or arguing with her.
- *Curiosity* – showing a non-judgemental interest in the patient's thoughts, feelings and behaviours.
- *Acceptance* – acknowledgment of the child's experiences as being valid representations of her sense of self.
- *Humility* – the ability to acknowledge the absence of a full understanding of the situation and an absence of all the answers.
- *Flexibility* – the ability to adopt different approaches as required, often within a very short period of time, even during one conversation.
- *Honesty* – it should be self-evident that the clinician should at all times be honest; any evidence of dishonesty will impair trust and impede the development and maintenance of the therapeutic alliance.
- *Supportiveness* – facilitates the establishment of a relationship based on collaboration and is the opposite of coercion.

Externalisation

This is the process of making a clear distinction between the child and her illness. All too often young people with eating disorders are considered to be choosing to behave as they do and that if they so wished they could revert to normal eating and behaviour. A teenage girl with anorexia nervosa is often thought simply to be responding to media and peer group pressure, with a belief that persuasion and coercion should be sufficient to get her to 'see sense'. When these prove insufficient, anger and frustration ensue. In turn the teenager herself experiences a multitude of conflicting thoughts and feelings, which can leave her feeling confused and frightened. Similarly, the difficulties experienced in swallowing by those with functional dysphagia, or in trying new foods by those with selective eating, may be responded to with persuasion or coercion, with subsequent increased resistance by the child.

Many people with anorexia nervosa are able to make such a distinction for themselves, for example by talking about 'A', 'my anorexia', 'the anorexic voice', 'my thoughts', or in some cases giving it a name. Others lack such awareness and cannot perceive themselves as ill. The same may apply to parents, with some being fully aware that their daughter is ill, but others seeing their daughter as having complete control over her behaviour and choosing to behave in the way she does.

The utilisation of externalisation involves explaining to the child and parents that just as a child with a chest infection does not choose to have a cough, a fever and pain when breathing, so the child with anorexia nervosa does not choose to see herself as fat and to become terrified of weight gain. Instead, just as the chest infection is conceptualised as a distinct entity so is 'the anorexia'. Some parents have likened it to an uninvited guest in the family.

It is helpful for the clinician to reiterate that 'my job is to help your parents to help you to fight the anorexia'. When a child with anorexia nervosa appears vigorously to be resisting attempts to help her or is expressing terror at the thought of having to eat, the clinician (or parent) can say something along the lines of 'the anorexia is giving you a particularly hard time today' or 'the anorexic voice sounds really strong just now'.

Externalisation may be used during any conversation: for example, when a child says, 'I can't eat, I am too fat', a helpful question can be, 'Is that you or your anorexia speaking?' When things are going well it is useful to make a comment such as, 'Seems like you are getting the better of the anorexia today.'

Initially such comments may irritate the child (as do most comments) but in time they become more acceptable and appear to help. Gradually she starts using the same 'language'. The parents often value such an approach, not only because they can begin to understand that their child is indeed gripped by an illness, rather than being difficult, but also it gives them a language with which to speak to her.

Communication

How we talk with our patients is a crucial factor in the creation and maintenance of therapeutic engagement. In this section we briefly discuss some important principles when considering communication. These are incorporated into our therapeutic stance, as outlined above, and delivered through clear, honest, empathic and respectful language.

Communication is always a two-way process with both verbal and non-verbal components. How and what we communicate will invariably affect our patients' responses. As Watzlawick (1972) stated 'it is impossible not to communicate'. Although there is often a tendency to focus on the verbal, the non-verbal is just as, and sometimes, even more important. Thus all behaviour is a communication, be it verbal or non-verbal, audible (clear words or a sigh, a sob, a groan) or non-audible, active or passive, facial expression, body posture, motor activity or any other component of body language or indeed the full range of human behaviour. Each of these may be, and often are, significant communications.

For example a patient who is slumped in her chair, silent, head bowed and face hidden behind long hair, is communicating just as powerfully as if she were actually shouting. A clinician who sits upright in his chair, immediately opposite the patient, arms crossed and silently awaiting her contribution is communicating a very different message from the clinician who arranges the chairs so there is not direct eye contact, and gently comments on how upset the patient appears.

In the next section we explore the pragmatics of communication through the use of motivational language and techniques.

Motivational language and techniques

> *The sun and the wind were having a dispute as to who was more powerful. They saw a man walking along and they had a bet as to which of them could get him to remove his coat. The wind started first and blew up a huge gale, the coat flapped but the man only fastened the buttons and tightened up his belt. The sun tried next and shone brightly making the man sweat. He took off his coat.*

> (Anonymous)

The story of the sun and the wind highlights the importance of motivation. The wind's coercive approach simply increased the man's resistance to change; the sun's approach led the man to *want* to take off his coat.

The growing focus on motivation in eating disorder services is linked to the fact that patients with eating disorders, and especially anorexia nervosa, are commonly resistant to change, despite everyone's best efforts to help them understand their situation and its dangers. Motivational approaches have their origins in the substance misuse field and were initially based upon the observation that substance users commonly lack motivation to change. Central is the premise that only the client has the power to bring about substantive change and that resistance is not a trait that exists within a person, but rather something that characterises an inter-personal process (Miller and Rollnick, 2002). Motivational approaches are partially based upon the observation that directly attempting to influence behaviour in individuals who lack motivation can lead to increased resistance and to the absence of behavioural change (the sun and the wind).

Within the field of motivational approaches there are a number of terms in common use. Unfortunately, they are increasingly being used inconsistently and their meanings are often confused. Their original meanings have historical and research validity but are not used with the same meaning in clinical practice. In consequence we use here definitions that seem most clinically relevant. However because of the potential confusions we have chosen, for the purposes of this chapter, to use whenever possible the more generic term 'motivational language and techniques'.

Motivation

Motivation is the process that initiates, guides and maintains goal-oriented behaviors. It is what causes us to act, whether it is eating to assuage hunger or avoiding eating to reduce weight. It involves biological, emotional, social and cognitive forces that activate or inhibit behaviour.

Motivation for change

Motivation for change is a construct for which there are many measures, definitions, and conceptions. At its simplest it means the degree of desire the patient has to overcome her eating disorder.

Readiness for change

This is a closely linked but distinct concept by which is meant the individual's readiness to overcome her eating disorder.

Motivational interviewing

Motivational interviewing (MI) is a collaborative approach that considers individuals as experts about themselves and their experiences It draws upon the client's own values, motivations, abilities and resources (Miller and Rollnick, 2002).

Motivational enhancement therapy

Motivational enhancement therapy (MET) was initially designed as a brief treatment based upon principles of MI with the addition of clinical feedback provided to clients (Miller and Rollnick, 2002). Now it is practised in many different contexts and formats.

Motivational approaches

Motivational approaches are characterised by a focus on the patient's wishes in regard to whether or not to relinquish a problem, be that a compulsive behaviour, an addiction, adherence to treatment or an eating disorder. Such approaches explore the competing incentives to change and to stay the same and have the ultimate aim of enhancing motivation to change. They are characterised by a collaborative relationship that places as much responsibility as possible in the hands of the patient and is devoid of argument or coercion. They are informed by the therapeutic stance (see above) and are based upon the transtheoretical model of change, originally described by Prochaska and DiClimente (1983).

Transtheoretical model of change

The transtheoretical model of change offers a framework for considering motivation/readiness in 'treatment-resistant individuals'. According to this model, motivation/readiness status can be described according to a series of stages:

- *Pre-contemplation* – unaware that there is a problem, or unwilling or unable to change.
- *Contemplation* – aware that there is a problem, but unwilling or unable to change.
- *Preparation* – aware that there is a problem, and intending to change soon.
- *Action* – actively working to change.
- *Maintenance* – working to prevent relapse.

For a clinical illustration of these stages, see the section on 'advantages and disadvantages' (p. 205). The stages are shown diagrammatically in Figure 11.1, which demonstrates an average time frame (in months) for the progression of an adolescent with anorexia nervosa through the stages, the tendency to move between them throughout the process and the overlap between them. It is important to

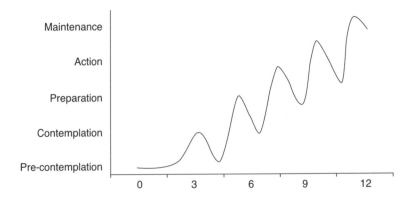

Figure 11.1 Stages of readiness to change.

emphasise that Figure 11.1 is an approximation and that there is considerable variation with some/patients progressing much more rapidly and others more slowly. Occasionally relapse does occur with regression to earlier stages. However, in this younger population it is unusual to see regression all the way to pre-contemplation once action has been reached. Clinical experience supports the utility of this model.

Assessment of motivation

Obtaining an accurate assessment of stage of change is useful because readiness to change been shown to predict clinical outcome in adolescents and adults, including the decision to engage in intensive symptom reduction treatment, symptom change post-treatment, dropout and relapse (Geller et al., 2001; Geller et al., 2004). Such information helps inform the most appropriate treatment for that patient.

The assessment of readiness for change can be conducted using various instruments or through clinical interviewing or a combination of the two. In child and adolescent eating disorders, a number of measures have been used, e.g. PCAN (Serpell et al., 2003), MSCARED (Gusella et al., 2003).

Motivational approaches with children, adolescents and their parents

Motivational approaches for adults with eating disorders have been in use now for many years (e.g. Geller et al., 2003) and are based upon the principles outlined by Miller and Rollnick (2002). Results are promising (e.g. Fel et al., 2001; Dunn et al., 2006; Geller et al., 2011). The application of motivational approaches for children and adolescents with eating disorders is based upon the same principles as those used for adults. There are many similarities in their application with the younger population but also some differences. These are generally determined by developmental issues such as the need to simplify language and concepts as well as the need to work closely with parents. In this section we present, discuss and illustrate some of the ways in which motivational approaches are applied when working with the younger population.

Little has been written about the application of motivational approaches for younger patients and their parents (e.g. Lask, 2003), but they are of particular importance in the assessment and treatment of this population for a number of reasons. First, many of this age group are in pre-contemplation and either do not recognise they are ill or have no wish to change. It is common for them to be seeing a clinician because their parents have chosen that course of action and have not made this decision themselves. Resistance to treatment for an eating disorder in this age group is the norm. This is intensified by the age-appropriate tendency of adolescents to resist authority, to insist on their rights to as much autonomy as possible and to assess the supremacy of their own views and values over those of adults. Finally, the developmental status of children and adolescents renders them far more vulnerable to the physical sequelae of an inadequate diet and therefore more liable to rapid physical decompensation (see Chapter 5).

Clinical applications

Motivational approaches incorporate a number of techniques. To describe these let us consider a fairly typical example of a teenager with anorexia nervosa being seen for the first time.

Lisa, aged 14, presented to an early onset eating disorders programme with a history of food restriction and marked weight loss. Her parents said that they were concerned about her low weight, moodiness, and overall health. They described Lisa as an overachiever in all domains of her life – an excellent student at school, successful in her competitive gymnastics club and very popular. In response to their growing concern, Lisa's parents had tried a number of techniques to get her to eat more, including persuasion, bribes and threats. On a few occasions her father had lost his temper and stormed out of the house. Both parents said they were sick with worry about her and feared that she might die. Lisa said, 'I like me the way I am. My parents are making a big deal out of nothing. Why won't they just leave me alone?'

Let us now consider some of the motivational techniques we can use in working with Lisa. It should be noted that the therapeutic stance outlined earlier applies throughout. In addition, when working motivationally, though it might feel counter-intuitive, it is important to adopt a stance of low investment in change. If Lisa experiences pressure from us to change she will feel coerced and will resist. Clinicians find this very hard but need to be aware that a high investment in change when working with motivation is counter-productive. However they can utilise their therapeutic energy by having a high investment in trying to understand Lisa, but not to change her.

Open questions

These are questions that do not require a yes or no answer, but rather allow for a wide range of answers. So instead of asking 'Do you think that you are too thin?' the clinician might ask Lisa 'What for you are the good things about being thin?' Other such questions include 'Can you tell me more about that?' and 'Can you help me to understand that better?' Such questions are not challenging and reflect the stance of curiosity.

Reflective listening

This involves repeating what the patient has said, using very slightly different words but retaining the essence of her reply. For example, Lisa answered the question 'What for you are the good things about being thin?' by saying 'I feel good about myself.' When asked to explain further, she said 'It makes me feel strong, like I have willpower', to which the clinician replied 'So, for you, being thin equals being strong and disciplined.' Such a response helped Lisa feel understood.

Affirmation

Should Lisa give a positive reply to the therapist's reflection above, this might be followed by 'It must feel great to be strong and disciplined.' Affirmation is warm and respectful validation of the patient's views and attitudes. It adds to the sense the patient may be experiencing of being listened to and understood and complements this with a sense of being accepted.

Tracking

This involves the therapist not having a specific agenda but rather following the patient's thoughts and feelings, regardless of what these are. It incorporates the therapeutic stance of flexibility. For example, if after the therapist had said to Lisa 'It must feel great to be strong and disciplined' she had replied 'Yes', the therapist might ask another open-ended question such as 'Can you tell me more about that?' However, if Lisa had replied by saying 'It's not always great to be the strong one', the therapist might respond with a reflection such as 'So it sounds like there are times when it's not great to be strong.' Alternatively, had Lisa replied 'But I am not always as strong and disciplined as I should be', the therapist would need to utilise sufficient flexibility to track this change of 'direction'. A tracking reply might be 'Let me make sure I understand – you feel great about being strong and disciplined, but sometimes you worry that you are not as strong and disciplined as you want to be.' In essence tracking is staying on the same track as the patient wherever the track leads, even if that involves the patient talking about something seemingly completely unrelated to the eating disorder, such as her favourite music.

Exploring mixed feelings

Most people with anorexia nervosa have mixed feelings about their illness, especially in the stages of contemplation and preparation. For example, if Lisa were to be in contemplation she might say something like 'One part of my mind tells me to eat and the other tells me not to as I am too fat.' The therapist might respond to that by acknowledging empathically the ambivalence and asking her to talk more about 'these divided feelings'. The acknowledgement of ambivalence is in itself supportive but also allows for further exploration, especially in relation to the advantages and disadvantages of change.

The advantages and disadvantages

Central to the ambivalence so commonly seen in those with eating disorders are the competing advantages and disadvantages of the disorder. When those with anorexia nervosa are in contemplation, although they can see advantages and disadvantages to being thin, even one important advantage that restricting offers can outweigh many disadvantages. Examples of what they might say include:

- I feel in control.
- Being thin comforts me.
- I look good when I am thin.
- I feel good when I am thin.
- Eating gives me stomach pains; if I don't eat I don't get the pain.
- Eating makes me feel sick; if I don't eat I don't feel sick.
- I get a sense of achievement when I lose weight.
- I feel proud of myself when I lose weight.
- Not eating keeps stress away.
- I feel ashamed when I eat so not eating keeps that feeling away.
- I feel disgusted with myself if I see fat when I look in the mirror so if I am thin I don't have that problem.
- I feel special when I am thin.

When asked about possible disadvantages, those in pre-contemplation are usually unable to think of any. Once they have reached contemplation or beyond they are more able to mention disadvantages such as:

- I feel tired all the time.
- I feel cold even when it's hot.
- I don't have the energy I used to have.
- I get dizzy when I stand up.
- I can't lead my usual life.
- I am fed up with worrying about my weight and what I eat.
- I can't stop thinking about my weight and shape.
- People are always nagging me.
- My mum and dad are always freaking out.
- I worry about what's happening to my bones.
- I'm scared I may not be able to have children.
- I want to get back to my old self and not be worried all the time.

The balance between advantages and disadvantages varies depending upon the stage of readiness to change. In pre-contemplation, only advantages can usually be considered. In contemplation, disadvantages emerge and in preparation there is some sort of balance between them. In action and maintenance, the disadvantages outweigh the advantages. When using a motivational approach disadvantages are best discussed only if the patient mentions them or appears ready to consider them.

In Lisa's case she could initially only see advantages, saying she felt much fitter being thin, had just the right weight for her gymnastics and that her friends wished they could be like her. 'I feel much more in control – people are always trying to control me; this way it all feels much better.' She was clearly in *pre-contemplation*.

Initially her treatment explored the perceived advantages of restricting and the consequences of Lisa expecting herself to be strong and disciplined all the time. After some sessions, Lisa noted that she didn't have the same amount of energy that she used to have. She also became aware that this made it hard to convince herself and others that she was strong. Someone had mentioned that if she fell during her gymnastics she might break a bone: 'That worries me but I am not going to put on any weight 'cos I prefer myself the way I am' (*contemplation*).

A few weeks later she commented that her gymnastics coach had told her she was too thin and that she couldn't be successful if she didn't gain some weight. She felt she was working harder and harder to feel strong and disciplined, but the feeling of strength was eluding her. She was wondering how to cope with what was becoming obvious to her – 'that I need to gain weight but I am so worried about getting fat' (*preparation*).

Shortly after this, Lisa asked for help. She said she wanted to learn how to better communicate with her parents and friends. She was ready to try eating again. She had come to the conclusion that although she still wanted to be thin and considered herself overweight, she could also acknowledge that her low energy and unhappiness were spoiling her life. On balance she felt that it was better to find a way of coping with weight gain rather than maintaining a weight that was too low for her to be healthy (*action*).

As she resumed a normal diet and started gaining weight her anxieties increased and from time to time she was very upset and scared about being 'forced to eat'. Her parents discussed with her different ways in which they could help her to cope with her distress. She chose to have her mother holding her hand during each meal and for her father not to be in the room (*maintenance*).

Summarising

Just as reflective listening involves repeating what the patient has just said, using very slightly different words but retaining the essence of her reply, summarising involves a reflection of the essence of what the patient has been saying throughout the session. For example, in Lisa's case toward the end of their fourth meeting the therapist said: 'Let me see if I have understood what you have been saying. It seems like you want to be thin because it helps you feel good about yourself, you feel much stronger and disciplined, and fitter being thin, have just the right weight for your gymnastics and you feel much more in control. You feel your parents are making an unnecessary fuss and wish they would get off your back. Is that approximately right'? Lisa nodded her agreement, at which the therapist asked if there was anything he had forgotten or got wrong. Lisa reminded the therapist that she had told him that her friends wished they could be like her but also that she was a bit worried about the danger of breaking a bone.

Summarising has many advantages. It helps the patient feel listened to, understood and acknowledged, allows her to correct the therapist when mistakes are made or particular points are forgotten and to reflect upon what she has been saying. The option of summarising from time to time also encourages the therapist to focus even more on what is being said, which in turn enhances the chances of understanding and remembering.

Draining

Patients often feel that they are not understood and are overwhelmed by the demands of the illness. Draining is a technique designed to help with these phenomena, and involves a thorough exploration of the advantages of the illness (e.g. feeling proud, having a sense of achievement, feeling in control, feeling attractive). The purpose of the draining technique is to explore all ways in which eating disorder symptoms may be helpful. Without this shared understanding the patient's energy is often spent protecting the status quo, and they are left stuck and pre-contemplative. Increased understanding can set the stage for consideration of alternatives and possibly discussion of the disadvantages of their illness. Critical to draining is the therapist placing no pressure on the patient and conveying that they have all the time in the world to listen to what the patient has to say. The process of draining will not only leave patients feeling understood by the therapist, but they will also have a better understanding of themselves, and much of the shame and guilt of their disorder will be alleviated. In Lisa's case part of the conversation went along these lines:

Therapist: You have said that there are many good things for you in losing weight – I wonder if we can just discuss them a bit more.

Lisa: Well I have already told you I feel more in control if I don't eat and my friends envy me.

Therapist: More in control?

Lisa: Yes, I eat what I want and if I don't want to eat then I don't, and no one can control me. I am fed up with people always telling me what to do and when.

Therapist: Who is controlling you?

Lisa: My dad especially and he's always commenting on my weight – first he said I was getting fat, now he's saying I am too thin. Why can't he leave me alone? It's my body not his!

Therapist: So your dad tries to control you by commenting on your weight.

Lisa: Yes and it pisses me off – he's always done that, ever since I can remember.

Therapist: So one of the good things in not eating is that you can control your dad.

Lisa: Yes. He is such a control freak and he needs to know what it's like.

Therapist: Seems like having some control over him is a really good feeling.

Lisa:	You bet.
Therapist:	Can you tell me about some of the other good things about being more in control.
Lisa:	I feel stronger in myself.
Therapist:	Stronger?
Lisa:	Yes, I feel really powerful and like I can do anything.

The conversation continued along these lines for another ten minutes. The therapist is using motivational techniques such as open questions, reflective listening, affirmation and tracking. In addition he is encouraging Lisa to talk as much as possible about the particular theme of control. Eventually he asks if there is anything else Lisa wants to say about being in control:

Lisa:	No.
Therapist:	Sure?
Lisa:	I think so.
Therapist:	Well we can always come back to control whenever you want. Meantime you also mentioned earlier on that your friends envy you.
Lisa:	They all want to be thin, all girls do. I don't think I'm the thinnest but I seem to get the most attention.
Therapist:	Attention?
Lisa:	Katie's always going on about how she'd like to be as thin as me and has tried but can't do it – she keeps asking how I do it.
Therapist:	How does that feel for you?
Lisa:	Good – like I am better than her.
Therapist:	Better?
Lisa:	Well she's very smart and pretty and everyone admires her and I always felt envious of her, but now it's like the other way round.
Therapist:	Sounds like that feels really good for you.
Lisa:	Uh huh.
Therapist:	So being thin helps you feel in control and admired. Are there any other things that make you feel good about yourself?
Lisa:	When I do well in school.
Therapist:	Yes, your mum mentioned that you are an excellent student! What do you like most about school?
Lisa:	I like it when I work hard on something and get top marks.
Therapist:	It sounds like school is something that you are really good at and provides a sense of accomplishment. Is there anything else that makes you feel good about yourself?
Lisa:	Yes, gymnastics!
Therapist:	Ya, I can see from the smile on your face that gymnastics is a good thing in your life. What is it about gymnastics that makes you feel good about yourself?
Lisa:	I love winning competitions; I love being able to do a perfect landing.

Therapist: Sounds like there are lots of things about gymnastics that make you feel good about yourself . . . What else?

The conversation proceeds along these lines giving Lisa the chance to say all she wants about why she loves gymnastics. Lisa is then 'drained' of other things that make her feel good about herself, including spending time with friends, horseback riding and taking care of her little sister.

After a while Lisa reflects, 'Gymnastics is the biggest thing for me. Trouble is, although I look better now since I got thin, I don't seem to be as strong as I used to be. Do you think my strength will come back?'

At some point the therapist needs to make a decision as to whether to try to continue the draining about things that make Lisa feel good about herself or invite Lisa to talk about the disadvantage of being thin. If the therapist focuses exclusively on the disadvantages, there is the danger of Lisa feeling controlled and even coerced. However, once Lisa has hinted at disadvantages it is useful to follow up with open questions about them.

Transfer

This involves exploring other areas of the patient's life, to which the advantages of anorexia nervosa might be applied; for example, feeling in control and feeling special. This allows the patient to consider how she might achieve the good feelings associated with maintaining a low weight without having to endanger her health. In Lisa's case:

Therapist: You have said how important it is to you to have control and that you only seem to have it through not eating.
Lisa: Yes, I never have control.
Therapist: So in what parts of your life would you like control?
Lisa: My dad's always telling me what to do, what to wear, who I can see, when I've got to be home.
Therapist: Sounds very annoying.
Lisa: He never lets up. He's got some sort of hang-up.
Therapist: So what would you like to tell him?
Lisa: To leave me alone and mind his own business.
Therapist: Mind his own business . . . .
Lisa: Yeh, why does he have to interfere so much?
Therapist: Why do you think?
Lisa: Well I know he loves me and he worries about me but he has a funny way of showing it.
Therapist: So how would you like him to show it?
Lisa: Well he could stop nagging me for a start.
Therapist: I wonder if you could ask him to stop.
Lisa: He wouldn't listen.

Therapist:	So he doesn't listen when you ask him to stop, and he doesn't listen when you restrict – sounds like neither strategy is working.
Lisa:	Yeh, nothing works with him.

Not all children or adolescents are as co-operative or willing to speak as Lisa. Many young patients with eating disorders are angry, denying or silent and the application of a motivational approach in such scenarios is associated with many challenges. In the following section examples are given of how to work motivationally with Jane, an angry 16 year old, Pat, a 15 year old in pre-contemplation and Sue, a silent 13 year old.

Jane, 16, third meeting

Therapist:	Hi Jane – good to see you.
Jane:	It's not good to see you – it's a waste of time.
Therapist:	A waste of time?
Jane:	What's the point – you just want me to put on weight, just like everyone else does. You all pretend you care and want to help but all you really want is to turn me into a fat pig.
Therapist:	A fat pig?
Jane:	That's what you all want. No one cares about what I want.
Therapist:	You seem very angry today.
Jane:	I don't seem angry – I am angry.
Therapist:	Can you help me to understand some of what's making you so angry?
Jane:	I've already told you, just now. Don't you listen to anything I say? Obviously you can't understand if you don't listen.
Therapist:	Any possibility of another chance?
Jane:	What's the point?
Therapist:	So it's all pointless?
Jane:	Congratulations, at least you got that right.
Therapist:	So maybe I can try a bit more?
Jane:	That's up to you.
Therapist:	Well I'm hoping we can work on this together.
Jane:	That would be a first.
Therapist:	So no one wants to work *with* you?
Jane:	They say they do but they're all liars.
Therapist:	That sounds really hard for you if you can never believe anyone.
Jane:	It's hardly surprising I get so angry with everybody.
Therapist:	No, not surprising at all – I would feel very angry if I thought everyone was lying to me.
Jane:	Would you?
Therapist:	Absolutely.
Jane:	So why can't you all be honest and just admit you want to fatten me up?

Therapist:	I'm wondering what's so awful for you about people wanting you to put on weight.
Jane:	It's up to me what weight I should be, not all you apologies for doctors and psychologists.
Therapist:	Yes, of course you should decide what weight you should be.
Jane:	So why don't you all just let me be 38 kilos. I keep telling you that's what I want to be.
Therapist:	How would it be if you weighed more?
Jane:	Awful, really awful, and I am NOT going to put on weight.
Therapist:	Because?
Jane:	Because I'd be fat and ugly and disgusting.
Therapist:	So putting on weight means being fat, ugly and disgusting.
Jane:	Wow, you are listening.
Therapist:	Can you tell me a bit more about disgusting?
Jane:	Fat is disgusting. It shows you are greedy and it looks gross.
Therapist:	Gross?
Jane:	Yes, like a fat pig.
Therapist:	So can I just check I've understood correctly – you can't trust anyone because they are all liars and all they really want is to make you put on weight. And if you do that you will be fat, ugly and disgusting.
Jane:	Have you been taking lessons or something?
Therapist:	So I got something right for a change?
Jane:	For a change!
Therapist:	Okay, whilst I am on a roll, can I try to understand a bit more?
Jane:	If you want.

At this point Jane's anger seems to be subsiding, associated with the therapist taking her anger full on, acknowledging and affirming it. By continuing in the same vein it should be possible for Jane and the therapist to have a useful conversation around readiness and motivation (or lack of them).

Pat, 15, first meeting

Therapist:	Hi Pat, nice to meet you.
Pat:	Why do I have to be here?
Therapist:	What did your parents tell you?
Pat:	Dunno.
Therapist:	Okay – they told me they were worried about you not eating and losing a lot of weight.
Pat:	Where do they get that idea from?
Therapist:	I guess we will have to ask them.
Pat:	They're stupid.
Therapist:	Sometimes parents can seem very stupid.

Pat:	They just imagine things. I am eating fine.
Therapist:	So it must be strange for you that they say you aren't.
Pat:	Well I eat normally, just the same as my sister and my friends.
Therapist:	So how can you convince your parents there is nothing to worry about?
Pat:	I don't know – you tell them.
Therapist:	Well that would be hard for me to do as I don't know anything about your eating.
Pat:	Well do you think I am too thin? They say I am but I know they are lying.
Therapist:	Lying?
Pat:	Yes, they know how much I hate being fat so they pretend I am not.
Therapist:	What do you hate about being fat?
Pat:	It's yukky, gross, horrible.
Therapist:	Can you tell me more about that?
Pat:	No one wants to be fat. They all look at you and laugh at you.
Therapist:	What do they say?
Pat:	Oh I don't know. Why do you ask all these questions?
Therapist:	Well I am trying to understand how it is for you. It seems like you are having a very tough time at the moment.
Pat:	No one believes me and they are just trying to make me fatter.
Therapist:	I am wondering how things would be better for you if you could be the size you wanted.
Pat:	The thinner you are the more popular you are – the thin girls are much more popular.
Therapist:	That sounds like you don't feel you are popular.
Pat:	Well I am not – most of the girls in my class hate me.
Therapist:	You reckon that if you could be the size you want they are more likely to like you.
Pat:	Dunno.
Therapist:	Well it's important to feel liked.
Pat:	I wouldn't know.
Therapist:	Well may be I can try to understand all this better. Can you tell me some other good things about being thinner?
Pat:	I'd be more successful. All the people on the telly are thin . . .
Therapist:	And in the magazines . . .
Pat:	Yeh, everywhere. You just can't get anywhere if you're fat and no one likes you and you feel stupid.
Therapist:	Maybe I can just check that I have understood – you are worried about being fat but your parents say you are too thin and that you need to put on weight. The idea of being fat is yukky. People would look at you and laugh at you and you can't be popular and successful, you would just be stupid. Is that roughly how you see it?

In this dialogue the therapist has made no attempt to convince Pat she is thin, nor got into any arguments with her, despite her lack of insight. Instead he has simply tracked her thoughts and feelings, using curiosity, open questions, reflection, affirmation and summarising. This has facilitated a conversation about the perceived advantages for her in being thin and the disadvantages of being fat. Continuation of the dialogue over a number of meetings was associated with a gradual transition to contemplation.

Sue, 13, second meeting

Sue is sitting silently, her head bowed and her face hidden behind long hair. The therapist, who is sitting a metre away from her and at an angle to her, is speaking slowly, with long pauses.

Therapist: Good to see you again, Sue.
Sue remains silent.
Therapist: I am wondering how things have been since we last met.
Sue remains silent.
Therapist: Seems like you don't want to talk today.
Sue shrugs her shoulders.
Therapist: That's okay and of course you don't have to if you don't want to.
Sue remains silent.
Therapist: Sue, I am not expecting you to talk and that's absolutely fine. If you want to say anything, of course you can, but as I said I am not expecting you to.
Sue remains silent.
Therapist: But you know I have this funny habit of thinking aloud and I hope you won't mind if I do this now.
Sue shrugs her shoulders.
Therapist: And what I am thinking is that Sue really doesn't want to be here today and it's all a waste of time.
Sue gives no response.
Therapist: And that she wishes everyone would just leave her alone to get on with her life how she wants . . . that it's a complete pain when people interfere and tell her what she should and should not do . . . and no one will ever understand her properly . . . I think that's a horrible situation to be in.
Sue shows an almost imperceptible nod of her head.
Therapist: And it's even worse because people are trying to make her put on weight when she desperately wants to lose weight.
Sue turns her head very slightly toward the therapist.
Therapist: So, I am wondering what I can do to be helpful.
Sue gives no response.
Therapist: I am not even sure if it's okay to continue thinking aloud.
Sue: [irritated mumble] Whatever.

After an initial and almost complete unresponsiveness, Sue's nonverbal responses indicate a grudging interest in what is being said. The use of the third person, talking about Sue as if she is not there, rather than addressing her directly, is deliberate. Because it is indirect it takes the pressure off Sue to respond. Any pressure is experienced as coercive and the natural response is to resist. The therapist can continue in this manner, being especially sensitive to the nonverbal communications, cautious about saying too much and ensuring adequate time between each comment for Sue to consider what is being said. (For a more detailed exploration of working with the silent child, see Lask, 2012.)

Including parents

A potential problem in utilising motivational approaches when working with children and adolescents is that the parents may be excluded. Consequently they may not be able to understand the therapeutic aims. The child may convey to her parents that the therapist is being supportive of her maintaining a low weight and there is every possibility of inconsistency in what is said. Therefore it is far better to include the parents in the therapeutic process. This has the advantage of helping them to understand better what is driving their daughter to starve herself and learning how best to talk with her.

Sara, 15, has had anorexia nervosa for about six months and the following dialogue occurred during the initial assessment when her parents were present:

Therapist: I am wondering if you could help me to understand a bit more about your wish to lose weight.

Sara: I am just so fat, I've got to lose weight; I look disgusting and . . .

Father: Sara, I've told you so many times, you aren't fat, you are desperately thin.

Therapist: Maybe we can just let Sara explain to us how it is for her, then you can let me know how you see things. Is that okay?

Father: Okay.

Therapist: You were saying Sara that you feel you look disgusting . . .

Sara: Yes, I've got all this fat and I hate myself. I am so ugly.

Mother: Darling you aren't ugly – you are the most beautiful girl in the world.

Therapist: Again it may be helpful if we just let Sara say what she thinks first. Then we can discuss it further. Sara, sorry, you were saying you hate yourself.

Sara: Anyone this fat would hate themselves.

Therapist: Can you tell me more about ugly and hating yourself?

Sara: If you eat too much you get fat and ugly and that means you are greedy and disgusting.

Father: But she doesn't eat too much . . .

Therapist: Maybe you can help your parents understand how it feels to be you.

Sara: What's the point – they don't listen.

Therapist: Well maybe I can help them to listen.

Sara: They never do.

Therapist [to Sara and parents]: How about we all try to work on this together?

Father: That's why we came here but Sara has got to be honest, she never . . .

Therapist: Well I think the best way forward is that we let Sara explain how she sees things. Then each of you can have your turn . . .

Mother [to therapist]: He gets so worried about her.

Therapist: I think everyone has their own worries and we should make sure everyone has a chance to share them and feel understood. Sara, you were saying that you are desperate to lose weight, that you feel fat, ugly and disgusting, and that you hate yourself . . .

Sara: And no one understands. I can't eat more – it will ruin my life . . .
Father leans forward to speak.

Therapist: Can you explain to your parents how it would ruin your life, and [to parents] can you just let her tell you about that?

Sara: You don't understand how I hate being fat. You don't even believe me and I eat and I know you think I throw up all the time but I don't . . .

Father: You know that's not true. We can smell it in the bathroom . . .

Therapist: I tell you what Sara, maybe we should let your dad have his say first, so he can get it off his chest, and then maybe your mum, then you can have your say? Or would you prefer mum to have her say first?
Sara shrugs.

Therapist: Who wants to go first?

Mother: He should.

Therapist [to Sara and father]: Okay?
Both nod.

Therapist [to father]: You are obviously very worried about Sara . . .

Father: If she carries on like this she will die. I can't bear to see her looking so ill and inflicting it on herself. She looks like something out of Belsen. We've got to do something.

Therapist: It must be awful for you seeing this happening.

Father: You can't imagine, you feel so helpless and all she does is fight us when we try to help . . .

Sara: You don't help, you just get angry and yell at me . . .

Therapist: How about we let him finish Sara, then you can tell him where he got it wrong.

Sara: Okay.

Therapist: Sounds like the biggest problem is that you feel she's going to die and that you feel there is nothing you can do to help her.

Father: Any father would feel that way. It's dreadful seeing her this way.

The therapist continues to encourage Sara's father to 'offload' his concerns, using the same stance and similar techniques, especially open questions, affirmation, reflection, tracking and draining. Later:

Father:	I hope you've been listening Sara and that you'll listen to the doctor.
Sara:	Can I speak now?
Therapist:	Yes, maybe you can tell dad where you reckon he got it wrong, and maybe also any bits he got right.
Sara:	Well for a start I don't make myself sick, it was just once or twice and he thinks it's after every meal. And I don't do all those press-ups, I just want to have a flat tummy. What's wrong with that?
Therapist:	Maybe you can explain to dad about the flat tummy . . .
Sara:	Everyone wants a flat tummy . . .

And so the dialogue proceeds. Later Sara's mother is encouraged to give her account. When there is considerable interruption, as illustrated above, the therapist can help the family to decide who should 'go first', promising that everyone can have their say. It can take several sessions for progress to be made and it's important for everyone to be aware of this time frame. It can be helpful for the therapist to educate parents about research on readiness and motivation, including evidence suggesting that changing for others is associated with relapse. This can help parents recognise that pushing too hard can be counterproductive.

There can be a fine line between working motivationally with child and parents together and more conventional family therapy with its focus on family relationships (see Chapter 12). There need be no rules about what should be the primary focus, but generally speaking in the early stages of the assessment process it is likely to be more helpful to focus on motivation, although the experienced therapist should be sufficiently skilful and flexible to be able to work on both.

Integrating motivational approaches with other aspects of treatment

Motivational approaches are not an exclusive treatment but rather a complement to other approaches. Whilst motivational sessions can be used as a specific inter- vention, just as might be family therapy (Chapter 12), cognitive behavioural therapy (Chapter 13), psychodynamic psychotherapy (Chapter 14), or cognitive remediation therapy (Chapter 15), they can also be used alongside, or as a precursor to, other therapies and integrated into the whole treatment regimen. It is perfectly reasonable to combine motivational techniques with, for example, the use of externalisation. This is particularly pertinent at meals and other times when compensatory behaviours such as purging or excessive exercising are being used. Once a treatment plan, including the non-negotiables, has been agreed, every effort should be made to avoid getting caught up in the inevitable arguments. Rather the motivational stance can be adopted as illustrated in the following example. Jenny, 14, with anorexia nervosa, in contemplation, is finding it very hard to adhere to the agreed meal plan:

Jenny: I can't eat all this – it's far too much. They've given me far more than I need. I'm not eating all this.

Nurse: It's really hard for you to eat all you need.

Jenny: I don't need this much – can't you hear me?

Nurse: Yes, I can hear you Jenny and I am sorry you are so upset.

Jenny: Then do something about it. I don't need to eat this much.

Nurse: Seems like the anorexia is giving you a really tough time today.

Jenny: It's nothing to do with anorexia, I just don't need this much.

Nurse: We have already agreed your meal plan and this is part of it, so I am wondering how I can help you to eat it.

Jenny: You can't – you're just useless. We agreed I only needed half a potato so why have they given me a whole one.

Nurse: It must be awful for you to be so worried about half a potato.

Jenny: So would you be if they lied to you about what they were going to give you.

Nurse: I see how upset you are and I know you are terrified of putting on weight, but this is what has been agreed and it's not going to help for us to argue. I wonder what else I can do to help you with this.

Jenny: If I eat this can I have more exercise time afterwards?

Nurse: I know you don't see it this way but I see your anorexia really getting at you today. I wonder what would be the worst thing for you about finishing this meal?

Jenny: Then I would have given in to you all and let myself down.

Nurse: Given in and let yourself down?

Jenny: Yes, I promised myself I wouldn't give in to you all.

Nurse: I can see how awful that feels to you.

Jenny: So why don't you do something about it?

Nurse: Well I was thinking how difficult it must be to have anorexia telling you one thing and us all telling you the opposite. It sounds like being pulled two ways at once.

Jenny: Yes, that's just it, so why don't you all stop pulling me and let me do what I want.

Nurse: I guess that would be us giving into the anorexia and letting it get the better of you.

Jenny: I don't want anyone getting the better of me.

Nurse: Absolutely. So what can we do to make sure the anorexia doesn't?

Jenny: Do you promise I won't put on weight?

Nurse: Anorexia doesn't want you to put on weight; but what do *you* want for yourself – to be tormented by anorexia and the fear of weight gain or to get out of here and get on with a normal life?

Jenny: Yes, I just want to get out of here.

Nurse: And to do that you need to be able to show your parents you can eat okay and they have nothing to worry about. So how can I help you to do that?

The nurse avoids arguing about content (either of the meal or other aspects of the eating disorder) and instead uses a motivational stance and externalisation. There are many variations on this approach, the detail of which can be adapted to suit the circumstances. For example after the meal Jenny may be determined to exercise excessively to compensate for her calorie intake:

Jenny: I've got to go for a walk now and I know you'll say no, but please, please let me.

Nurse: It's hard to have to wait for your walk.

Jenny: I am getting so fat.

Nurse: As we have already all agreed that you have to wait an hour for the walk, let's talk instead about how it feels to have to wait.

Jenny: Why do you torment me?

Nurse: I think it's the anorexia that torments you. Seems like it never leaves you alone for a minute. What's the worst thing it says to you?

Jenny: That I am a fat, disgusting pig.

Nurse: Wow, that's quite some insult.

Jenny: Well I am.

Nurse: It sounds as if you feel that taking a walk now may help you feel less fat and disgusting.

Jenny: Now you're at last beginning to understand so why don't you let me do what I need to?

Nurse: Can you help me to understand why it's so hard to wait an hour?

Other eating disorders

The focus in this section has been on how to engage the child with anorexia nervosa. However, the techniques are also applicable for the other eating disorders. For example, the resistance to trying new foods in selective eating, or to swallowing in functional dysphagia, or to eating more in food avoidance emotional disorder can all be explored using the stance and techniques described above. All the same principles apply including parental involvement.

In summary, motivational approaches focus on the patient's wishes in regard to whether or not to relinquish the eating disorder. Once motivation has improved there is more willingness to accept treatment for the eating disorder. They can be used in all age groups and for all eating disorders. The main aims are to enhance motivation rather than reduce symptoms. The approaches are characterised by a collaborative relationship that places as much responsibility as possible in the hands of the patient. In particular they avoid the use of challenge or coercion. Moving through the stages of readiness to change can be a slow process with much fluctuation between the stages. The therapeutic stance requires sufficient patience and flexibility to accommodate to these quite often dramatic fluctuations. Motivational approaches can and indeed should be used throughout the treatment process. They can be used in combination with many other treatments and might better be seen as a treatment principle rather than a stand-alone treatment.

When applied to children and adolescents it is important to include the parents in the treatment process so that they can better understand their daughter's illness, her ambivalence and help her with the battle against it. Although not yet empirically evaluated in the younger population, clinical experience suggests that the motivational approach is of considerable value and should be available in any early onset eating disorder programme.

Summary

- Our task is to help the child fight the illness and to help the parents to help their child in this endeavour
- Therapeutic engagement is essential requiring a good therapeutic alliance, externalisation, good quality communication and a focus on motivation.
- Achieving a good therapeutic alliance requires warmth, curiosity, supportiveness, empathy, respect, humility and flexibility.
- Externalisation involves distinguishing between the illness and the child
- Communication is 2-way, includes both verbal and non-verbal components and should include listening carefully and sympathetically to what the patient and parents are saying.
- A focus on motivation enhances engagement and the therapeutic process.

References

Dunn, E., Neighbors, C., and Larimer, M. (2006). Motivational enhancement therapy and self-help treatment for binge eaters. *Psychology of Addictive Behaviours, 20*, 44–52.

Feld, R., Woodside, D., Kaplan, A., Olmstead, M., and Carter, J. (2001). Pre-treatment motivational enhancement therapy for eating disorders. *International Journal of Eating Disorders, 29*, 393–400.

Geller, J., Brown, K., and Srikameswaran, S. (2011). The efficacy of a brief motivational intervention for indviduals with eating disorders. *International Journal of Eating Disorders, 44*, 497–505.

Geller, J., Brown, K. E., Zaitsoff, S. L., Goodrich, S., and Hastings, F. (2003). Collaborative versus directive interventions in the treatment of eating disorders: Implications for care providers. *Professional Psychology: Research and Practice, 34*, 406–413.

Geller, J., Cockell, S. J., and Drab, D. (2001). Assessing readiness for change in anorexia nervosa: The psychometric properties of the readiness and motivation interview. *Psychological Assessment, 13*, 189–198.

Geller, J., Drab-Hudson, D., Whisenhunt, B. L., and Srikameswaran, S. (2004). Readiness to change dietary restriction predicts short and long term outcomes in the eating disorders. *Eating Disorders: The Journal of Treatment and Prevention, 12*, 209–224.

Gusella, J., Bird, B., and Butler, G. (2003). Tipping the scales: Is decision making related to readiness to change in girls with eating disorders? *The Canadian Child and Adolescent Psychiatry Review*, *12*, 110–112.

Lask, B. (2003). Motivating children and adolescents to improve adherence. *Journal of Pediatrics*, *143* (4), 430–433.

Lask, B. (2012). Musings with the silent child. In: *The Silent Child: Communication without Words* (ed. Magagna, J.) Karnac: London.

Miller, W. R., and Rollnick, S. (2002). *Motivational Interviewing: Preparing People for Change*. New York: Guilford Press.

Prochaska, J., and di Clemente, C. (1983). Stages and processes of self-change of smoking: Towards an integrative model of change. *Journal of Consulting and Clinical Psychology*, *51*, 390–395.

Serpell, L., Neiderman, M., Haworth, E., Emmanueli, F., Lask, B. (2003). The use of the pros and cons of anorexia nervosa (P-CAN) scale with children and adolescents. *Journal of Psychosomatic*, *54*, 567–571.

Chapter 12

Nutrition and refeeding

Melissa Hart

Overview

Nutrition intervention is one of the central components of treatment of any eating disorder, and is associated with significant physical and psychological risk. Informed understanding of the complexities involved and appropriate strategies for intervention are crucial. A comprehensive nutrition assessment is vital, with consideration given to the specific information required and how this is collected. When considering intervention, clear communication, refeeding safely, therapeutic alliance, facilitating change towards normal, healthy eating and involving the patient and family are key considerations.

Introduction

This chapter deals with nutritional assessment and the establishment and maintenance of adequate nutrition and healthy eating patterns. Such components of management are best provided by a dietician, although not all services have access to one. The role of the dietician may vary depending on many factors including the expertise of the dietician involved, the role of other members of the team, the needs of each individual patient and the overall treatment plan.

Assessment

A pre-requisite of nutritional rehabilitation is a comprehensive assessment. Nutrition assessment in patients with an eating disorder involves collecting specific nutritional information to inform the assessment, as well as consideration of how the information is collected. Incorporation of aspects of the clinical assessment and physical complications (see Chapter 6) which have nutritional implications is essential. Other specific information includes assessment of nutritional intake and eating behaviour, along with factors that may influence food choice and eating behaviour. Involving the family (see Chapter 13), therapeutic alliance (see Chapter 11) and avoiding exclusive focus on weight and eating are important considerations when collecting information.

Assessment of nutritional intake and eating behaviour

Assessing current and past dietary behaviour can assist in establishing a more realistic and physically safe nutrition plan. Diet histories are often used by dieticians to assess the nutritional adequacy of the diet, to provide a detailed description of eating behaviour and to explore attitudes and beliefs towards food and eating of the patient and family.

A focus of enquiry should include the adequacy of specific nutrient intakes and food groups. Restriction or exclusion of dietary fat, total energy, carbohydrates, protein and fluid may be evident. Alternatively, intakes of these could be excessive if the patient is bingeing. Dietary fibre intake may be low due to poor intake or high due to excessive use of high fibre foods. Dietary intake may be low in a range of micronutrients, including calcium, iron, folate and Vitamin B_{12}. The contribution of vitamin and mineral supplements to dietary intake should be assessed. Artificially sweetened substances (including chewing gums and sweets) may have a laxative effect and their use should be ascertained.

The regularity of meals and snacks or presence of chaotic eating behaviour throughout the day will also need to be determined. Periods of restriction or unusually large intake should be explored. Clarifying the changes in eating behaviour that have occurred over time (including types and quantities of foods or fluids) may also provide useful information regarding the development of thoughts associated with specific foods or nutrients. Vegetarianism, 'dislike' of certain foods and 'allergies' to specific foods may be reported. The timing and context of such occurrences need to be ascertained. If they arose after the onset of the eating disorder, they may be part of the eating disorder psychopathology rather than true vegetarianism, dislikes or allergies. Other behaviours that can provide useful information include calorie counting, recording, weighing or measuring food or fluid, arranging food in a certain way, excessive use of condiments, cutting food into small pieces, fiddling with food on the plate, or keeping a food diary. Finally, compensatory behaviours should also be explored. Restricting, purging or excessive exercise may directly influence nutritional status and requirements. It should also be borne in mind that past bingeing or purging practices may re-emerge during treatment.

Consideration of the factors influencing food choice and eating behaviour is also important. Aside from the eating disorder, other factors which influence eating and nutrition should be considered as part of assessment and may include stages of growth and development, food availability, family beliefs and practices, socio-economic pressures and socio-cultural influences.

Many biological influences on eating arise during childhood. Children experience continual growth each year and relatively high nutrient requirements in relation to size (McVeagh and Reed, 2001; Patchell, 2000). A high quality diet is required to achieve optimal growth and development during this time. Many children may have small appetites, however, and selective food refusal and food fads are often seen. The nutritional requirements of adolescence are also high due to the growth spurt and physical maturation. This is a nutritionally vulnerable period of life, with a greater demand for nutrients and a period of psychosocial and developmental change (McVeagh and Reed, 2001; Patchell, 2000). Adolescence is a period of striving for independence and having a stronger need to conform with peers regarding food choices and eating behaviour. There may be increased interest in dietary fads and dieting behaviour. Body image dissatisfaction also is common. Typical adolescent eating behaviour may include missing meals, snacking to accommodate the higher energy requirements, increased fast food intake and consumption of high energy foods, including foods high in fat, soft drinks and sports drinks (Patchell, 2000).

Many other factors affecting eating need to be considered. Foods available in the home, in schools and in fast food restaurants can directly affect food choices, along with family dietary patterns and beliefs. Socio-economic influences may include economic status, education of parents or carers, family structure, ethnic origin and social attitudes (Patchell, 2000). Advertising, portrayal of slimness in the media, fashion and body shape beliefs of family and friends may also influence body image concern and dieting behaviour (McVeagh and Reed, 2001).

Consideration of how the information is collected

How nutritional information is collected can influence the quality of information gathered and the success of future nutrition interventions. Family involvement, a therapeutic approach and avoiding exclusive focus on weight and eating are important considerations.

Parental involvement in assessment and treatment planning is essential. Parents or carers have a key role in assisting their child with eating and are an essential source of knowledge regarding the eating history. Consequently parents should always be involved in the assessment process, including clarifying past and current eating behaviours and changes in eating over time. Family views on what constitutes normal, healthy eating and their attitudes to dieting should be ascertained. Food preparation practices should be clarified, including how food is purchased, who is responsible for meal preparation and how much influence over purchasing or preparation of food their child has. It is helpful to know about types of meals and snacks consumed, whether the family eats at the dinner table, whether meals are eaten together as a family and how family members react to restrictive or chaotic eating. Finally, it is also useful to determine whether and how family eating practices have changed during the illness.

One of the most important aspects of the nutrition assessment is *how* the interview is conducted. The style of interviewing will influence the amount and accuracy of the information obtained and may either foster or damage the therapeutic alliance. The interview should aim to proceed in the least threatening way possible, and questioning should be sensitive, empathic and validating (see Chapters 10 and 11 for further discussion of these issues). The therapeutic alliance is a key issue in nutrition intervention and essential in fostering a collaborative working relationship over time. A collaborative experience with a dietician can be invaluable for anyone with an eating disorder, and may mean the patient will seek appropriate nutritional assistance when ready to make further change. Early in the interview, an enquiry of how the patient feels about discussing food and eating can be helpful. It is also important to gain some understanding during the interview of whether the patient feels there are certain aspects of eating that they would like to change. This can assist in clarifying aims and motivation.

The therapeutic alliance can be hindered by an over-emphasis on weight and food intake, to the exclusion of other aspects of life. An exclusive focus on weight and nutrition can be perceived by the patient as intrusive, challenging and of no immediate benefit. The patient may be anticipating that the nutrition intervention will involve '*making* me eat' and '*making* me fat'. If this is not handled sensitively it may lead to an increase in resistance and power struggles. Bearing this in mind may also assist in ensuring our own expectations of change or adherence to the nutrition plan remain realistic. At times of heightened clinician anxiety or frustration, it can be easy to become more directive and to focus more intently on weight gain or increased oral intake. Also, clinicians who are well versed in advising patients to increase physical activity and reduce dietary fat and energy may find it difficult to give the 'near enough eating is good enough' message (Beumont, Beumont, Touyz and Williams, 1997).

By the end of the nutrition assessment, there should be some clarity regarding the current nutritional risk, whether eating behaviours are consistent with healthy eating, patient and family beliefs around eating, body weight and shape, readiness for change and patient and family strengths to facilitate nutritional change.

Management

Key components of nutritional management may include conveying a clear understanding of key principles, involving the family and patient, guiding nutritional change and refeeding.

What is normal, healthy eating

Before embarking on nutritional change, it is important to be clear about what is it that we are working towards. Healthy eating can be difficult to define and varies between individuals. Food beliefs, emotions, access to food, cultural background, stage of development and individual physical differences may all determine what constitutes normal, healthy eating for each individual. There are many factors involved in considering normal, healthy eating, including:

- maintaining a healthy body through eating in a relaxed and flexible way;
- consuming a reasonably adequate nutritional intake;
- eating a wide variety of foods;

- eating regular meals and snacks that would be considered normal in type and amount (this may mean eating three meals per day or eating smaller amounts at more frequent time intervals throughout the day);
- eating in a way that responds to internal cues of hunger and satiety;
- choosing foods that are desired or liked and eating them without guilt;
- consuming a regular, healthy amount of 'junk' food without significant feelings of guilt;
- eating out socially with minimal anxiety;
- avoiding compensatory behaviours;
- eating meals that would be considered culturally appropriate in different social contexts (such as religious celebrations or birthdays).

It is also important to consider what is not normal, healthy eating. This includes:

- counting calories or fats;
- measuring or weighing what is eaten;
- spending a large proportion of the day thinking about food, eating or body weight;
- eating having much more significance than other activities;
- continually following a rigid eating plan;
- having rigid rules around eating;
- using supplements in place of whole foods.

It is also important to be mindful that our perception of healthy eating may differ to that of the patient, their family or to other members of the treating team, and most certainly will differ to that of anorexia nervosa. Consistently conveying key principles of healthy eating behaviour is important. People with an eating disorder may be well versed in dieting and continual self-questioning of their own dietary intake and physical activity. As clinicians we need to be mindful when communicating nutrition messages that we convey healthy approaches towards eating and physical activity, rather than reinforcing dieting or rigid thinking. For example, rather than encouraging thoughts such as 'have I had too much fat or too many calories', a healthier way of thinking about dietary intake would be 'have I had enough of the good, healthy foods such as breads and cereals, dairy, fluids and so forth'. With this in mind, important principles to convey would include:

- appreciation of body diversity and individuality;
- thinking in food terms as opposed to nutrients or calories;
- aiming for a healthy lifestyle approach to living with everything in moderation, as opposed to a 'dieting approach';
- an appreciation of the influences on eating behaviour that children and adolescents face, including psychological issues, family dietary beliefs and practices, peer influence, media and socio-economic issues.

Involving the family and patient

A second important consideration in facilitating nutrition change is inclusion of the family and the patient. Parents are usually best placed to facilitate restoration of healthy eating behaviours, are important members of the treating team and can be active participants in nutrition treatment, especially at home. Facilitating agreement on approaches to managing nutrition at home should as much as possible be a collaborative process. Wherever possible, parents should be empowered to make appropriate decisions regarding nutritional management at home. Decisions may be made about issues such as the types and quantity of foods to be eaten, the timing of meals and snacks, where foods will be eaten, the time allowed for meals and snacks, who is to attend mealtimes and how difficulties around mealtimes will be managed. Strategies may also need to be made for managing bingeing, purging and exercise. In the nutritional management of children and adolescents with anorexia nervosa, carers should be included in any dietary education or meal planning (National Institute for Clinical Excellence, 2004).

In some instances an individual approach is warranted, whereby the change process is patient-centred. An essential aspect of this process is the therapeutic alliance and consideration of patient readiness for change (see above and Chapters 7 and 11). It is unwise to avoid launching into nutritional treatment when the patient's readiness and motivation for change has not been addressed. This raises the likelihood of further resistance. An example of this may be the provision of education on nutrition and normal eating when the patient is clearly stating that they do not want to hear about nutrition and that they have no intention of beginning to eat.

Once goals have been agreed, a useful way forward is to ask a question such as: 'if you were able to begin to move towards these goals, how would you like to do this?'

A conversation may occur such as:

> One of the goals you had mentioned is to be able to have a healthy body to do all the fun things that you like, like going horse riding and going out with friends. What do you think would need to change for that to be able to actually happen?

They might suggest a change that could assist in improving energy levels such as being able to have some breakfast. A response may be something like:

> If you were to consider being able to have some breakfast each day, what do you think would be a comfortable way of doing that? Is that something you might be able to try over the next week?

The dialogue needs to be focussed as much as possible on what the patient thinks they can achieve and how they might achieve it.

Providing nutrition education

Nutrition education is an ongoing process and may be used to support positive and sustainable behaviour change. People with an eating disorder may have varying levels of knowledge regarding food, nutrition, health and weight. Ideas may have become distorted over time and knowledge may be highly selective and obtained from dubious sources (Beumont et al., 1997). Provision of appropriate information can assist with reducing misconceptions around eating and reducing fears associated with improved oral intake.

The type of information provided will depend upon the level of knowledge, the information requested and the stage of treatment of the patient. Early in an admission, for example, education to assist with reducing fear around eating and weight gain would be appropriate. This may include explaining expected weight fluctuations due to fluid shifts and glycogen storage, understanding potential physical feelings such as gastric discomfort and the effect of metabolic changes on nutritional requirements. Education may then progress to the effects of poor nutrition on physical and mental health, defining normal, healthy eating, the role of food groups in health, nutritional requirements to maintain health and energy balance. Finally, helpful information may include establishing regular eating patterns, meal planning, responding to hunger and satiety, establishing flexibility in eating, social eating, defining a healthy amount of 'junk' food and longer term maintenance of healthy nutrition.

The type of information provided to parents should depend upon the needs of each family. Support and coaching around nutrition and eating should be sensitively offered. Information may include the healthy lifestyle approach to food and physical activity (as opposed to the dieting approach), nutritional requirements for age and stage of development, what is normal, healthy eating, creating a positive eating environment and eating at school and in social settings. Other discussions may include ways to assist the child in recovery by being mindful of imparting 'healthy' as opposed to 'dieting' messages, and ensuring that other family activities are not displaced by an over-emphasis on food and eating.

Facilitating positive nutrition change

Establishing gradual changes towards the longer-term goals of normal, healthy eating should be family- and patient-centred and facilitated by the dietician in collaboration with other members of the team. Consideration should be given to the agreed goals and phase of treatment. Regular, short-term plans should be established and communicated clearly to all involved. This may include for example, gradually increasing the type or quantity of foods included at mealtimes or snacks, gradually introducing feared foods, being able to eat at the dinner table with others, reducing compensatory behaviours or being able to attend social occasions involving food.

Any change in eating behaviour should work towards a normal, healthy outcome. Small but regular changes towards healthy eating should be made to allow for physical and psychological adjustment. A good place to start may be working towards being able to include some foods regularly throughout the day. This may progress to including foods from each of the food groups, and gradually being able to consume the amounts required within food groups to sustain health and growth. Finally, the focus may move to being able to eat regular (though not excessive) amounts of 'junk' food and eating out socially without feelings of guilt (e.g. at the movies, eating 'junk' food at a friend's party or having take away meals with friends).

Other areas requiring consideration include the use of low fat and diet products, patient dislikes and vegetarianism. Being able to consume full fat products (such as regular-fat dairy products or margarine) is considered part of normal, healthy eating and is not dissuaded. Some treatment settings will not allow the use of low fat products for patients, while others allow a transition period between use of low-fat and full-fat products. The use of 'diet' products is generally not recommended for patients with eating disorders. Specific foods may not have been 'disliked' prior to the onset of the eating disorder, though have become a 'dislike' subsequently. Similarly, the patient may have become a vegetarian or developed 'allergies' to specific foods (such as cheese) during the course of the eating disorder. In such instances this may be more a component of the eating disorder, and would need to be worked through as part of recovery. Potential food allergies should be discussed with the medical team to ensure physical safety.

Offering choice may reinforce the importance of variety and flexibility in eating and may also allow the patient to take more responsibility around eating. Providing a range of choice in non-safety related areas may also improve the treatment alliance. If, however, in the face of choice and negotiation, patients become increasingly anxious or demanding, the number of choices and the negotiations offered may need to be reduced.

Some components of treatment may be considered as 'non-negotiable' (see Chapter 10). 'Non-negotiables' may include weekly weight gains and consuming a specified amount of nutrition at meals and mid-meals. Lengthy discussions and negotiations around this should be dissuaded to avoid collusion with the eating disorder and increasing disordered eating thoughts and behaviours. Choice, however, could be offered around the *process* of refeeding, as an example. What can be negotiable (within reason) is how the nutrition plan may be achieved (e.g. would it be more preferable to consume a larger volume of food at mealtimes or the use of supplements or more energy-dense foods?). Options for refeeding can be discussed, including consuming food and fluid orally with the assistance of a menu plan, use of oral nutritional supplements or nasogastric feeding. If nasogastric feeding is likely to be required, a time-limited trial of oral feeding could be offered. Time will need to be allocated to talking about this and in providing the opportunity to consume food and fluids orally before proceeding with nasogastric feeding. A conversation regarding refeeding may be something like:

'We are *very* concerned for your health and would like to work towards improving this. To do this we need to improve your nutrition and weight, which I know is going to be very difficult for you. This is something that we simply *cannot* negotiate on. What we can do though is to talk about how you would like this to happen'.

Many psychological symptoms and social behaviours attributed to eating disorders are the result of starvation and return to normal with restoration of a healthy body weight. This does not, however, automatically alleviate abnormal eating or disturbed attitudes towards food and weight (American Psychiatric Association, 2006; Windauer, Lennerts, Talbot, Touyz and Beumont, 1993). Ongoing nutritional care may assist the patient to establish sustainable and appropriate eating behaviour.

Refeeding

Refeeding involves replenishment of adequate nutrition and hydration and is indicated when there is evidence of significant weight loss, delayed growth, nutritional deficiency, dehydration, circulatory failure or electrolyte disturbances. The primary and immediate aim of refeeding is to alleviate the shorter and longer term physical and psychological sequelae of malnutrition and restore normal growth. The first stage of treatment should focus on the correction of hypoglycaemia, electrolyte disturbance and dehydration, and stabilization of cardiovascular function, while the second stage the correction of nutrient deficiencies and the third the correction of body composition (Royal College of Psychiatrists, 2005). Vigorous efforts to achieve weight gain in the early stages have potential physical dangers and may be psychologically intolerable to the patient.

Nutritional requirements and refeeding

A dietician is best placed to determine the nutritional requirements at different stages of weight restoration. Consideration will need to be given to requirements for total energy intake and intakes of fat, protein, carbohydrate, fluid, fibre, vitamins and minerals. Total energy intakes are important for normal growth and development and are particularly important for those requiring refeeding. Determining appropriate energy requirements for weight gain can be difficult, however, due to physical changes occurring during refeeding (including metabolic rate), actual energy consumed and actual energy lost (through activity or purging behaviours). Protein is essential for normal growth and development and may be compromised in people with an eating disorder. Carbohydrates are the body's preferred source of energy and should be consumed regularly throughout the day. Fluid is essential for survival and patients may become acutely unwell with restricted fluid intake. Consideration should be given to the dietary fibre requirements and the gradual re-introduction of fibre in those with low intakes. A range of vitamins and minerals will also need to be considered.

Electrolyte supplementation is often required and micronutrient supplementation is recommended. Iron supplements, however, may be dangerous during the early stages of treatment (Royal College of Psychiatrists, 2005).

Consideration should be given to the quantity of nutrition that the patient has been able to consume. The amount of nutrition the child may tolerate, both physically and psychologically, should be assessed before proceeding with refeeding. When refeeding commences, the initial calorie intake should be based upon the average daily consumption in the previous week or two. Generally, it is wise to have an increase of only about 200–300 calories. Anything greater increases the risk of refeeding syndrome, based upon hidden biochemical deficiencies (see Chapter 6 for fuller explanation and see below for management) and may in any event be either physically or psychologically intolerable. This may mean starting with only 600 to 900 calories per day with intake spread throughout the day to minimise excessive nutritional load. In the case of nasogastric feeding or other forms of enteric feeding (see below) this could involve continuous 24 hour feeds (Brooks and Melink, 1995; Beumont et al., 1997).

Nutritional intake can be increased by gradual amounts (usually about 200–300 calories) every third day until the final requirements have been met. Less emaciated patients who have been tolerating reasonable amounts of nutrition may be commenced on a higher nutritional intake (Beumont et al., 1997). It should be borne in mind that until calorie intake reaches between 1,500 and 2,000 calories daily, weight is unlikely to increase and may even drop in the early stages of refeeding. This is simply a reflection of an inadequate diet and, providing physical health is not immediately endangered, should be tolerated. If the patient is at immediate risk of severe physical decompensation then a higher intake will be necessary, but this should be supervised by a paediatrician.

A weekly weight gain of 0.5–1.0 kg is often suggested for in-patients and 0.5 kg for out-patients. However, energy requirements may also increase after the first few weeks of refeeding due to increases in the metabolic rate and increased physical activity. They may be as high as 3,500 to 4,500 calories depending on individual requirements (Andersen, Bowers and Evans, 1997). Once an adequate weight has been achieved, nutritional intake can be reduced accordingly.

Meal plans

In some instances, particularly in the in-patient setting, a meal plan may be a useful way to provide structure for the day's eating, to provide guidance around the timing and content of meals and snacks and to ensure consistency in the team approach. Meal plans are not suitable for every patient and consideration should be given to the needs of each individual. If the meal plan contributes to increased rigidity or preoccupation with eating, increased anxiety or family conflict, its use should be reconsidered. Establishing the meal plan should also be a process that is facilitated (rather than imposed) by the dietician.

Meal plans can lead to splitting and important steps need to be taken to mini-mise this happening. One important aspect of meal planning is documenting and communicating the plan clearly for the patient, parents and other members of the treating team. This may also include sending the documented meal plan to the general practitioner for out-patients.

In constructing a meal plan there are a few key points to keep in mind:

- involve regular meals and snacks;
- meals and snacks should be appropriate in type, content and timing (timing will need to take into consideration the normal family routine);
- allow for variety, flexibility and spontaneity in eating;
- include foods from each of the foods groups;
- provide structure for the days eating;
- involve the patient and parents.

A sample meal plan for a healthy, moderately active adolescent is provided below. The content would need to be adjusted for those on a very restricted intake with the aim of a gradual increase every few days.

Sample Meal Plan

Breakfast (between 6.30am and 8.30am)
1 bowl of cereal with milk
1–2 slices of toast (or 1–2 slices of fruit toast, ½–1 average bread roll
    or ½–1 breakfast muffin) with margarine and spread (*or no cereal
    and 2–4 toast*)
1 glass of juice

Morning Snack (roughly half way between breakfast and lunch)
1–2 snacks and 1 glass water

Lunch (between 12 noon and 1.30pm)
1–2 sandwiches or bread rolls with filling (e.g. meat, cheese and salad)
Piece of fruit or tub of yoghurt
1 glass water

Afternoon Snack (roughly half way between lunch and dinner)
1–2 snacks and 1 glass water

Dinner (between 5.30pm and 7.30pm)
¼ plate meat, fish, chicken or alternative
¼ plate potato, rice, pasta or bread

½ plate mixed vegetables
dessert (e.g. tinned fruit and custard/yoghurt/ice cream)
I glass water

Supper
1–2 snacks and I glass water

Snacks
Examples include: I piece of fruit, I tub of yoghurt (approx 200g), 4
    crackers with cheese, I glass of milk, a handful of dried fruit and
    nuts, ½ sandwich or I slice of toast.

Extras
Examples include: a 50g packet of chips or 60g bar chocolate 3 times per
    week. Takeaway meal or meal out (e.g. fish and chips) once per week.

Fostering appropriate eating and providing meal support

Whenever possible, refeeding interventions should be aimed at fostering normal, healthy eating behaviour – such as sitting at the dinner table to eat, consuming appropriate types and quantities of foods at meal and snack times, eating within an acceptable time period, avoiding compensatory behaviours after eating, and maintaining adequate weight. However restoration of physical well-being is the top priority and this should be achieved by whatever means the patient finds tolerable. Refeeding can be a highly distressing process, and means for minimising distress should be always be considered. The level of distress should be monitored and a collaborative stance around ways to minimise distress for the patient should be adopted.

Providing meal support can be an important tool in assisting patients to improve nutritional intake and to facilitate appropriate weight restoration and eating behaviour. This involves providing support before, during and after meals and snacks. Key components to consider include communicating clear expectations regarding food quantities and time taken to consume foods, providing encouragement around eating, providing empathy and understanding, using distraction techniques and discouraging discussion of calories, dieting or eating disorder thoughts (Couturier and Mahmood, 2009). This can involve being both a cheerleader and coach for the patient.

The route of refeeding

Oral refeeding is the preferred option and should always be offered as a first choice. However some patients simply cannot manage an adequate intake orally.

In such cases enteral feeding (e.g. nasogastric or even gastrostomy feeds) may be necessary. In some situations, patients may actually prefer the assistance of nasogastric feeding and feel they simply cannot consume the required amount of nutrition orally.

Oral refeeding

Oral refeeding would normally consist of a combination of food and drinks. The amount and type of nutrition required will be determined by the urgency of the situation (e.g. dehydration or medical instability) and the amount the child has been able to manage over the preceding few days or weeks (having realistic expectations). The nutrition plan should be appropriate in timing, type and quantity for normal eating, and higher energy choices may be added to allow for weight gain. Once acceptable growth has been achieved, higher energy choices can be reduced.

Medical requirements of refeeding may determine how directive refeeding will need to be and how much room there is for offering choice and negotiation. A more directive approach will be indicated for a patient at high risk of medical compromise, whereas a more collaborative stance may be adopted for less urgent situations. For example, if a patient has consumed one apple per day and minimal fluids over the preceding two weeks, there will be a higher risk of medical compromise and less opportunity for offering choice. For a patient who has been consuming half of all meals and is medically stable, increased choice may be offered.

The boundaries of choice will need to be clear and the meal planning should remain a guided process. For a child at high risk of medical compromise, for example, there may be a specified period of time (e.g. the next eight hours) to consume a pre-determined amount of food and fluid at each meal and snack time. The requirements may be something like five cups (5 × 250mls) of fluid and a specific amount of food at each meal (e.g. half portion of protein, half sandwich, half serving of cereal with milk or one tub of yoghurt). For a patient who is at a low risk of medical instability, more choice may be offered. The patient may need to consume three healthy meals each day, for example, and there could be choice around how this could be achieved. Requirements will need to be very clear for all involved, along with what will need to happen if the patient is unable to achieve this. Time should be spent with the patient, parents or carers and staff to ensure clarity in approach towards refeeding and to avoid potential splitting.

Oral nutritional supplements

Oral supplements can be helpful when beginning oral refeeding or when moving from nasogastric feeding. They may be an easier alternative to increased oral intake, and may be less invasive than nasogastric feeding. In the early stages of refeeding and once nearing a healthy weight, energy intakes can be so substantial that patients find it difficult to ingest enough food orally to meet nutritional requirements (Russell, Baur, Beumont, Byrnes and Zipfel, 1998). Nutrient-dense oral supplements, such as high-energy drinks and puddings, can be a useful and acceptable solution. Supplements may be added to food intake as a high energy extra, then gradually reduced for weight maintenance.

When progressing from nasogastric feeding, oral supplements can be a useful transitional step. Supplements may be offered as a complement to, or in place of, enteric feeds as a way of encouraging improved oral intake and reducing reliance on the nasogastric feed. A system may be documented whereby a pre-determined amount will be deducted from the nasogastric feed for each specified quantity of oral supplement consumed. The plan should, however, include a plan for consuming oral foods as early as is practical.

Nasogastric feeding

Nasogastric feeding is sometimes quite wrongly equated with 'forced feeding'. Forced feeding is literally that – feeding by physical force, against the patient's wishes. It is rarely required, providing the patient's eating disorder is managed appropriately, with a good therapeutic alliance, the use of externalisation and the motivational approach (see Chapters 10 and 11). Nasogastric feeding is indicated when oral intake is inadequate despite all attempts to render it tolerable. Occasionally patients prefer nasogastric feeds, sometimes because they simply feel unable to eat adequately and other times because those with anorexia nervosa may feel less guilty. When a patient states a preference for nasogastric feeds they should be supported until such time as their medical state has improved. An audit of children and adolescents who had undergone nasogastric feeding for anorexia nervosa showed that although many of them initially found it an unpleasant experience, the majority were grateful that it had been carried out (Neiderman, Richardson, Farley and Lask, 2001).

Nasogastric feeds may be commenced as the sole source of nutrition or may be accompanied by oral nutrition if the patient can so manage. Feeds are usually commenced at a low, continuous rate to reduce the nutritional load, and gradually increased as tolerated. Once tolerating an adequate amount of feed has been achieved, feeding may then become intermittent (e.g. overnight) or may progress to bolus feeding (administering a particular volume of feed at regular intervals). Overnight feeding (e.g. from 7pm to 7am) may be used as a step towards bolus feeding. This may allow for increased appetite during the day and prove to be an acceptable step towards bolus or oral feeding. There may, however, be increased opportunity for tampering with overnight feeding. Patients may alternatively move directly from continuous to bolus regimens. Bolus feeding can be given at meal and snack times to mimic physiologically normal eating patterns.

Plans for progressing to oral feeding should form an ongoing component of the nutrition plan. Improved oral intake and normal, healthy eating should be encouraged and facilitated wherever possible. A plan may be negotiated, for example, that if the patient is able to consume a quarter of each meal orally for three consecutive days, this is good evidence of being able to manage more nutrition orally. The nasogastric feed may then be reduced accordingly. The plan may then progress to attempting half of the meals and so forth. Once the patient is consuming a full meal plan, a three day trial may commence for ceasing the nasogastric feed while leaving the nasogastric tube in situ. The tube may then be removed and a trial of full oral feeds resumed.

Gastrostomy feeding

A gastrostomy is the insertion of a tube into the stomach for the purpose of administering feeds directly to the stomach. They are very rarely indicated in eating disorders, although are quite commonly used in certain chronic diseases such as cystic fibrosis. However, in some circumstances, especially in anorexia nervosa, they may be life-saving. Some patients with anorexia nervosa may be so terrified of refeeding that they not only refuse all oral feeds but may even repeatedly withdraw the nasogastric tube. A gastrostomy tube is much harder to withdraw, as it can be secured much more firmly. The management of gastrostomy feeds is similar to that of nasogastric feeds. A fuller description of their use is provided by Neiderman, Zardy, Tattersall and Lask (2000). The legal and ethical issues associated with enteral feeding are discussed in Chapter 17.

Refeeding safely (refeeding syndrome)

Refeeding syndrome (see Chapter 6) is a potential complication of refeeding and may be fatal. Patients most at risk are those with a low body weight (e.g. a body mass index of 14 or less), prolonged malnutrition or rapid weight loss (Melchior, 1998). Other factors which may contribute include hypophosphatemia, thiamine deficiency and prolonged QT intervals on ECG (Melchior, 1998; Ornstein, Golden, Jacobson and Shenker, 2003). Medical monitoring and routine observations during refeeding are essential in preventing and detecting refeeding syndrome. This should include food and fluid intake and output, vital signs, rapid weight gain (which may indicate fluid overload), electrolytes, oedema, gastrointestinal complications and congestive heart failure (American Psychiatric Association, 2006).

Standardised protocols for managing refeeding syndrome have not been established due to limited available data. A suggestion for managing those at risk of refeeding syndrome may involve the following:

- Before commencing enteral nutrition support, correct electrolyte deficiencies and carefully restore circulatory volume (Sobotka, 2010).
- Commence prophylactic supplementation such as phosphate, thiamine and multivitamin supplements prior to and during refeeding (Bhraonáin and Lawton, 2011; Birmingham and Beumont, 2004; Royal Australian and New Zealand College of Psychiatrists, 2004).

- Avoid consumption of high carbohydrate fluids (soft drinks, fruit juices and cordials) to minimise the risk of reducing serum phosphate levels.
- Monitor biochemistry daily for the first week and second daily for the second week. Alterations in biochemistry and observations prior to and during refeeding must be addressed (Birmingham et al., 2004; Kohn, Golden and Shenker, 1998).
- Feeding should be introduced slowly and gradually increased as tolerated (see section on Nutritional Requirements and Refeeding).
- If symptoms of refeeding syndrome arise, nutrient intake should be reduced or suspended until further continuation is medically indicated (Royal Australian and New Zealand College of Psychiatrists, 2004).

Conclusion

Nutritional intervention is one of the central components of the treatment of any eating disorder. This can, however, be associated with potential physical risk and does have the potential to exacerbate disordered eating behaviour. Therefore careful and knowledgeable consideration of the complexities involved and strategies required to refeed and to foster healthy eating behaviour are essential. Key components for successful intervention in nutrition include a therapeutic alliance, family involvement, refeeding safely and facilitating normal, healthy eating behaviour.

Summary

- Nutrition intervention is a central component of treatment of any eating disorder, and is associated with significant physical and psychological risk.
- Informed understanding of the complexities involved and appropriate strategies for intervention are crucial
- A comprehensive nutrition assessment is vital, with emphasis on the specific information required and how this is collected.
- Clear communication, refeeding safely, therapeutic alliance, facilitating change towards normal, healthy eating and involving the patient and family are key considerations for intervention.

References

American Psychiatric Association (2006). *Treatment of Patients with Eating Disorders* (3rd ed.). Online. Available http://psychiatryonline.org/data/Books/prac/EatingDisorders 3ePG_04-28-06.pdf (accessed 16 August 2011).
Andersen, A. E., Bowers, W., and Evans, K. (1997). Inpatient treatment of anorexia

nervosa, In *Handbook of Treatment for Eating Disorders* (2nd ed., Ch. 17). London: The Guilford Press.

Beumont, P. J. V., Beumont, C. C., Touyz, S. W., and Williams, H. (1997). Nutritional counselling and supervised exercise, In *Handbook of Treatment for Eating Disorders* (2nd ed., Ch. 9). London: The Guilford Press.

Bhraonáin, S. N., and Lawton, L. D. (2011). Chronic malnutrition may in fact be an acute emergency, *The Journal of Emergency Medicine*, article in press.

Birmingham, C. L., and Beumont, P. (2004). *Medical Management of Eating Disorders*. Cambridge: Cambridge University Press.

Brooks M., and Melink G. (1995). The refeeding syndrome: An approach to understanding its complications and preventing its occurrence, *Pharmacotherapy*, 15 (6), 713–726.

Couturier, J., and Mahmood, A. (2009). Meal support therapy reduces the use of nasogastric feeding for adolescents hospitalized with anorexia nervosa, *Eating Disorders*, 17, 327–332.

Kohn, M. R., Golden, N. H., and Shenker, I. R. (1998). Cardiac arrest and delirium: Presentations of the refeeding syndrome in severely malnourished adolescents with anorexia nervosa, *Journal of Adolescent Health*, 22, 239–243.

McVeagh, P., and Reed, E. (2001). *Kids Food Health, Nutrition and Your Child's Development: From School-Age to Teenage*. Sydney: Finch Publishing.

Melchoir, J. C. (1998). From malnutrition to refeeding during anorexia nervosa, *Current Opinions in Clinical Nutrition and Metabolic Care*, 1 (6), 481–485.

National Institute for Clinical Excellence (2004). *Eating Disorders, Core Interventions in the Treatment and Management of Anorexia Nervosa, Bulimia Nervosa and Related Eating Disorders*. London: The British Psychological Society and Gaskell.

Neiderman, M., Richardson, J., Farley, A., and Lask, B. (2001). Naso-gastric feeding in early-onset eating disorders, *International Journal of Eating Disorders*, 29, 441–448.

Neiderman, M., Zardy, M., Tattersall, M., and Lask, B. (2000). Enteric feeding in early-onset anorexia nervosa, *International Journal of Eating Disorders*, 28, 470–475.

Ornstein, R. M., Golden, N. H., Jacobson, M. S., and Shenker, I. R. (2003). Hypophosphatemia during nutritional rehabilitation in anorexia nervosa: Implications for refeeding and monitoring, *Journal of Adolescent Health*, 32 (1), 83–88.

Patchell, C. (2000). Feeding school-age children and adolescents, In *Nutrition and Child Health* (Ch. 5). Sydney: Baillière Tindall.

Royal Australian and New Zealand College of Psychiatrists (2004). Australian and New Zealand Clinical Practice Guidelines for the Treatment of Anorexia Nervosa, *Australian and New Zealand Journal of Psychiatry*, 38, 659–670.

Royal College of Psychiatrists (2005). *Nutritional Guidelines for Anorexia Nervosa*. Council Report 130 (CR 130). Online. Available http://www.rcpsych.ac.uk/files/pdfversion/cr130.pdf (accessed 16 August 2011).

Russell, J., Baur, L., Beumont, P., Byrnes, S., and Zipfel, S. (1998). Refeeding of anorexics: Wasteful not wilful, *The Lancet*, 352 (9138), 1445–1446.

Sobotka, L. (2010). Basics in clinical nutrition: Refeeding syndrome. *e-SPEN, the European e-Journal of Clinical Nutrition and Metabolism*, 5, e146–e147.

Windauer, U., Lennerts, W., Talbot, P., Touyz, S. W., and Beumont, P. J. V. (1993). How well are 'cured' anorexia nervosa patients? *British Journal of Psychiatry*, 163, 195–200.

Chapter 13

Family approaches

Cecile Rausch Herscovici

Overview

Family approaches have consistently appeared to be an important component for child and adolescent eating disorders. Notwithstanding the limitations of the available evidence, there is general agreement that family interventions should be offered whenever possible, and especially for adolescents with anorexia nervosa. This chapter reviews family treatment models and the available research evidence.

Introduction

Since the 1970s, family-oriented approaches have appeared to have most value for adolescent anorexia nervosa. Family approaches have been researched more than any other model of treatment for this age group and current knowledge informs not only of their efficacy, but also of the components that seemingly contribute to outcome and the clinical circumstances that render them more effective. The latter is important because it is that sort of information, coupled with knowledge regarding the processes underlying the resulting changes that leads to specific targets for intervention. This chapter will focus on the rationale that has sustained family approaches through time and on the clinical implications of the contents derived from both quantitative and qualitative research. Little information is available on the application of family-oriented approaches to other forms of disturbed eating behaviour and there is scarce evidence-based research relating to their response to treatment (Bryant-Waugh, Markham, Kreipe, and Walsh, 2010). Hence, the family approaches that will be discussed subsequently refer only to the classical eating disorders of anorexia nervosa, bulimia nervosa and their variants.

History of family approaches

The pioneering work carried out with families dates back to the 1950s when Bateson and his team (Bateson, Jackson, Haley, and Weakland, 1956), while studying families with a schizophrenic member, described the family as an organized system whose members behaved according to rules that dictated interpersonal behaviours and communications. Family systems therapy was designed to challenge and disrupt unhelpful patterns of interaction. A major breakthrough of this contextual approach was that it involved not only the identified patient, but also the wider system, and most commonly the family.

Family therapy for anorexia nervosa (often referred to as the Maudsley model) is an adaptation of Minuchin's family therapy pioneered at the Philadelphia Child Guidance Clinic in the 1970s with few key differences. Minuchin and colleagues proposed a 'psychosomatic paradigm' as typical of families with a member affected by anorexia nervosa (Minuchin, Rosman, and Baker, 1978). According to that conceptual framework, the presenting organization of these families was characterized by enmeshment, overprotection, conflict avoidance, rigidity, and triangular involvement of the identified patient in parental conflict. Noteworthy, in most cases these observations of family interaction were carried out when the disease was present, making it difficult to determine whether the patterns of interaction were the cause or the consequence of the eating disorder. In fact, later studies showed that such characteristics are common (though not universal) in families who have children with any chronic illness. In other words, these are not necessarily pre-existing (or causal) conditions but more often ways in which the family adapts to the strains and requirements of a chronic disorder (Wood et al., 1989).

Often the original concept was misinterpreted as presuming a family aetiology with distinction between causal and maintenance factors becoming blurred (Eisler et al., 2005). Worth mentioning is that a causative attribution is contrary to the mutual interdependence of factors inherent to the systems approach. It is only fair to its creators to emphasize that the approach was not set on blaming the parents but rather on changing the family structure because it was considered a context that favoured both the development and most importantly the maintenance of the anorexia nervosa. From that standpoint, the main goal of therapy was to 'normalize' the family dynamics (Cook-Darzens, Doyen, and Mouren, 2008).

In the 1980s, a seminal group of clinical researchers at the Maudsley Hospital in London, Russell, Eisler and Dare furthered this approach and conducted research that consistently informed the field on the intricacies of the model. Aside from the treatment trials, the observational and naturalistic studies that followed showed that there was no consistent pattern of family structure nor of family functioning in families with an eating disordered member (Eisler, 1995). In fact, as others have shown, these families comprise a heterogeneous group, in terms of not only their patterns of interaction, but also of their emotional climate. Indeed they are more similar to control families than to any other group (Cook-Darzens, Doyen, Falissard, and Mouren, 2005; Kog, Vertommen, and Vandereycken, 1987; Roijen, 1992).

Family therapy for the treatment of eating disorders has also received the input of other theoretical orientations including most notably Milan Systemic (Selvini-Palazzoli, 1974), strategic (Madanes, 1981) and narrative (White, 1989). However, no direct comparisons of these approaches has been made and the only systematic evaluation done was the follow-up study of a Milan oriented treatment (Stierlin and Weber, 1987).

How theory informs practice

Epistemology refers to the rules we utilize to get to know and understand the world and our experience. Cybernetic epistemology is considered to have been a turning point in the behavioural sciences. It introduced the idea that systems maintain their stability by means of self-regulatory mechanisms that also become manifest in the processes of human communication and interaction. This understanding of human behaviour emphasizes the role of the social context in shaping the individual's behaviour, emotions and ideas. General systems theory deals with the study of the relation among the parts that interact in a context, stressing that they are a part of a whole that is not equal to the sum of its components.

Circular causality, derived from this frame, differs from traditional linear causality in that it takes place in a context of relationships in such a way that each cause is at the same time effect of a prior cause. Consequently, instead of searching for the historical explanation of the current problems, one looks for the maintaining factors that operate on the current interactions. The actual context contributes to maintain the problem either by active participation of its members (e.g. dysfunctional family interactions regarding symptom management) or due to deficits in essential resources of the natural context (e.g. parents who feel helpless and declare themselves incompetent in helping their daughter). Because from this perspective, insight per se does not bring about change, the proposed change aims at behaviour rather than cognitions or emotions. Therefore the focus of intervention is on current observable interactions that perpetuate the problem, rather than on alleged causal factors. Problems are not only discussed, but are often enacted (brought into the therapy room as a live performance). This allows the therapist to intervene directly, with the potential for a more positive interactional outcome. In this sense, the therapist has an active role in promoting change and sometimes turns to crisis induction as a way of facilitating change, especially when the system is stuck in unhelpful interactions. The lunch session, originally described by the Philadelphia Child Guidance team (Rosman, Minuchin, and Liebman, 1975) is a classic example of the latter, has been used over many years, and is even incorporated in the manualised version of the Maudsley model (Lock, Le Grange, Agras, and Dare, 2001).

A significant implication of this focus on the here and now is that treatment of anorexia nervosa is more likely to be effective when informed by models of the maintenance of the disorder rather than by accounts of its development (Shafran and de Silva, 2003). Consequently, the family becomes the focus of treatment, not because they have caused the problem, but because they have become a part of it. Thus, while intervening, we are not looking at the family characteristics that brought on the eating disorder, but rather at how they have reorganized around it. As in its earlier days, the main thrust of this treatment is to promote a parental unified stance in dealing with the eating disorder.

The most important change introduced in recent years by the Maudsley group has been to place a major emphasis on alleviating the parents' sense of blame. Seeing and treating people in a family context can mistakenly carry strong connotations of blame, under the assumption that they are summoned because they have caused or contributed to the problem. Frequently, when a child or adolescent is diagnosed with an eating disturbance or an eating disorder, the parents are often overcome by a sense of guilt and failure that typically undermines their ability to respond effectively to the requirements of the presenting problem. Hence, a crucial goal of the clinician working with parents is to empower them for this task, a goal that is accomplished by eliciting their strengths and resources.

Removal of the parental sense of blame is achieved mainly by an intervention originally named by White (1989), as *externalizing the problem*. This consists essentially of distinguishing between, on the one hand, the pathology, and on the other, the identity of the patient. This facilitates the creation of a united front to challenge the disorder. In so doing the therapist joins the family in stressing that they are not to blame for the disorder, but rather its victims, and that their help is needed in order to free the patient from the illness.

Another component of the family-oriented approach is that of psycho- education, in which the therapist informs the patient and family of the effects of starvation and current knowledge about the disorder, emphasizing its multidimensional nature and elusive aetiology, with the two fold goal of understanding what they are up against and of ruling out any self-blaming attitude (Lask, 2000). Another noteworthy difference is the encouragement of the adolescents' cooperation with treatment, enriched lately by the motivational approach (see Chapter 11).

Clinical goals

The main clinical goals are:

I. Anxiety relief/containment

It is critical that the therapeutic process strikes a balance between containing the fear, frustration, and anxiety that inevitably accompany the parents and the patient affected by an eating disorder, while at the same time keeping a sufficient level of tension that enables them to move forward and challenge the status quo. The containment provided by the therapist's expertise and empathic support will assist them in managing the disorder. Because the parents and the siblings are usually overwhelmed, stressed, and frustrated by the hardships caused by the eating disorder, it is advisable to address these burdens, as a way not only of joining the system, but mainly to assist in dealing with them. This will contribute to helping the family regain a feeling of competency.

2. Getting acquainted with the disorder

It is of paramount importance that both the parents and the identified patient acknowledge the nature of disorder, its feature of being temporarily beyond her control, and consequently the necessity of parental involvement in its management.

3. Empowering the parents

The therapist strives to empower the parents to handle the everyday contingencies related to the eating disorder (dieting, purging, hyperactivity, and conflict around mealtimes). This often requires challenging unhelpful interactions regarding food intake and symptom management and supporting the parents in the sustained effort that is required. In order for the parents to achieve a sense of competency, the therapist promotes a coherent and cohesive parental team and remains focused on symptom management during the initial stage of treatment. Reinforcing the parental subsystem and working separately with the identified patient can contribute to a favourable outcome.

4. Conflict management skills

Given the frequent occurrence of conflict in eating disorders, the development of conflict management skills within the family is often beneficial, not only regarding the contingencies of symptom management, but also as a specific resource designed to enhance relapse prevention

5. Addressing other problematic issues

When the eating disorder has become manageable, therapy can proceed to identify and work through developmental issues such as autonomy and independence, and any longstanding problematic interpersonal interactions, belief systems, and role expectations that may contribute to maintenance of the eating disorder.

However, it should be noted that none of the above will suffice to resolve the eating disorder and the focus on eating behaviour and underlying issues needs to be maintained until symptom management has been attained.

Family oriented treatment for adolescent bulimia nervosa is very similar to that for anorexia nervosa. The salient differences relate to the usually older age of the affected adolescent, her expectably greater autonomy, and the ego dystonic nature of the bulimic features. Hence, instead of encouraging the parents to take charge of normalizing the eating patterns and preventing the occurrence of purging behaviours, the therapist proposes a collaborative approach enlisting the patient and the parents in the pursuit of challenging the bulimia nervosa.

In Lock and Le Grange's manual (2001), treatment usually entails about 20 family sessions, lasts between four and six months, and consists of three stages. As in the treatment for anorexia nervosa, initially parents are encouraged to disrupt disordered eating behaviours, and therapy deals with separating these behaviours from the adolescent's self-identity. In the second stage, control of the symptomatic behaviour is passed on from the parents to the adolescent. The final stage involves addressing the effects of the bulimia nervosa on the adolescent's developmental processes.

Family therapy and family interventions

In clinical practice, a range of different interventions and models for involving parents and/or families in treatment have been developed including family therapy, parental counselling, separate family counselling, multi-family group treatment and group psycho-education for parents of adolescents.

Different models of family therapy for eating disorders have utilized an array of techniques and strategies, largely dependent upon each model's theory of change. For example the structural approach (Minuchin, Rosman and Baker, 1978) from which the 'Maudsley Model' is derived focuses on reinforcing the parental sub-system. Narrative therapists focus on distinguishing between the illness and the patient (see above) and assist patients to emerge from therapy with a sense of empowerment that enables them to take a proactive role as agents of change in their community. (White, 1991), The feminist perspective (Brumberg, 1988; Bryant-Waugh, 2000; Walters, Carter, Papp, and Silverstein, 1988) challenges the malevolent influence of certain values and cultural practices such as the stereotypes and gender inequalities. From this standpoint, women are under social pressure to be concerned with social judgments about their appearance and girls are often brought up to put the needs of the other before their own. These patriarchal structures shape gender differences, and the disproportionate gender representation of eating disorders is a dramatic expression of this bias.

The nature, type, and intensity of family involvement needs to be tailored to the developmental stage of the patient and also depends on the degree of involvement patients have with their families. The main goal of the most effective family interventions is the restoration of effective parenting functioning, one that will enable the parents to work consistently towards helping their child attain a healthy body weight and symptom free eating habits. There is general agreement that a family approach is advisable in the majority of cases of adolescent eating disorders, as long as the identified patient is living at least with one parent. Possible exceptions might include if either the patient or a parent is psychotic, or if there is ongoing violence or abuse.

Additionally, there are specific indicators for including the siblings; most notably:

- When it seems advisable to provide a space for them to express how the eating disorder is affecting them. Consequently the therapy can contribute to working out arrangements that protect them from that prolonged turmoil. On other occasions, the siblings can provide an emotional support system for their sister at a time when she feels challenged by the parent's demand of changes in the eating behaviour.

- When the identified patient needs help in attaining a validating presence in the family context that is not based on her illness. Often this is related to the developmental or structural arrangements within the family (e.g. parents who lack confidence in their child's ability to become increasingly independent and/or intergenerational coalitions that keep the identified patient attached to one parent at the expense of her autonomy).

A combination of a family approach with individual therapy is suitable when the eating disorder has had a protracted presence in the patient's life and it has become an integral part of her identity, impairing her ability to imagine a future without an eating disorder and thus making it even more difficult to let go of it. On the other hand, working alone with the parents is advisable when longstanding marital difficulties hinder the possibility of agreeing on management strategies. The common denominators of these interventions are containment of parental anxiety, alleviation of parental guilt, and involvement of the parents as co-therapists.

Parental Counselling

Parental counselling has been described by Lask and Bryant-Waugh (1997) not as an intervention in itself, but rather as an attitude that should prevail in parental management of a child's eating disorder, regardless of the preferred family therapy model (Lask and Bryant-Waugh, 1997). The key suggested components of parental counselling are what the authors call the four Cs: Cohesion, Consistency, Communication, and Conflict resolution.

- *Cohesion* alludes to the parents working together as a team.
- *Consistency* refers to the finding of a mutually agreed approach between both parents, which is applied over time. Consistency enhances the chances of a better outcome and that is why it is advisable for parents to be supported in their effort to persevere in spite of the inevitable early opposition of the child.
- *Communication* that is open and direct will contribute to a clearer under-standing of both the feelings involved and of the issues to be resolved.
- *Conflict resolution* is a key area of healthy family functioning and is likely to contribute to earlier resolution of the eating disorder.

Parental counselling is most commonly provided without the children present. This is very often a frustrating and trying experience for the parents, related not only to the possible feeling of guilt and blame, but most likely to the anger and helplessness resulting from the child's manipulations, denial, and sometimes violent outbursts. It is not infrequent for parents to describe their child as seeming to be 'possessed' at times, using language and attitudes totally foreign to their family life. Additionally, a hostile environment will probably undermine both the child's self esteem and also the results of the therapeutic effort. Therefore, it is advisable to contemplate having meetings with the parents alone so that these feelings can be dealt with and the parents helped in working out disagreements between them. The differences between parental counselling and family therapy may at times be blurred, but so long as the therapist is clear about the goals of the therapy this need not be a problem.

Multi-family day treatment

Multi-family day treatment involves parents or whole families in the therapeutic process instead of or complementary to "typical" family-oriented treatment. This kind of approach is in part inspired by the Minuchin team, who pioneered the idea of 'enacting' the eating problems concretely (Rosman et al., 1975). A number of outpatient programs have been developed, either as an alternative to hospitalization or as an outpatient extension of inpatient treatment. The active involvement of the parents required by the structure of the program, facilitates connection with other families, who provide feedback and support, thus contributing to overcoming the sense of loneliness and stigmatization that often affects these families. The time frame, the group context, and the intensity of the treatment program require the patients and their parents to adapt continually to new situations, thus enabling the development of an effective 'hands on' approach to symptom management (Scholz and Asen, 2001). Typically a programme consists of an initial intensive 2–5 day presence that is subsequently tailored to shorter monthly meetings tapered down throughout one year (Eisler, 2005; Scholz, Rix, Scholz, Gantchev, and Thömke, 2005).

Group Psycho-education

Some treatment centres have developed psycho-education programs involving parents in the therapeutic process as an adjunct to outpatient treatment. In one program, parents of children receiving treatment attended 16 session group meetings, which adapted elements of cognitive and behavioural theory. Parents reported that these meetings had a profound impact on their management of their child's eating disorder and on decreasing the burden they experienced (Zucker, Marcus, and Bulik, 2006). This kind of approach may represent a useful and economic method in the multimodal treatment of eating disorders.

Evidence for family approaches in anorexia nervosa

Since Minuchin and colleagues (1978) published the first follow-up study of 53 adolescents treated with family therapy and reported that 86 per cent had recovered, subsequent uncontrolled studies have produced comparable findings. The case series of the Philadelphia group presented a short duration of illness (mean, ~8 months) and was treated mostly on an outpatient basis, albeit some were also briefly admitted to the paediatric unit.

Two studies in which family therapy was the main form of treatment combined individual and inpatient treatment. A five-year follow-up of study of 25 adolescents with anorexia nervosa with a short duration of illness (mean: 8.1 months) conducted in Toronto (Martin, 1985) revealed a good outcome for 80 per cent of the patients according to the Morgan and Russell criteria (Morgan and Russell, 1975). In Buenos Aires, a series of 30 anorexia nervosa patients (mean age: 14.7 years; mean duration of illness: 10.3 months) were treated and followed-up 4–8.6 years after first presentation (Rausch Herscovici and Bay, 1996). Although 40 per cent of these had been hospitalized, at end of treatment outcome was good for 60 percent, intermediate for 30 percent, and poor for 10 per cent of the patients, assessed with the above mentioned criteria.

Another case series of 45 children and adolescents (mean age: 14.5 years) were compared at pre and post treatment after receiving an average of 17 manualised family–based treatment sessions (Le Grange, Binford, and Loeb, 2005). Using the Morgan Russell outcome criteria (weight and menstrual status) at post treatment, 56 per cent had a good outcome, 25 per cent had and intermediate outcome, and 11 per cent responded poorly.

An open trial aimed at assessing the feasibility of effectively delivering the manualised version of family-based treatment, assessed and treated twenty adolescents (ages 12–17) with anorexia nervosa or sub-threshold anorexia nervosa (Loeb et al., 2007). After an average of one year of treatment, for the 75 per cent patients that completed treatment, end of the study analysis showed a significant improvement in percentage of ideal body weight (from 82.3 to 93.6) and of menstrual status (an increase from 11 per cent to 67 per cent of those attaining regular menses).

Depending on the selection criteria of each review, the number of randomized controlled trials evaluating family therapy for adolescent samples is variable. Altogether there are eleven published studies comprising fewer than 600 patients. Although family therapy is frequently used for adolescents with anorexia nervosa, the only model that been systematically tested to date in randomized controlled trials is the one pioneered by Minuchin et al., later refined by the Maudsley group (Dare, 1985; Dare and Eisler, 1997) and then manualised as the 'family-based treatment' or 'Maudsley Approach' (Lock et al., 2001). This approach has been tested in nine trials with adolescents and outcomes indicate it is effective for this age group with most patients (80–90 per cent) showing good to excellent progress (Eisler et al., 2000; Le Grange, Eisler, Dare and Russell, 1992; Lock, Agras, Bryson, and Kraemer, 2005; Rausch Herscovici, 2006). Additionally, at longer term follow-up treatment effects were sustained. (Eisler et al., 1997; Eisler, Simic, Russell, and Dare, 2007; Le Grange et al., 2005; Lock, Couturier, and Agras, 2006). However, it is not clear whether this treatment would be appropriate for older adolescent patients living away from home.

The effectiveness of the Maudsley approach and of other forms of family therapy has been compared to other treatments. Three studies found family therapy to be superior (Lock et al., 2010; Robin et al., 1999; Russell, Szmukler, Dare, and Eisler, 1987), and for three other studies, the differences were not significant (Ball and Mitchell, 2004; Espina, Ortego Saenz De Calderon, and Ochoa De Alda Apellaniz, 2000; Geist, Heinman, Stephens, Davis, and Katzman, 2000). Notably, some differences favouring family therapy seem to diminish at longer term follow-up, suggesting that over time, those treated with other methods could attain a comparable outcome (Eisler et al., 1997; Robin et al., 1999). The more recently published trial involving 121 adolescents compared family-based treatment with adolescent-focused individual therapy (Lock et al., 2010). However only those with mild illness were included (ill for less than a year and a weight loss of less than 25%) and there is no evidence of effectiveness of this approach for moderately or severely ill patients.

A recent Cochrane Review included 13 randomized controlled trials of any age, most of which have been mentioned above. Eight trials compared family therapy to other psychological interventions. The derived evidence suggests that family therapy might be more effective than treatment as usual in the short term, albeit it does not suffice to indicate whether this effect persists in the long term. Only one of these trials segregated participants by age and level of chronicity suggesting family therapy had better responses among the younger, less chronic group (Russell et al., 1987). Hence, a conclusion about the effect of family therapy on chronicity or on age of onset remains elusive.

The other five trials compared different forms of family therapy. One of these applied a 'specific family approach' to individual families, and 'systems family therapy' for the group setting (Whitney et al., 2011; NB: the data provided to the Cochrane Review had been unpublished at the time).

The other family treatments evaluated were theoretically very similar, with one differing element: short-term versus long term (Lock et al., 2005); conjoint versus separated family therapy (Le Grange et al., 1992; Eisler, 2000), and family therapy with and without a family meal (Rausch Herscovici, 2006). The review concluded it was not possible to determine whether there are differences between different types of family therapy due to the scarcity of trials and usable data, coupled with the lack of specificity of the theoretical underpinnings of the family therapy used in a number of trials (Fisher, Hetrick, and Rushford, 2010).

Of particular note is a critical analysis of the research corpus which concluded that the true value of family therapy for adolescent anorexia nervosa has yet to be established, because of small sample sizes and other methodological weaknesses such as strict inclusion, which limit the interpretation and generalisability of the findings (Fairburn, 2005). Fairburn concludes that based on available evidence, it is not clear that any effects of treatment are due to the involvement of the family or to other the components of treatment.

The only case series of family therapy for children with anorexia nervosa published to date (Lock, le Grange, Forsberg, and Hewell, 2006) indicates that this approach is equally effective for 9- to 12-year-old-children with anorexia nervosa as it is for 13 to 18 year olds suggesting that both age groups benefit from a family-based approach to treatment.

Evidence of family therapy for bulimia nervosa

Only two studies have examined family interventions designed for bulimia nervosa in adolescents. When family therapy was compared to cognitive behavioural therapy guided self-care at six months, bingeing had decreased significantly in the latter group. However, at 12 months this difference had disappeared and no other differences between groups were found either in behavioural or attitudinal eating disorder symptoms. Because direct cost of treatment was lower for cognitive behavioural therapy guided self-care, that form of treatment seems to offer a slight advantage by decreasing bingeing behaviours more rapidly and proving more cost effective (Schmidt et al., 2007).

When family therapy adapted for bulimia nervosa was compared to individual supportive psychotherapy, the former performed better in terms of abstinence of bulimic symptoms at end of treatment although at follow-up this advantage was no longer statistically significant (Le Grange, Crosby, Rathouz, and Leventhal, 2007).

These studies may not generalize to younger adolescent patients with bulimia nervosa.

Evidence of family-based therapy for other eating disorders

Using current diagnostic criteria, more than half of children and adolescents with eating disorders are diagnosed as 'eating disorders not otherwise specified'. It has been suggested that they should be treated using approaches with evidence of effectiveness for the full-syndrome of anorexia nervosa and bulimia nervosa (Le Grange et al., 2006; Lock et al., 2010). Taking into account that some of the controlled trials have included sub-threshold cases, coupled with some data indicating that family therapy is useful for patients under the age of 12 presenting with symptoms of anorexia nervosa, the family approach has been advised for this subgroup also (Lock, 2010).

There have been as yet no controlled treatment studies of binge eating disorder in this younger population. A case report described the treatment of an adolescent with binge eating disorder using dialectical behavioural therapy modified to include four family sessions. Although binge-eating episodes decreased, weight concerns worsened (Safer, Couturier, and Lock, 2007). Because too little is known about this disorder in adolescents and further clinical research is required, it is not possible to draw conclusions regarding treatment (Rutherford and Couturier, 2007).

In summary, reviewers have consistently concluded that in the absence of evidence for other treatments, family therapy should be used for treating adolescents and ought to be considered a promising resource for other eating problems in children and adolescents (Berkman et al., 2006; Keel and Haedt, 2008). Notwithstanding the limitations of the accumulated evidence, the National Institute of Clinical Evidence of the United Kingdom and a position paper of the

Academy for Eating Disorders in the United States recommend that family inter-ventions should be offered in the treatment of younger patients with eating disor-ders whenever possible, and especially for adolescents with anorexia nervosa (Le Grange, Lock, Loeb, and Nicholls, 2010; NICE, 2004).

There is preliminary evidence that the multi-family day treatment is a cost effective approach yielding positive results thus providing a valuable alternative to inpatient care for many cases and a multi-centre, multi-national research project is currently under way (Asen and Scholz, 2010). Meanwhile a Canadian study has compared the relative efficacy of eight sessions of multi-family therapy with the same number of individual family sessions in 25 hospitalized adolescents (Geist et al., 2000). Although both therapeutic modalities produced similar levels of improvement, multi-family treatment appears advantageous when taking into account the cost-effective aspect.

Moderating factors

Moderators of treatment are factors that have a significant influence on the effects of treatment although they are independent of the treatment condition. Potential moderators are age, co-morbidity, chronicity, therapist characteristics, etc. Exploratory studies of moderators of outcome of family treatments for anorexia nervosa suggest that intact families respond more favourably to treatment than single parent and separated or divorced families. Additionally, co-morbid psycho-pathology predicts dropout and remission (Lock et al., 2006). Further, adolescents with very high levels of obsessive-compulsive features may not fare as well as those without these features and tend to require more time in treatment (Lock, Couturier, and Agras, 2006).

Regarding family interactions, there is indication that problematic family behaviours may hinder remission. Conversely, healthier family relationships seem to have an important effect on therapeutic engagement and outcome. Not surprisingly, newer models emphasize the interpersonal component in the main-tenance of anorexia nervosa (Schmidt and Treasure, 2006). Expressed emotion is a measure that reflects the amount of criticism, hostility, and emotional over-involvement expressed by family members towards the patient. Studies indicate that families displaying higher levels of expressed emotion are often more diffi-cult to engage in therapy and more likely to drop out. Taking into account that this variable not only affects adherence to treatment and outcome, but also seems to be amenable to improvement with family therapy, a family approach appears warranted in cases of high parental criticism and aggressiveness. As noted earlier, available evidence underscores that this subgroup of patients from families with high expressed emotion have a better outcome if these family dynamics are initially tackled in separate sessions (Eisler et al., 2000; Eisler et al., 2005; Eisler, Simic, Russell, and Dare, 2007; Szmukler et al., 1985; Uehara, Kawashima, Goto, Tasaki, and Someya, 2001).

Regarding bulimia nervosa, moderators of outcome of family treatment so far identified are age and eating-related psychopathology. Family therapy has been found to be more acceptable to younger adolescents (Schmidt et al., 2007) and one study showed that when the parents were not involved in treatment, the patient tended to perceive the mother as having a more negative attitude towards the illness (Perkins et al., 2005).

On the other hand, patients with less severe associated psychopathology seem to do better with family-based therapy as compared to individual supportive therapy. However for those with greater psychopathology, treatment type seems not to make a difference (Le Grange, Crosby, and Lock, 2008). Regarding predictors of outcome, patients with fewer episodes of binge/purge at baseline were found to be more prone to a better outcome, and those who do not show early reductions in bulimic symptoms are unlikely to have remitted at end of treatment or at follow-up (Le Grange, Doyle, Crosby, and Chen, 2008).

Qualitative studies

There is scarce information regarding both how patients perceive family treatments as a whole, and what they think of its components. Taking into account that patient satisfaction plays a central role in the therapeutic alliance and outcome, exploration of this area appears warranted. This is especially so given adolescents with anorexia nervosa typically deny their illness, are rarely motivated to initiate treatment, and are very reluctant to gain weight. Additionally, from a motivational perspective, placing the parents in charge of weight restoration could undermine the therapeutic alliance with any patient in pre-contemplation or contemplation (see Chapter 11). This is not to say that refeeding should not be implemented but rather careful consideration needs to be given to ensuring a good therapeutic alliance in such circumstances.

Evidence derived from qualitative studies reveals interesting information that might contribute to refine and enhance family approaches. Overall, studies conducted to this date show that many young patients and their carers developed a strong therapeutic alliance and rated treatment as successful (Krautter and Lock, 2004; Pereira, Lock, and Oggins, 2006; Zaitsoff, Doyle, Hoste, and le Grange, 2008). The expertise of the specialist seems to add to the sense of being understood and ability to trust the therapist (Roots, Rowlands, and Gowers, 2009). One study showed that even though patients found treatment to be overall acceptable, adolescents would have liked it explore the causes of the illness and to focus on other personal problems (Le Grange and Gelman, 1998). In another study parents reported being more pleased with the therapists than were the patients and valued the family sessions more than the patients (Paulson-Karlsson, Nevonen, and Engström, 2006).

These findings point to the advantage of keeping a flexible frame of treatment, contingent on the requirements of the stage of treatment and of the issues to be addressed; a structure that also allows for seeing the patient individually when judged clinically appropriate.

A study designed to evaluate the patient's and parent's perception of the components of family based treatment, found that the family meal (a key intervention in the manualised version of the Maudsley approach) was not mentioned by either, whilst the therapeutic relationship was rated as the most valued aspect (Rausch Herscovici, Torrente, and Kovalskys, 2009). This finding suggests that the family meal may not be an essential component of family therapy, contrary to common reports in the literature.

Summarizing, given the nature of the data available to this date, it becomes clear that the scientific evidence is currently weak for factors associated with efficacy of treatment and is unavailable with regard to how socio-demographic factors affect outcome. Notably, of the 13 studies documented by the Cochrane Review, only two were from non-English speaking countries. However, from a clinical standpoint, it becomes apparent that parents being in charge of restoring the child's normal eating habits, and temporarily taking control of symptom management, is a vital component.

Additionally, the focus placed by the family approach on maintenance factors of the eating disorder is probably the concept that best addresses the different themes of intervention at each stage of treatment, e.g. the self-perpetuating nature of the eating disorder, of unhelpful family interactions related to symptom management, of conflict avoidance, of failure in conflict resolution, etc.

Albeit often overlooked, intrinsic to this approach and pre-requisites for therapeutic efforts to succeed, are the early establishment of a therapeutic alliance (see Chapter 11 and 12) and excellent team work (see Chapter 11). The team needs to be cohesive, consistent, and focused. A useful metaphor for all those involved is to describe the endeavour they face when entering a game (hockey, football, or whatever sports team they best relate to), a game in which the eating disorder is the sole adversary. The team's success at defeating this formidable opponent is contingent on its ability to remain always alert (focused), consistently supporting each other (cohesive) and tenaciously striving to attain the supreme goal of victory.

A fair amount of creativity might be required for this venture, as there is seldom a 'one size fits all' approach for dealing with eating disorders. In other words, even though the family approach is obviously important, it will probably be enhanced by the therapist's ability to be flexible and eclectic. The clinician needs to use an array of interventions that best suits the specifics of the situation and the age of the patients involved, and continually to assess the impact of each intervention on patient and family.

Conclusion

The available evidence indicates that family therapy remains an essential component of the treatment of child and adolescent eating disorders. However there is emerging evidence of suggesting the need to tailor the treatment to the characteristics of each family and of each patient. Hence, family therapy models will need to become more eclectic as they integrate a variety of interventions. The crucial role assigned to the family in the improvement and recovery of young patients with eating disorders has shifted the locus of family intervention from a deficit-based model (normalising family pathology) to a resource-based approach (aimed at mobilising family competencies). Hence, the main aim of family therapy is to render the family resources available for challenging the eating disorder.

Summary

- Family interventions are a necessary component of the treatment of eating disorders.
- Current evidence for treatment efficacy is weak, but consistently suggests that family interventions should be offered in the treatment of younger patients with eating disorders whenever possible, and especially for adolescents with anorexia nervosa.
- The family approach addresses maintenance factors of the eating disorder at each stage of treatment.
- The therapy team needs to understand, empathise with, and respect the family's position, be supportive, but also focused on explicit goals.
- The richness of the family approach is contingent on the therapist's ability to take into account the specifics and idiosyncrasies of each particular family and construct the interventions according to each individual family's needs.

References

Asen, E., and Scholz, M. M. (2010). Eating Disorders, psychosis and mood disorders. *Mutiple-Family Therapy: Concepts and Techniques* (pp. 121–135). New York: Taylor & Francis.

Ball, J., and Mitchell, P. (2004). A randomized controlled study of cognitive behavior therapy and behavioral family therapy for anorexia nervosa patients. *Eating Disorders: The Journal of Treatment and Prevention, 12*, 303–314.

Bateson, G., Jackson, D. D., Haley, J., and Weakland, J. (1956). Toward a theory of schizophrenia. *Behavioral Science, 1*, 251–264.

Berkman, N. D., Bulik, C. M., Brownley, K. A., Lohr, K. N., Sedway, J. A., Rooks, A., et al. (2006). Management of eating disorders. *Evidence Report/Technology Assessment (Full Report), 135*, 1–166.

Brumberg, J. J. (1988). *Fasting Girls: The History of Anorexia Nervosa*. Cambridge, MA: Harvard University Press.

Bryant-Waugh, R. (2000). Developmental-systemic feminist therapy. In K. J. Miller and J. S. Mizes (Eds), *Comparative Treatments for Eating Disorders* (pp. 160–181). New York: Springer.

Bryant-Waugh, R., Markham, L., Kreipe, R., and Walsh, T. (2010). Feeding and eating disorders in childhood. *International Journal of Eating Disorders, 43* (2), 98–111.

Cook-Darzens, S., Doyen, C., Falissard, B., and Mouren, M.-C. (2005). Self-perceived family functioning in 40 French families of anorexic adolescents: implications for therapy. *European Eating Disorders Review, 13* (4), 223–236.

Cook-Darzens, S., Doyen, C., and Mouren, M.-C. (2008). Family therapy in the treatment of adolescent anorexia nervosa: current research evidence and its therapeutic implications. *Eating and Weight Disorders, 13* (4), 157–170.

Dare, C. (1985). The family therapy of anorexia nervosa. *Journal of Psychiatric Research, 19* (2–3), 435–443.

Dare, C., and Eisler, I. (1997). Family therapy for anorexia nervosa. In D. M. Garner and P. E. Garfinkel (Eds), *Handbook of Treatment for Eating Disorders* (2nd ed., pp. 307–324). New York: The Guilford Press.

Eisler, I. (1995). Family models of eating disorders. In G. Szmukler, C. Dare and J. Treasure (Eds), *Handbook of Eating Disorders. Theory, Treatment and Research* (pp. 155–176). Chichester: John Wiley & Sons.

Eisler, I. (2005). The empirical and theoretical base of family therapy and multiple family day therapy for adolescent anorexia nervosa. *Journal of Family Therapy, 27* (2), 104–131.

Eisler, I., Dare, C., Hodes, M., Russell, G., Dodge, E., and Le Grange, D. (2000). Family therapy for adolescent anorexia nervosa: the results of a controlled comparison of two family interventions. *Journal of Child Psychology and Psychiatry, 41* (6), 727–736.

Eisler, I., Dare, C., Hodes, M., Russell, G. F. M., Dodge, E., and Le Grange, D. (2005). Family therapy for adolescent anorexia nervosa: The results of a controlled comparison of two family interventions. *Focus, 3* (4), 629–640.

Eisler, I., Dare, C., Russell, G. F., Szmukler, G., Le Grange, D., and Dodge, E. (1997). Family and individual therapy in anorexia nervosa. A 5-year follow-up. *Archives of General Psychiatry, 54* (11), 1025–1030.

Eisler, I., Simic, M., Russell, G. F. M., and Dare, C. (2007). A randomised controlled treatment trial of two forms of family therapy in adolescent anorexia nervosa: a five-year follow-up. *Journal of Child Psychology and Psychiatry, 48* (6), 552–560.

Espina, E., Ortego Saenz De Calderon, M., and Ochoa De Alda Apellaniz, I. (2000). A controlled trial of family interventions in eating disorders. Changes in psychopathology and social adjustment. *Anales de Psiquiatria, 16* (8), 322–336.

Fairburn, C. G. (2005). Evidence-based treatment of anorexia nervosa. *International Journal of Eating Disorders, 37* (S1), S26–S30.

Fisher, C. A., Hetrick, S. E., and Rushford, N. (2010). Family therapy for anorexia nervosa. *Cochrane Database Syst Rev* (4), CD004780.

Geist, R., Heinman, M., Stephens, D., Davis, R., and Katzman, D. K. (2000). Comparison of family therapy and family group psychoeducation in adolescents with anorexia nervosa. *Canadian Journal of Psychiatry, 45* (2), 173–178.

Keel, P., and Haedt, A. (2008). Evidence-based psychosocial treatments for eating problems and eating disorders. *Journal of Clinical Child and Adolescent Psychology, 37* (1), 39–61.

Kog, E., Vertommen, H., and Vandereycken, W. (1987). Minuchin's psychosomatic family model revised: a concept-validation study using a multitrait-multimethod approach. *Family Process, 26* (2), 235–253.

Krautter, T., and Lock, J. (2004). Is manualized family-based treatment for adolescent anorexia nervosa acceptable to patients? Patient satisfaction at the end of treatment. *Journal of Family Therapy, 26*, 66–82.

Lask, B. (2000). Overview of management. In B. Lask and R. Bryant-Waugh (Eds), *Anorexia Nervosa and Related Eating Disorders in Childhood and Adolescence* (2nd ed., pp. 167–185). Hove: Psychology Press.

Lask, B., and Bryant-Waugh, R. (1997). Prepubertal Eating Disorders. In D. Garner and P. Garfinkel (Eds), *Handbook of Treatment for Eating Disorders* (2nd ed., pp. 476–483). New York: Guilford Press.

Le Grange, D., Binford, R., and Loeb, K. L. (2005). Manualized family-based treatment for anorexia nervosa: A case series. *Journal of the American Academy of Child and Adolescent Psychiatry*, *44* (1), 41–46.

Le Grange, D., Binford, R. B., Peterson, C. B., Crow, S. J., Crosby, R. D., Klein, M. H., et al. (2006). DSM-IV threshold versus subthreshold bulimia nervosa. *International Journal of Eating Disorders*, *39* (6), 462–467.

Le Grange, D., Crosby, R. D., and Lock, J. (2008). Predictors and moderators of outcome in family-based treatment for adolescent bulimia nervosa. *Journal of the American Academy of Child and Adolescent Psychiatry*, *47* (4), 464–470.

Le Grange, D., Crosby, R. D., Rathouz, P. J., and Leventhal, B. L. (2007). A randomized controlled comparison of family-based treatment and supportive psychotherapy for adolescent bulimia nervosa. *Archives of General Psychiatry*, *64* (9), 1049–1056.

Le Grange, D., Doyle, P., Crosby, R. D., and Chen, E. (2008). Early response to treatment in adolescent bulimia nervosa. *International Journal of Eating Disorders*, *41* (8), 755–757.

Le Grange, D., Eisler, I., Dare, C., and Russell, G. F. M. (1992). Evaluation of family treatments in adolescent anorexia nervosa: A pilot study. *International Journal of Eating Disorders*, *12*, 347–357.

Le Grange, D., and Gelman, T. (1998). The patient's perspective of treatment in eating disorders: A preliminary study. *South African Journal of Psychology*, *28*, 182–186.

Le Grange, D., Lock, J., Loeb, K., and Nicholls, D. (2010). Academy for Eating Disorders position paper: The role of the family in eating disorders. *International Journal of Eating Disorders*, *43*, 1–5.

Lock, J. (2010). Treatment of adolescent eating disorders: Progress and challenges. *Minerva Psichiatrica*, *51* (3), 207–216.

Lock, J., Agras, W. S., Bryson, S., and Kraemer, H. C. (2005). A comparison of short- and long-term family therapy for adolescent anorexia nervosa. *Journal of the American Academy of Child and Adolescent Psychiatry*, *44* (7), 632–639.

Lock, J., Couturier, J., and Agras, W. S. (2006). Comparison of long-term outcomes in adolescents with anorexia nervosa treated with family therapy. *Journal of the American Academy of Child and Adolescent Psychiatry*, *45* (6), 666–672.

Lock, J., Couturier, J., Bryson, S., and Agras, S. (2006). Predictors of dropout and remission in family therapy for adolescent anorexia nervosa in a randomized clinical trial. *International Journal of Eating Disorders*, *39* (8), 639–647.

Lock, J., Le Grange, D., Agras, S. W., and Dare, C. (2001). *Treatment Manual for Anorexia Nervosa: A Family Based Approach*. New York: The Guilford Press.

Lock, J., Le Grange, D., Agras, W. S., Moye, A., Bryson, S. W., and Jo, B. (2010). Randomized clinical trial comparing family-based treatment with adolescent-focused individual therapy for adolescents with anorexia nervosa. *Archives of General Psychiatry*, *67* (10), 1025–1032.

Lock, J., Le Grange, D., Forsberg, S., and Hewell, K. (2006). Is family therapy useful for treating children with anorexia nervosa? Results of a case series. *Journal of the American Academy of Child and Adolescent Psychiatry*, *45* (11), 1323–1328.

Loeb, K. L., Walsh, B. T., Lock, J., Le Grange, D., Jones, J., Marcus, S., et al. (2007). Open trial of family-based treatment for full and partial anorexia nervosa in adolescence: evidence of successful dissemination. *Journal of the American Academy of Child and Adolescent Psychiatry, 46* (7), 792–800.

Madanes, C. (1981). *Strategic Family Therapy.* San Francisco, CA, and London: Jossey-Bass.

Martin, E. F. (1985). The treatment and outcome of anorexia nervosa in adolescents: a prospective study and five year follow-up. *Journal of Psychiatric Research, 19,* 509–514.

Minuchin, S., Rosman, B. L., and Baker, L. (1978). *Psychosomatic Families: Anorexia Nervosa in Context.* Cambridge, MA: Harvard University Press.

Morgan, H. G., and Russell, G. F. (1975). Value of family background and clinical features as predictors of long-term outcome in anorexia nervosa: four-year follow-up study of 41 patients. *Psychological Medicine, 5* (4), 355–371.

NICE (2004). *Eating Disorders: Core Interventions in the Treatment and Management of Anorexia Nervosa, Bulimia Nervosa and Related Eating Disorders.* London: National Institute for Clinical Excellence.

Paulson-Karlsson, G., Nevonen, L., and Engström, I. (2006). Anorexia nervosa: treatment satisfaction. *Journal of Family Therapy, 28* (3), 293–306.

Pereira, T., Lock, J., and Oggins, J. (2006). Role of therapeutic alliance in family therapy for adolescent anorexia nervosa. *International Journal of Eating Disorders, 39,* 677–684.

Perkins, S., Schmidt, U., Eisler, I., Treasure, J., Yi, I., Winn, S., et al. (2005). Why do adolescents with bulimia nervosa choose not to involve their parents in treatment? *European Child and Adolescent Psychiatry, 14* (7), 376–385.

Rausch Herscovici, , C. (2006). Lunch session, weight gain and their interaction with the psychopathology of anorexia nervosa in adolescents. *Vertex, 17* (65), 7–15.

Rausch Herscovici, , C., and Bay, L. (1996). Favorable outcome of anorexia nervosa patients treated in Argentina with a family approach. *Eating Disorders: The Journal of Treatment and Prevention, 4,* 59–66.

Rausch Herscovici, C., Torrente, F., and Kovalskys, I. (2009). *Components of a Family-based Treatment for Adolescent Anorexia Nervosa from the Patients' Perspective: A Qualitative Study.* Paper presented at the The 9th London International Eating Disorders Conference.

Robin, A., Siegal, P. T., Moye, A. W., Gilroy, M., Dennis, A. B., and Sikand, A. (1999). A controlled comparison of family versus individual therapy for adolescents with anorexia nervosa. *Journal of the American Academy of Child and Adolescent Psychiatry, 38,* 1482–1489.

Roijen, S. (1992). Anorexia nervosa families – a homogeneous group? A case record study. *Acta Psychiatr Scand, 85* (3), 196–200.

Roots, P., Rowlands, L., and Gowers, S. G. (2009). User satisfaction with services in a randomised controlled trial of adolescent anorexia nervosa. *European Eating Disorders Review, 17* (5), 331–337.

Rosman, B. L., Minuchin, S., and Liebman, R. (1975). Family lunch session: An introduction to family therapy in anorexia nervosa. *American Journal of Orthopsychiatry, 45,* 846–854.

Russell, G. F., Szmukler, G. I., Dare, C., and Eisler, I. (1987). An evaluation of family therapy in anorexia nervosa and bulimia nervosa. *Archives of General Psychiatry, 44* (12), 1047–1056.

Rutherford, L., and Couturier, J. (2007). A review of psychotherapeutic interventions for children and adolescents with eating disorders. *Journal of Canadian Academy of Child and Adolescent Psychiatry*, *16* (4), 153–157.

Safer, D. L., Couturier, J. L., and Lock, J. (2007). Dialectical behavior therapy modified for adolescent binge eating disorder: A case report. *Cognitive and Behavioral Practice*, *14* (2), 157–167.

Schmidt, U., Lee, S., Beecham, J., Perkins, S., Treasure, J., Yi, I., et al. (2007). A randomized controlled trial of family therapy and cognitive behavior therapy guided self-care for adolescents with bulimia nervosa and related disorders. *American Journal of Psychiatry*, *164* (4), 591–598.

Schmidt, U., and Treasure, J. (2006). Anorexia nervosa: Valued and visible. A cognitive-interpersonal maintenance model and its implications for research and practice. *British Journal of Clinical Psychology*, *45* (3), 343–366.

Scholz, M., and Asen, E. (2001). Multiple family therapy with eating disordered adolescents: Concepts and preliminary results. *European Eating Disorders Review*, *9*, 33–42.

Scholz, M., Rix, M., Scholz, K., Gantchev, K., and Thömke, V. (2005). Multiple family therapy for anorexia nervosa: Concepts, experiences and results. *Journal of Family Therapy*, *27* (2), 132–141.

Selvini-Palazzoli, M. (1974). *Self-starvation: From the Intrapsychic to the Transpersonal Approach to Anorexia Nervosa*. London: Chaucer Publishing.

Shafran, R., and de Silva, P. (2003). Cognitive-behavioural models. In J. Treasure, U. Schmidt and E. V. Furth (Eds), *Handbook of Eating Disorders*. Chichester: Wiley.

Stierlin, H., and Weber, M. (1987). Anorexia nervosa: Lessons from a follow-up study. *Family Systems Medicine*, *7*, 120–157.

Szmukler, G. I., Eisler, I., Russell, G. F. M., and Dare, C. (1985). Anorexia nervosa, parental expressed emotion, and dropping out of treatment. *British Journal of Psychiatry*, *147*, 265–271.

Uehara, T., Kawashima, Y., Goto, M., Tasaki, S. I., and Someya, T. (2001). Psychoeducation for the families of patients with eating disorders and changes in expressed emotion: A preliminary study. *Comprehensive Psychiatry*, *42* (2), 132–138.

Walters, M., Carter, B., Papp, P., and Silverstein, O. (1988). *The Invisible Web: Gender Patterns in Family Relationships*. New York: Guilford Press.

White, M. (1989). The externalizing of the problem and the re-authoring of lives and relationships. *Dulwich Centre Newsletter*, (2), 5–28.

White, M. (1991). Deconstruction and therapy. *Dulwich Centre Newsletter*, *3*, 21–40.

Whitney, J., Murphy, T., Landau, S., Gavan, K., Todd, G., Whitaker, W., et al. (2011). A practical comparison of two types of family intervention: An exploratory RCT of family day workshops and individual family work as a supplement to inpatient care for adults with anorexia nervosa. *European Eating Disorder Review*, *20* (2), 142–150.

Wood, B., Watkins, J. B., Boyle, J. T., Nogueira, J., Zimand, E., and Carroll, L. (1989). The 'Psychosomatic Family' model: An Empirical and theoretical analysis. *Family Process*, *28* (4), 399–417.

Zaitsoff, S. L., Doyle, A. C., Hoste, R. R., and Le Grange, D. (2008). How do adolescents with bulimia nervosa rate the acceptability and therapeutic relationship in family-based treatment? *International Journal of Eating Disorders*, *41* (5), 390–398.

Zucker, N. L., Marcus, M., and Bulik, C. (2006). A group parent-training program: A novel approach for eating disorder management. *Eating and Weight Disorders*, *11* (2), 78–82.

Chapter 14

Cognitive behavioural approaches

Beth Watkins

Overview

Cognitive Behavioural Therapy (CBT) is an umbrella term used to describe therapies that share a theoretical basis in behaviourist learning theory and cognitive psychology, and which utilise methods of change derived from these theories. Whilst different, these theoretical approaches found common ground in that their focus is on the here and now and symptom reduction. Some therapies are more focused on behavioural interventions, where the objective is to identify and effect change in habitual behaviour. Others are more focused on cognitive interventions, where the objective is to identify, monitor and challenge dysfunctional, inaccurate or unhelpful thoughts, assumptions, and beliefs that accompany difficult feelings and unhelpful behaviours. This chapter describes the history and development of CBT; considers the cognitive behavioural theory of eating disorders and describes how this model can be applied when working with children and adolescents. In addition, the chapter considers how cognitive and behavioural principles can be applied to eating difficulties in children and adolescents when weight and shape concerns are not present. Throughout the chapter, the overarching aim is to attend to the need for a developmental perspective on CBT, taking into account that children are part of families and the need to consider the interface of CBT with other interventions.

History and development of cognitive behavioural therapy

Behavioural learning theory assumes that the outcome of learning is a change in observable, measurable behaviour (response), and that this is shaped by features and events in the environment (stimulus). The theory also assumes that contiguity and reinforcement are central to explaining the learning process. Operant conditioning (e.g. Skinner, 1953) is a learning process that occurs through reinforcement of a behaviour by a reward or a punishment (which increases and decreases the likelihood of a behaviour recurring, respectively), leading to an association being made between a behaviour and a consequence for that behaviour. The goal of reinforcement is to strengthen the desired behaviour and increase the likelihood that it will occur again in the future. When and how frequently the behaviour is reinforced can have an impact on this. In the initial stages of learning, it is usually necessary to continually reinforce the behaviour, and when the behaviour has been learned, a partial reinforcement schedule, where the behaviour is not reinforced on every occasion, can be implemented. Learned behaviours are acquired more slowly with *partial reinforcement*, but the response is more resistant to extinction

Cognitive psychology is the study of how people think, perceive, remember and learn, and acknowledges how important mental processes, such as thoughts, beliefs, imagery and interpretation of events, are in influencing behaviour. Theorists proposed that people could learn behaviour by watching others (observational learning, Bandura, 1962) and could change behaviour by using positive self-talk rather than negative or upsetting self-talk (self-instructional training, Meichenbaum and Goodman, 1971). Ellis (1957) developed Rational Emotive Therapy which proposes that unrealistic and irrational beliefs cause many emotional problems. It suggests that it is not events, but rather the beliefs that people hold, that cause emotional distress. Beck (1975) took these ideas a stage further and proposed a cognitive model of emotional disorders, which describes how people's spontaneous (automatic) thoughts about, or perceptions of, situations influence their emotional (and often physiological), and behavioural reactions. When distressed, people's automatic thoughts and perceptions are often distorted and dysfunctional; however, they can learn to identify, evaluate and correct their automatic thoughts and perceptions so that their thinking more closely resembles reality. This usually results in a decrease in their distress, enabling them to behave more functionally.

Beck's cognitive model is longitudinal and provides a framework within which to understand both the onset and the maintenance of a presenting problem (see Figure 14.1).

Westbrook, Kennerley and Kirk (2007) summarised the principles of CBT. The cognitive principle suggests that it is the interpretations of events, not events themselves, which are crucial. Events do not give rise to emotions; cognitions follow the event and give rise to the ensuing emotion. The behavioural principle suggests that what we do has a powerful influence on our thoughts and emotions; behaviour can maintain or change thoughts and emotions. The continuum principle suggests that mental health problems are exaggerated or extreme versions of normal processes, rather than pathological states that are qualitatively different, which means that these problems can happen to anyone. The 'here and now' principle suggests that it is more fruitful to focus on current processes rather than on the past, noting that tackling current maintaining factors can reduce symptoms. The interacting systems principle suggests that it is helpful to look at problems as interactions between thoughts, feelings, behaviour and physiology in the context of the environment in which the person operates. Finally, the empirical principle suggests that it is important to evaluate both theories and therapies empirically so that treatment is based on well-established theories and that those having treatment can be told if treatments are likely to be effective.

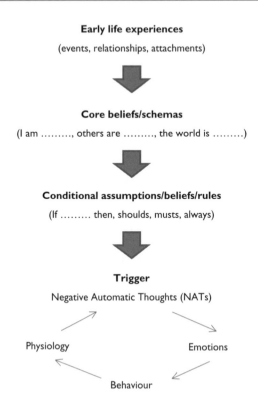

Early life experiences

(events, relationships, attachments)

Core beliefs/schemas

(I am ...., others are ...., the world is ....)

Conditional assumptions/beliefs/rules

(If .... then, shoulds, musts, always)

Trigger

Negative Automatic Thoughts (NATs)

Physiology

Emotions

Behaviour

Figure 14.1 Beck's cognitive theory of emotional disorder.

Cognitive behavioural theory of eating disorders

Garner and Bemis (1982) proposed a cognitive behavioural model of anorexia nervosa, based on the principles of Beck's (1975) cognitive theory of depression. They suggested that at the onset of the illness, causal factors converge and result in the belief that it is absolutely essential to be thin. Maintenance of low weight and fear of loss of control over eating are then established as core beliefs, and the 'overvalued ideas' of the importance of weight and shape can account for the behaviours observed. The typical behaviours associated with eating disorders, such as exercise, vomiting and using laxatives serve as negative reinforcement to the removal of the aversive stimulus of fear of fatness (Garner and Bemis, 1982).

Slade (1982) added that a need for control is central to the development and maintenance of anorexia nervosa, and is manifested in dieting. Positive reinforcement is gained from succeeding in dieting, and negative reinforcement gained through fear of weight gain and avoidance of other difficulties. This results in an intensification of the dieting coupled with further weight loss, which serves to maintain the disorder.

Fairburn, Shafran and Cooper (1999) proposed a cognitive behavioural theory of the maintenance of anorexia nervosa, which also suggests that a need for control is at the core of the disorder, but that the influence of concerns about weight and shape is an important maintaining factor. This maintenance model proposes that attempts to restrict eating are reinforced through three main feedback mechanisms with the result that the disorder becomes self-perpetuating. The first mechanism is that dietary restriction enhances the sense of being in control, i.e. success in restricting food intake positively reinforces the sense of being in control. The second mechanism is that aspects of starvation encourage further dietary restriction, i.e physiological and psychological changes can promote further dietary restriction by undermining the sense of being in control. For example, increased feelings of hunger due to insufficient food intake may be perceived as a threat to control over eating. The third mechanism is that extreme concerns about weight and shape encourage dietary restriction, i.e. failure to control body weight and shape, particularly in cultures where it is common for people to judge their self-worth in terms of weight and shape, leads to dietary restriction.

More recently, Fairburn, Cooper and Shafran (2003) have proposed a 'transdiagnostic' theory of eating disorders. They suggest that anorexia nervosa, bulimia nervosa and Eating Disorder Not Otherwise Specified (EDNOS) share the same distinctive psychopathology and, based on evidence from longitudinal outcome studies (e.g. Fairburn, Norman, Welch et al., 1995; Sullivan, Bulik, Fear et al., 1998), individuals with anorexia nervosa, bulimia nervosa and eating disorders not otherwise specified move between diagnostic states over time. This theory suggests that the maintenance of anorexia nervosa, bulimia nervosa and eating disorders not otherwise specified in some individuals is driven by one or more common mechanisms: 'clinical perfectionism', core low self-esteem, mood intolerance and interpersonal difficulties (Shafran, Cooper and Fairburn, 2002).

Perfectionism is hypothesised to be a major predisposing factor (e.g. Bruch, 1978) for eating disorders as well as a key maintaining factor for severe anorexia nervosa in adults (Fairburn, Cooper and Shafran, 2003). Shafran, Cooper and Fairburn (2002) suggest that 'clinical' perfectionism is intrinsically linked with self-evaluation and the pursuit of personally demanding standards, despite adverse consequences. Perfectionism is commonly seen in young people with eating disorders and it can be useful to distinguish between helpful and unhelpful (clinical) perfectionism when addressing the role of perfectionism in the maintenance of the eating disorder.

There are a number of developmental changes that occur during puberty which can prove difficult to negotiate in those who may already be vulnerable to the development of an eating disorder. Young people will face the challenge of adjusting to biological and physical changes, developing relationships, coping with increased responsibility, becoming independent and developing an identity. For example, physical changes include a rise in the average proportion of body fat and a rise in body weight. Girls in middle childhood have a mean proportion of body fat of 8 per cent and this rises to 22 per cent after puberty (Tanner, 1989). In addition, the period of maximum growth usually occurs between the ages of 11 and 13 years, during which time body weight rises by about 40 per cent (Tanner, 1989). Whilst boys also experience this weight gain, much of it is accounted for by an increase in muscle tissue. A neurodevelopmental model of anorexia nervosa which includes consideration of both the biological changes and the psychosocial transitions faced by young people as they go through puberty, suggests that, during puberty, the rigidity of those vulnerable to anorexia nervosa may be challenged by change, resulting in increased vulnerability to dysregulation in relevant biopsychosocial systems (Connan, Campbell, Katzman, et al., 2003).

Evidence base for CBT in adolescents with eating disorders

Whilst there is some support for individual CBT approaches in adolescents with bulimia nervosa and other binge eating syndromes, this is not the case in anorexia nervosa. Indeed, the evidence base for CBT for anorexia nervosa in adults is limited and in adolescents, is very much in its infancy. Nevertheless, eating disorders represent a perfect example of how abnormal thoughts and behaviours combine to result in physical and social impairment and thus, in theory, cognitive behavioural approaches could provide an effective strategy for treating these disorders (Gowers and Green, 2009). Further research is necessary in order to explore this idea.

Suitability for CBT

The evidence base should be considered if CBT is to be the only treatment offered. However, if individual CBT is to be offered as part of a wider treatment package, other factors need to be taken into account when considering suitability. If there are multiple presenting problems that need to be addressed, it is important to ensure that there is a supportive framework around the child first, before embarking on CBT. Consideration of the degree to which systemic factors may contribute to the maintenance of the problem is paramount, as this informs whether a systemic, rather than a child-focused approach would be more suitable.

The child's linguistic and cognitive development also needs to be taken into account. CBT requires the ability to 'think about thinking' and to identify, challenge and generate alternative ways of thinking (Stallard, 2005). CBT can be quite complex and by adolescence, young people can usually engage in sophisticated processes requiring abstract conceptual thinking, such as cognitive restructuring. However, the ability to reason effectively about concrete issues is all that is required for many of the tasks in CBT, and thus children as young as seven years should be able to manage simple, clearly explained concrete techniques. Specific to eating disorders, the effects of starvation should be considered when assessing for suitability for CBT. Starvation appears to have a significant effect on cognitive functioning, with impaired concentration, alertness, comprehension and judgement being observed in those who are in a state of semi-starvation, and in addition, semi-starvation leads to increased preoccupation with food (Garner and Garfinkel, 1997). Nevertheless, CBT may still be a suitable approach as long as techniques and materials used in sessions are adapted to suit the young person's current cognitive functioning.

Consideration needs to be given to who is motivated for the young person to make change. Often, the parents or carers want change whilst the young person may not think that change is necessary. Assessing whether the young person is motivated to make change and whether they want to play an active role in effecting this change is necessary when considering whether CBT may be an appropriate intervention.

Assessment and case formulation

Initial assessment

The initial assessment provides an opportunity to begin to engage with the young person and their family. A comprehensive assessment should consist of the following components:

- current eating disorder symptoms and their impact on family, school and social functioning;
- history and development of the eating disorder;
- co-morbid disorders and associated problems; general emotional and behavioural difficulties;
- physical health;
- family assessment;
- developmental history;
- educational history and current functioning;
- social functioning;
- strengths and protective factors;
- standardised questionnaires and/or interviews for assessment and evaluating outcome.

During the assessment, it is helpful to track a recent example in the context of a CBT framework, identifying the trigger for the event, and plotting the sequence of events including thoughts, feelings, behaviour and physiological responses. Throughout the assessment, it is important to begin to identify maintaining factors and to look for themes that might suggest underlying rules for living that may be driving the maintenance of the difficulties.

Case formulation

It is useful to produce a brief formulation in the assessment as this shows the young person and their family that the therapist has gained an understanding of the difficulties and creates some hope that change is possible. The case formulation should:

- create some understanding of the current difficulties and the relationship between them;
- draw on psychological theory;
- be developed collaboratively with the young person;
- not be too complex;
- be considered a work in progress and present ideas rather than the absolute truth;
- incorporate positive strengths and abilities.

Involvement of parents

Generally, there is increasing evidence to suggest that involving parents in CBT with children may produce additional benefits (Barrett et al., 1996; King et al., 1998; Toren et al., 2000). Specific parental roles vary; the parent may be a facilitator (to aid transfer of skills from sessions to home), a co-therapist (a more active role where the parent may prompt, monitor and review their child's use of cognitive skills), or a client (the parent may learn new skills such as behaviour management skills or learn how to cope with their own problems, such as managing anxiety). Barrett et al. (1996) described a systemic model to empower parents and children to form an 'expert team'. Parents can be taught to recognize the effect of their own behaviour on the development and maintenance of their child's problem and how to address their own anxiety. The parent's role in the intervention, and thus the extent and nature of their involvement needs to be clarified and agreed at the outset.

If the child's difficulties are inappropriately perceived as responsible for all of the family's difficulties, individual CBT would not be appropriate as it would not address the wider family issues. If the child's perceived cognitive distortions reflect limited parental capabilities or maladaptive parental views, assessment needs to determine whether these represent a cognitive distortion or an accurate reflection of dysfunction within the family.

The involvement of parents is important in supporting young people with eating disorders when they engage in a course of CBT, as it allows parents to take responsibility for some of the behavioural aspects of the treatment that the young person may not be ready or able to take responsibility for immediately. Much of the desired behavioural change in eating disorders is related to eating and behaviours during mealtimes. Whilst some young people may be able to take responsibility for this behavioural aspect of the treatment, it is important to consider the age of the young person, the severity of the eating disorder and how socially limiting the current eating behaviour is, when considering how involved the parents should be in this aspect of treatment. It is fairly usual for parents to take responsibility for change in eating behaviour at the beginning of treatment, with a view to there being a gradual transition of responsibility back to the young person over the course of treatment.

A behavioural approach to fussy or selective eating

Token charts draw on the principles of operant conditioning, and there is much evidence to show that they are extremely useful in eliciting behaviour change in young children. However, parents often report that they have used token charts without success. This can be for a number of reasons, such as not explaining to the child what they must do to earn a token, or setting unrealistic goals. Using token charts with selective or faddy eaters can work very well in effecting behaviour change. Working with parents to follow the guidelines below will ensure that the use of a token chart has the best possible chance of success.

- Design a personalised token chart.
- Be clear and specific about what behaviour earns a token (the 'target' behaviour) – for example, 'trying one teaspoonful of a new food at meal-times' is a clear and specific goal, whilst 'eating new foods' is less clear.
- Ensure the child understands what they have to do to earn a token.
- Keep the token chart in a place easily seen by the child.
- If the child is unable to earn a token in the early days of trying, then make the first step easier, to try to encourage them. This could be (for example) trying a slightly different variation of a food that they like, rather than trying a completely new food.
- Always praise the child when they earn a token and allow him or her to stick the token on the chart at once.
- Even if the child doesn't like the new food that is tried, praise them for trying. Praise should be very directed and specific, for example 'I am so proud of you for trying that food'.
- If the child is disappointed that they haven't earned a token, a parent should sympathise, and encourage them by saying 'You can try again'.
- It is important for parents not to get cross or upset and to remain positive.
- Tokens should not be removed for bad behaviour – once a token is earned it should NEVER be removed.
- Use the chart to reward the child. Never use the chart in a negative way.

The child can also keep a list of foods tried and write 'OK' or 'Yuk' next to each food. Parents can encourage the child to try these foods again on a regular basis so that they become integrated into their diet.

With regard to rewards, the parents should decide how many tokens the child needs to collect to get a small reward. It should not be too hard to earn a reward – for example, asking a child to collect 20 tokens when they only have the opportunity to earn a maximum of one token per day can make a child lose interest very quickly as the reward is too far away. Rewards do not need to be expensive and should be appropriate for the child. Some rewards can, and should, be free, for example, allowing the child to choose which DVD to watch or doing something special, such as having a sleepover. However, do not make privileges that the child already enjoys become rewards. For example, if the child usually gets to choose which DVD to watch, this should not now become a 'reward'. Small rewards that cost money can be decided upon at the parent's discretion – these may be things such as comics or small toys.

If the child has some initial success but then begins to lose interest in earning stars, it can be a good idea to introduce 'spot prizes'. This utilises the principle of a partial reinforcement schedule, in that there may be a 'spot prize' at any time. This will often encourage a child to persevere with the target behaviour, as they could get rewarded at any time.

Creative token charts

Using a flower can help to record exactly what foods the child has tried. Using coloured sticky paper cut out a number of petal shapes (both small and large). Start with a drawing of a flower with no petals and then add the petal shapes to the flower each time the child tries a new food. The food that that the child has tried should be written on the petal shape along with the words 'OK' or 'Yuk' to record whether they liked the tried food. Petal sizes can vary according to the amount of food that the child tried, for example, a small petal can represent a tiny taste, whilst a larger petal can represent a larger spoonful of a new food.

The placemat reward chart acts both as a reward chart, and also allows for thinking about a nutritionally balanced diet. Use a large circle of cardboard (bigger than the child's plate) and colour four sections which represent the basic food groups of protein, carbohydrate, fruit and vegetables. Using stickers in these four colours, the child can add a number of stickers to the placemat throughout the course of their meal and every time they takes a bite of something from her plate, they can take a sticker of the corresponding colour to stick around the outer edge of the mat. This approach may be a little ambitious at first, but could be something that could be used once the child has established trying new foods using one of the other reward chart approaches noted above.

The token chart method should be tried for approximately two to four weeks. It is important to trouble shoot any difficulties that come up during this time so that the use of a token chart can be maximally effective.

A cognitive behavioural treatment approach to eating disorders

Beginning treatment

It is important to be transparent about the therapy process, explaining when confidentiality has to be broken and why, and explaining that there are likely to be some parts of treatment that are 'non-negotiable', such as being weighed. If the young person is anxious about being weighed, this can be worked through by exploring the negative thoughts that are associated with being weighed. Recognising the personal experiences that the young person brings to the therapeutic relationship allows the therapist to balance being the expert with being able to learn from the young person. Being interested in the young person, having a desire to understand their experience and believing change is possible are all factors that contribute to a good engagement with the young person. Many young people are ambivalent about recovery from an eating disorder, so the clinician needs to take a curious stance, thinking with the young person about the pros and cons of change without applying pressure to do so.

The initial stage of treatment focuses on supporting the young person to re-establish normal eating patterns, and, in the case of anorexia nervosa, regain weight. Depending on the diagnosis and the severity of the eating disorder, the extent of the family role in this initial stage of treatment may vary. For example, the family of a young adolescent with anorexia nervosa may be offered family-based treatment, whilst the role of the family of an older teenager with bulimia nervosa may be to support the individual CBT treatment.

Goal setting

Identifying goals for treatment as early in the process as possible is important. The young person may easily be able to identify things they would like to change and these may not all be related to eating, weight and shape. If it is difficult for the young person to identify a goal that would directly contribute to their recovery from an eating disorder, the therapist should take a motivational approach to explore any ambivalence about making change. Therapists should also be clear that there are some goals that they are unable to collaborate with the young person on, such as losing weight or maintaining an unhealthily low weight. The therapist can clearly and empathically explain that they are unable to collaborate on these goals, because of the consequences to physical health of low weight, and work with the young person to find goals that they can work on together.

Psychoeducation

Psychoeducation is useful in the engagement process and throughout the course of therapy. 'Information meetings' can be a good way of delivering general information about eating disorders, and giving all members of the family an opportunity to ask questions. The young person and their family can be given written information to take home, and encouraged to use a highlighter pen to identify things that they may want further information about or have questions about.

Motivation

Motivation to make change is made up of two parts: desire to change and confidence that change is possible. Thus motivation to change should be elicited from the young person, rather than imposed upon them. Motivational interviewing (Miller and Rollnick, 2002, 2009) can be a powerful tool in enhancing intrinsic motivation to change by exploring and resolving ambivalence. As motivation can fluctuate significantly from day to day, a motivational approach should continue throughout the course of treatment. It can be useful to measure motivation (desire and confidence) at the beginning of each session – this can help the therapist to gauge whether they need to primarily attend to enhancing motivation in the session.

Desire	Confidence
0------------------------------10	0------------------------------10

These ratings can be used to look back over changes in motivation through-out the course of therapy, which, in itself, can be motivating for the young person.

Trying to persuade the young person to make change by stressing the benefits of change, can increase resistance because the young person may feel misunder-stood or 'wrong'. It is important to recognise and accept confusing and contradic-tory thoughts that the young person may have. Resistance to change indicates that the therapist may be assuming greater readiness to change than the young person feels, and is a sign that the therapist may need to spend more time working with motivational strategies with the young person, by identifying or reviewing and mobilising the young person's intrinsic values and goals to stimulate behaviour change.

Motivational techniques

Pros and cons of change

The young person makes a list of the advantages and disadvantages of changing or maintaining the eating disorder, allowing them to consider the potential value of change. Often young people will discover that the majority of the advantages of maintaining the eating disorder provide only short term, rather than long term, benefits.

Friend or foe letters (Serpell, Treasure, et al., 1999)

The young person writes two letters to the eating disorder; one as a friend and one as an enemy. This can enhance motivation by enabling the young person to reflect on how the eating disorder hinders them in their life. This technique can also strengthen the engagement with the therapist, as the therapist acknowledges that there are also aspects of the eating disorder that the young person values. For younger children it can be useful to do this exercise thinking of the eating disorder as the best friend and the worst bully.

Longer term plans

The thoughts of young people with eating disorders tend to become very detail focused, making it difficult for the young person to view the 'bigger picture' in relation to how the eating disorder might impact on their life in the longer term. This technique asks the young person to consider where they want their life to be in one year's time, taking into account the following areas: school, friendships, relationships, family life, health, self-esteem, leisure and hobbies. They are then asked to predict how things will be in each of these areas if they still have an eating disorder. This exercise can be repeated over different timeframes, relevant to the individual young person. This enables the young person to take a step back and view the 'bigger picture' and helps to identify valued directions in their life. This also allows the young person to consider the impact that the eating disorder may have on their long term goals.

Self-monitoring

Self-monitoring helps to identify thoughts, feelings and behaviours which cause distress, and the links between them, and provides the most accurate picture of how the eating disorder is maintained and how it can be changed. Self-monitoring enables the young person to identify the situations which lead to difficult thoughts, feelings and behaviours, allowing them to become aware of harmful patterns that maintain the eating disorder, and see that these patterns are not just arbitrary and automatic. This can lead to an increase in motivation, as the young person begins to see that change is possible. In addition, it can be useful to look back over diary sheets over time, to see how things have changed. Designing the young person's thought diary in session helps to personalize and ensure that the method of self-monitoring is realistic for the individual young person. For example, it may be helpful for a young person to have a 'checklist' of feelings that they can tick, or a face that they can draw a feeling on to. Using technology, such as email and text messaging can be a useful way for young people to self-monitor.

Problem eating and compensatory behaviours

Changing eating behaviours

In anorexia nervosa, the aim is to increase the amount of food eaten in order to facilitate weight gain and to begin to address fears about eating and weight gain. A regular eating pattern should be introduced which includes both meals and snacks. If the young person is eating regular meals, but eating a reduced amount of food, the aim would be to increase intake across all meals, or to introduce snacks between meals.

In bulimia nervosa, the initial emphasis should be on establishing a regular pattern of eating. Introducing regular eating tackles the trigger of hunger and thus the urge to binge will be reduced. This, in itself, can enable some young people to reduce the frequency of their binge episodes. However, the young person may specifically need to address triggers for binge eating, such as cravings for particular foods, which may occur if they are avoiding or restricting certain types of foods, or emotional triggers for binge eating. A clear formulation of the triggers and maintaining factors for binge eating behaviour is essential at this stage.

Dietary advice should be given, where possible, from a dietitian. Meal planning is essential, as making spontaneous decisions about what to eat can be extremely anxiety provoking for both the young person and their family. When faced with changing eating behaviours, it can be helpful for the young person to have a list of the reasons why they want to recover, and review this list when finding it difficult to make these changes. Distraction techniques, such as playing cards with family members after mealtimes, can help the young person to manage any difficult thoughts and feelings they may have after a meal, and also distract from urges to engage in compensatory behaviours following eating.

Dealing with compensatory behaviours

I. SELF-INDUCED VOMITING

Information should be given about the adverse physical consequences of self-induced vomiting, and how self-induced vomiting is not an effective method of managing weight. This information can be helpful in enhancing the young person's motivation to eliminate this behaviour.

II. LAXATIVE AND DIURETIC USE

Similarly, information regarding the nature of weight loss attributable to laxatives or diuretics should be given to the young person. Laxatives and diuretics cause fluid loss, which only produces a temporary weight loss that is reversed as soon as the body is rehydrated.

III. EXERCISE

Excessive exercise is a common behaviour in young people with eating disorders, particularly those with anorexia nervosa. This can take the form of overt exercise, such as running; covert exercise, such as doing star jumps out of sight of others; or constant movement, where the young person may, for example, avoid sitting, jiggle their leg whilst sitting, or make numerous trips to and from the bathroom on the pretext that they have forgotten something.

The maintenance model for compulsive exercise (Meyer, et al., 2011) suggests that a number of factors contribute to the maintenance of excessive exercise:

- weight and shape concerns;
- perfectionism;
- psychological dependence on exercise for mood regulation;
- compulsivity;
- behavioural rigidity.

Some young people may hold unhelpful beliefs that make their exercise behaviour extremely resistant to change. If this is the case, it is helpful to collaboratively construct a maintenance formulation specifically related to the exercise behaviour and to address the thoughts and beliefs associated with exercise in the same way as addressing thoughts and beliefs associated with eating, weight and shape.

Automatic thoughts, assumptions and core beliefs

Identifying automatic thoughts

Self-monitoring allows the young person to identify automatic thoughts. However, it may be difficult for them to access their thoughts. If so, the therapist can take the role of the 'thought catcher' (Turk, 1998) by identifying important cognitions as they occur and bringing them to the attention of the young person.

Another way to access thoughts is for the therapist to 'follow the feeling', by paying particular attention to changes in mood in the session. These changes in mood can be brought to the young person's attention, which may help them to notice what is going through their mind. The therapist can note, for example, 'You seem to be thinking about something that is making you sad.'

Typical examples of automatic thoughts that young people with an eating disorder might have are:

> 'When I lose some more weight, people will like me.'
> 'Once I start eating, I won't be able to stop.'

During the course of treatment, young people may have automatic thoughts that are positive, if they have used behaviours to control their weight or shape. Examples of these thoughts are:

> 'Losing weight makes me feel more in control.'
> 'Exercise has helped me maintain my weight.'

Once automatic thoughts have been identified, whether negative or positive, it is important to check whether these thoughts are consistent with the young person's goals for therapy.

Identifying assumptions and core beliefs

Often, young people make conditional assumptions, such as 'If I get thin, then I will be happy/accepted/have achieved something'. Beliefs that are commonly held by young people with eating disorders tend to become 'rules' by which the young person controls their behaviour, and are usually rigidly adhered to. These rules tend to focus on achievement, approval and/or control. Typical 'rules' that young people report are:

- I must always eat less than anyone else.
- I must not eat carbohydrates.
- I must not eat after 6pm.
- I must weigh all my foods.
- I must stick to a particular number of calories per day.

Addressing unhelpful thoughts, assumptions and beliefs

When unhelpful thoughts, assumptions and beliefs have been identified, the next step is to look for factual evidence for and against the validity and usefulness of the thought, assumption or belief. It is important to identify whether there are any thinking errors that may be contributing to the young person's thought being biased or unhelpful. Typical thinking errors in eating disorders are as follows:

Black and white thinking (categorical rather than continuum thinking):
I'm either totally in control or totally out of control of my eating.

Overgeneralizing (making assumptions based on one event):
I sat down for five minutes therefore I am a lazy person.

Catastrophising (focusing on the worst possible outcome):
If I eat a biscuit I will lose control and binge all day.

Selective attention (focusing on one aspect of a situation instead of looking at the whole picture):
One girl is thinner than me.

Mind reading (assuming that others perceptions are negative):
They think that I am greedy.

Magnification/Minimisation (magnifying the negative/weaknesses and minimising the positive/strengths):
It doesn't matter that I didn't binge all week – I ruined it by bingeing today.

Jumping to conclusions (in the absence of any factual evidence):
People will only like me if I am thin.

Double standards (setting higher standards for self than others):
It's acceptable for others to be a normal weight, but it's not OK for me.

Emotional reasoning (feeling something makes it true):
I 'feel' fat so I must be fat.

When the young person finds that their thought may be biased and unhelpful, they can arrive at a balanced conclusion about this thought and develop an alternative thought which is more accurate. They can then gather evidence to support or refute this alternative thought.

Continuum lines are a good way to challenge black and white thinking, as a 'grey' area is introduced. Orthogonal lines can be an objective way of looking at the relationship between two characteristics, and thus addressing conditional beliefs. For example, the young person may hold the conditional belief 'If I am thin, then I will be happy'. Positive data logs can be used to test whether young people's negative beliefs are accurate or not. By keeping a log of positive things about themselves, others and the world, a young person can become more conscious of the positive things that they may be overlooking, which can help them arrive at a more balanced decision about their negative belief.

Helping the young person to identify and address their rules about eating is an important part of treatment. The young person could write a list of their rules as a homework task and then the therapist can explore with the young person whether their rules are helpful and whether they can let some rules go, whilst modifying others to become more helpful guidelines.

Behavioural experiments

Behavioural experiments allow for testing predictions which arise from the young person's assumptions and core beliefs. They provide experiential evidence for and against the predicted outcome of the young person's thoughts and beliefs. Both planned and accidental behavioural experiments can promote greater cognitive, behavioural and emotional change than verbal cognitive techniques used in isolation.

Surveys can be used to test young people's beliefs about what other people consider to be important, by using feedback from others. For example, a young person might believe that boys only find extremely thin girls attractive. The therapist and young person can devise a brief questionnaire that would test this belief and then both the young person and therapist can ask a number of people they know to complete their questionnaire. They can then look at whether the results of the survey provide evidence for or against the young person's belief.

Discovery experiments deal with unfamiliar situations, in which there are no clear predictions of outcome. These experiments allow the young person to find out what would happen if they were to do something that they had not done before or if they acted differently in a situation that they were familiar with. For example, the young person may rigidly stick to meals at particular times, but may not be sure of what will happen if they eat at a slightly different time. The young person could try eating some meals at slightly different times and see what happens.

Hypothesis testing experiments are those that test out the validity of a specific thought or belief. For example, a young person with anorexia nervosa might believe that sitting down directly after a meal will double their weekly weight gain. This belief can be tested by gradually increasing the frequency of sitting down after meals and checking whether their weekly weight gain does indeed double as they increase the frequency of sitting down after meals.

It is important to design behavioural experiments in collaboration with the young person and, where appropriate, to enlist their parents to support them as they embark on these experiments.

Over-evaluation of eating, weight and shape

Whilst most young people will evaluate themselves on a range of aspects of themselves and their lives, young people with eating disorders place significantly more emphasis on eating, weight and shape in their self-evaluation. A self-evaluation pie chart can be a useful way to explore how much emphasis the young person places on eating, weight and shape when evaluating themselves, and increase their awareness of this emphasis. The young person constructs a pie chart representing proportionally their different domains for self-evaluation. Usually, a significant proportion of the young person's pie chart will be taken up with aspects related to the eating disorder.

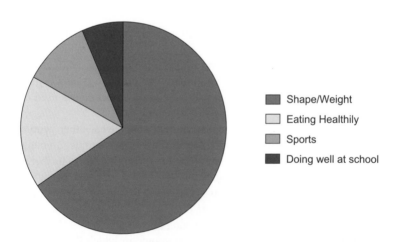

The therapist and young person then explore the potential difficulties that arise from this emphasis on eating, weight and shape and the therapist can explain that judging themselves almost entirely in one domain creates an 'all the eggs are in one basket' situation. This puts pressure on the young person to achieve in that particular domain and if anything goes wrong, the young person is likely to feel really bad. The goals set are often unachievable, setting the young person up to fail (see perfectionism, below). Other important domains in life are replaced by the overvalued domains leading to the young person missing out on other, perhaps more helpful, domains for self-evaluation.

A second pie chart can then be constructed to represent how the young person would like their life to be. These pie charts are used together to think with the young person about how they could move from the 'now' pie chart to the 'ideal' pie chart.

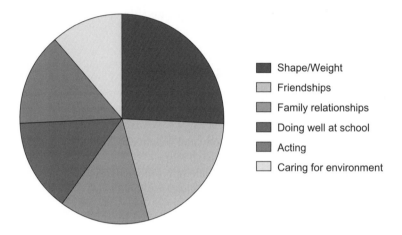

- Shape/Weight
- Friendships
- Family relationships
- Doing well at school
- Acting
- Caring for environment

Body and weight checking and avoidance

Preoccupation with weight and shape is likely to occur when a young person's self-worth is based on eating, weight and shape, and their ability to control these things. Body and weight checking maintains this preoccupation, which in turn reinforces the young person's over-evaluation of controlling their eating, weight and shape. Usually, the young person will report that the purpose of body and weight checking is to reassure them that they are not fat/heavier than they want to be. However, this is rarely the outcome of these behaviours.

Examples of body and weight checking behaviours are:

- measuring parts of the body;
- checking body in a mirror;
- pinching parts of the body;
- repeated weighing;
- comparing self to others who are thinner;
- repeatedly trying on the same clothes.

Body and weight avoidance can also be unhelpful, acting as a safety behaviour that serves to reinforce the young person's distorted assumptions and beliefs about their body and their weight.

Examples of body and weight avoidance behaviours are:

- avoiding looking in the mirror;
- wearing loose clothing;
- avoiding clothes shopping;
- avoiding weighing;
- avoiding close physical contact with others.

Often, young people are not aware of the extent of their body and weight checking/ avoidance, as these behaviours become a habit.

Reducing body and weight checking and avoidance

- Identify the purpose and predicted effects of checking/avoidance behaviour (e.g. 'Looking in the mirror will reassure me that I am not fat and make me feel better').
- Monitor the extent and frequency of body and weight checking/avoidance.
- Construct a hierarchy of behaviours to challenge.
- Set specific goals to reduce, limit, eliminate or postpone a behaviour.
- Test predictions made about the effects of checking behaviours.

'Feeling Fat'

Negative feelings such as guilt, anger, boredom and distress are commonly misla-belled as 'feeling fat'. When a young person identifies negative feelings as 'feeling fat', their focus is brought back to their dissatisfaction with their body which maintains their preoccupation with body shape and weight. Explaining that fat is not a feeling is extremely important, and that by learning to identify and label feelings correctly, it is possible to then address the true nature of the feeling. Using a diary to identify situations in which the young person 'feels fat' can be helpful as this helps to identify which situations are likely to trigger 'feeling fat' and enables the young person to explore what other feelings they may have been experiencing at that time.

Perfectionism

Unhelpful perfectionism is maintained when the young person makes a biased evaluation of their performance. If their performance meets the standard that had been set, they reappraise this standard as being insufficiently demanding, and raise the standard. If their performance does not meet the high standard that had been set, the young person perceives this to be a failure and becomes highly self-critical and may avoid tasks or procrastinate over tasks related to the domain in which they have perceived themselves to have failed.

The following steps are suggested to tackle unhelpful perfectionism:

- detailed discussion of the advantages and disadvantages of perfectionism;
- addressing the maintaining behaviours;
- tackling beliefs and unhelpful cognitive styles;
- historical review of the development of perfectionism.

Overcoming obstacles

Difficulties grasping abstract concepts

Using play and drawing can be a helpful way to turn abstract concepts into concrete understandable examples. Metaphors also provide a way in which abstract concepts can be described and understood in concrete terms.

'I can't cope'

Imagery using positive coping images which build on the young person's existing interests can be useful if the young person does not believe that they can cope with the anxiety that the challenges of treatment may present.

'I don't want to talk about it'

It may be difficult, for whatever reason, for the young person to talk about their difficulties with the therapist. It is important to adapt materials so that they are accessible to the young person. Using blackboards, flipcharts, playing and drawing can help the young person to express thoughts and feelings. A board game, 'All About Me' (Hemmings, 1991) can be helpful as the young person and the therapist play together, enabling the therapist to model that it is safe to talk about feelings. Talking about the young person's difficulties as if they belonged to a third person can be helpful too, as this allows the young person to begin to explore the difficulties in a way that may feel less threatening. It is important that the therapist is creative in using the session time, as sitting in silence may feel extremely difficult for the young person.

Homework compliance

Most of the change process in CBT happens outside the sessions, and so homework is a cornerstone of CBT. There are many obstacles to homework compliance, including practical obstacles (no time, lost the homework), comprehension obstacles (too complex, not relevant or meaningful to the young person), emotional obstacles (avoidance due to the belief that it will make the young person feel worse, hopelessness, lack of motivation), and systemic obstacles (no-one to support the young person completing homework, fear that others will read the homework).

The therapist should be open in talking about homework and realistic in what can be undertaken. Homework should be developed collaboratively, relevant to the young person's problem/goal and well-explained and broken down into smaller tasks if necessary. Time should be devoted to assigning and reviewing homework so that its importance is clear. The therapist should acknowledge potential avoidance or anxiety about completing homework and brainstorm overcoming homework obstacles in session. Homework can be facilitated by the young person using a notebook in sessions, using technology such as email and text messaging, trying out the homework assignment in session, and asking the young person to plan where and when they will do the homework. The therapist can also do the homework with the young person, for example, if the homework is to gather information to test the validity of a particular thought, such as 'chocolate makes you gain weight faster than any other food', both the young person and the therapist can gather this information and share it in the next session.

Relapse prevention

Relapse prevention planning involves exploring strategies for maintaining progress made. It is useful to review what has been helpful in treatment, and identify which strategies the young person can continue to use to minimize the risk of relapse. Writing a list of high risk situations that may occur over the next year is also important. Once a list has been compiled, the therapist and young person can explore the warning signs that might suggest that eating behaviour is becoming problematic, for example, if the young person begins to skip meals. Finally, drawing on the strategies that the young person found helpful in treatment, a plan to either avoid or cope with high risk situations can be compiled.

Conclusion

Whilst there is some support for individual CBT approaches in adolescents with bulimia nervosa, this is not so in anorexia nervosa. Nevertheless, it would appear that eating disorders represent a perfect example of how abnormal thoughts and behaviours combine to result in physical and social impairment and thus, in theory, cognitive behavioural approaches could provide an effective strategy for treating these disorders (Gowers and Green, 2009). Further research is necessary in order to explore this idea.

Summary

- CBT is an umbrella term used to describe therapies that share a theoretical basis in behaviourist learning theory and cognitive psychology.
- CBT is case formulation driven, and the involvement and role of parents in the intervention may vary depending on the formulation.
- A number of factors need to be considered when assessing suitability for CBT, including systemic factors, and who is motivated for the young person to make change.
- Behavioural and cognitive techniques and strategies should be tailored to the individual young person, based on the formulation.
- It is important to attend to motivation and obstacles throughout the intervention.

References

Bandura, A. (1962). *Social Learning through Imitation*. Lincoln, NE: University of Nebraska Press.

Barrett, P. M., Dadds, M. R., and Rapee, R. M. (1996). Family treatment of childhood anxiety: A controlled trial. *Journal of Consulting and Clinical Psychology*, *64* (2), 333–342.

Beck, A. T. (1975) *Cognitive Therapy and the Emotional Disorders*. International Universities Press.

Bruch, H. (1978). *The Golden Cage: The Enigma of Anorexia Nervosa*. Cambridge, MA: Harvard University Press.

Connan, F., Campbell, C., Katzman, M., Lightman, S. L., and Treasure, J. (2003). A neurodevelopmental model for anorexia nervosa. *Physiology and Behaviour*, *79* (1), 13–24.

Ellis, A. (1957). Rational psychotherapy and individual psychology. *Journal of Individual Psychology*, *13*, 38–44.

Fairburn, C. G., Cooper, Z., and Shafran, R. (2003). Cognitive behaviour therapy for eating disorders: A transdiagnostic theory and treatment. *Behaviour Research and Therapy*, 509–528.

Fairburn, C., Shafran, R., and Cooper, Z. (1999). A cognitive behavioural theory of anorexia nervosa. *Behavioural Research and Therapy*, *37*, 1–13.

Fairburn, C. G., Norman, P. A., Welch, S. L., O'Connor, M. E., Doll, H. A., and Peveler, R. C. (1995). A prospective study of outcome in bulimia nervosa and the long-term effects of three psychological treatments. *Archives of General Psychiatry*, *52*, 304–312.

Garner, D. M., and Bemis, K. M. (1982) A cognitive-behavioural approach to anorexia nervosa. *Cognitive Therapy and Research*, *6*, 123–150.

Garner, D. M., and Garfinkel, P. E. (1997). *Handbook of Treatment for Eating Disorders*. New York: Guilford Press.

Gowers, S. G., and Green, L. (2009). *Eating Disorders: Cognitive Behaviour Therapy with Children and Young People*. London: Routledge.

Hemmings, P. (1991). *All About Me*. London: Barnardo's.

King, N. J., Tonge, B. J., Heyne, D., Rollingd, S., Young, D., Myerson, N., et al. (1998). Cognitive behavioural treatment of school-refusing children: A controlled evaluation. *Journal of the American Academy of Child and Adolescent Psychiatry, 37* (4), 395–403.

Meichenbaum, D. J., and Goodman, J. (1971). Training impulsive children to talk to themselves: A means of developing self-control. *Journal of Abnormal Psychology, 77,* 115–126.

Meyer, C., Taranis, L., Goodwin, H., and Haycraft, E. (2011), Compulsive exercise and eating disorders. *European Eating Disorders Review, 19,* 174–189.

Miller, W. R., and Rollnick, S. (2002) *Motivational Interviewing: Preparing People for Change* (2nd ed.), New York: Guilford Press.

Miller, W. R., and Rollnick, S. (2009). Ten things that motivational interviewing is not. *Behavioural and Cognitive Psychotherapy, 37* (2), 129–140.

Serpell, L., Treasure, J., Teasdale, J., and Sullivan, V. (1999). Anorexia nervosa: Friend or foe? *International Journal of Eating Disorders, 25,* 177.

Shafran, R., Cooper, Z. and Fairburn, C. G. (2002). Clinical perfectionism: A cognitive behavioural analysis. *Behaviour Research and Therapy, 40,* 773–791.

Skinner, B. F. (1953). *Science and Human Behavior*. Oxford: Macmillan.

Slade, P. (1982). Towards a functional analysis of anorexia nervosa and bulimia nervosa. *British Journal of Clinical Psychology, 21,* 167–179.

Stallard, P. (2005). *A Clinician's Guide to Think Good Feel Good: Using CBT with Children and Young People*. Chichester: Wiley-Blackwell.

Sullivan, P., Bulik, C., Fear, J., and Pickering, A. (1998). Outcome of anorexia nervosa: A case-control study. *American Journal of Psychiatry, 155,* 939–946.

Tanner, J.M. (1989) *Foetus into Man: Physical Growth from Conception to Maturity* (2nd ed.). Ware: Castlemead.

Toren, P., Wolmer, L., Rosental, B., Eldar, S., Koren, S., Lask, M., et al. (2000). Case series: Brief parent-child group therapy for childhood anxiety disorders using a manual based cognitive-behavioural technique. *Journal of the American Academy of Child and Adolescent Psychiatry, 39* (10), 1309–1312.

Turk, J. (1998). Children with learning disabilities and their parents. In P. Graham (ed.), *Cognitive Behaviour Therapy for Children and Families* (1st ed.). Cambridge: Cambridge University Press.

Westbrook, D., Kennerley, H., and Kirk, J. (2007). *An Introduction to Cognitive Behavioural Therapy: Skills and Applications*. London: Sage Publications Ltd.

Chapter 15

Individual psychotherapy

Cathy Troupp

Overview

This chapter describes the role and process of individual psychotherapy for children and young people with eating disorders, in the context of a multi-disciplinary, out-patient, specialist child and adolescent mental health team. The evidence base is briefly examined. Key psychoanalytic writing and conceptualisations about eating disorders are reviewed. Psychotherapy research is discussed with a particular focus on change-promoting factors, such as therapeutic alliance. There then follows a section charting the therapeutic process, emphasising the importance of early engagement and ways in which this may be achieved with children and young people with eating disorders. Case vignettes are used for illustration, and one longer case study, which highlights what can be learned from, firstly, psychodynamic attention to the therapeutic relationship, and secondly, collaborative goal setting.

Introduction

It makes intuitive sense to offer individual psychotherapy as a treatment for children and adolescents with anorexia nervosa and other eating disorders. Surely, one would think, something must be troubling a child deeply for her to behave as self-destructively and irrationally as refusing to eat and apparently not wanting to be healthy. One-to-one psychotherapy would seem an obvious means to understand more about her inner world, the thoughts and feelings, fears and anxieties that lead her to deny herself the sustenance required for life.

Parents sometimes express a hope that a psychotherapist will get to know their child and what is 'going on inside' her, when they themselves feel so bewildered, frightened, and shut out. Parents often speak about the shock they feel when they realize that their child has been tricking and lying to them for a period of time. Suddenly, they feel that they don't know their child and have lost contact with her. They are forced to respond by withdrawing their trust in their own child and feel terrible about doing so (Cottee-Lane et al., 2004; Nicholls and Magagna, 1997). Some parents hope that a 'specialist' may succeed where they feel that they have failed. They may hope that the psychotherapist will gain the trust of their child sufficiently to wield the influence that they feel they have lost, and make their child see the madness of her behaviour, start to see sense, and eat.

But the reality is that it is often difficult to engage a child with an eating disorder in individual psychotherapy. It is difficult to build a therapeutic relationship based on trust, because the very nature of the eating disorder works against it. This is a serious barrier, as both clinical experience and research into the determinants of change in psychotherapy tell us that the quality of the therapeutic relationship, or therapeutic alliance as it is also called, is one of the primary agents of change in psychotherapy for children as for adults (Shirk et al., 2011). Engaging a child with an eating disorder in individual psychotherapy can be a great challenge, requiring the therapist to demonstrate confidence, experience, a sound theoretical and technical grounding as well as the flexibility to adapt this to the individual personality and needs of each child. In particular, the therapist needs to be skilled at finding ways of communicating and understanding that do not rely on asking questions. Many children in the pre-treatment stage of an eating disorder cannot explain their behaviour, what they are thinking, and how they are feeling.

Evidence-based practice and practice-based evidence

'Children and adolescents with anorexia nervosa should be offered individual appointments with a health care professional separate from those with their family members or carers', is the only specific recommendation touching on individual psychotherapy in the NICE guidelines (2004), and this is a level C (expert opinion) recommendation, not one based on controlled clinical trials. There is no nationally or internationally agreed guidance on what should constitute individual psychotherapy for young people with eating disorders, because the research that could establish individual psychotherapy as an evidence-based treatment is lacking. The barriers to research have been comprehensively documented by Gowers and Bryant-Waugh (2004). It is also the case that with multi-disciplinary treatment held to be the gold standard for children, through practice-based evidence, controlled trials proposing to offer only individual therapy in one treatment arm, or further, to compare individual therapy modalities, would most likely be considered unethical.

A recent study comparing the outcome of family-based treatment on the one hand, with individual therapy ('adolescent focused psychotherapy') with parallel parent work on the other (Lock et al., 2010), yielded complex findings, particularly when it is taken into account that the group randomized to individual psychotherapy appeared to have been overall at a lower weight, and with lower scores on the Eating Disorder Examination (EDE; a measure of eating disorder psychopathology, see Chapter 7), at the start of treatment. Both treatments were equally effective at the end of treatment, but family-based treatment seemed to be more effective on the 'full remission' measure at 6 and 12 months' follow-up, though not on the 'partial remission' measure. Family-based treatment was superior at end of treatment but not at follow-up in terms of EDE scores. In other words, both treatments were effective and both showed significant, but different, 'sleeper effects'. This quantitative study calls for a qualitative follow-on study elucidating what factors cause some patients respond better to one type of treatment over another; the 'what works for whom?' question. Nevertheless, this study does establish that individual psychotherapy offered in combination with parent work can be an effective treatment. The findings of this study are important, as the faster pace of research in family-based treatments was increasingly being misconstrued as proving that individual therapy did not work.

One reason for the onward march of research in family-based treatment has been the existence of a treatment manual (Lock, 2001). Individual therapy research has suffered from the absence of a manualised treatment protocol (for an exception, see Bryant-Waugh, 2006). Fitzpatrick et al. (2010) wrote a companion paper describing the individual 'adolescent focused' therapy that was used in the Lock et al. (2010) trial and promising a manual. This type of therapy derives from the American school of 'self-psychology' which has much in common with psychodynamic or psychoanalytic psychotherapy. It is described as addressing 'key deficits in development' associated with anorexia nervosa. It emphasises that young people with anorexia nervosa are viewed as using food and weight to avoid negative emotions associated with adolescent development which they find intolerable. It posits the aims of therapy as being to help young people identify their emotions in the first place, and then learn to tolerate them, particularly negative ones. It also highlights the arrested emotional and psychological development that is the consequence of an eating disorder.

In this chapter, the aims of individual psychotherapy are formulated similarly:

1   To help the young person understand herself better and develop 'emotional language'.
2   To support the young person's development in terms of individuation, and integration with peers and the social world.
3   To help the young person find ways to communicate her internal states to her parents, in ways that are acceptable to both.

This last goal, that of improving the adolescent or child's capacity to express herself to her parents, was not highlighted in Fitzpatrick's study, but it is essential. Family and individual treatments need to be integrated and therapists need to ensure that compatible treatment goals are set, subsequently communicating continually about the progress of treatment. Individual therapy supports the child's effort to communicate her feelings and views to her parents while family therapy supports the parents' ability to hear, and sometimes bear, what their child has to say to them.

Individual therapy for eating disorders is mostly grounded in the cognitive-behavioural or the psychodynamic schools, both of which have an evidence-base for the treatment of other mental health problems in children, such as anxiety, depression, and attachment-related problems and trauma (for psychodynamic child psychotherapy, see Midgley and Kennedy, 2011; for CBT for children and adolescents, see Muños-Solomando et al., 2008) This chapter, written by a psychoanalytic child psychotherapist, favours a description of the psychodynamic approach to individual therapy in the context of the specialist, multi-disciplinary, out-patient eating disorders team.

This chapter continues with a review of key psychoanalytic writing and thinking about eating disorders. This is followed by a brief review of relevant literature from the field of psychotherapy research, particularly focusing on change-promoting factors within child and adolescent psychotherapy such as therapeutic alliance. There then follows a section charting the therapeutic process, emphasising the importance of early engagement and ways in which this may be achieved with children and young people with eating disorders. Case vignettes have been used to illustrate various points, and the chapter ends with a longer case history, focusing particularly on what could be learned from, firstly, psychodynamic attention to the therapeutic relationship, and secondly, collaborative goal setting in this context.

The psychoanalytic theoretical framework

There have been some fascinating accounts of early psychoanalytic treatment of adults with anorexia (Binswanger, 1944; Thomä, 1967), mostly of in-patients. Psychoanalytic psychotherapists have been influenced also by the work of Bruch (1978), particularly by her understanding of self-starvation as an attempt to solve the contradiction for young women of the early feminist era who both wanted to model themselves on their mothers and simultaneously carve out a different identity in the world. Bruch's work also demonstrates an at the time unusually compassionate, non-punitive stance towards the patients themselves. Crisp (1995) introduced the 'regression hypothesis', the idea that anorexia represents an attempt to avoid the demands of adolescent sexual development and to 'stop the clock' and remain a child. This idea is still integral to a range of theoretical thinking, not least because it chimes with daily clinical experience.

Current psychoanalytic thinking about eating disorders takes as its starting point the observations we make time and again about the way an eating disorder interferes with the making and sustaining of good relationships – within the family, with friends, and with the social world. Further, these problems seem to derive from an impoverished sense of self and self-worth. Children and young people with anorexia nervosa withdraw from relationships. They seem not to care very much that their lives have become as restricted as their diets, that they have no interests and little to talk about beyond their wish to be thinner, that they seem unable to think about their future. Sometimes they don't even seem to mind that they may not be able to go to school or see their friends, or that they are no longer able to talk to their parents.

In psychoanalytic formulations of eating disorders, it is common to compare having anorexia nervosa to being part of a cult or a gang, led by a despotic leader or tyrant (e.g. Williams 1997a and 1997b, Lawrence 2008). The tyrant is an internal one, inhabiting the child's own mind. In anorexia, trust, dependence and loyalty are shifted away from parents, family, peers and school, to a malign internal figure. This figure poses as a friend, a leader, while in reality having only destruction of the personality, and the concomitant increase in its own power, as the aim. One could say that in eating disorders, the 'deal' offered by the internal tyrant runs like this: 'If you give me your allegiance and obedience, and don't eat and become thinner and thinner, I will in turn protect you from all difficult emotions and painful thoughts. You will not have to think or feel, as long as you do what I tell you.'

This conceptualization tallies well with the description of adolescent focused therapy by Fitzpatrick et al. (2010). The emotions that come with dependent, but changing, relationships are felt, for some reason, to be intolerable to children and adolescents with eating disorders. Therefore they turn to themselves for the fulfilment of all their needs. One might imagine that the need for food is denied precisely because it is so intimately connected with the child's dependency on its parents, particularly mother. The offer by the 'internal tyrant' to protect them against all psychological pain and difficulty is irresistible to someone who, for a variety of reasons, struggles to bear the vagaries of dependent relationships.

The idea that there is a destructive, anti-relational, part of the personality at large in eating disorders, in not confined to psychoanalytic theory, but is a common way of conceptualizing the internal situation of a child or young person with an eating disorder. Phrases such as 'the unhealthy part', or 'the anorexic part', are often used in clinical settings, but there is no generally agreed term for this familiar clinical observation. Different specialist teams, and indeed individual patient-therapist pairs, develop their own preferred way of describing what all recognize as near-universal characteristic of eating disorders.

Psychoanalytic thinking also fits well with qualitative research carried out by Serpell et al. (1999) in which participants were asked to write two letters, one to anorexia as a friend, and one to anorexia as an enemy ('Anorexia nervosa: Friend or foe?'). The results yielded the finding that positive experiences of having anorexia primarily included feeling looked after or protected, gaining a sense of control, and feeling special. Negative experiences included constant thoughts about food, feeling taken over, and the damage done to personal relationships. Nearly all participants spoke about anorexia as a protector, with a typical statement being, 'Anorexia, my friend . . . you are the source of my security, my guard . . .' We can see that the idea of an internal tyrant is present in the experience of being 'protected', and the 'narcissistic' element present in the experience of feeling special.

Case example

A 17-year-old patient said that whenever she struggled with her confidence in a group of people her own age, she only had to tell herself, 'I am thinner than every one of you', to feel better. She said, 'I had expected that everything would come right when I turned 16 – that I would be beautiful, popular, and have a boyfriend. None of those things happened.' She turned to weight loss and body control as a means of numbing the pain of a sense of failure, finding herself without the resources to resolve the confidence problems commonly associated with adolescent development.

Most likely all therapists working with people with eating disorders will try to bring their patients' attention to this internal tyrant or 'unhealthy part'. This can be done by talking in terms of 'parts' of the self, or by structured externalization exercises. It is difficult to know to what extent it is fruitful to try to persuade the patient to side with the therapist against the 'internal tyrant' and to fight its domination. Clinical experience suggests, in the words of one patient, that 'you can put me in a boat but you can't make me row out onto the lake'. (For parents' experience of this feature of eating disorders, see Cottee-Lane et al., 2004.) In other words, only the patient can make the ultimate decision to jettison the internal tyrant. But once this decision has been made, the therapist can strongly support the process by helping the young person to become more self-aware and to notice the link between troubling emotions and the temptation to turn to anorexic behaviour and cognition.

The term 'no-entry defence' coined by Williams (1997a and 1997b) refers to the idea that *some* children may develop anorexia as a way of enacting a closure of their minds to overwhelming stimuli, just as they refuse to allow food to enter their bodies. Williams hypothesizes that children who have not experienced understanding and containment of their emotions in their early years, or who have felt particularly misunderstood, turn away from the expectation of intimate communication altogether. Their subjective experience of communication becomes one of being intruded upon by another's emotions, and their solution is to erect a kind of 'no entry' barrier, both psychologically and physically. In this context, 'containment' is a specific term, referring to an influential psychoanalytic theory (Bion, 1959) about the needs of infants to be 'contained' by their mothers by means of sensitive attention and responsiveness to their communications, thus supporting the infant to develop of a sense of itself as a being with agency who can communicative meaningfully and make itself understood, from birth onwards. Most mothers perform this 'containing' function quite naturally (cf. Winnicott, 1958, on 'good-enough' mothering) but there is research evidence that mothers with mental health difficulties cannot attend to their infants' communications adequately (Hobson, 2002). Such research also shows that one of the actions infants perform in the presence of poorly attuned mothering is to literally turn away their heads, faces and gaze. This research suggests the possibility of observational corroboration for the theory of the 'no-entry defence', although in no way shows that this kind of early experience would be a factor unique to eating disorders.

However, adverse early experience contributes to insecure attachment in childhood, and there is evidence from the adult literature on eating disorders that a larger proportion of adults with eating disorders than in the normal population can be categorized, through the Adult Attachment Interview (AAI) (Main et al., 1985; George et al., 1985), as being insecurely attached (O'Shaughnessy and Dallos, 2009). It may be that future research will identify particular, subtle, aspects of early parenting experience that predispose towards an eating disorder, but at present there are no broad categories – such as, for example, trauma, maltreatment, sexual, physical or emotional abuse – that have been associated with the development of eating disorders.

Psychoanalytic psychotherapy assumes that mental illness is meaningful. Self-destructive and irrational behaviour is seen as a symptom of mental conflict, and is interpreted as communication, though it may take some time to figure out what each individual patient is 'saying' through their symptoms. With older children and adults, therapy can help to create a meaningful narrative in words. Younger children, and many children of all ages with eating disorders, can usually put into words very little about their feelings at the start of treatment. Hence communication is primarily through, on the one hand, eating disordered behaviour and, on the other, through 'counter-transference', that is, through the responses evoked in the therapist, which the therapist then uses as a signpost to the states of mind that the patient herself cannot access.

Not all those working with eating disorders believe that the symptoms are meaningful in their own right. Perhaps because the communication, if that is what it is, is so opaque and difficult to interpret, there is a tendency in current treatment not to search for meaning but to take the symptoms as 'given'. The current research in the neurobiological factors in eating disorders may inadvertently encourage the idea that there is no psychological or emotional meaning to the child's behaviour. The meaning has to be sought with each individual patient, in the first instance, and it may often not become clear what was troubling the child until she is able to look back and put her difficulties into words. This may be with the benefit of hindsight or after a period of psychotherapy in which she has been helped to translate bodily enactment into mental phenomena.

Therapeutic alliance

Therapeutic alliance is a term that refers to the relationship between patient and therapist. The relationship needs to be characterized by enough warmth and respect to feel trustworthy to the patient, and can then serve as foundation for collaborative therapeutic work (Shirk et al., 2011). This does not mean that there is no room for hostility, irritation, anger, mistrust, and disappointment. These kinds of emotions need to surface and be named and accepted in therapy.

One might argue that attention to negative emotions is particularly important in eating disorders, because it is precisely these emotions that children and young people have such difficulty tolerating, and which they try to do away with by obliterating all emotion. The eating disorder itself works against the formation of a trusting therapeutic relationship. The therapist has to address the child's withdrawal from close relationships in therapy as much as in 'real' life. In psychodynamic psychotherapy in particular, the therapeutic relationship itself is one of the topics for observation and periodic discussion (Blagys and Hilsenroth, 2000, 2002; Shedler, 2010; Schneider et al., 2009), and is considered one of the mediators of change. The intention is that fears about relating to others will be 'lived out' in relation to the therapist also. The therapy setting allows direct focus on the relationship in a controlled setting, different from the to and fro of everyday life. What the child learns about how she or he relates to the therapist will resonate with her wider relationships, and increase her self-awareness. However, negative emotions need to be relatively temporary states in the context of a generally positive relationship in order for this kind of work to feel safe.

Research in the field of alliance in child and adolescent psychotherapy is less developed than in adult psychotherapy. It has become a commonplace to state that the findings from adult psychotherapy show that it is the quality of the therapeutic alliance, above all other factors, that determines the outcome of the therapy, but there is increasing evidence that the same may be true of child and adolescent psychotherapy (Shirk et al., 2011). There is also increasing evidence that clinicians from different schools do not adhere strictly to their core theoretical and technical components but adapt their treatments to the patient (Schneider et al., 2009). For an up-to-date and thorough exposition of how taking the therapy 'brand' at face value can undermine meaningful research into psychotherapy, see McQueen and Smith (2012). The underlying question seems to be, as Norcross and Lambert (2011) put it, 'Do treatments cure disorders or do relationships heal people?' They go on to dismiss this as a false dichotomy and to argue for the view that it is the patient (above all), the therapist, their relationship, the treatment method and the context that *all* contribute to the success (and failure) of the treatment. Relationship and therapeutic technique are interwoven, or 'Treatment methods are relational acts' (Safran and Muran, 2000).

Comparing anorexia nervosa to membership of an 'internal gang', though a metaphor, makes sense of why it can be so difficult to engage a child or adolescent with an eating disorder in individual therapy. The offer of a new, therapeutic, relationship, is experienced as direct threat to the internal system and therefore viewed with suspicion on the one hand. On the other hand, most children with eating disorders also want help even if their 'internal tyrant' will not allow them to ask for it. The way around this ambivalence, for most, is to become passive and allow others – parents and professionals – to take the lead in seeking help and offering treatment.

Therefore, individual therapy often has to start without the child's explicit consent. The ambivalence about getting help may be enacted by conflicting messages, for example, insisting that they are 'fine' while also saying that they 'don't mind' being offered individual sessions, or even just by accompanying the therapist to her room for an exploratory meeting. This kind of 'passive consent' cannot provide a firm foundation for purposeful and goal-focused work in the long run, but may be the best that can be expected at the beginning of the process.

Psychotherapy process

Engagement and basic stance

Psychotherapy with children with eating disorders doesn't differ from psycho-therapy for other kinds of problems in its fundamentals: a regular time and set place for a session, the therapist's punctuality, a predictable length of session, a familiar greeting, the same therapist each time, notice and careful consideration for holidays and breaks in therapy, and so on. A respectful, kind, open-minded attitude with an emphasis on understanding how things look and feel from the young person's own point of view, is another fundamental to the therapeutic stance in all models of child and adolescent therapy.

The range of clinicians available in the multi-disciplinary team will to some extent determine to what extent individual therapy can be ring-fenced as a confi-dential, exploratory space, relatively free from the pressures and immediate demands imposed by considerations of medical safety and physical health.

Ideally, the individual therapy space would not, at least at the beginning, be the arena for discussion of meal plans and weight gain targets. These should ideally be negotiated in a family session. Similarly, education about the physical risks should, preferably, be carried out by a doctor or dietitian. That said, a joint session with a doctor or dietitian can be very dynamic, as the therapist's knowledge and under-standing of the young person's irrational beliefs about the body, eating, food and nutrition can helpfully inform the discussion and the therapist can actively track the young person's response to the information provided by the physician. The individual therapist needs to be free to establish a stance that demonstrates a genuine openness to hearing how it is for the young person, without being prompted to argue, cajole or exhort. At the same time, the therapist needs to make clear that she is not, of course, an ally of the eating disorder. This is a fine balance to tread requiring clear and careful choice of words and tone, on repeated occasions.

Clinical example

A 12-year-old girl, Lydia, who was very underweight, had a joint session with the team's pediatrician and her individual therapist. Lydia's therapist explained that Lydia believed that all food converted into fat inside her body. The paediatrician was then able to explain how the body used energy and nutrition to build up bone, muscle, heart activity, and so on, before it became fat. Further on in the session, the therapist drew attention to the fact that Lydia had never imagined herself as an adolescent, something she knew about from Lydia's individual sessions. This allowed the doctor to focus on the inevitability and necessity of development from the physiological perspective. The combination of Lydia's personal anxieties with the information given by the paediatrician made it more difficult for Lydia to dismiss the information as not being relevant to her. In fact, Lydia referred back this session in individual therapy and periodically requested another session with the doctor whenever she had to tolerate a physiological change in the interests of getting better, such as weight gain and menstruation.

Psychological treatment for eating disorders is a multi-disciplinary treatment and this raises questions about the boundaries between the different components of treatment. All child psychotherapy is founded on limited confidentiality – that is, the therapist will not keep confidential any information that indicates that the child is being harmed by others, either physically, sexually or emotionally, or indeed, is harming others. This should always be stated explicitly at the beginning of therapy. This limitation is often live in eating disorders work and negotiating its parameters case by case may require regular consultation with managers, team members and clinical supervisors. However, the details of the sessions, and in particular, information about the child's emerging thoughts and feelings, must be kept confidential in the usual way. There can be no expectation that parents are entitled to know, through the individual therapist, what their child is thinking, feeling, or indeed worrying about. The individual therapist will need to judge on a session-by-session basis what is usefully shared with the rest of the team.

One aim of individual psychotherapy is to enable to child to speak more openly to her parents, but for many children, this is hard to do and the channels of communication may develop only slowly. Parents do, of course, know a great deal about their children, but there may be things that the child is deliberately keeping secret, or feels ashamed to talk about.

Regular team case discussion is an essential prerequisite for an integrated therapeutic approach. In particular, family therapist and individual therapist need to 'touch base' regularly to check that treatment is proceeding along coherent lines, without overstepping the boundaries of confidentiality of the respective therapeutic settings. The family therapist and individual therapist often have perspectives that differ in the relative weight given to the child's and the family's feelings, wishes, and viewpoints. These can be brought together by case discussion. When they are not aired, there is a danger that perspectives get polarized and 'splitting' occurs.

Early engagement needs to be characterized by a combination of gentleness, firmness and flexibility. The therapist needs to be gentle in her use of language, for example, avoiding shocking turns of phrase, along the lines of, 'you do realize that if you carry on like this you may die?' This is worth mentioning as the eating disorder itself often provokes people to try to 'shock' the child out of it. These kinds of statements do upset children with eating disorders, but they do not cure them. Children with eating disorders do not learn and adapt their behaviour according to emotional experience. Unpleasant emotions only prompt the child with an eating disorder to redouble her efforts at control, in accordance with her belief that the more restrictive she can be, the less anxiety and psychological disturbance she will suffer.

Gentleness can be coupled with more robust discussion further into therapy, but in the engagement phase it is important to tailor one's stance to the child's level of anxiety about engagement.

Firmness is required in negotiating boundaries of behaviour within the session, and also the boundaries of confidentiality. For example, the therapist may insist that a child who exercises compulsively sits down and remains seated and as still as possible in the session. Sometimes, children insist that they do not want to be separated from their parents in order to come into their session. The therapist can insist that the session cannot take place with parents present. Experience does tend to show that this separation anxiety is similar to that shown by children going to nursery and that as soon as the separation is effected, the child can engage with the therapist.

Flexibility is not the opposite of firmness, but a necessary pragmatic tool. Sessions may need to be moved or shortened in order to accommodate a child's anxiety, and various kinds of technical modifications or innovations may be helpful. This is where a psychodynamic therapist may need to step out of her preference for following the patient's lead and be willing to set structuring tasks, and conversely, the cognitive-behavioural therapist may need to allow an open free-flowing session if that seems to be what the child needs. Non-verbal techniques such as play for children at the younger end of the spectrum, as well as role play, and the use of drawing and crafts, can all be drawn on.

Addressing bodily sensations and perceptions may be very helpful in the engagement phase, rather than an exclusive focus on talking, given that putting things into words is precisely what is so difficult for the child or young person. Statements about feeling fat, having a huge stomach, and so on, may need to be accepted as the conversational currency for the time being and attempts to 'translate' the bodily sensations into mental phenomena need to be undertaken with a light touch.

Flexibility should not become a euphemism for a mish-mash of approaches, however. The therapist needs to keep in mind both an underlying theoretical formulation, and the aims of therapy.

Clinical example 1: Addressing the body

Danielle, a girl of 11 with anorexia nervosa, could not sit still in her early therapy sessions as continuous exercise was part of her self-imposed regime. Her therapist asked her to agree to be still just for one minute, and to focus on what came into her mind. Danielle reported that she could feel her waistband touching her stomach and this made her feel fat. She became tearful. The therapist later repeated the exercise, asking Danielle to lean back in her chair, stating explicitly that she might then not feel her waistband. This time Danielle reported a memory from a summer holiday when she was still well, and said that she wished she could be happy again in the way that she used to be. It could be seen that starting where Danielle 'was at' allowed her to move from her preoccupation with her body to some mental representation.

Clinical example 2: Addressing feelings in the therapeutic relationship

Jasmine, aged 13, looked suspicious when greeted by her new therapist in the waiting room and was unwilling to go with her. She explained gruffly that she felt fine. She said that she did not want to talk to anyone outside her family. The therapist acknowledged that Jasmine was being faced with two unpleasant demands: to talk about eating, and to talk to a new person, outside her family. She hazarded that this made Jasmine feel 'suspicious' and as if she were being 'intruded upon'. Jasmine agreed, and relaxed slightly. Jasmine then became able to describe all the demands for engagement, including from school and friends, that she wished to avoid. It can be seen that in order to begin constructing a therapeutic alliance, the therapist had to address immediately the negative feelings that Jasmine brought to the first encounter.

Engagement phase: summary

The beginning phase of individual therapy is characterized by:

1   A robust framework, that is, a regular time, place and the same therapist each week.
2   A kind, respectful, open-minded stance, with a willingness to engage wherever the child herself 'is at'.
3   A gentle, firm and flexible approach, bearing in mind that children with eating disorders may find it very difficult to put words to feelings.
4   Clarity in the team regarding the boundaries of confidentiality.
5   Clarity in the team about the respective tasks of family therapy and individual therapy.
6   Clarity about where and when multi-disciplinary case discussion will take place.

Goal setting and collaboration

Goals or aims of therapy can be set in all models of psychotherapy; in psychodynamic psychotherapy the focus might be more on internal change while in cognitive-behavioural therapy goals might be put in terms of external change. In other words, psychodynamic goals might be about feeling differently, and in behavioural treatment, about doing things differently. Ideally, the two sorts of goals should be brought together, so that the changed feeling and changed behaviour are linked up. For example:

Goal: *I would like to feel more confident in my peer group* (this represents internal change). *For example, I would like to be able to stay at my friend's house for a sleepover* (behavioural change).

In the first few sessions it is helpful to formulate goals for the first phase of therapy. This can be achieved in a structured manner (e.g. Law, 2007) or through discussion and mutual agreement. Goals can be determined by the patient although the therapist will usually help to bring certain themes to the fore and may also prohibit some 'goals' as being impossible to achieve, or anti-therapeutic. For example, 'lose more weight' would not be a permissible goal for therapy with a young person with an eating disorder! A 'magical' goal, and therefore not permissible, would be 'never to be unhappy again'. The young person can rate where she is in relation to the goal, for example on a scale of 0–10, at the start of therapy, and then after an agreed number of months or at the end of treatment, whichever is sooner. When the patient judges that the goal has been adequately reached, a new goal can be set. Using goal setting and monitoring of progress in this way can assist in the evaluation of therapy, but is also useful clinically not only for helping patients to formulate their own goals, but also for keeping the aims of therapy in mind, enhancing the patient's sense of engagement and 'ownership' of the therapy, and for motivation. When patients come to review their goals, they are often surprised at how far they have come. 'Did I really feel that? That's not a problem anymore!' is quite a common reaction to looking at goals from a few months before. In the psychodynamic framework, goals need not explicitly be referred to at every session, but this may differ in other models.

It can be hard to agree goals with children with eating disorders. Children who have come far in terms of their weight restoration, physical health and school engagement, may still cling to the idea that all they want is to lose weight again. Sometimes it may be helpful to allow the new, healthier eating and lifestyle to become habitual without pinpointing it cognitively, but eventually the mind needs to embrace what the body is doing. There is evidence that patient-therapist consensus about goals, and collaboration to reach them, leads to better therapeutic outcomes. If it turns out to be impossible to set goals in the first phase of therapy, the therapist should try again at regular intervals.

The middle phase

This section will be illustrated by means of a longer case example. The middle phase of therapy is perhaps the most amorphous, because with the engagement and therapeutic alliance in place, the content of the work can take as many directions as there are individuals. Nevertheless, there are some familiar themes in terms of both content and process, and these will be highlighted in the case example that follows.

Case example: Alice

Alice was nearly 13 when she began individual psychotherapy. She had been diagnosed with anorexia nervosa at the age of nine and had had several hospital admissions where her weight was restored, although she always relapsed after a few months. Despite her long illness, Alice and her family had not accessed a comprehensive programme of psychological therapy before, and so this was her first time in individual psychotherapy.

Alice's presentation in early sessions followed a pattern. She would start the session in a cheerful, chatty manner. Halfway through the session she would fall silent, become restless, and fall to doing stylized doodles. Attempts to elicit information about what was troubling her now led to little verbal response. The therapist's countertransference followed a parallel pattern, beginning with a lively response, hopeful about deepening contact. When Alice withdrew, the therapist's countertransference was of bewilderment and anxiety. She felt uncertain and as if she had done something 'wrong' to provoke this withdrawal.

The first phase of work focused on this communication of 'two halves'. Alice could not answer direct questions about what prompted her withdrawal or what she felt during it, in keeping with a child with eating disorders who communicates through behaviour rather than words. The withdrawal, silence and doodling *were* the communication, or rather half of it, along with the other, cheerful half. The therapist needed to find ways of understanding these.

In early sessions, Alice and her therapist worked on formulating goals. As can be seen, two of her four goals focused on her worries about the therapeutic relationship itself.

Alice, 13	Time 1: Start of therapy	T1
Goal 1	To know when I'm stressed and why then I think I'm fat.	4
Goal 2	To be able to tell my therapist what is and isn't helpful.	5
Goal 3	To feel less anxious about coming to therapy.	3
Goal 4	To be able to think through my emotions.	2

It could be expected that Alice's worries about how to engage with her therapist were connected to her silences and pattern of withdrawal in the second part of her session. The therapist examined her countertransference and distinguished between times when she felt that conversation simply petered out as if Alice's wellspring of things to say had run dry, and other times, when Alice's silence felt hostile, and the therapist felt as if she had been clumsy and got it wrong. She began tentatively to put these experiences into words, in what is called a 'therapist-centred' (Steiner, 1994) interpretation, for example: 'Sometimes when you fall silent it feels as though it has something to do with what I've said, as if I've got something wrong. I wonder if we could think about that, whether sometimes I say things that annoy you but which you may not want to point out because you don't want to sound critical.' The therapist-centred form is intended to demonstrate the therapist taking responsibility for her own feelings and being careful not to 'blame' the patient. It also avoids direct questioning ('Why have you stopped talking?'), which can feel persecuting.

This approach was helpful with Alice. Through a few sessions it became understood that it was actually the therapist's lively response to Alice's cheerful chatter in the first half of the session that felt 'wrong' and was annoying to Alice. Alice interpreted this as the therapist only liking her cheerful side and not being interested in her hostile, angry, confused feelings. Although Alice continued to start sessions in the same chatty manner, the therapist was now able to say, with humour, that she needed to be on her guard not to give the impression that lively chat was all that she wanted.

In the middle phase, Alice became genuinely interested in the contents of her mind, why she felt the way she did, and how she could ensure that her adolescent years were better than her recent childhood. She began to bring to therapy stories, events and issues from her everyday life to discuss and think about, issues to do with friends, parents, siblings, and teachers. She seemed to have 'come alive'.

However, the danger of enjoying her talking and progress continued to require attention. If the therapist seemed too engaged, too responsive, and acted too much as if Alice was a regular teenager, a hostile silence would ensue. She might then report a wish to lose weight or a difficulty following her meal plan.

This dynamic was also observed by the therapist, put into words, and recognized by Alice. Discussion at quite a deep level followed, about Alice's fear that if she were seen to be an ordinary teenager, functioning well, it would be forgotten that she needed special care and attention and that she could feel fragile and anxious. Being 'healthy' might mean no longer being special. This is a familiar fear of children and young people in the process of recovering from an eating disorder. The disordered eating behaviour has been so powerful and, in a sense, successful, in activating a care system, that it is frightening to give it up.

Nevertheless, Alice's Goal Based Outcome Measure after five months of therapy showed the following positive changes in her self-ratings:

Alice, 13	Time 2: After five months of therapy	T1	T2
Goal 1	To know when I'm stressed and why then I think I'm fat.	4	7
Goal 2	To be able to tell my therapist what is and isn't helpful.	5	8
Goal 3	To feel less anxious about coming to therapy.	3	9
Goal 4	To be able to think through my emotions.	2	8

Some of the themes of Alice's individual therapy were fed into the multi-disciplinary team discussion and to inform the family work, and similarly, developments in family work were made known to the individual therapist. In particular, the themes of needing to ensure that her wish to be specially cared for and understood was not forgotten, was live in the family, in her relationship with her parents and her siblings. She found it difficult to share in the family context and continued to resort to withdrawal or restrictive eating behaviour to signal her need. Alice also felt unsure whether her mother really wanted to know her 'darker' side or whether she would prefer just to have a 'happy girl', and her mother's attitude to this dilemma of Alice's was able to be thought about in family sessions.

At this stage of therapy, Alice set new goals, as follows:

Alice, 13 Time 2: New goals		T2	T3
		5/12	9/12
Goal 1	To feel more comfortable in school and with peers.	6	7
Goal 2	To put into words when I am struggling with eating and to persevere when they (parents) don't understand.	4	8
Goal 3	To give myself treats when I feel like it.	3	8

These were re-rated as shown above, at the end of therapy, which lasted nine months.

Themes in therapy

Fear of being assumed to be well: We have noted already the fear that children and young people with eating disorders have, that if they abandon the restrictive eating that arouses so much anxiety, their parents and the professionals will 'forget' about their needs. This was evident in Alice's therapy, and both her parents and her therapist came to understand that withdrawal was her way of signalling a need for contact and concern. Her second goal on her new form (above), that of persevering in her communication with her parents, showed a willingness to try to find more constructive methods of showing her needs.

Difficulty sharing: Another familiar difficulty was with sharing: sharing attention in the family, sharing herself with her therapist and her parents. Alice's mixed feelings about allowing her therapist to enjoy their conversation was put into words by her when she said, 'Sometimes when I tell you something, I regret it and wish that I could take back my words.' Another time, she explained how, if her mother asked her to lay the table, she wanted to retrieve the 10 minutes that she had thus 'given' to her mother. Sharing is not felt like sharing but like having something stolen. It can take a long time for patients to realize the pleasures that come from sharing.

Middle phase: summary

The therapeutic alliance is established and collaborative goal setting achieved.

The therapeutic relationship provides opportunities for developing self-awareness in relationships in general.

Feelings can be identified and named.

Eating-related behaviour can be linked to feelings.

The young person shows interest in self-reflection.

Sharing thoughts, feelings and information with the therapist becomes possible.

Sharing insights, thoughts and feelings with her family, both in family sessions and at home, becomes possible.

It is possible to discuss anxieties connected with 'getting better', both perceived losses and gains.

Ending phase

Most therapists working with eating disorders patients would probably agree that the ending usually takes place before the work is properly 'finished'. What a complete therapy would look like is difficult to define; as difficult as it is to define a fully recovered patient. Often, we have to content ourselves with knowing that the patient is somewhat better and hope that progress continues in the next phase of life. Much attention needs to be given to the supportive framework for the child or young person upon leaving therapy. In particular, the individual therapist needs to ask, 'Will my patient be able to tell people what she is thinking and feeling, and ask for the help she needs, when I am no longer available?'

The framework for ending is no different in eating disorders work than in therapy for other problems. The end date needs to be set well in advance and should never arrive abruptly. Ideally, the date should be known before a holiday break in therapy, so that the child or young person can have a 'rehearsal' and come back and report on how the break went, knowing that the ending is in view. There may be more focused attention to thinking about how the child will cope when difficult situations arise in the future. Some therapists write ending letters that the child can refer to should the need arise. Patient and therapist review progress together, and a goal based outcome measure, for example, provides a useful framework for this.

It is a common clinical observation that old problems rear their heads as the ending draws near. This can be understood as a wish to go over things properly before the therapist is no longer available, as well as, perhaps, wanting to make sure that the professional network remains alert.

The relapse rate of eating disorders is high, as we know, and therefore no therapist approaches the end of treatment with equanimity. Every therapist hopes that their patient will have learned skills and developed inner resources for coping when faced with future challenges. Some therapies show a sleeper effect (Midgley and Kennedy, 2011; Trowell et al., 2007) where the positive work of psychotherapy continues under the patient's own steam. Such an outcome is surely the best that any therapist could hope for.

Summary

- The goals of treatment are to enhance the patient's ability to identify emotional states, develop a language of the emotions, and communicate her feelings and needs to others, especially her parents.

- The therapist needs a coherent formulation at start of treatment as an essential framework for therapy. This formulation will vary according to the therapist's own theoretical orientation.
- Specialist knowledge and experience of eating disorders is especially necessary in the engagement phase of therapy.
- The characteristic ambivalence of eating disorders persists throughout treatment.
- Family and individual therapies need to be well integrated in the team for best outcomes.

References

Binswanger, L. (1944). The case of Ellen West. In R. May, E. Angel, and H. Ellenberger (Eds), *Existence*. New York: Basic Books, 1958.

Bion, W. R. (1959). Attacks on linking. *International Journal of Psychoanalysis*, 40, 308–315.

Blagys, M. D., and Hilsenroth, M. J. (2000). Distinctive activities of short-term psychodynamic-interpersonal psychotherapy: A review of the comparative psychotherapy process literature. *Clinical Psychology: Science and Practice*, 7, 167–188.

Blagys, M. D., and Hilsenroth, M. J. (2002). Distinctive activities of cognitive-behavioral therapy: A review of the comparative psychotherapy process literature. *Clinical Psychology Review*, 22, 671–706.

Bruch, H. (1978). *The Golden Cage: The Enigma of Anorexia Nervosa*. Cambridge, MA: Harvard University Press.

Bryant-Waugh, R. (2006). Pathways to recovery: Promoting change within a developmental-systemic framework. *Clinical Child Psychology and Psychiatry*, 11, 213–224.

Crisp, A. H. (1995). *Anorexia Nervosa: Let Me Be*. London: Routledge.

Cottee-Lane, D., Pistrang, N., and Bryant-Waugh, R. (2004). Childhood onset anorexia nervosa: The experience of parents. *European Eating Disorders Review*, 12, 169–177.

Fitzpatrick, K., Moye, A., Hostee, R., Le Grange, D., and Lock, J. (2010). Adolescent Focused Psychotherapy for adolescents with anorexia nervosa. *Journal of Contemporary Psychotherapy*, 40, 31–39.

George, C., Kaplan, N., and Main, M. (1985). Adult Attachment Interview protocol. *Unpublished manuscript*, University of California, Berkeley, CA.

Gowers, S., and Bryant-Waugh, R. (2004). Management of child and adolescent eating disorders: The current evidence base and future directions. *Journal of Child Psychology and Psychiatry*, 45 (1), 63–83.

Hobson, P. (2002). *The Cradle of Thought: Exploring the origins of thinking*. London: Macmillan.

Law, D. (2007) Goal based outcome measure, *CAMHS Outcome Research Consortium* (CORC), www.corc.uk.net.

Lawrence, M. (2008). *The Anorexic Mind*. London: Karnac.

Lock, J., Le Grange, D., Agras, W. S., and Dare, C. (2001). *Treatment Manual for Anorexia Nervosa: A Family-Based Approach.* New York: Guilford Publications.

Lock, J., Le Grange, D., Agras, W. S., Moye, A., Bryson, S. W., and Jo, B. (2010). Randomized clinical trial comparing family-based treatment with adolescent-focused individual therapy for adolescents with anorexia nervosa. *Archives of General Psychiatry, 67* (10), 1025–1032.

Main, M., Kaplan, N., and Cassidy, J. (1985). Security in infancy, childhood, and adulthood: A move to the level of representation. *Monographs of the Society for Research in Child Development, 50* (1–2, Serial No. 209), 66–104.

McQueen, D., and St. John Smith, P. (2012) NICE recommendations for psychotherapy in depression: of limited clinical utility. *Psychiatrike,* in preparation.

Midgley, N., and Kennedy, E. (2011). Psychodynamic psychotherapy for children and adolescents: a critical review of the evidence base. *Journal of Child Psychotherapy, 37,* 232–260.

Muñoz-Solomando, A., Kendall, T., and Whittington, C. J. (2008). Cognitive behavioural therapy for children and adolescents. *Current Opinion in Psychiatry 21* (4), 332–337.

Nicholls, D., and Magagna, J. (1997). A group for the parents of children with eating disorders. *Clinical Child Psychology and Psychiatry, 2* (4), 565–578.

Norcross, J. C., and Lambert, M. J. (2011): Psychotherapy relationships that work II. *Psychotherapy, 48* (1), 4–8.

NICE Guidelines. National Collaborating Centre for Mental Health (2004) *Eating Disorders. Core Interventions in the Treatment and Management of Anorexia Nervosa, Bulimia Nervosa and Related Eating Disorders.* London: National Institute for Clinical Excellence.

O'Shaughnessy, R., and Dallos, R. (2009). Attachment research and eating disorders: A review of the literature. *Clinical Child Psychology and Psychiatry, 14* (4), 559–574.

Safran, J. D., and Muran, J. D. (2000). *Negotiating the Therapeutic Alliance.* New York: Guilford Press.

Schneider, C., Pruetzel-Thomas, A., and Midgley, N. (2009). Discovering new ways of seeing and speaking about psychotherapy process: The Child Psychotherapy Q-Set, in N. Midgley, J. Anderson, E. Grainger, T. Nesic-Vuckovic, and C. Urwin, (Eds), *Child Psychotherapy and Research: New Approaches, Emerging Findings.* London: Routledge.

Serpell, L., Treasure, J., Teasdale, J., and Sullivan, V. (1999). Anorexia nervosa: friend or foe? *International Journal of Eating Disorders, 25* (2), 177–186.

Shedler, J. (2010) The efficacy of psychodynamic psychotherapy. *American Psychologist, 65* (2), 98–109.

Shirk, S. R., Karver, M. S., and Brown, R. (2011). The alliance in child and adolescent psychotherapy. *Psychotherapy, 48* (1), 17–24.

Steiner, J. (1994). Patient-centred and analyst-centred interpretations: some implications of containment and countertransference. *Psychoanalytic Inquiry, 14,* 406–422.

Thomä, H. (1967). *Anorexia Nervosa.* New York: International Universities Press.

Trowell, J., Joffe, I., Campbell, J., Clemente, C., Almqvist, F., Soininen, M., et al. (2007). Childhood depression: A place for psychotherapy. An outcome study comparing individual psychodynamic psychotherapy and family therapy. *European Child and Adolescent Psychiatry, 16* (3), 157–167.

Williams, G. (1997a). *Internal Landscapes and Foreign Bodies*. London: Duckworth.

Williams, G. (1997b). Reflections on some dynamics of eating disorders: no-entry defences and foreign bodies. *International Journal of Psychoanalysis*, *78*, 927–942.

Winnicott, D. W. W. (1958). *Through Paediatrics to Psychoanalysis: Collected Papers*. London: Tavistock Publications.

Chapter 16

Cognitive Remediation Therapy

*Isabel Owen, Camilla Lindvall Dahlgren
and Bryan Lask*

Overview

This chapter focuses on the application of Cognitive Remediation Therapy (CRT) for children and adolescents suffering from anorexia nervosa. We consider its origins and underlying rationale, describe the techniques commonly used, discuss the research evidence and explore future directions.

Introduction

The last few decades of psychological research have seen a growing interest in the relationship between mind and brain, between conscious experience and the cells, connections and pathways that are its physical, cognitive, emotional and behavioural correlates. Research into eating disorders is no exception – see Chapter 8 for an overview of the neuroscience of eating disorders. Few treatments have specifically targeted the underlying neurobiological phenomena. Cognitive remediation therapy is a relatively new treatment that targets the underlying cognitive styles that seem to contribute to the pathogenesis and maintenance of anorexia nervosa.

Definition

Cognitive remediation therapy aims to increase awareness of cognitive weaknesses through a combination of practice and meta-cognition – 'thinking about thinking'. In anorexia nervosa it targets neurocognitive abilities such as central coherence, visuo-spatial memory, cognitive flexibility, planning and other executive functions.

Origins

Cognitive Remediation Therapy (CRT) developed from a tradition of neuro-psychological assessment and was originally used for patients undergoing neurorehabilitation after brain damage (see Cicerone et al., 2005). Initially, it focused on simple, repetitive, drill-and-practice exercises aimed at improving areas of brain functioning in a similar way to an athlete performing repetitive weight lifts to strengthen a muscle. These exercises were designed to help repair damaged functions, with the overall aim of improving the quality of life or social functioning of the patient. Examples include tasks such as the participant being read a random list of numbers, asked to memorise them and then repeat them back in the correct order, or a traditional Stroop task, when names of colours are written in contrasting coloured inks and the participant has to either state the written word or its ink colour (see the WAIS-R [Wechsler, 1981] and Stroop, 1935 respectively).

Following apparent success in this field, CRT was applied to other illnesses where neurocognitive weaknesses or impairments have been identified, such as schizophrenia (Delahunty and Morice, 1993; Wykes and van der Gaag, 2001; Wykes, 2007), dyslexia (Broom and Doctor, 1995) and more recently, ADHD (O'Connell et al., 2006) and those whose treatment for cancer has left them with cognitive difficulties (Spencer, 2006). The nature of the therapy in many of these settings lends itself to being administered by computer, with all the attendant benefits of cost and convenience, but lacking a therapeutic relationship and the potential remediating power of interpersonal communication.

Rationale for the use of CRT in anorexia nervosa

More recently anorexia nervosa has become a focus of attention in CRT research. Underlying neuro-psychological weaknesses, such as poor cognitive flexibility (Roberts et al., 2007), weak central coherence (Lopez et al., 2008) and impaired visuo-spatial processing (Lask et al., 2005; Lena et al., 2004), have been assumed to contribute both to the development, and to the maintenance of anorexia nervosa. For a detailed review see Chapter 8. It is possible that the poor prognosis often associated with anorexia nervosa could be due in part to the fact that previous treatments have not addressed these weaknesses. A lack of cognitive flexibility could contribute to the inability to shift from repetitive thoughts of worthlessness or self-hatred, and to the inability to change ineffective behavioural patterns such as excessive excersise or rigid meal routines. Someone who lacks good central coherence will have a tendency to focus on the fine detail to the detriment of seeing the bigger picture – i.e. they cannot see the wood for the trees. It is possible that this way of thinking in anorexia nervosa could result in a focus on small details such as even the most minimal of fat deposits on the thighs or lower abdomen, with an inability to see these in the wider context of an emaciated body. Poor visuo-spatial memory could contribute to a distorted body-image.

CRT has been adapted to address these cognitive differences in anorexia nervosa, initially for adults (e.g. Tchanturia et al., 2007; Tchanturia and Davies, 2008) and more recently for children and adolescents (Lindvall and Lask, 2011; Wood et al., 2011; Owen et al., 2011).

Clinical application

CRT is usually carried out as a session-based intervention with a trained therapist. It can be used at any point in the treatment process, and can be used separately from, or in parallel with, other components of the treatment programme. CRT can be applied in a number of contexts when working with children and adolescents, including individually, in groups, with the family and on in-patient units (Wood et al., 2011, Lindvall et al., 2011). The main focus is on the patient engaging in specific activities, which are experienced as playing games or solving puzzles, often with the therapist, but sometimes independently. During each such exercise the therapist helps the patient to reflect upon her/his thinking style, starting with how they approached solving the puzzle. The therapist uses a few guiding questions, examples of which are listed in Table 16.1. The questions are not prescriptive but may serve as an illustration:

A number of core principles inform the clinical application of CRT for this population:

1 The primary focus of CRT is on the underlying cognitive styles

It combines practical exercises, such as games, puzzles and paper-and-pencil tasks, with reflections about *how* the exercises are tackled. It is an intervention that focuses on the *process* rather than the *content* of thought and perception – the *how* rather than the *what*. By addressing the *process* of thinking rather than the *content* (for example eating disorder thoughts about weight or shape) it encourages the development of an awareness of one's own thinking styles – metacognition. The areas that the games target are based on research findings which suggest that neuropsychological deficits affect approximately two-thirds of patients with anorexia nervosa; namely visuo-spatial memory, central coherence and some components of executive functioning (see Chapter 8).

2 Consideration of how cognitive styles are applied in everyday life

CRT can help patients to consider their cognitive styles by undertaking simple cognitive tasks, reflecting on how these relate to real life, exploring

Table 16.1 Guiding questions

1 How did you go about trying to solve the puzzle?
2 Can you think of a different way of approaching it?
3 Do you use this particular way of thinking or doing things in other areas of your life?
4 Could you try the different approach you suggested, in your real life?
5 What do you think are the pros and cons of each approach?

alternative strategies, their pros and cons, and considering the possibility of applying new skills and strategies in real life to achieve personal goals. Examples of this can be found later in the chapter, in the section on patient feedback.

3 The use of games and puzzles

The adaptation of CRT described here involves the use of exercises, tasks, games and puzzles which have been selected and developed specifically for use with children and adolescents. Their inclusion is informed by age, developmental status and cognitive style. This form of CRT has a strong focus on making the sessions fun and enjoyable for children and adolescents with anorexia nervosa. Our patients consistently report this as being helpful to them and therapists report that engagement in the therapeutic process is far easier than when using other approaches. The games that have been developed and sourced are appealing and fun with a variety of levels of difficulty aimed specifically to be appropriate for children and adolescents aged 8–18. Examples of these games and puzzles, from Owen et al. (2011) are provided later in the chapter.

4 A deliberate lack of focus on eating, weight and shape

This approach determinedly avoids a deliberate focus on weight, shape and eating. If the patient raises these issues we listen, acknowledge and accept the concerns and link these to the immediate work being done.

Examples of exercises

The games and puzzles that can be used in CRT are numerous. We like to think of them as a resource pack, or cupboard of games, which can be chosen as and when they are needed, rather than a series of exercises which are set in stone. A few examples are set out below to illustrate the range of games and puzzles that can be useful. All are intended to be followed by a discussion involving the sort of guiding questions listed above.

Visuo-spatial memory

A significant number of our young patients struggle with visuo-spatial memory. The *visuo-spatial* domain refers to object recognition (what is it?), spatial location (where is it?) and visual memory (what did it look like?). Practising cognitive abilities in this domain includes exercises like remembering a route or complex shapes, and rotating a map or picture in one's head. We have sourced and developed a number of tasks around these themes. The following is an example of a game that can be used to help with this cognitive domain.

FINDING YOUR WAY

In this visuo-spatial task, the patient is asked find the way from one end of the pathway to the other, stating whether each turn would be a left or a right turn, without physically rotating the paper (Figure 16.1). The same game can also be played using a street map, and asking the patient to navigate between two points of their choice. There are many possible variations; another option is to ask the patient to keep count of the number of left and right turns as they work through the task, or to ask them to get from one point on a map to another, without taking any left turns.

Central coherence

Central coherence is a complex function that allows us to see both the fine detail and the bigger picture. It allows us to 'zoom in' on specific features, and to 'zoom out' to see how they all fit together. Central coherence is an extremely important function that underlies many of our day-to-day tasks both as children and adults. It is an ability that develops throughout childhood and adolescence. Evidence is emerging that people who suffer from anorexia appear to have a cognitive style

Figure 16.1 Finding your way.

that is focused on the fine detail rather than the global picture, or to put it another way, they may find they 'miss the wood for the trees'. A number of games and puzzles can be used to help with this, including the ones below. Both Geometric Figures and the Main Idea game were first used with adults with anorexia nervosa at King's College London (see Tchanturia and Hambrook, 2010).

Geometric figures

The therapist gives the patient a selection of geometric figures (see Figure 16.2). The therapist asks the patient to choose one of the figures in the pile. They then tell the patient that she/he will be in charge in this game, and will get to tell the therapist what to do! The patient is then asked to describe the figure to the therapist, whose job is to draw a picture guided by the patient's words. The patient cannot see what the therapist is drawing and the therapist is not allowed to ask any questions. The patient and therapist then compare their figures, and explore the strategies used to describe the figure.

Summarizing

This task targets the patient's central coherence by asking them to find the main points of a story or letter. In a session, the therapist presents the patient with a

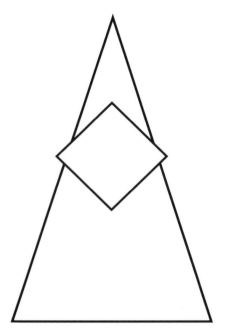

Figure 16.2 Geometric figure.

story or a letter. They give the patient some time to read it through, or offer to read it to them. They then ask the patient to summarize the story or the letter. The patient can also be asked to do this in three short sentences, then three short phrases and finally just three words. The stories are chosen to be interesting and appealing to children and adolescents, including traditional tales such as 'Rumplestiltskin':

> In a beautiful green valley, by a crystal stream, there lived a miller and his daughter. The daughter was kind, caring and had hair the colour of finest gold. Her father, on the other hand, was not an honest man. He was often to be heard boasting and telling all sorts of lies to his friends. He even began to tell people that his daughter was so clever she could spin simple straw into real gold. People were so impressed by this tale that they told their friends, who then told their friends. And so word spread far and wide of the girl who could spin straw into gold until, at last, it reached the ears of the Crown Prince himself. The Prince rode out to find her, and seeing the kindness in her eyes asked her to marry him. They were married that same day, and everyone in the Kingdom rejoiced.
>
> The couple were happy and content, until a few weeks after the wedding, when the Prince needed some more gold to decorate his palace. So he had a mountain of straw taken up to the tallest tower, with a spinning wheel, and asked his new wife to spin it into gold. Left on her own in the tower, the princess wept. She had never been happier, but now the prince would find out it was all a lie, and she would lose him forever.

Executive functioning

There are many components to executive functioning (see Chapter 8) including: (1) planning, (2) flexibility and (3) inhibition.

1 Planning

A number of patients with anorexia nervosa exhibit difficulties with both abstract and concrete planning, whether that is in the short term, day-to-day, or in the longer term. Some of the patients seem to prefer to work on a trial-and-error basis, and to take things as they come rather than to foresee and plan in advance, whereas others stick rigidly to pre-organised plans and agendas. There are a number of games and puzzles that have been developed and sourced to work with these different ways of approaching problem solving and planning, including the selection given below. In addition, a number of games that require the use of strategy or forward planning, including backgammon, croquet and a variety of mazes can be used.

PHOTO SEQUENCING PUZZLE

In this simple game, the participant has to place a series of photos in the correct order (see Figure 16.3). This allows for consideration of planning strategies.

Figure 16.3 Photo sequencing.

PLANNING AND PRIORITISING GAMES

These are two simple games to help someone who struggles with the more abstract tasks involved in planning. In the first, the participant is asked to pick one of the following tasks and think about the steps they need to take to:

- Make a cup of tea.
- Plan a birthday party for a friend.
- Plan a short story.
- Go to a concert.
- Apply for a job.
- Go to a football game.
- Visit a friend who lives out of town.
- Go to the hair dresser.
- Plan a trip to the cinema for themselves and 3 friends.

In the next activity, the participant is given a fictitious scenario, with a number of problems that all need solving. They are asked to think through the different solutions, and which order to go about them. For example:

Imagine you are at home one evening:
- You have homework due in the next morning.
- You are due to meet a friend later that evening, but need to call to tell them you will be late.
- You spill a glass of water over the table you are working on.

What order do you sort things out in?
Why?
Could you have prioritised differently?
What would be the results of prioritising differently?

2 Flexibility

Flexibility includes things like the ability to switch between jobs or tasks, or to interrupt one way of thinking to see a perspective from another angle. This domain comes into play in many areas of a patient's life, for example when they are planning a revision schedule or thinking through a point of view in a conversation.

Many games can be used that require a flexible approach or several concurrent actions that require you to swap between them. These include traditional Stroop tasks (when names of colours are written in contrasting coloured inks and you have to either say the written word or its ink colour, or switch between the two), and visual illusions where the participant has to try to see two different images within the same picture, and then switch between the two. An example of another game is given below.

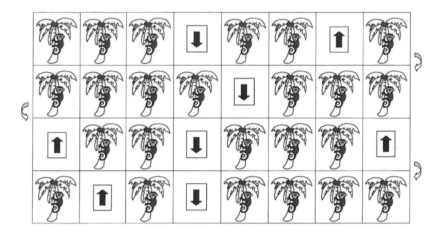

Figure 16.4 Up and Down.

UP AND DOWN

Patients are presented with the picture in Figure 16.4. They are asked to count up from 1 until they get to a square with an arrow in it. If the arrow points down, they then have to start counting down rather than up. As an added complexity, when they get to a square with an arrow in it, they have to state the direction rather than the number, for example, 1, 2, 3, 4, down, 3, 2 . . .

3 Inhibition

Inhibition concerns the ability to ignore a distracting stimulus in order to complete a task. It essentially requires us to stop a thought process, consciously or otherwise. Many tasks can be used to target inhibition, as long as they have an element that requires a blocking or stopping of attention or response to an irrelevant stimulus. One of the most commonly used tasks is the Stroop Task, where participants have to read a list of names of colours which have been written in contrasting coloured inks, for example the word 'blue' is in fact written in red ink, and the participant has to either state the written word or its ink colour (Stroop, 1935).

CRT sessions

Each of the activities described here can be used as a one-off, or different variants tapping the same neurocognitive ability can be revisited through the course of therapy. Generally patients receive between 8–10 CRT sessions,

Table 16.2 Course structure

Session number	Description
1	Introduction to CRT; What does the process/structure look like, what is the goal/the aims of this intervention, what will be the therapist's and the patient's tasks during the sessions. Which important issues might emerge, how do we tackle these issues, the need for sharing information with other relevant health care takers and/or family members.
2–9	Identification of cognitive styles. Identifying ineffective thinking patterns and exploring new ways of thinking. Promoting thinking about thinking (i.e. meta-cognition). Implementation of small behavioural changes (Homework).
10	Completion, summarizing the course of intervention, discussion, feedback.

each lasting approximately 30–45 minutes. The structure and content are flexible and can be tailored to meet each patient's specific needs. An example of how a course of CRT might be structured over 10 sessions is shown in Table 16.2.

Modes of delivery

There are a number of potential modes of delivery including: individual, group-based, family-based and within an in-patient milieu (Wood et al. 2011; Lindvall and Lask, 2011). So far, all seem promising with high levels of engagement reflected in good session attendance and many reports of enjoyment. Different contexts for delivering CRT are likely to have different advantages. For example, individually delivered CRT allows for in-depth exploration of each patient's difficulties and problem-solving skills. Group-based delivery can encourage peer-group support, enhance the morale of the whole group and appears to be both time- and resource-efficient. Family-based delivery can help parents to understand better their child's difficulties and also sometimes highlights intergenerational patterns in relation to areas of neurocognitive strength and weakness.

Patient and Therapist Feedback

At the end of the intervention, the therapist encourages the patient to write a short letter, commenting and reflecting upon their experience in terms of the process, positives and negatives, and to express their thoughts regarding what could have been different or better.

Here is a feedback letter from a 16-year-old patient.

Dear (Name of Therapist),

CRT for me has been like nothing I have ever experienced before, but it has been very useful. It was very exciting to do all the tasks and games which focused on my way of thinking in different situations, and how I solve problems. I really liked talking to you about how I think, because that is something I usually don't do.

CRT has not changed me in any major ways, but I have been able to make some small changes, and the therapy has challenged my way of thinking. I have become more aware of why I approach different situations in certain ways, and it has made me realize that there are things that I want to change in my everyday life. I really liked the homework tasks, because I enjoyed challenging myself in different situations, without having to succeed at the first attempt.

I feel that the discussions we had after each task were very helpful, because I have never talked about my experiences regarding issues such as making decisions in everyday life, planning and analysing. You were honest and interested in listening to me, and I liked that. It has been a bit complicated for me at home, because my family does not know much about CRT (except for the information they received during the information meeting), and it's difficult for me when I feel I can't talk about what we do during the sessions. I think my parents still think it's difficult to speak about the eating disorder, and try to 'cure' me by feeding me huge amounts of food. But they do not understand the rest, and what actually happens in my head. And that's why it has helped coming to you.

I think I would have liked a few more sessions with more concrete challenges. But I would absolutely recommend this treatment to others, because you start to reflect lot on yourself as a person, and why you choose to be the person you are, and do the things you do, and this is important. An even if you're a bit sceptical at the start, it doesn't hurt to try it out!

From,

(Name of Patient)

The therapist also writes a feedback letter, but focuses more on what has been observed during the sessions, potential changes in thinking and behavioural styles, and suggestions for future work.

Dear (Name of Patient),

When we met in our last CRT session we decided it might be helpful to think about what CRT is and ways in which it might have helped you.

Cognitive Remediation Therapy is a collection of games and puzzles, like visual illusions, sorting games, mazes and map games. We use them to help explore people's 'thinking' styles. 'Thinking style' means things like: the way you solve problems; how you plan; dealing with sudden changes; being flexible; learning and remembering new information; picking up rules; and whether you focus more on the fine details or 'the big picture'.

Why is it helpful to do this? Some people's thinking style might make it harder to manage their eating disorder. CRT should give you a better understanding of how you tend to think, and also give you some different ways of thinking about things.

In our CRT sessions you have worked hard, and as a result have made some very subtle but important changes in your thinking style that I think you can be really proud of. I've put some examples below.

The first game we played had some letters written by different people, and also a busy picture with a lot of things happening in it. We looked at these and in all of them you could see the main themes, and didn't get too distracted by the detail – you could see the 'big picture'. One of the letters was a bit trickier, and you reflected that in real life there were times when it was hard to see the whole picture, especially with body image. You thought that if you saw a bit of fat on one part of your body then it felt as you were fat all over, and it was harder to 'zoom out' and see the whole picture.

The next game we played was the Penguin game where you had to remember a number of penguins dressed in silly outfits. It was quite difficult (there was a lot to remember) but you concentrated hard and managed to remember very successfully indeed. You had a range of strategies for remembering and recalling, like using the names of things rather than trying to recall the picture itself; or telling a story about the different pictures. It is very handy to have a number of different strategies to call on like this, and you thought you had used them before very successfully, like with GCSE exam revision.

We played the Maze Game next. This was a selection of mazes that got harder and harder! You found your way out of all the mazes but there were times on some of the really hard ones when you got a stuck in dead ends. You thought that a different way of approaching it would have been to plan a bit more, and then you would have seen the dead ends earlier. You thought that in real life you tended to get started and then dealt with the options as you came across them. We thought a bit about whether there was another way of approaching this in real life too.

In the next game, we had to arrange a number of different blue and green tiles in a way that made them into a joined-up loop. This had some pretty challenging levels too. You thought that you tended to start with the bits that you could do easily first, and then have a go at the rest, rather than planning it all in one go. You thought that in real life it could be quite like this too- with unpacking in your new room you started with the bits that you knew where you wanted to put them, and then had a go at the rest.

You reflected for a bit on the different strategies you had for planning and thought that you had a range of different strategies, and could acknowledge when one wasn't working and try something different. In real life, you felt this was also the same and was something that you have really worked on here at (Name of Hospital). This is a really useful thing to be able to do and also an ability to be very proud of.

We played the Map Game where you had to find three different routes between the same two points. You could do this, although you noticed that they were quite similar, and it was tricky to go a long way from what you felt was the most obvious route. You had a go at doing it really differently, and found a route that was wasn't obvious at all, but this felt a bit frustrating. In real life you thought it might be a bit like this, that there was one route that seemed the most obvious to you, and making little changes was easier than doing it completely differently which could feel frustrating. This seemed like an important thing to know about yourself.

In difficult levels of this! You worked really hard and persevered even when it got really tough. At one point we thought about having a look at the clue as it was very hard to work out the puzzle without it. You thought it felt a bit like cheating, and this reminded you of a time in real life when you had tried really hard to do something difficult, finding a job, and had asked your Mum for help. When she found one, it had felt a bit like all the work you had done was pointless and that it was a bit like cheating to ask for help. We thought for a bit about how successful people often have whole teams of people helping them to do difficult things, and how that feels in comparison. You thought that sometimes in real life you might have kept more of an open mind and asked for help more. This seems like an important thing to know about yourself too.

I hope that this has made CRT a bit clearer, and I also hope that I have described some of your personal thinking skills- both your very impressive strengths and some things that it would be helpful to think about for the future.

From,

(Name of Therapist)

How could CRT work? Possible mechanisms

CRT has been hypothesised to be effective by either strengthening and refining neural circuits, or bypassing weakened or damaged circuits to create new pathways, and by learning and transferring new cognitive strategies to appropriate situations (Demily et al., 2008; McGurk et al., 2007). Its usefulness in treating anorexia nervosa is based on the assumption that specific cognitive styles (see Chapter 8) may contribute to the development or maintenance of the disorder. These cognitive styles in turn may reflect less than optimal functioning of specific neural circuits. The key question for CRT is therefore whether it can help strengthen the existing pathways or aid the development of alternative pathways.

Future directions

The research evidence in adults with anorexia nervosa is promising. Early pilot studies have found that CRT can be helpful for adults with anorexia nervosa (Tchanturia et al., 2007), even for those who have been ill for some time. Improvements have been reported in cognitive functioning and eating disorder psychopathology. Furthermore patients find it a very acceptable form of treatment and commonly it seems to enhance motivation (Whitney et al., 2008; Davies and Tchanturia, 2005; Tchanturia et al., 2007)

To date, there are no reported quantitative studies of CRT for children and adolescents with eating disorders. A single case study in 2009 reported that CRT was acceptable for use with adolescents, and that the early indicators suggested improvement on some psychopathology and cognitive scores (Cwojdzińska et al., 2009). We have run CRT sessions with children and adolescents (30 patients, aged 13–19), focusing on providing age-appropriate CRT for this patient group across three different centres. Though not yet formally evaluated again the responses seem promising. Some specific clinical details are provided in Wood et al. (2011).

However there are many unanswered questions:

1   Does CRT lead to improvement in psychopathology, neuropsychological function, and motivation in this population?
2   If so are there particular subgroups who respond better than others?
3   Are there differences dependent upon mode of delivery, e.g. individual v group v family?
4   Which mode of delivery works better for whom?
5   When is CRT best offered, early in the treatment process or later?
6   What is the optimal number and length of sessions?
7   How is CRT best integrated with other treatments?
8   Is 'homework' useful?
9   If new cognitive skills are learnt, do they transfer to real life and how long are they retained?
10 Are top-up sessions useful?
11 Should interventions be based specifically on the ascertained cognitive weaknesses or might they cover other domains?

12   How can potential changes be measured reliably?
13   If CRT is of value, what are the mechanisms at work?

Conclusion

CRT, based on a neuropsychological model of predisposition and maintenance, seems to be a promising way forward as part of the treatment package for anorexia nervosa. For a disorder with such serious physical complications and risks, and no clear first line treatment, it is encouraging to have an approach which is yielding promising early results. Sessions are usually experienced as fun and non-threatening due to lack of explicit focus on food, weight or shape, and many therapists confirm that it can enhance engagement and motivation. It has been found to be acceptable to child and adolescent patients, parents and therapists alike. However, more research is needed to confirm the extent of its effect on neuropsychological function, eating disorder psychopathology and quality of life as well as to systematically consider a variety of theoretical, practical and methodological questions.

Summary

- Cognitive Remediation Therapy is emerging as a promising approach for children and adolescents with anorexia nervosa.
- Unlike most other therapies, it systematically and directly targets the underlying cognitive styles that seem to be associated with anorexia nervosa.
- The approach described here focuses on the use of a 'resource pack' of fun and practical games and exercises to explore meta-cognition and thus the possibility of overcoming unhelpful thinking styles.
- Early clinical experience suggests that CRT for children and adolescents with anorexia nervosa may become a useful addition to their treatment, albeit with many interesting questions to be answered.

References

Broom, Y. M., and Doctor, E. A. (1995). Developmental phonological dyslexia: A case study of the efficacy of a remediation programme. *Cognitive Neuropsychology, 12* (7), 725–766.

Cicerone, K. D., Langenbahn, D. M., Braden, C., Malec, J. F., Kalmar, K., Fraas, M., et al. (2005). Evidence-based cognitive rehabilitation: updated review of the literature from 2003 through 2008. *Archives of Physical Medicine and Rehabilitation, 86* (8), 1681–1692.

Cwojdzińska, A., Markowska-Regulska, K., and Rybakowski, F. (2009). Cognitive remediation therapy in adolescent anorexia nervosa – a case report. *Psychiatria Polska 43* (1), 115–124. [Article in Polish]

Davies, H., and Tchanturia, K. (2005). Cognitive remediation therapy as an intervention for AN. *European Eating Disorders Review*, *13*, 311–316.

Delahunty, A., and Morice, R. (1993). *A Training Programme for the Remediation of Cognitive Deficits in Schizophrenia*. Albury, NSW: Department of Health.

Demily, C., and Franck, N. (2008). Cognitive remediation: a promising tool for the treatment of schizophrenia. *Expert Review of Neurotherapeutics*, *8*, 1029–1036.

Lask, B., Gordon, I., Christie, D., Frampton, I., Chowdhury, U., and Watkins, B. (2005). Functional neuroimaging in early-onset anorexia nervosa. *International Journal of Eating Disorders*, *37*, S49–S51.

Lena, S. M., Fiocco, A. J., and Leyenaar, J. K. (2004). The role of cognitive deficits in the development of eating disorders. *Neuropsychology Review*, *14* (2), 99–113.

Lindvall, C., and Lask, B. (2011). Clinical applications. In B. Lask and I. Frampton (Eds), *Eating Disorders and the Brain*. Chichester: Wiley/Blackwell.

Lopez, C., Tchanturia, K., Stahl, D., and Treasure, J. (2008). Central coherence in eating disorders: a systematic review. *Psychological Medicine*, *38* (10), 1393–1404.

McGurk, S. R., Twamley, E. W., Sitzer, D. I., McHugo, G. J., and Mueser, K. T. (2007). A meta-analysis of cognitive remediation in schizophrenia. *American Journal of Psychiatry*, *164*, 1791–1802.

O'Connell, R. G., Bellgrove, M. A., Dockree, P. M., and Robertson, I. H. (2006). Cognitive remediation in ADHD: Effects of periodic non-contingent alerts on sustained attention to response. *Neuropsychological Rehabilitation*, *16* (6), 653–665.

Owen, I., Lindvall, C., and Lask, B. (2011). *Cognitive Remediation Therapy for Children and Adolescents*. Ellern Mede Centre, Totteridge, UK, and Oslo University Hospital, Norway. Available at www.ellernmede.org

Roberts, M. E., Tchanturia, K., Stahl, D., Southgate, L., and Treasure, J. (2007). A systematic review and meta-analysis of set-shifting ability in eating disorders. *Psychological Medicine*, *37*, 1075–1084.

Spencer, J. (2006). The role of cognitive remediation in childhood cancer survivors experiencing neurocognitive late effects. *Journal of Pediatric Oncological Nursing*, *23* (6), 321–325.

Stroop, J. R. (1935). Studies of interference in serial verbal reactions. *Journal of Experimental Psychology*, *18* (6), 643–662.

Tchanturia, K., Davies, H., and Campbell, I. C. (2007). Cognitive Remediation Therapy for patients with anorexia nervosa: Preliminary findings. *Annals of General Psychiatry*, *6*, 14.

Tchanturia K., and Davies H. (2008). *Cognitive Remediation Programme for Anorexia Nervosa: A Manual for Practitioners*. London: NHS Foundation Trust.

Tchanturia, K., and Hambrook, D. (2010) Cognitive Remediation Therapy for Anorexia Nervosa. In C. M. Grilo and J. Mitchell (Eds), *The Treatment of Eating Disorders: A Clinical Handbook*. New York: Guilford Press.

Whitney, J., Easter, A., and Tchanturia, K. (2008). The patients' experiences in cognitive exercise intervention for anorexia nervosa: Qualitative findings. *International Journal of Eating Disorders*, *41* (6), 542–550.

Wood, L., Al-Khairulla, H., and Lask, B. (2011). Group cognitive remediation therapy for adolescents with anorexia nervosa. *Clinical Child Psychology and Psychiatry*, *16* (2), 225–231.

Wykes, T. (2007). Cognitive remediation therapy in schizophrenia: Randomised controlled trial. *British Journal of Psychiatry*, *19*, 421–427.

Wykes, T., and van der Gagg, M. (2001). Is it time to develop a new cognitive therapy for psychosis-cognitive remediation therapy? *Clinical Psychology Review, 21,* 1227–1256.

Chapter 17

Ethical and legal issues

Anne Stewart and Jacinta Tan

Abstract

This chapter describes common ethical and legal dilemmas in eating disorders in children and adolescents using three clinical vignettes to illustrate. The dilemmas are discussed using the Four-Framework Grid, a tool for considering ethical and legal issues in eating disorders that covers clinical, ethical, legal and resource perspectives. Practical application of this grid is described and a treatment decision-making algorithm for inpatient admission is presented. Finally a series of recommendations for good practice are highlighted including the crucial importance of collaborative decision-making.

Introduction

Management of eating disorders in children and adolescents is frequently complex, difficult and demanding. The physical, social and psychological consequences of the disorder can be serious, yet at the same time the young person may acknowledge neither the disorder nor the need for treatment. This poses difficult clinical and ethical dilemmas for both clinicians and parents. Initiating and maintaining a therapeutic alliance is clearly a key aspect to treatment (see Chapter 11). However, clinicians can feel overwhelmed by the dilemmas they face in treating young people with eating disorders and may be unsure how best to proceed. The aim of this chapter is to clarify these dilemmas and to provide a framework for an ethical approach to treatment that takes into account legal boundaries, clinical effectiveness and service issues.

The chapter begins with a summary of the UK National Institute for Health and Clinical Excellence (NICE) guidelines relevant to this area and the broad principles for treatment. Three case vignettes are then presented, illustrating a range of different dilemmas. A framework for understanding and resolving ethical dilemmas is put forward, making reference to relevant research. This includes a discussion of how to facilitate competence and healthy treatment decision making within service limitations. Finally, recommendations are made to enhance ethical practice within teams and develop effective collaboration with young people and families.

Summary of NICE guidelines regarding broad principles for good practice, compulsory treatment and confidentiality

A number of countries have now developed guidelines for management of eating disorders (e.g. American Psychiatric Association, 2006; NICE, 2004). The NICE guidelines for eating disorders were developed in the United Kingdom following extensive review of the literature and appraisal of the best evidence available. They are intended to provide evidence-based guidance regarding the management of anorexia nervosa (AN), bulimia nervosa (BN) and related presentations in individuals aged 8 years and over. The guidelines highlight a number of broad principles for good practice. These include the need to provide information to young people and families on aspects of eating disorders and their treatment, and the need to work collaboratively as far as possible. Building up a treatment alliance is emphasised as a cornerstone of treatment.

The guidelines also make specific reference to the issues of compulsory treatment and confidentiality. They state that where a young person is refusing treatment, consideration should be given to the use of mental health legislation or parental consent to enable treatment to take place. The guidelines state that parental consent should not be used indefinitely, because this does not confer protection of the child's rights that are found in the use of formal legislation. Also, the legal basis under which treatment is given should be carefully recorded in the notes. If children or adolescents are refusing essential treatment, it is recommended that a second opinion is sought from an eating disorder specialist. Finally, if both a young person with anorexia nervosa and her parents are refusing treatment, when this is clearly in her best interests, consideration should be given to the use of childcare legislation to override the parental decisions in the light of their difficulties in exercising their parental responsibilities. The NICE guidelines also state that young people's confidentiality should be respected wherever possible. Adopting these broad guidelines can enhance effective management of young people with eating disorders.

Case vignettes

Miriam, age 17

Miriam is a 17 year old with a two-year history of anorexia nervosa. She lives at home with her parents and younger siblings and developed eating problems following an increase of weight in puberty. At the same time she had experienced bullying at school and the loss of a close friend who moved away. Her mother had also suffered an eating disorder as a young adult. Miriam was referred to the outpatient department with her family and attended reluctantly with her parents.

On assessment, Miriam was found to be very low in weight, lacking in energy and suffering dizzy spells. Outpatient treatment was commenced, involving family therapy focusing on the eating problem, as well as supportive individual sessions. An initial aim was to build up a therapeutic alliance. Her parents were encouraged to help Miriam establish regular eating, find ways of decreasing the tension at home and build up channels of communication. During an individual session, Miriam disclosed that she occasionally cut herself to relieve stress, but asked the therapist not to tell her parents.

Miriam's eating improved a little. However, after three months of treatment, her weight was much the same as when first seen. Her parents were encouraged to provide more support at meal times. However, they found this difficult and could not manage the conflict that arose. They raised the possibility of inpatient admission for more intensive treatment. Miriam was strongly against admission, saying that she would stop eating altogether if this happened. She maintained that she was fine at her current weight, and just needed to be left alone to get on with her life. Her parents reported separately to the therapist that she was very unhappy at school, had not made any new friends and rarely went out.

The weeks went by and Miriam failed to gain weight. Meanwhile a bone scan showed very low bone density. Her parents were aware of the long term consequences for her health and asked again if Miriam could be admitted to hospital. A case review was held, involving the outpatient team, Miriam, her parents, her school teacher and a member of the inpatient unit. The meeting raised different views on the way forward. On the one hand, her individual therapist felt that the main focus should be to continue to engage and motivate Miriam, whilst helping her family to provide support. The therapist felt that admission might damage the alliance that they were beginning to make. On the other hand, there was concern about her deteriorating physical state, lack of progress and the risk of the disorder becoming entrenched, indicating the need for intensive treatment as an inpatient.

Shona age 15

Shona is a 15-year-old athlete. Since the age of 10 she has been training 2 hours a day four times a week and competing at county and regional level in running, while achieving excellent grades at school. Running is her life and she has no friends or hobbies outside it. Because of the demands of the discipline, Shona, like all her peers, has always watched her food intake and been concerned about eating healthily. She had menarche at 14 years but her periods are irregular and often absent.

A few months ago Shona had a viral illness during which she was too ill to train and lost her appetite, resulting in weight loss. On recovery, she found it difficult to regain her weight, but at the same time was desperate to make up for the loss of training in order to regain condition and achieve her ambition of gaining a place in the junior national team. Her weight decreased further, and her parents and coach became concerned about her physical health. She was referred to a Child and Adolescent Mental Health Service who diagnosed anorexia nervosa and due to concern about her rapid weight loss and poor physical state, recommended a reduction in her training in order to facilitate gradual weight restoration. Shona refused, disagreeing that she has an eating disorder and arguing that if only she could increase her training she would be able to eat more again and return to her old self.

Her coach told her that if she reduced her training she may need to be dropped from the team for this season. Shona is devastated saying that this is her life and she has to get back in the team. She is not willing to attend for treatment for her eating disorder because of the time commitment involved. Moreover, she objects to the target weight, suggested by the treatment team, as unacceptably high, arguing that it is much higher than the weight she previously maintained while competing and is also higher than the weight of her fellow athletes.

Christopher age 13

Christopher is a 13 year old who has had difficulties with eating since the age of 7. He was referred to the Child and Adolescent Mental Health Service at the age of 11 and after a period of unsuccessful outpatient treatment was admitted to an inpatient mental health unit where he required nasogastric feeding. He was discharged at his target weight, and initially maintained his weight. However, over the next few months he gradually lost weight again and, despite intensive work by the outpatient team, his eating problems once more became entrenched.

He is an only child born to parents after many years of infertility treatment and much loved by both his parents. Early development milestones were normal but he had a history of selective eating as a child and there was some concern about his growth. There is no family history of eating disorders.

Christopher's weight continued to decline and his physical state deteriorated. His weight was now 70 per cent for height and he had a very low blood pressure and pulse rate. He was admitted voluntarily to another inpatient unit. There, he gained weight steadily. However, he was ambivalent about getting better and insisted that he should opt out of treatment and go home. At this stage his health was no longer life-threatening, although staff felt that he would be likely to deteriorate again if he left hospital prematurely.

Christopher's parents were very anxious not to lose his affection. At the same time they had difficulty supervising meals and ensuring adequate food intake at home and were concerned about his long term outcome, particularly in relation to puberty and growth. Christopher did not want his parents involved in the treatment as he believed that family sessions were causing deterioration in his relationship with them.

Ethical dilemmas arising from the vignettes

A range of ethical dilemmas arises in the treatment of young people with eating disorders, as illustrated by the cases of Miriam, Shona and Christopher. They are all ambivalent about treatment, in common with many young people with eating disorders. As with most adolescents, they are struggling with issues of control and are reluctant to subject themselves to a treatment which they perceive takes away their control. In addition they are at a developmental stage when the impulse of the present moment, such as the drive to lose weight, is more important than a distant goal, such as the prospect of recovery. Miriam initially felt better about herself when her weight dropped. However, over time she felt increasingly bad about herself, and failed to develop a positive sense of identity. Giving up her eating disorder would be hard if there is no clear sense of an identity without the eating disorder (Tan, Hope, and Stewart, 2003a).

Clinicians treating Miriam, Shona and Christopher may experience a dilemma between allowing them to make their own decisions or taking away their choice due to a desire to protect and treat. Their parents also may experience similar dilemmas. Christopher's parents were very anxious not to lose his affection. In order to recover and remain in a healthy state, young people need to be actively involved in their own treatment. But before that can happen, they may need to be supported in a way that feels intrusive or controlling to them (Tan, Stewart, Fitzpatrick, and Hope, 2010). It can be hard to know to what extent and how early in treatment the young person should be able to make treatment choices. It may be difficult to assess how competent the young person is to make choices, particularly when they appear intellectually able to rationalise, yet are making decisions that are clearly not in their interest.

With Miriam, who is nearly 18, there may be pressure to allow her to make what she perceives as a lifestyle choice, as evinced by the 'pro-anorexic' movement (Charland, 2004; Udovitch, 2002). Similarly, Shona, though only 15, has body image, weight and eating issues that have been normalised within certain elite sports, and her choices are driven by her elite running career, which would be generally viewed as a positive, high achievement lifestyle. There have been debates about whether adult patients with anorexia nervosa should be allowed to refuse treatment even if death is the likely result, or offered palliative care as opposed to treatment aiming for recovery (Draper, 2000; Russon and Alison, 1998; Williams, Pieri, and Sims, 1998). Using compulsory treatment or more informal coercion raises ethical dilemmas regarding the rights of adolescents to choose. Moreover, compulsory admission can be carried out using different legal means and the clinician is faced with a difficult choice concerning which route to pursue. Differences of opinion within the team may impair the treatment decision-making process.

Finally, issues relating to confidentiality frequently emerge in treatment. Adolescents may wish to keep aspects of their treatment confidential, which raises a dilemma for clinicians who have to balance this wish with the need to keep parents adequately informed, particularly with younger patients. The issues affecting Miriam, Shona and Christopher will be discussed in detail using the Four-Framework Grid, a theoretical tool that will now be described.

The Four-Framework Grid: a theoretical tool for considering ethical and legal issues in eating disorders

The authors have developed a theoretical tool for considering ethical and legal issues alongside the clinical context and resource issues called the 'Four-Framework Grid' (Tan, 2004; Tan and Stewart, 2003) shown in Figure 17.1. This tool provides an overview of the relevant issues to be considered in working with any patient in the healthcare setting, but is particularly applicable to young people with eating disorders. The four key areas in the grid concern the frameworks for the arenas of ethical, legal, clinical and resource issues. The content of each framework can be modified to suit each particular clinical context. The grid provides a structured way to consider each arena in turn while acknowledging the interaction between all the arenas. Each framework will be discussed in turn.

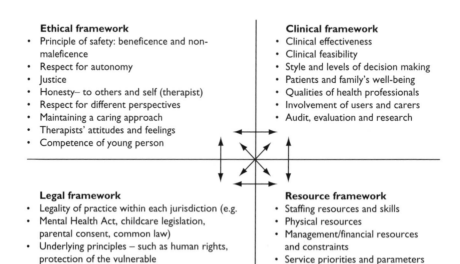

Ethical framework
- Principle of safety: beneficence and non-maleficence
- Respect for autonomy
- Justice
- Honesty– to others and self (therapist)
- Respect for different perspectives
- Maintaining a caring approach
- Therapists' attitudes and feelings
- Competence of young person

Clinical framework
- Clinical effectiveness
- Clinical feasibility
- Style and levels of decision making
- Patients and family's well-being
- Qualities of health professionals
- Involvement of users and carers
- Audit, evaluation and research

Legal framework
- Legality of practice within each jurisdiction (e.g.
- Mental Health Act, childcare legislation, parental consent, common law)
- Underlying principles – such as human rights, protection of the vulnerable
- Interpretation of legal principles in case law, which is always evolving
- Balancing different legal principles

Resource framework
- Staffing resources and skills
- Physical resources
- Management/financial resources and constraints
- Service priorities and parameters
- Information for patients

Figure 17.1 The Four-Framework Grid.

Ethical Framework

Central to this ethical framework is the consideration of Beauchamp and Childress' Four Principles (Beauchamp and Childress, 2001), namely: beneficence, non-maleficence, respect for autonomy and justice. Other relevant ethical principles include:

- being honest with the family, young person and oneself;
- respecting the different perspectives of the patient and other family members;
- maintaining a caring approach;
- cultivating an awareness of one's own feelings and attitudes and working ethically within teams.

Finally, assessment and promotion of decision-making competence is also discussed within this framework.

Beneficence

Beneficence, the doing of good to the patient, involves ensuring the safety of the patient and prevention of adverse consequences of the illness. It is important, therefore, to determine the potential risk of the eating disorder. Physical assessment and investigation should be carried out to determine whether there is any immediate physical risk (indicated by rapid weight loss, collapse, bradycardia, exercise-induced chest pain, diminishing exercise tolerance, muscle weakness or low urine output) as well as the longer-term risks, for example reduced bone density. As well as consideration of physical risks, there needs to be assessment of psychiatric morbidity, including risk of suicide, as well as possible social and educational risks.

Alongside determination of risk and need for treatment, the beneficial effect of the proposed treatment needs to be ascertained. Unfortunately, there is, to date, relatively little published treatment outcome research in adolescent eating disorders (Gowers and Bryant-Waugh, 2004). However, the evidence basis there is should guide the clinician in formulating a treatment proposal that includes strategies with known beneficial effects, for example the involvement of the family within treatment (see Chapter 13).

The relative lack of efficacy of current treatments means that it can be difficult to help a sizeable minority of patients to achieve good functioning, let alone full recovery. This raises the ethical issue of whether there is true benefit in engaging in strenuous attempts to deliver treatment where patients have longstanding illness with a long history of treatment attempts and refusal of further treatment. Yet, the research suggests that improvement and recovery can still occur after long periods of illness, which implies that it may be problematic to conceptualise anorexia nervosa as a permanent or terminal disorder for which the clinician should offer no further treatment. This is particularly the case for the younger age group where it may be inappropriate and unhelpful to think in terms of chronicity and/or irreversibility.

Non-maleficence

Non-maleficence is the avoidance of doing harm to the patient. Having assessed the risks of the eating disorder and determined the need for treatment, it is important to discuss with the young person and the family the potential harm of treatment as well as the benefits. As previously stated, there is limited research on treatment outcome. Moreover, research concerning the benefits or otherwise of inpatient treatment is almost non-existent, and it has been suggested that there may be adverse consequences following this form of treatment (Gowers, Weetman, Shore, Hossain, and Elvins, 2000). These include individual aversive aspects of admission, lack of social contact, disruption of schooling and family life, as well as the experience of being controlled and reduced autonomy for the young person. The potential effects of inpatient treatment have to be taken into consideration before deciding on the way forward for Miriam or Christopher. The short-term benefits of improved physical state will have to be balanced against the possible harm of inpatient treatment. In addition, the long term outcome of compulsory treatment is not really known, although short term effects are generally good. Indeed weight restoration can be life-saving.

The lack of clear outcome research means that other factors, such as patient preference and clinical feasibility, need to be more prominent in the decision making. This especially applies when it is difficult to demonstrate benefit to the interventions, which may actually be harmful. Some clinicians believe that apart from issues of the deprivation of liberty, the use of compulsory treatment is harmful both to patients and to the therapeutic alliance (Rathner, 1998).

Autonomy

In the treatment of eating disorders a common dilemma is how to balance up respect for autonomy with the need to take care of the young person. We would argue that as well as respecting autonomy, it needs to be promoted and developed. Young people become autonomous if they grow up in a context of appropriate protection, opportunity to develop and explore choice, and an experience of nurturing (Stewart, 2000). In the same way, the context of treatment for the young person with an eating disorder should ideally contain all these elements in order to promote the development of autonomy. In other words, the professional will need, wherever possible, to provide a combination of caring and boundaries, constantly being aware of the need for the young person to make choices. Thus the dilemma between care taking and autonomy can be reframed as the need for appropriate care taking *and* respect for autonomy. The skill for clinicians is working out where the balance needs to lie at any particular time. Making these dilemmas overt to the young person and family can be enormously helpful in steering a course away from the battleground of having to care for and protect versus respect for autonomy.

The autonomy of the family is another issue to be considered, particularly for younger adolescents, which is also framed as the right to family life as upheld in the Human Rights Act 1998.[1] Families often make decisions as a group and it is important that the integrity of the family unit should be respected where possible and appropriate, which also helps to support the young person while promoting his or her development of autonomy (Stewart, 2000; Tan, 2005).

Clinicians should also be mindful of cultural differences between different ethnic groups, religious groups and individual family groups with respect to how much decision-making is individual, consensual or influenced by each other's views. There are certain cultures, such as (but not exclusively) Asian or Oriental, where patients may be much more respectful and accepting of doctors' opinions (Moazam, 2000). Some Asian families may also appear to defer or prioritise the views of other members, with family relationships being much more interdependent; in such families, autonomy may have to be viewed from a relational construct rather than an individual one (Ho, 2008; Tan, Syahirah, Lee, Goh, and Lee – submitted; Tan and Chin, 2011). Some cultures may also have different approaches to truth-telling and disclosure to patients seen as vulnerable and needing protection (Ho, 2008; Tan and Chin, 2011; Fan, 2000). Parents in such families may also appear to dominate decision-making with their children appearing passive and submissive, this dominance being largely an expression of concern and care and a wish to protect the patient (Tan and Chin, 2011; Fan, 2000). It is important for teams to be sensitive to family styles and values which may differ from their own, and to learn to both understand and respect these styles and values. In such cases, teams need to negotiate carefully with and between members of the family, in particular between parents and their adolescent children, and to be able to identify and deal with the rare cases of unhelpful or even abusive oppression without unintentionally disrupting supportive and caring patterns of relationships between family members (Ho, 2008).

Even if compulsory admission is being contemplated, with potential loss of autonomy, it is possible to relate to the young person in a way that promotes her autonomy. This can be done by taking time to listen to her views, to give information, and to go carefully through the risks and benefits of each option. The desire for confidentiality also raises important issues of autonomy. During the process of therapy Miriam disclosed issues regarding self-cutting that she wished to keep secret from her parents. This posed a dilemma for the therapist as to whether to override her wishes and inform her parents, or respect her desire for confidentiality. The NICE guidelines emphasize the important principle of confidentiality. However, this has to be balanced with the responsibility of parents for the welfare of their children and the need for them to be kept informed. In a situation where the young person is self-harming, the clinician needs to weigh up the respect for confidentiality with the safety of the young person and the adverse impact of maintaining secrets within the family. Thus the right to confidentiality, which is part of respecting autonomy, has to be balanced against considerations of non-maleficence, beneficence and protection.

Justice

Beauchamp and Childress (2001) suggest that justice has different aspects: distributive justice; respecting rights; respecting the rules of law; and reparative justice. In the current treatment environment of managed care or limited resources, there are dilemmas of how to engage in ethical practice with respect to meeting the needs of all patients, whilst working within constraints imposed by the relative scarcity of funding, scarcity of skills and time, and differential funding for different services or individuals. The consideration of compulsory treatment should also be done while bearing in mind issues of justice with respect to human rights, patient dignity and the rights of access for the patient, as well as those around her, to the appropriate treatment and support.

Honesty

It is important to be open with the patient and family about the limitations of the treatment proposed and the dilemmas concerning treatment. Being truthful can sometimes be painful for the young person and family, particularly if there is bad news about the consequences of the illness. Giving the information in manageable chunks, dealing with one's own fear of telling bad news, providing the right setting and supporting the young person and family, can all be helpful. It is important to be aware that the manner in which we convey information may have a major impact on how the young person and family interpret this information.

Respect for different perspectives

It is important to listen to the perspectives of the young person, her parents, siblings, the general practitioner and others involved. Refusal of admission by the young person or parents may in fact be reasonable. The parents may be aware how difficult separation from home will be for their daughter and may prefer to continue with the treatment programme at home. Alternatively, the parents may be reluctant to agree to admission because of the difficulty in taking a decision that is counter to their daughter's wishes. If this is the case, they may need support to take this difficult decision.

Maintaining a caring and respectful approach

Throughout the process of treatment decision making, the relationship between the professional and the young person is key. A caring approach that respects the individual's views is important to patients and is likely to promote collaboration with treatment (Stewart and Tan, 2005). Many young people with anorexia nervosa struggle with the notion of who they really are and to what extent the illness is part of their authentic self or an alien identity (Hope, Tan, Stewart, and Fitzpatrick, in press). Allowing the young person to give voice to these conflicts can be enormously helpful.

Taking account of therapists' feelings/attitudes

Therapists may experience a wide range of emotional responses within the therapeutic context. These feelings may arise from previous experience or background or may be linked to their own confidence in dealing with eating disorders. Being faced with a stubborn young person who is refusing to eat, and with a distraught family, may evoke anger, distress, irritation and/or intense empathy. Indeed, patients with anorexia nervosa generate more anger, distress and feelings of helplessness in health professionals than do other patients (Brotma, Stern, and Hertzog, 1984). It is important for therapists to acknowledge the feelings that arise when treating eating disorders and be open about the impact of their own background and personality.

Being aware and taking account of therapist reactions and attitudes, rather than ignoring them, can illuminate the therapeutic process and also help the therapist to understand some of the feelings expressed by the parent, and to avoid punitive attitudes towards patients. Most patients with eating disorders are female and reflection on how gender of both the patient and the therapist might affect the treatment process is also important.

Treatment is often long term and some therapists are at risk from over-involvement with families or even burnout. Therapists need to be aware of powerful counter-transference feelings that may arise (see Chapter 11), and ensure that they have regular supervision in order that they can remain effective in therapy, tailoring their involvement to what is helpful to the young person and family.

Developing ethical practice within teams

Treatment of eating disorders should involve teamwork. Relationships within, and between, treatment teams can become difficult, particularly if the young person poses a high risk (Jarman, Smith, and Walsh, 1997) and differences of opinion can exacerbate splits within the family. Developing an ethical way of working within teams can facilitate effective and efficient clinical work. There are a number of ways in which teams can do this (see Table 17.1). Developing a shared reflectiveness about the work, including an awareness of one's own motivation and values is important, as is being up to date on the evidence for different treatment approaches and being aware of the relevant legal boundaries. It is important for team members to respect each other's views and engage in a collaborative approach regarding decision – making with each other, as well as with the family and young person. Being open about the dilemmas within the team in balancing competing principles and frameworks can also be very helpful for the family.

Table 17.1 Ethical practice within teams

- Being reflective about the work
- Knowledge of recent literature on effectiveness
- Awareness of relevant legal boundaries
- Ability to respect and value different perspectives and value systems within the team
- Collaborative approach regarding decision-making
- Openness about the dilemmas in weighing up competing principles and frameworks
- Good communication between all team members involved in treatment of each patient and family
- Willingness to seek appropriate external supervision and support when delivering emotionally difficult treatment
- Clarity regarding team leadership structure and how decisions are made especially contentious or controversial decisions

Competence of the young person to make a choice

Whether or not a young person is competent to make her own choice about treatment has to be considered. Confusingly, there are two different terms which are frequently used interchangeably – 'capacity', and 'competence', and usage also varies between countries (Tan and Jones, 2001). In the UK, 'capacity' tends to refer to the legal concept of the ability to make treatment decisions, the criteria of which are laid down in case law and statute law. 'Competence' tends to refer to a looser clinical notion of this ability. This is the usage that we will employ here. 'Capacity' has various definitions in the law of different countries, but generally encompasses the ability to understand treatment information, process this information to arrive at a choice, and to communicate the choice. 'Competence', in contrast, is poorly defined, but many clinicians would consider additional factors such as consistency of a decision over time, the impact of mental disorders such as depression, the basis of relevant beliefs (for instance, whether they are grounded in delusions), and the ability to apply information to the self (Grisso and Appelbaum, 1998).

Weithorn and Campbell (1982) found that the criteria for capacity, which are largely intellectual in nature, were fully satisfied to adult standards by the age of 14 and with simplified information by the age of 9 years. Young people with eating disorders should be encouraged to make their own decisions where possible. The key components of competence are: understanding the relevant information, appreciating the situation as it relates to them, being able to weigh up the information, coming to a rational decision and communicating choice (Grisso and Appelbaum, 1998).

Competence in young people with eating disorders may be hard to assess. The young person may be intellectually able to make a choice. However, the eating disorder may be affecting her value system or identity in a way that compromises her ability to make informed choices (Tan, Hope, and Stewart, 2003a, 2003b). This impact may increase with severity of the disorder, and needs to be taken into account in assessing whether a young person is able to make her own treatment decisions. A questionnaire survey of psychiatrists (Tan, Doll, Fitzpatrick, Stewart, and Hope 2008) found that compared to 'mild' anorexia nervosa, psychiatrists generally were less likely to feel that patients with 'severe' anorexia nervosa were intentionally engaging in weight loss behaviours, were able to control their behaviours, wanted to get better, or were able to reason properly. However, eating disorder specialists were less likely than other psychiatrists to think that patients with 'mild' anorexia nervosa were choosing to engage in their behaviours or able to control their behaviours.

There are a number of factors that facilitate competence and healthy treatment decision making in young people (See Table 17.2). First, building up a trusting relationship with the young person is a crucial part of this process. It is important that the young person feels respected rather than coerced (Stewart and Tan, 2005). Second, it is important to provide information and carefully go through the risks and benefits of each option within a setting that is free of distractions. Having adequate time is essential in order to provide full explanations and answer any questions. Third, taking a motivational approach can facilitate the decision making process (see Chapter 11). This includes encouraging the young person to weigh up the advantages and disadvantages of change or no change, identify areas of concern and clarify future goals and ways of achieving them. Finally, sufficient time needs to be allowed for the young person and family to make the decision. It is helpful to consider decision making as an evolving process as the young person develops a stronger relationship with the treatment team.

Table 17.2 Strategies to facilitate competence in young people

- Provision of information
- Carefully go through risks and benefits of each option
- Having adequate time for full explanations and answers to questions
- A setting free of distractions or interruptions
- Assess consent for different things separately, allowing the opportunity to choose wherever possible
- Respect of young person's views
- Building up a trusting relationship with the young person and family
- Absence of coercion
- Motivational approach with young person/family
- Make overt the decision-making dilemmas
- Facilitate the decision making process
- Conceptualise treatment refusal as an evolving process
- Allow sufficient time to make decision
- Reassurance of their choice and right to withdraw (although making it clear what the bottom line is)
- Allow joint or shared decision-making according to family style and young person's preference

Legal Framework

In this framework, clinicians need to be aware of the legality of practice within the specific jurisdiction, and the underlying principles such as human rights and protection of the vulnerable. The status of the law concerning consent of legal minors of different ages and capacity to treatment should also be thoroughly understood. Different legal principles need to be balanced against each other. The potential use of mental health legislation, parental consent, common law and childcare law all need to be considered carefully. The legal framework described in this chapter is for England and Wales (different statutes apply in other countries). Readers from other jurisdictions are encouraged to apply the principles in this framework to the legislation relevant to their own particular settings.

Balancing different legal principles – the legal framework with minors

In England and Wales, the legal framework around which decisions regarding children and young people are made are based on the Children Act 1989 and 2004, the Family Law Reform Act, 1969, the Mental Health Act 1983 and 2007, the Mental Capacity Act, 2005 and common law derived from case rulings. Table 17.3

Table 17.3 Summary of the law relating to consent in young people in England and Wales

---

Those under 16
- Presumed not to have capacity to consent unless they satisfy health professionals that they do have capacity (also known as 'Gillick competence').
- If they are 'Gillick competent', they can give valid consent to medical treatment although parental involvement is recommended.
- If the patient refuses consent, those with parental responsibility or the courts can give consent to treatment in the child's best interest (Children Act 1989).

Those age 16 and 17
- Presumed to have capacity to give valid consent to medical treatment unless the contrary is shown (Family Law Reform Act 1969).
- Parental consent is needed if they do not have capacity.
- If the patient refuses consent, then those with parental responsibility, or those with proxy powers to consent under the Mental Capacity Act 2005, or the courts can give consent in the young person's best interest

Those over 18
- Patients lacking capacity can have decisions made on their behalf by proxy decision-makers under the Mental Capacity Act 2005.

For all ages
- The Mental Health Act 2007 can be used to treat patients without their consent in the presence of mental illness if they are at risk of serious harm

---

provides a summary of the law relating to consent in young people in England and Wales, which will not be discussed in detail in this chapter. Interested readers can read Hope, Savulescu, and Hendrick (2003) for an account of the relevant legal aspects; this account will instead focus on the principles of the legal basis for treatment without consent.

In the area of psychiatric treatment for children and in particular adolescents, there is a convergence of several disparate statutes which differ in spirit but are equally applicable to the treatment of children: first, childcare law with its emphasis on the welfare of the child and parental responsibility; second, case law and legislation concerning consent to treatment that emphasises capacity and autonomy of individuals who possess capacity and treatment in best interests of those who do not; third, mental health legislation with its emphasis on protection of the mentally disordered. Mental health professionals treating young patients with eating disorders must navigate this complex legal landscape by balancing the different legal principles contained in all the different statutes, even though they can often only use one statute at a time.

The law in most countries allows treatment without consent for children and adolescents, if they lack the capacity to make a treatment decision or have serious mental illness. In addition, in most jurisdictions, parents generally have the right to provide consent on behalf of their offspring. It is often appropriate for children and adolescents with eating disorders to have treatment under their parents' consent, although the Mental Health Act, 2007 does not allow for young people with capacity to be admitted under parental consent. Where the young person lacks capacity it may be a relief to experience clear boundaries laid down by their parents. Parents may need help to develop the confidence to be clear with their children about what is required. Patients report that the notion of informal compulsory treatment is acceptable to them (Tan, 2006). Usually, when a child is admitted to hospital under parental consent, they comply with the treatment. However, for those that continue to resist, the relatively informal process of parental consent may be inappropriate because there is no right of appeal and in such cases, clinicians may need to consider the use of more formal legal means to impose treatment, such as mental health legislation, guardianship orders or treatment orders.

Alternatives to compulsory treatment

Before deciding that compulsory treatment is necessary it is important to explore systematically all the possible alternatives. These include: engaging the patient and family; listening to the patient and being empathic; understanding the difficulties but at the same time taking an encouraging and firm approach. A greater intensity of outpatient involvement including home treatment or day-patient programmes may be preferable (if resources allow). However, despite these alternatives, compulsory treatment may sometimes be essential.

Interpretation of legal principles in case law

Case law tends to consist of extreme or unusual cases which have caused sufficient controversy or conflict to be brought to court. At the same time, the precedents set by case law are often applied to medical practice as general principles. It is important that there should be careful distinction between the facts of the particular cases taken to court and the aspects of the judgements that relate to the specific circumstances, and the more general principles laid out or confirmed by the judges. There is a possibility for clinicians to be conservative in their interpretations of the scope or application of case rulings, because of a wish to avoid litigation over failure to observe the law. These factors work together to make the awareness, careful interpretation and application of case rulings to everyday clinical practice an important issue.

Factors influencing the route of compulsory treatment chosen

There are a number of factors that may influence which route to compulsory treatment is chosen, including the age of the young person, the degree of behavioural disturbance or resistance, whether there is support from parents, the context in which the disturbance occurs, whether there is time to facilitate consent and whether the adolescent is competent to make a decision. The potential advantages and disadvantages of the various routes, as just described, will need to be taken into account. The competence of the professional team and availability of a range of treatments may also affect choice of route to be taken. Finally, there is evidence that psychiatrists in different sub-specialities have different attitudes towards best interests and compulsory treatment in anorexia nervosa. Tan, Doll, Fitzpatrick, Stewart and Hope (2008), found that psychiatrists generally supported a role for compulsory measures under mental health legislation in the treatment of patients with anorexia nervosa. Child and adolescent psychiatrists were more likely to have a positive view of the use of parental consent and compulsory treatment for an adolescent with anorexia nervosa. With younger adolescents or children it may be appropriate to encourage parental consent. With older adolescents, particularly if there is a high degree of resistance, mental health act legislation may need to be used. Where there is lack of support or neglect in the parents, a care order obtained from the courts may need to be used. Where there is support from parents but a difficulty in enabling the child to have treatment an inherent jurisdiction of the High Court may be supportive to parents and provide a helpful legal structure to enable the child to receive treatment. In an emergency, common law may need to be used in the first instance. Some aspects of treatment such as essential physical investigations may be done using mental capacity legislation if the young person lacks the capacity to decide on the relevant aspect of treatment.

The therapeutic alliance and compulsory treatment

Where compulsory treatment is used, it is essential to maintain the therapeutic alliance with young people and their parents (see Chapter 11). Providing information, listening to the young person and their family and respecting their views and concerns will help with this process. Tan, Stewart, Fitzpatrick, and Hope (2010) in a qualitative study of young people with anorexia nervosa found that they view compulsory treatment as appropriate when the condition is life threatening. Moreover, their perception of compulsory treatment was influenced by the nature of their relationship with professionals. What mattered most to patients was having a supportive, trusting and respectful relationship with professionals.

Clinical Framework

Clinical effectiveness

In working with eating disorders there needs to be a consideration of the evidence base for the treatment (see Chapters 9 and 10). Despite many advances in the understanding of anorexia nervosa, the disorder remains difficult to treat. Many different forms of treatment have been tried over the years, but it is still not clear what are the most effective approaches (Gowers and Bryant-Waugh, 2004). There is, however, accumulating evidence for the efficacy of family therapy (Robin, Siegel, Moye, Gilroy, Dennis et al., 1999). The recent NICE guidelines as well as the APA guidelines recommend this.

With regard to inpatient treatment, operant behavioural techniques gained popularity in the 60s and 70s but these approaches were later challenged and considered to be unnecessarily harsh (Steinhausen, 1994). Young people gained weight in hospital but tended to lose it after discharge. Inpatients who gain weight under the pressure of persuasion and within a context of fear very often relapse after discharge. There is some evidence that less coercive programmes with less emphasis on rapid weight gain can be more productive (Touyz, Beumont, and Dunn, 1987). The challenge for inpatient units is to be able to operate a structured programme, which respects the individual and promotes autonomy rather than enforces compliance. A number of studies report that patients themselves report that programmes including bed rest and a firm approach can be helpful, although when applied too rigidly or harshly can be unhelpful (Griffiths et al., 1997; Tan, 2006).

Gowers et al. (2007) compared inpatient treatment with clinical care as usual and a specialised form of outpatient treatment and found that neither the inpatient treatment nor the specialised outpatient treatment were more effective than clinical care as usual (on intention to treat analysis), although clinical care as usual resulted in more inpatient admissions as a result of failure to progress. Inpatient treatment predicted poor outcomes whether randomised first line or secondary to failed outpatient treatment. Specialised outpatient treatment was found to be the most cost effective of the three approaches (Byford et al., 2007).

Clinical experience suggests that inpatient admission may be essential in terms of providing an immediate safe environment for refeeding. The short-term outcome and needs have to be balanced against the possible longer term outcome. This has to taken into consideration before deciding to undertake a programme of intensive treatment in hospital. In terms of balancing the advantages and disadvantages of admission, the short-term difficulties may be necessary to save life or overcome an impasse in order to promote a long-term healthy outcome.

In summary, the evidence basis for inpatient care and the evidence for the effectiveness of different forms of outpatient treatment need to be carefully considered. In all cases, there should be discussion with the young person and family on the advantages and disadvantages of the various options, and respect for their views.

Clinical feasibility

As well as being aware of the evidence base, it is important to assess whether a treatment is clinically feasible; for example, whether there are appropriate clinicians available to carry out the work, or whether there is an inpatient unit easily accessible.

Levels and style of decision making

It is helpful to be aware of the style of decision-making with which the patient is comfortable. Tan (2005) found that young people may prefer either a largely individual decision-making style or a group decision-making style. In relation to treatment decisions in eating disorders, some young people prefer to make the decision themselves, whilst others prefer to make a decision along with parents and professionals. Age, personality characteristics and severity of illness may all influence this preference.

In addition, the level of the decision to be made needs to be clarified. The young person and family may have agreed to admission and treatment for the eating disorder. However, when it comes to meal times, the strong 'anorexic urge' can take over and make it difficult for the patient to choose to eat. Predicting this makes it easier for her to be given support and encouragement at this time. Knowing that overall the patient wants to get better can make it easier for parents and professionals to cope with the inevitable distress that s/he may express at being 'made' to eat.

Well-being of patient and family

Miriam and Christopher were reluctant for their parents to participate in the therapy. Research indicates the importance of involving the family in treatment that directly relates to the eating disorder. The NICE guidelines also indicate the importance of involving the family in treatment that directly relates to the eating disorder. Clearly, it is important to involve the parents wherever possible. Nevertheless, the young person may still insist that their parents are not involved and very occasionally may even ask for help without their parent's knowledge (more commonly in bulimia nervosa rather than anorexia nervosa). With younger adolescents it is very clear that parents do need to be involved wherever possible, even if the young person is reluctant. However, for those age 16 and 17, the situation is less clear. The clinician may face a dilemma of having to balance the right of the adolescent to have individual treatment with the duty of the parent to take parental responsibility (enshrined in the Children Act 1989).

Another important consideration is whether the treatment is acceptable to patients and their families. Adequate time is needed to listen to the wishes and concerns of the family and the young person. Families who have a son or daughter with an eating disorder often feel helpless and guilty, blaming themselves for the eating disorder. Working with such families can be very challenging. Many issues come to the surface that are mirrored in society as a whole, including power imbalances, the role of women, the role of parents and the importance of body weight and shape (Orbach, 1978; Russell, 1995). Being aware of these issues and having regular supervision can make it easier to deal with them.

Qualities of health professionals

The qualities of the health professional may significantly affect clinical decision-making. Tan (2006) and Stewart and Tan (2005) have indicated the qualities in the health professionals that are likely to be important in helping patients to progress clinically. Those qualities which patients themselves had found helpful are shown in Table 17.4. These include: being kind and approachable; being able to empathize with and understand the painful experience that is being endured; being respectful of the individual and able to discern a person's real personality and wishes in the middle of difficult situations; being able to stand firm and not be hoodwinked by the protestations that anorexia nervosa may cause a person to have, for example: lying or refusing treatment, even if he/she might want treatment; able to understand and respect a person's individual needs and tailor treatment accordingly, for example the level of restriction or freedom needed and the pace of treatment; able to decisively take control and protect the person from herself if she is out of control and not able to help herself; being fair to all patients and not favouring one over another, particularly in an inpatient setting where patients compare treatment; and finally, able to offer patients confidentiality in their therapy, but at the same time willing to offer parents support, advice and help.

Table 17.4 Qualities in professionals that assist recovery (Tan, 2006)

- Kind and approachable
- Able to empathise
- Able to respect the young person and see the individual behind the eating disorder
- Able to stand firm and consistent
- Able to be flexible in approach and modify treatment approach to suit the situation and individual patient and family
- Able to understand and respect the young person's needs
- Able to take control where necessary
- Fair to all patients
- Able to offer confidentiality – with appropriate, clear caveats about limits of confidentiality
- Able to manage anxiety in themselves and in the young person/family
- Able to respect different family cultures

Involvement of patients and carers

Ideally, patients and carers within a service should be involved in all aspects of management, including contributing to staff interviews, development of audits and service development. They may have useful ideas to contribute, and the process of involving them enables them to take some ownership for the service that is being offered. Once involved in developing services and programmes, the treatment decisions may be easier to negotiate. There may be variants of who is considered a 'carer' and should be involved in management discussions, some of which can be challenging for clinicians. For example, Shona has a running coach who is 'in loco parentis' and highly involved in all decisions concerning her training programme and lifestyle with a great deal of power with regard to her sporting future. Other children may split their time living with separated parents, who may each have different parenting styles or may communicate poorly with each other. Still others may live with other carers such as relatives or foster parents, but also have parents who continue to have parental responsibilities and the right to be informed about their care. In such cases, clinicians have to negotiate the relationships within the network of carers around the patient with the best interests of the patient firmly in mind, and to determine how best to communicate clearly with all the important parties and to avoid confusion or collusion with any particular parties.

Need for audit, evaluation and contribution to research

It is important to set up structures for evaluation and audit of the service. Professionals need to be aware of the outcome of treatment in order to extend their learning and adapt the service accordingly. Given the sparseness of knowledge about effective treatments for child and adolescent eating disorders, services have a responsibility to encourage the development of evaluative research, and to contribute wherever possible.

Resource Framework

Health professionals as gatekeepers and providers of services

There are potentially conflicting ethical issues of justice, resource allocation and duty of care when health professionals are responsible for all three. It is important to consider what resources are actually available, as providing the most effective treatment can depend on the availability of resources. The clinician may be in the difficult position of deciding between the need for intensive treatment of one individual and the need to provide treatment for others who are seriously ill and still on the waiting list. For Miriam and Christopher, the decision to move towards inpatient treatment may be partly affected by what resources are available in the community.

As well as staffing resources, it is important to pay attention to the physical resources. Within inpatient units, the environmental setting needs to be conducive to recovering from an eating disorder, with attention paid to comfort as well as ease of access to school and other facilities. Care should be taken to provide meals that are attractive and tailored to the individual's needs.

Service parameters and priorities

Political and economic pressures can have a profound effect on the development of treatment programmes. Clinicians and managers have to work within a financially restricted and target-driven climate that can hamper long-term work with eating disorders. The goals of managers may differ from those of clinicians. Separation of management and clinical work can lead to decision-making at a level which is divorced from the reality of clinical treatment. This may reduce innovation and lead to more rigid structures and systems. Ethical values need to be at the cornerstone of service delivery. However, a service that is significantly financially restricted may make it more difficult for the patient to gain trust. This can result in difficulties with engagement or formal complaints. Maintaining a close partnership between managers and clinicians is essential and can aid development of services.

The development of specialist eating disorder services can lead to fragmentation of local care. Inpatient admissions generate income and have therefore flourished, even though the need for intensive community care is well known. Indeed, the lack of resources for community treatment may increase the need for inpatient admission. Time devoted to service development, including provision of services across a whole community, may lead to a more efficient and cost-effective service in the long term.

Information for patients

There is a need to provide accessible written material for patients, their parents and siblings, and teachers. There are new opportunities but also threats to be found in the new technologies for communication and information which are becoming increasingly accessible to a majority of the population. Many professional and eating disorder organisations have produced materials for patients and their families to read (Beat, 2010), including material specially produced for adolescents (Royal College of Psychiatrists, 2004, 2006). Internet-based resources for treatment delivery and self-help strategies have also been growing (Eating Disorders Association, 2006; Murphy, Frost, Webster, and Schmidt, 2004). However, this free access to information has its dangers, as exemplified by the 'pro-anorexia' movement. Websites produced by individuals ascribing to this philosophy have varying stances about whether anorexia nervosa is desirable, but generally agree that anorexia nervosa is a life-style choice. In some of these sites, people suffering from anorexia nervosa exchange tips and suggestions, which, along with media images of excessively thin role models, can be particularly hazardous to impressionable young people (Fox, Ward, and O'Rourke, 2005; Morrison, 2003).

Using the Four-Framework Grid

Managing refusal of treatment by an adolescent with an eating disorder

Children and adolescents with eating disorders may be seriously ill and require intensive outpatient treatment or inpatient admission, yet may refuse this treatment. There are a number of factors to be taken into account when deciding whether a young person can refuse treatment, which involves all four domains contained in the Four-Framework Grid.

In the consideration of clinical factors, the potential risk of the illness needs to be ascertained. This requires a careful assessment of the physical and psychological consequences of the eating disorder and consideration of all the possible treatment options, the evidence basis for these options, and the best fit of options to the situation, as well as acceptability to the particular patient and family. The likely benefit and harm of the treatment need to be considered. A compulsory admission may be life-saving in the short term, but the longer term effects are less certain. There may be specific individual difficulties relating to the young person's dislike of being in a unit away from home as well as reduced contact with local friends, family and school. She will have less autonomy and responsibility and may feel over-controlled.

The benefits and harms relating to outpatient treatment need consideration in the same way.

It is important to check what the young person knows about the proposed treatment including the process of admission, if inpatient treatment is recommended, and what their fears are about this. The clinician should take time to ascertain the wishes of the adolescent and her parents. The young person's understanding of inpatient admission and her reasons for refusing it need to be discussed. If the parent also refuses consent, are the reasons sensible? It is important to clarify whether the young person is willing to engage in other treatment options. If admission is not to occur it is important to consider whether the parents will be able to keep her safe and promote recovery at home.

All clinical issues should be considered with respect to which option provides the greatest long- and short-term benefit as opposed to the least long- and short-term harm. The physical or psychiatric risks may indicate the need for admission. If the young person is unwilling to be admitted, it is important to try alternatives to compulsory admission first. Identifying the reasons for refusal and providing careful explanations within the context of a motivational approach can be helpful. It is important to avoid getting into battles with a young person and scare tactics are generally not helpful. The aim throughout is to promote healthy autonomy and competence.

An assessment of the competence of the young person to make a decision is important. The eating disorder and any co-morbid conditions such as depression may be affecting her ability to decide for herself (Tan et al., 2003a, 2003b, 2003c). The treatment team needs to ensure that it is fair both to the patient and family but also fulfilling its duties of care, including providing adequate respect of autonomy while protecting vulnerable patients.

With regard to resources the options need to be considered against the constraints of the resources available. At the same time, ethical issues such as balancing issues of distributive justice and duties to the individual patient will need to be discussed in collaboration with management.

Finally, in consideration of the legal factors, along with the importance of understanding the legal rulings and statutes applicable to the issue of treatment of eating disorders in young people, the principles and spirit of the law should always been borne in mind. These usually appeal to ethical principles and these should be considered in deciding which legal routes to use.

A treatment decision-making algorithm for inpatient admission

Figure 17.2 shows an algorithm for decision-making regarding inpatient care.

The first step is to engage the patient and her parents and to seek to understand the context. A comprehensive assessment of physical and psychological state is essential. The second step is to provide information on the disorder and options for treatment, to build trust and promote healthy decision-making. The risks and benefits of treatment need to be discussed with all concerned and the decision-making dilemmas identified. Anxiety about the process in patients, carers and professionals needs to be understood and managed. Hopefully, this will lead to a process of joint decision-making. Other relevant adults, for example school-teachers or other family members, may also contribute to this process. In cases where it is not possible to agree, an assessment needs to be made as to whether the

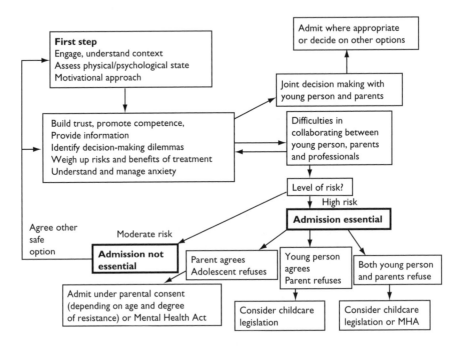

Figure 17.2 Treatment decision-making algorithm for inpatient admission.

treatment, for example hospital admission, is advisable or essential. If it is advisable but not essential, another safe option can be agreed, and further work done to engage the young person and build up trust and motivation. Regular assessments need to be carried out. If at some point, admission is considered to be essential, then the decision to undertake compulsory admission may need to be taken. If the parents agree to the admission despite refusal of the patient, she may be admitted under parental consent if she lacks capacity, although if there is a high degree of resistance and the adolescent is older, there needs to be consideration of the use of the Mental Health Act. In contrast should the young person agree to admission but the parents disagree, despite the risks of not being treated, there may need to be consideration of compulsory treatment under child care or guardianship legislation. Where both the patient and parents refuse essential treatment, a care order, The Mental Health Act or intervention by the courts may be needed.

Conclusion

The treatment of children and adolescents who suffer from eating disorders can be difficult because of the range of clinical, ethical and legal issues involved. We suggest that having a systematic way of considering these can be helpful, particularly as issues in one arena usually affect issues in another. We have outlined some key recommendations in Table 17.5.

Table 17.5 Practical recommendations

Treatment alliance
A firm treatment alliance with the young person and the family is the cornerstone of treatment. Time needs to be spent building up this alliance.

• **Information about the eating disorder and treatment**
It is important to make sure that the young person and their family are aware of the symptoms and consequences of an eating disorder and what the treatment involves.

• **Collaborative decision making**
Wherever possible, it is important to work collaboratively, identifying the options with the young person and family and weighing up with them the benefits and risks of the different options. Making decisions in advance can be helpful.

• **Least invasive treatment**
Bearing in mind the principle of no harm, the treatment chosen should be the least invasive whilst at the same time being potentially beneficial for the patient.

• **Ethical team working**
A reflective working practice within teams can enhance the clinical work.

• **Openness about dilemmas**
Being open about the dilemmas with the young person and the family can improve the treatment alliance and collaborative working.

• **Promote autonomy and competence**
Keeping the goal of promotion of autonomy and competence in mind can enhance treatment decision making.

• **Listen to and respect the young person**
It is important to be aware of the young person's views and their reasons for treatment refusal.

• **Take time**
Unless there is serious risk it is possible to take time to make decisions, allowing the chance to build up a relationship and collaborative way of working.

Summary

• Ethical and legal dilemmas are common in the treatment of eating disorders.
• The treatment alliance is the cornerstone of treatment.
• Ethical working requires consideration of clinical, ethical, legal and resource frameworks.
• An important aim is to promote competence and healthy decision making in the patient and family.
• Collaborative decision making is crucial.
• Respect is needed for the different views of young people and parents.
• Openness about the dilemmas can facilitate collaboration.

Acknowledgements

The authors would like to thank Professor Tony Hope for his comments on an earlier draft for this chapter. We would also like to thank Professor Walter Vandereycken for his helpful comments on the algorithm (Figure 17.2). Much of the recent research by Tan et al. cited in this chapter has been conducted with funding from the Wellcome Trust.

Notes

The National Institute for Health and Clinical Excellence (NICE) is the independent organisation responsible for providing national guidance for the United Kingdom on the promotion of good health and the prevention and treatment of ill health. Although not accorded the status of strict policy, NICE guidance is usually adopted by the National Health Service as the standard for best practice, and is thus highly significant to clinicians working within the National Health Service in the United Kingdom, who would have to justify any deviation of clinical practice from the guidelines.

The Human Rights Act 1998 Article 8: Right to respect for private and family life:

1   Everyone has the right to respect for his private and family life, his home and his correspondence.
2   There shall be no interference by a public authority with the exercise of this right except such as in accordance with the law and is necessary in a democratic society in the interests of national security, public safety or the economic well-being of the country, for the prevention of disorder or crime, for the protection of health or morals, or for the protection of the rights and freedoms of others.

References

American Psychiatric Association (2006, May). *Practice Guidelines for the Treatment of Eating Disorders*. Retrieved July 4, 2006, from http://www.psych.org/psych_pract/treatg/pg/prac_guide.cfm

Beat. (2010). *Beating Eating Disorders* Retrieved August 2011 from http://www.b-eat.co.uk

Beauchamp, T. L., and Childress, J. F. (2001). *Principles of Biomedical Ethics* (5th ed.), Oxford: Oxford University Press.

Brotman, A. W., Stern, T. A., and Herzog, D. B. (1984). Emotional reactions of house officers to patients with anorexia nervosa, diabetes and obesity. *International Journal of Eating Disorders*, *3*, 71–77.

Byford, S., Barrett, B., Roberts, C., Clark, A., Edwards, V., Smethurst, N., et al. (2007). Economic evalutation of a randomised controlled trial for anorexia enrvosa in adolescents. *British Journal of Psychiatry*, *191*, 436–440.

Charland, L. C. (2004). A madness for identity: Psychiatric labels, user autonomy, and the perils of the internet. *Philosophy, Psychology and Psychiatry, 11* (4), 335–349.

Draper, H. (2000). Anorexia nervosa and respecting a refusal of life-prolonging therapy: a limited justification. *Bioethics, 14* (2), 120–133.

Eating Disorders Association (2006). *Self Help Network.* Online. Available http://www.edauk.com/shn/index.htm (accessed 6 March 2006).

Fan, R. P. (2000). Informed consent and truth telling: the Chinese Confucian moral perspective. *Healthcare Ethics Committee Forum, 12*, 87–95.

Fox, N., Ward, K., and O'Rourke, A. (2005). Pro-anorexia, weight-loss drugs and the internet: an 'anti-recovery' explanatory model of anorexia. *Sociology of Health and Illness, 27* (7), 944–971.

Gowers, S. G., Weetman, J., Shore, A., Hossain, F., and Elvins, R. (2000). Impact of hospitalisation on the outcome of adolescent anorexia nervosa. *British Journal of Psychiatry, 176*, 138–141.

Gowers, S., and Bryant-Waugh, R. (2004). Management of child and adolescent eating disorders: the current evidence base and future directions. *Journal of Child Psychology and Psychiatry, 45*, 63–83.

Gowers, S. G., Clark, A., Roberts, C., Griffiths, A., Edwards, U., Bryan, C., et al. (2007). Clinical effectiveness of treatments of anorexia nervosa in adolescents. Randomised controlled trial. *British Journal of Psychiatry, 191*, 427–435.

Griffiths, R., Gross, G., Russell, J., Thornton, C., Beaumont, P. J. V., Schotte, D., et al. (1997). Perceptions of bed rest by anorexia nervosa patients. *International Journal of Eating Disorders, 23* (4), 443–447.

Grisso, T., and Appelbaum, P. S. (1998). Abilities related to competence. In T. Grisso, and P. S. Appelbaum (Eds), *Assessing competence to consent to treatment: A Guide for physicians and other health professionals* (pp. 31–60). Oxford: Oxford University Press.

Ho, A. (2008). Rational autonomy or undue pressure? Family's role in medical decision-making. *Scandinavian Journal of Caring Science, 22*, 128–135.

Hope, T., Tan, J., Stewart, A., and Fitzpatrick, R. (in press). Anorexia nervosa and the language of authenticity, *Hastings Centre Report, 41* (6).

Hope, T., Savulescu, J., and Hendrick, J. (2003). *Medical Ethics and Law: The Core Curriculum.* Edinburgh: Churchill Livingstone.

Jarman, M., Smith, J. A., and Walsh, S. (1997). The psychological battle for control: A qualitative study of health-care professionals' understandings of the treatment of anorexia nervosa. *Journal of Community and Applied Social Psychology, 7*, 137–152.

Moazam, F. (2000). Families, Patients and physicians in medical decision-making: a Pakistani perspective. *The Hastings Center Report, 30*, 28–37.

Morrison, G. (2003). *Fatal Trend: Pro-anorexia Nervosa Websites.* Retrieved 6 May, 2005, from http://preteenagerstoday.com/resources/articles/fataltrend.htm

Murphy, R., Frost, S., Webster, P., and Schmidt, U. (2004). An evaluation of web-based information. *International Journal of Eating Disorders, 35* (2), 145–154.

National Institute for Health and Clinical Excellence (NICE 2004). *Eating Disorders: Core interventions in the treatment and management of anorexia nervosa, bulimia nervosa and related eating disorders. Clinical Guideline 9.* Retrieved 25 July, 2005, from http://www.nice.org.uk/pdf/cg009niceguidance.pdf

Orbach, S. (1978). *Fat is a Feminist Issue*: London: Arrow Books.

Rathner, G. (1998). A plea against compulsory treatment of anorexia nervosa, In

W. Vandereycken, and P. J. Beumont (Eds), *Treating Eating Disorders: Ethical, Legal and Personal Issues* (pp. 179–215). London: Athlone Press.

Robin, A. L., Siegel, P. T., Moye, A. W., Gilroy, M., Dennis, A. B., and Sikand, A. (1999). A controlled comparison of family versus individual therapy for adolescents with anorexia nervosa. *Journal of the American Academy of Child and Adolescent Psychiatry*, *38*, 1482–1489.

Royal College of Psychiatrists (2004). *Leaflet 24, for Parents and Teachers. Eating Disorders in Young People*. Retrieved April 6, 2006, from http://www.rcpsych.ac.uk/info/mhgu/newmhgu24.htm

Royal College of Psychiatrists (2006). *Eating Disorders – New and Improved Leaflet*. Retrieved April 6, 2006, from http://www.rcpsych.ac.uk/info/help/anor/index.asp

Russell, D. (1995). *Women, Madness and Medicine*. Oxford: Blackwell.

Russell, G. F. M., Szmuckler, G.I., Dare, C., and Eisler, I. (1987). An evaluation of family therapy in anorexia nervosa and bulimia nervosa. *Archives of General Psychiatry*, *44*, 1047–1056.

Russon, L., and Alison, D. (1998). Does palliative care have a role in treatment of anorexia nervosa? Palliative care does not mean giving up. *British Medical Journal*, *317* (7152), 196–197.

Steinhausen, H. C. (1994). Anorexia and bulimia nervosa', In M. Rutter and E. Taylor, (Eds), *Child and Adolescent Psychiatry* (3rd ed., pp. 425–440). Oxford: Blackwell.

Stewart, A. (2000). *What is Adolescent Autonomy and How Can Clinicians Promote It?* Paper presented at the Fourth International Conference on Philosophy and Psychiatry: Madness, Science and Society, Florence, Italy.

Stewart, A., and Tan, J. (2005). *The Views of Patients Regarding the Treatment Decision Making Process in Anorexia Nervosa – Practical Implications of the Findings from an Empirical Medical Ethics Project*. Workshop at the 7th London International Conference on Eating Disorders, London, 4–6 April.

Tan, J. (2004). *Medical Ethics as a Tool in Treatment Dilemmas in Eating Disorders*. Paper presented at the Royal College of Psychiatrists Eating Disorders Special Interest Group meeting, London, 19 March.

Tan, J. (2005). *Can She REALLY Decide? An Ethical Approach to Choice and Compulsion in Anorexia Nervosa*. Presentation in plenary session Coercion, Collaboration and Choice (Chair, Stephen Touyz), at the 7th London International Conference on Eating Disorders, Imperial College, London, 4–6 April.

Tan, J. (2006). *Competence and Treatment Decision-making in Anorexia Nervosa*. Unpublished DPhil thesis, University of Oxford.

Tan, J. O. A., and Chin, J. J. L. (2011) Chapter 2: The role of the family. In: *What Doctors Say about Care of the Dying*. Lien Foundation, Singapore, 12–25. http://www.lienfoundation.org/publications_others.html

Tan, J. O. A., Doll, H., Fitzpatrick, R. Stewart, A., and Hope, T. (2008). Psychiatrists' attitudes towards autonomy, best interests and compulsory treatment in anorexia nervosa: a questionnaire survey. *Child and Adolescent Psychiatry and Mental Health*. *2* (40).

Tan, J., Hope, T., and Stewart, A. (2003a). Anorexia and personal identity: the accounts of patients and their parents. *International Journal of Law and Psychiatry*, *26*, 533–548.

Tan, J., Hope, T., and Stewart, A. (2003b). Competence to refuse treatment in anorexia nervosa. *International Journal of Law and Psychiatry*, *26*, 697–707.

Tan, J. O. A., and Jones, D. P. H. (2001). Children's consent. *Current Opinion in Psychiatry*, *14*, 303–307.

Tan, J., and Stewart, A. (2003c). *Ethical Issues in the Treatment of Eating Disorders*, Workshop at the London International Conference on Eating Disorders, Imperial College, London, 1–3 April.

Tan, J. O. A., Stewart, A., Fitzpatrick, R., and Hope, T. (2010). Attitudes of patients with anorexia nervosa to compulsory treatment and coercion. *International Journal of Law and Psychiatry*, *33*, 13–19.

Tan, J. O. A., Syahirah, B. A. K., Lee, H. Y., Goh, Y. L., and Lee, E. L. (Submitted) Cultural and ethical issues in the treatment of eating disorders in Singapore.

Touyz, S. W., Beaumont, P. J. V., and Dunn, S. M. (1987). Behaviour therapy in the management of patients with anorexia nervosa. A lenient, flexible approach *Psychotherapy and Psychosomatics*, *48*, 151–156.

Udovitch, M. (2002). *A Secret Society of the Starving*. Article in *The New York Times*, September 8.

Weithorn, L. A., and Campbell, S. B. (1982). The competency of children and adolescents to make informed treatment decisions. *Child Development*, *53* (6), 1589–1598.

Williams, C. J., Pieri, L., and Sims, A. (1998). Does palliative care have a role in treatment of anorexia nervosa? We should strive to keep patients alive. *British Medical Journal*, *317* (7152), 195–196.

Author Index

Heinman, M. 248
Helps, B. A. 98
Helverskov, J. L. 152
Hemmings, P. 277
Hendrick, J. 333
Henschel, A. 61
Herman, C. P. 63, 87, 135
Herpertz-Dahlmann, B. 97, 114, 152–3
Herring, S. 98
Hertz, S. M. 95
Herzog, D. 82, 106, 113, 117, 151
Herzog, W. 154, 168
Hetrick, S. E. 248
Hewell, K. 249
Heyerdahl, S. 155
Heymsfield, S. B. 94
Hick, K. 94
Higgs, J. 40
Hill, A. J. 64
Hill, L. S. 33
Hillman, J. B. 57
Hilsenroth, M. J. 288
Hinney, A. 56
Hirsch, R. 60
Hjern, A. 58
Ho, A. 327
Hobson, P. 286
Hodges, E. 107, 121
Hofmann, W. K. 93
Holland, A. J. 54
Holman, R. T. 93
Holtkamp, K. 97
Hope, T. 323, 329, 331, 333–5
Horrobin, D. F. 93
Hossain, F. 326
Hoste, R. R. 251
Hsu, L. K. 151, 155, 162–4
Hugo, P. 84, 88
Hultman, C. M. 58
Hutchinson, J. W. 78
Hutter, G. 93

Iacono, W. G. 55
Illing, V. 61
Irwin, M. 38
Isner, J. M. 94

Jabine, L. N. 163
Jackson, D. D. 239
Jackson, S. C. 113
Jacobi, C. 59
Jacobson, M. S. 95, 236, 238
Jacquemont, S. 54

Jarman, M. 329
Jarrell, M. P. 121
Jimerson, D. C. 88
Jocic, Z. 83
Johnson, M. 126
Jones, D. P. H. 330

Kalarchian, M. 36
Kaltiala-Heino, R. 59, 82, 114
Kanbur N. 99
Kaplan, E. L. 97
Katzman, D. 33, 83, 94, 96, 130, 248
Katzman, M. 66, 262
Kawashima, Y. 250
Kaye, W. 51, 53–4, 56, 128, 132, 158
Kazdin, A. 52
Keel, P. 83, 113, 249
Kemmler, G. 33
Kemps, E. 133, 135
Kendler, K. S. 53–4
Kennedy, E. 284, 297
Kennerley, H. 259
Kennerly, H. 66
Key, A. 61, 88, 95, 135
Killen, J. D. 59
Kilpatrick, D. G. 64
Kindler, J. 57
King, N. J. 264
Kipman, A. 56
Kirby, D. F. 93
Kirk, J. 259
Kiyohara, K. 97
Klostermann, B. K. 78
Klump, K. L. 54–5, 57, 61
Knibbs, J. 38, 107
Kog, E. 240
Kohn, M. 33, 237
Kotler, L. A. 64
Kouba, S. 154
Kovalskys, I. 252
Kozyrskyj, A. L. 64
Kraemer, H. 52, 247
Krautter, T. 251
Kreipe, R. 34, 239
Kroll, L. 44
Kumagai, L. F. 97
Kupfer, D. 52
Kurlan, R. 97

Lacey, H. 33
Lai, K. Y. 88
Lambe, E. 130
Lambert, M. J. 288

Subject Index

NEWPORT COMMUNITY
LEARNING & LIBRARIES

Taylor & Francis

eBooks

FOR LIBRARIES

ORDER YOUR FREE 30 DAY INSTITUTIONAL TRIAL TODAY!

Over 23,000 eBook titles in the Humanities, Social Sciences, STM and Law from some of the world's leading imprints.

Choose from a range of subject packages or create your own!

Benefits for you

▶ Free MARC records
▶ COUNTER-compliant usage statistics
▶ Flexible purchase and pricing options

Benefits for your user

▶ Off-site, anytime access via Athens or referring URL
▶ Print or copy pages or chapters
▶ Full content search
▶ Bookmark, highlight and annotate text
▶ Access to thousands of pages of quality research at the click of a button

For more information, pricing enquiries or to order a free trial, contact your local online sales team.

UK and Rest of World: **online.sales@tandf.co.uk**

US, Canada and Latin America:
e-reference@taylorandfrancis.com

www.ebooksubscriptions.com

ALPSP Award for BEST eBOOK PUBLISHER 2009 Finalist
sponsored by

Taylor & Francis eBooks
Taylor & Francis Group

A flexible and dynamic resource for teaching, learning and research.

8/1/13,

19/1/13

Newport Library and
Information Service
John Frost Square
Newport
South Wales NP20 1PA